GO!
with Microsoft®

Windows 7
Introductory

Shelley Gaskin

Prentice Hall

Boston   Columbus   Indianapolis   New York   San Francisco   Upper Saddle River
Amsterdam   Cape Town   Dubai   London   Madrid   Milan   Munich   Paris   Montreal   Toronto
Delhi   Mexico City   Sao Paulo   Sydney   Hong Kong   Seoul   Singapore   Taipei   Tokyo

Editor in Chief: Michael Payne
Associate VP/Executive Acquisitions Editor, Print: Stephanie Wall
Product Development Manager: Eileen Bien Calabro
Editorial Project Manager: Laura Burgess
Editorial Assistant: Nicole Sam
Director of Marketing: Kate Valentine
Marketing Manager: Tori Olson Alves
Marketing Coordinator: Susan Osterlitz
Marketing Assistant: Darshika Vyas
Senior Managing Editor: Cynthia Zonneveld
Associate Managing Editor: Camille Trentacoste
Production Project Manager: Mike Lackey
Operations Director: Alexis Heydt
Senior Operations Specialist: Natacha Moore
Senior Art Director: Jonathan Boylan
Text and Cover Designer: Blair Brown
Cover Photo: © Ben Durrant

Manager, Visual Research: Beth Brenzel
Manager, Rights and Permissions: Zina Arabia
Image Permission Coordinator: Richard Rodrigues
Manager, Cover Visual Research & Permissions: Karen Sanatar
Rights and Permissions Manager: Shannon Barbe
Text Permission Specialist: Christie Barros
AVP/Director of Online Programs, Media: Richard Keaveny
AVP/Director of Product Development, Media: Lisa Strite
Product Development Manager, Media: Cathi Profitko
Media Project Manager, Editorial: Alana Coles
Media Project Manager, Production: John Cassar
Supplements Editor: Lori Damanti
Full-Service Project Management: GGS Higher Education Resources, a Division of Premedia Global, Inc.
Composition: GGS Higher Education Resources, a Division of Premedia Global, Inc.
Printer/Binder: Courier/Kendallville
Cover Printer: Lehigh-Phoenix Color/Hagerstown
Text Font: Bookman Light

Credits and acknowledgments borrowed from other sources and reproduced, with permission, in this textbook appear on appropriate page within text.

Thanks to band members from The Skirts, Lynn Mayugba, Gerri Ranta, Cory Tozer, Wendy Powell, and Gitti Lindner, and cover artist Keara Fallon, for permission to use their album *Smashing the Sky*, which is pictured in this book.

Photo on page 228 courtesy of the author.

Microsoft® and Windows® are registered trademarks of the Microsoft Corporation in the U.S.A. and other countries. Screen shots and icons reprinted with permission from the Microsoft Corporation. This book is not sponsored or endorsed by or affiliated with the Microsoft Corporation.

Library of Congress Cataloging-in-Publication Data

CIP data on file.

10 9 8 7 6 5 4 3 2 1

Prentice Hall
is an imprint of

www.pearsonhighered.com

ISBN-10: 0-13-508903-4
ISBN-13: 978-0-13-508903-3

Contents

GO! System Contributors

We thank the following people for their hard work and support in making the GO! System all that it is!

Instructor Resource Authors

Sue Miner	Lehigh Carbon Community College
Joyce Thompson	Lehigh Carbon Community College
Paul Weaver	Bossier Parish Community College
Sharon Behrens	Mid-State Technical College
Julie Boyles	Portland Community College
Dawn Wood	
Jill Canine	Ivy Tech Community College

Technical Editor

Joyce Nielsen

Student Reviewers

Albinda, Sarah Evangeline	Phoenix College
Allen, John	Asheville-Buncombe Tech Community College
Alexander, Steven	St. Johns River Community College
Alexander, Melissa	Tulsa Community College
Bolz, Stephanie	Northern Michigan University
Berner, Ashley	Central Washington University
Boomer, Michelle	Northern Michigan University
Busse, Brennan	Northern Michigan University
Butkey, Maura	Central Washington University
Cates, Concita	Phoenix College
Charles, Marvin	Harrisburg Area Community College
Christensen, Kaylie	Northern Michigan University
Clark, Glen D. III	Harrisburg Area Community College
Cobble, Jan N.	Greenville Technical College
Connally, Brianna	Central Washington University
Davis, Brandon	Northern Michigan University
Davis, Christen	Central Washington University
De Jesus Garcia, Maria	Phoenix College
Den Boer, Lance	Central Washington University
Dix, Jessica	Central Washington University
Moeller, Jeffrey	Northern Michigan University
Downs, Elizabeth	Central Washington University
Elser, Julie	Harrisburg Area Community College
Erickson, Mike	Ball State University
Frye, Alicia	Phoenix College
Gadomski, Amanda	Northern Michigan University
Gassert, Jennifer	Harrisburg Area Community College
Gross, Mary Jo	Kirkwood Community College
Gyselinck, Craig	Central Washington University
Harrison, Margo	Central Washington University
Hatt, Patrick	Harrisburg Area Community College
Heacox, Kate	Central Washington University
Hedgman, Shaina	Tidewater College
Hill, Cheretta	Northwestern State University
Hochstedler, Bethany	Harrisburg Area Community College Lancaster
Homer, Jean	Greenville Technical College
Innis, Tim	Tulsa Community College
Jarboe, Aaron	Central Washington University
Key, Penny	Greenville Technical College
Klein, Colleen	Northern Michigan University
Lloyd, Kasey	Ivy Tech Bloomington
Moeller, Jeffrey	Northern Michigan University
Mullen, Sharita	Tidewater Community College
Nelson, Cody	Texas Tech University
Nicholson, Regina	Athens Tech College
Niehaus, Kristina	Northern Michigan University
Nisa, Zaibun	Santa Rosa Community College
Nunez, Nohelia	Santa Rosa Community College
Oak, Samantha	Central Washington University
Oberly, Sara	Harrisburg Area Community College Lancaster
Oertii, Monica	Central Washington University
Palenshus, Juliet	Central Washington University
Pohl, Amanda	Northern Michigan University
Presnell, Randy	Central Washington University
Reed, Kailee	Texas Tech University
Ritner, April	Northern Michigan University
Roberts, Corey	Tulsa Community College
Rodgers, Spencer	Texas Tech University
Rodriguez, Flavia	Northwestern State University
Rogers, A.	Tidewater Community College
Rossi, Jessica Ann	Central Washington University
Rothbauer, Taylor	Trident Technical College
Rozelle, Lauren	Texas Tech University
Schmadeke, Kimberly	Kirkwood Community College
Shafapay, Natasha	Central Washington University
Shanahan, Megan	Northern Michigan University
Sullivan, Alexandra Nicole	Greenville Technical College
Teska, Erika	Hawaii Pacific University
Torrenti, Natalie	Harrisburg Area Community College
Traub, Amy	Northern Michigan University
Underwood, Katie	Central Washington University
Walters, Kim	Central Washington University
Warren, Jennifer L.	Greenville Technical College
Wilson, Kelsie	Central Washington University
Wilson, Amanda	Green River Community College
Wylie, Jimmy	Texas Tech University

Contributors continued

Series Reviewers

Abraham, Reni	Houston Community College	Cannon, Kim	Greenville Technical College
Addison, Paul	Ivy Tech Community College	Carreon, Cleda	Indiana University—Purdue University, Indianapolis
Agatston, Ann	Agatston Consulting Technical College	Carriker, Sandra	North Shore Community College
Akuna, Valeria, Ph.D.	Estrella Mountain Community College	Casey, Patricia	Trident Technical College
		Cates, Wally	Central New Mexico Community College
Alexander, Melody	Ball Sate University		
Alejandro, Manuel	Southwest Texas Junior College	Chaffin, Catherine	Shawnee State University
Alger, David	Tidewater Community College Chesapeake Campus	Chauvin, Marg	Palm Beach Community College, Boca Raton
Allen, Jackie	Rowan-Cabarrus Community College	Challa, Chandrashekar	Virginia State University
		Chamlou, Afsaneh	NOVA Alexandria
Ali, Farha	Lander University	Chapman, Pam	Wabaunsee Community College
Amici, Penny	Harrisburg Area Community College	Christensen, Dan	Iowa Western Community College
Anderson, Patty A.	Lake City Community College	Clay, Betty	Southeastern Oklahoma State University
Andrews, Wilma	Virginia Commonwealth College, Nebraska University		
		Collins, Linda D.	Mesa Community College
Anik, Mazhar	Tiffin University	Cone, Bill	Northern Arizona University
Armstrong, Gary	Shippensburg University	Conroy-Link, Janet	Holy Family College
Arnold, Linda L.	Harrisburg Area Community College	Conway, Ronald	Bowling Green State University
		Cornforth, Carol G.	WVNCC
Ashby, Tom	Oklahoma City Community College	Cosgrove, Janet	Northwestern CT Community
		Courtney, Kevin	Hillsborough Community College
Atkins, Bonnie	Delaware Technical Community College	Coverdale, John	Riverside Community College
		Cox, Rollie	Madison Area Technical College
Aukland, Cherie	Thomas Nelson Community College	Crawford, Hiram	Olive Harvey College
		Crawford, Sonia	Central New Mexico Community College
Bachand, LaDonna	Santa Rosa Community College		
Bagui, Sikha	University of West Florida	Crawford, Thomasina	Miami-Dade College, Kendall Campus
Beecroft, Anita	Kwantlen University College		
Bell, Paula	Lock Haven College	Credico, Grace	Lethbridge Community College
Belton, Linda	Springfield Tech. Community College	Crenshaw, Richard	Miami Dade Community College, North
Bennett, Judith	Sam Houston State University	Crespo, Beverly	Mt. San Antonio College
Bhatia, Sai	Riverside Community College	Crooks, Steven	Texas Tech University
Bishop, Frances	DeVry Institute—Alpharetta (ATL)	Crossley, Connie	Cincinnati State Technical Community College
Blaszkiewicz, Holly	Ivy Tech Community College/Region 1		
		Curik, Mary	Central New Mexico Community College
Boito, Nancy	HACC Central Pennsylvania's Community College		
		De Arazoza, Ralph	Miami Dade Community College
Borger-Boglin, Grietje L.	San Antonio College/Northeast Lakeview College	Danno, John	DeVry University/Keller Graduate School
Branigan, Dave	DeVry University		
Bray, Patricia	Allegany College of Maryland	Davis, Phillip	Del Mar College
Britt, Brenda K.	Fayetteville Technical Community College	Davis, Richard	Trinity Valley Community College
		Davis, Sandra	Baker College of Allen Park
Brotherton, Cathy	Riverside Community College	Dees, Stephanie D.	Wharton County Junior College
Brown, Judy	Western Illinois University	DeHerrera, Laurie	Pikes Peak Community College
Buehler, Lesley	Ohlone College	Delk, Dr. K. Kay	Seminole Community College
Buell, C	Central Oregon Community College	Denton, Bree	Texas Tech University
		Dix, Jeanette	Ivy Tech Community College
Burns, Christine	Central New Mexico Community College	Dooly, Veronica P.	Asheville-Buncombe Technical Community College
Byars, Pat	Brookhaven College	Doroshow, Mike	Eastfield College
Byrd, Julie	Ivy Tech Community College	Douglas, Gretchen	SUNYCortland
Byrd, Lynn	Delta State University, Cleveland, Mississippi	Dove, Carol	Community College of Allegheny
		Dozier, Susan	Tidewater Community College, Virginia Beach Campus
Cacace, Richard N.	Pensacola Junior College		
Cadenhead, Charles	Brookhaven College	Driskel, Loretta	Niagara Community College
Calhoun, Ric	Gordon College	Duckwiler, Carol	Wabaunsee Community College
Cameron, Eric	Passaic Community College	Duhon, David	Baker College
Canine, Jill	Ivy Tech Community College of Indiana	Duncan, Mimi	University of Missouri-St. Louis
		Duthie, Judy	Green River Community College
Cannamore, Madie	Kennedy King	Duvall, Annette	Central New Mexico Community College

Ecklund, Paula — Duke University
Eilers, Albert — Cincinnati State Technical and Community College
Eng, Bernice — Brookdale Community College
Epperson, Arlin — Columbia College
Evans, Billie — Vance-Granville Community College
Evans, Jean — Brevard Community College
Feuerbach, Lisa — Ivy Tech East Chicago
Finley, Jean — ABTCC
Fisher, Fred — Florida State University
Foster, Nancy — Baker College
Foster-Shriver, Penny L. — Anne Arundel Community College
Foster-Turpen, Linda — CNM
Foszcz, Russ — McHenry County College
Fry, Susan — Boise State University
Fustos, Janos — Metro State
Gallup, Jeanette — Blinn College
Gelb, Janet — Grossmont College
Gentry, Barb — Parkland College
Gerace, Karin — St. Angela Merici School
Gerace, Tom — Tulane University
Ghajar, Homa — Oklahoma State University
Gifford, Steve — Northwest Iowa Community College
Glazer, Ellen — Broward Community College
Gordon, Robert — Hofstra University
Gramlich, Steven — Pasco-Hernando Community College
Graviett, Nancy M. — St. Charles Community College, St. Peters, Missouri
Greene, Rich — Community College of Allegheny County
Gregoryk, Kerry — Virginia Commonwealth State
Griggs, Debra — Bellevue Community College
Grimm, Carol — Palm Beach Community College
Guthrie, Rose — Fox Valley Technical College
Hahn, Norm — Thomas Nelson Community College
Haley-Hunter, Deb — Bluefield State College
Hall, Linnea — Northwest Mississippi Community College
Hammerschlag, Dr. Bill — Brookhaven College
Hansen, Michelle — Davenport University
Hayden, Nancy — Indiana University—Purdue University, Indianapolis
Hayes, Theresa — Broward Community College
Headrick, Betsy — Chattanooga State
Helfand, Terri — Chaffey College
Helms, Liz — Columbus State Community College
Hernandez, Leticia — TCI College of Technology
Hibbert, Marilyn — Salt Lake Community College
Hinds, Cheryl — Norfolk State University
Hines, James — Tidewater Community College
Hoffman, Joan — Milwaukee Area Technical College
Hogan, Pat — Cape Fear Community College
Holland, Susan — Southeast Community College
Holliday, Mardi — Community College of Philadelphia
Hollingsworth, Mary Carole — Georgia Perimeter College
Hopson, Bonnie — Athens Technical College
Horvath, Carrie — Albertus Magnus College
Horwitz, Steve — Community College of Philadelphia

Hotta, Barbara — Leeward Community College
Howard, Bunny — St. Johns River Community
Howard, Chris — DeVry University
Huckabay, Jamie — Austin Community College
Hudgins, Susan — East Central University
Hulett, Michelle J. — Missouri State University
Humphrey, John — Asheville Buncombe Technical Community College
Hunt, Darla A. — Morehead State University, Morehead, Kentucky
Hunt, Laura — Tulsa Community College
Ivey, Joan M. — Lanier Technical College
Jacob, Sherry — Jefferson Community College
Jacobs, Duane — Salt Lake Community College
Jauken, Barb — Southeastern Community
Jerry, Gina — Santa Monica College
Johnson, Deborah S. — Edison State College
Johnson, Kathy — Wright College
Johnson, Mary — Kingwood College
Johnson, Mary — Mt. San Antonio College
Jones, Stacey — Benedict College
Jones, Warren — University of Alabama, Birmingham
Jordan, Cheryl — San Juan College
Kapoor, Bhushan — California State University, Fullerton
Kasai, Susumu — Salt Lake Community College
Kates, Hazel — Miami Dade Community College, Kendall
Keen, Debby — University of Kentucky
Keeter, Sandy — Seminole Community College
Kern-Blystone, Dorothy Jean — Bowling Green State
Kerwin, Annette — College of DuPage
Keskin, Ilknur — The University of South Dakota
Kinney, Mark B. — Baker College
Kirk, Colleen — Mercy College
Kisling, Eric — East Carolina University
Kleckner, Michelle — Elon University
Kliston, Linda — Broward Community College, North Campus
Knuth, Toni — Baker College of Auburn Hills
Kochis, Dennis — Suffolk County Community College
Kominek, Kurt — Northeast State Technical Community College
Kramer, Ed — Northern Virginia Community College
Kretz, Daniel — Fox Valley Technical College
Laird, Jeff — Northeast State Community College
Lamoureaux, Jackie — Central New Mexico Community College
Lange, David — Grand Valley State
LaPointe, Deb — Central New Mexico Community College
Larsen, Jacqueline Anne — A-B Tech
Larson, Donna — Louisville Technical Institute
Laspina, Kathy — Vance-Granville Community College
Le Grand, Dr. Kate — Broward Community College
Lenhart, Sheryl — Terra Community College
Leonard, Yvonne — Coastal Carolina Community College
Letavec, Chris — University of Cincinnati
Lewis, Daphne L, Ed.D. — Wayland Baptist University
Lewis, Julie — Baker College-Allen Park
Liefert, Jane — Everett Community College

Lindaman, Linda	Black Hawk Community College	Meredith, Mary	University of Louisiana at Lafayette
Lindberg, Martha	Minnesota State University	Mermelstein, Lisa	Baruch College
Lightner, Renee	Broward Community College	Metos, Linda	Salt Lake Community College
Lindberg, Martha	Minnesota State University	Meurer, Daniel	University of Cincinnati
Linge, Richard	Arizona Western College	Meyer, Colleen	Cincinnati State Technical and Community College
Logan, Mary G.	Delgado Community College		
Loizeaux, Barbara	Westchester Community College	Meyer, Marian	Central New Mexico Community College
Lombardi, John	South University		
Lopez, Don	Clovis-State Center Community College District	Miller, Cindy	Ivy Tech Community College, Lafayette, Indiana
Lopez, Lisa	Spartanburg Community College	Mills, Robert E.	Tidewater Community College, Portsmouth Campus
Lord, Alexandria	Asheville Buncombe Tech		
Lovering, LeAnne	Augusta Technical College	Mitchell, Susan	Davenport University
Lowe, Rita	Harold Washington College	Mohle, Dennis	Fresno Community College
Low, Willy Hui	Joliet Junior College	Molki, Saeed	South Texas College
Lucas, Vickie	Broward Community College	Monk, Ellen	University of Delaware
Luna, Debbie	El Paso Community College	Moore, Rodney	Holland College
Luoma, Jean	Davenport University	Morris, Mike	Southeastern Oklahoma State University
Luse, Steven P.	Horry Georgetown Technical College		
		Morris, Nancy	Hudson Valley Community College
Lynam, Linda	Central Missouri State University		
Lyon, Lynne	Durham College	Moseler, Dan	Harrisburg Area Community College
Lyon, Pat Rajski	Tomball College		
Macarty, Matthew	University of New Hampshire	Nabors, Brent	Reedley College, Clovis Center
MacKinnon, Ruth	Georgia Southern University	Nadas, Erika	Wright College
Macon, Lisa	Valencia Community College, West Campus	Nadelman, Cindi	New England College
		Nademlynsky, Lisa	Johnson & Wales University
Machuca, Wayne	College of the Sequoias	Nagengast, Joseph	Florida Career College
Mack, Sherri	Butler County Community College	Nason, Scott	Rowan Cabarrus Community College
Madison, Dana	Clarion University		
Maguire, Trish	Eastern New Mexico University	Ncube, Cathy	University of West Florida
Malkan, Rajiv	Montgomery College	Newsome, Eloise	Northern Virginia Community College Woodbridge
Manning, David	Northern Kentucky University		
Marcus, Jacquie	Niagara Community College	Nicholls, Doreen	Mohawk Valley Community College
Marghitu, Daniela	Auburn University		
Marks, Suzanne	Bellevue Community College	Nicholson, John R.	Johnson County Community College
Marquez, Juanita	El Centro College		
Marquez, Juan	Mesa Community College	Nielson, Phil	Salt Lake Community College
Martin, Carol	Harrisburg Area Community College	Nunan, Karen L.	Northeast State Technical Community College
Martin, Paul C.	Harrisburg Area Community College	O'Neal, Lois Ann	Rogers State University
		Odegard, Teri	Edmonds Community College
Martyn, Margie	Baldwin-Wallace College	Ogle, Gregory	North Community College
Marucco, Toni	Lincoln Land Community College	Orr, Dr. Claudia	Northern Michigan University South
Mason, Lynn	Lubbock Christian University		
Matutis, Audrone	Houston Community College	Orsburn, Glen	Fox Valley Technical College
Matkin, Marie	University of Lethbridge	Otieno, Derek	DeVry University
Maurel, Trina	Odessa College	Otton, Diana Hill	Chesapeake College
May, Karen	Blinn College	Oxendale, Lucia	West Virginia Institute of Technology
McCain, Evelynn	Boise State University		
McCannon, Melinda	Gordon College	Paiano, Frank	Southwestern College
McCarthy, Marguerite	Northwestern Business College	Pannell, Dr. Elizabeth	Collin College
McCaskill, Matt L.	Brevard Community College	Patrick, Tanya	Clackamas Community College
McClellan, Carolyn	Tidewater Community College	Paul, Anindya	Daytona State College
McClure, Darlean	College of Sequoias	Peairs, Deb	Clark State Community College
McCrory, Sue A.	Missouri State University	Perez, Kimberly	Tidewater Community College
McCue, Stacy	Harrisburg Area Community College	Porter, Joyce	Weber State University
		Prince, Lisa	Missouri State University- Springfield Campus
McEntire-Orbach, Teresa	Middlesex County College		
McKinley, Lee	Georgia Perimeter College	Proietti, Kathleen	Northern Essex Community College
McLeod, Todd	Fresno City College		
McManus, Illyana	Grossmont College	Puopolo, Mike	Bunker Hill Community College
McPherson, Dori	Schoolcraft College	Pusins, Delores	HCCC
Meck, Kari	HACC	Putnam, Darlene	Thomas Nelson Community College
Meiklejohn, Nancy	Pikes Peak Community College		
Menking, Rick	Hardin-Simmons University		

Raghuraman, Ram	Joliet Junior College
Rani, Chigurupati	BMCC/CUNY
Reasoner, Ted Allen	Indiana University—Purdue
Reeves, Karen	High Point University
Remillard, Debbie	New Hampshire Technical Institute
Rhue, Shelly	DeVry University
Richards, Karen	Maplewoods Community College
Richardson, Mary	Albany Technical College
Rodgers, Gwen	Southern Nazarene University
Rodie, Karla	Pikes Peak Community College
Roselli, Diane Maie	Harrisburg Area Community College
Ross, Dianne	University of Louisiana in Lafayette
Rousseau, Mary	Broward Community College, South
Rovetto, Ann	Horry-Georgetown Technical College
Rusin, Iwona	Baker College
Sahabi, Ahmad	Baker College of Clinton Township
Samson, Dolly	Hawaii Pacific University
Sams, Todd	University of Cincinnati
Sandoval, Everett	Reedley College
Santiago, Diana	Central New Mexico Community College
Sardone, Nancy	Seton Hall University
Scafide, Jean	Mississippi Gulf Coast Community College
Scheeren, Judy	Westmoreland County Community College
Scheiwe, Adolph	Joliet Junior College
Schneider, Sol	Sam Houston State University
Schweitzer, John	Central New Mexico Community College
Scroggins, Michael	Southwest Missouri State University
Sedlacek, Brenda	Tidewater Community College
Sell, Kelly	Anne Arundel Community College
Sever, Suzanne	Northwest Arkansas Community College
Sewell, John	Florida Career College
Sheridan, Rick	California State University-Chico
Silvers, Pamela	Asheville Buncombe Tech
Sindt, Robert G.	Johnson County Community College
Singer, Noah	Tulsa Community College
Singer, Steven A.	University of Hawai'i, Kapi'olani Community College
Sinha, Atin	Albany State University
Skolnick, Martin	Florida Atlantic University
Smith, Kristi	Allegany College of Maryland
Smith, Patrick	Marshall Community and Technical College
Smith, Stella A.	Georgia Gwinnett College
Smith, T. Michael	Austin Community College
Smith, Tammy	Tompkins Cortland Community Collge
Smolenski, Bob	Delaware County Community College
Smolenski, Robert	Delaware Community College
Southwell, Donald	Delta College
Spangler, Candice	Columbus State
Spangler, Candice	Columbus State Community College
Stark, Diane	Phoenix College
Stedham, Vicki	St. Petersburg College, Clearwater
Stefanelli, Greg	Carroll Community College
Steiner, Ester	New Mexico State University
Stenlund, Neal	Northern Virginia Community College, Alexandria
St. John, Steve	Tulsa Community College
Sterling, Janet	Houston Community College
Stoughton, Catherine	Laramie County Community College
Sullivan, Angela	Joliet Junior College

Sullivan, Denise	Westchester Community College
Sullivan, Joseph	Joliet Junior College
Swart, John	Louisiana Tech University
Szurek, Joseph	University of Pittsburgh at Greensburg
Taff, Ann	Tulsa Community College
Taggart, James	Atlantic Cape Community College
Tarver, Mary Beth	Northwestern State University
Taylor, Michael	Seattle Central Community College
Terrell, Robert L.	Carson-Newman College
Terry, Dariel	Northern Virginia Community College
Thangiah, Sam	Slippery Rock University
Thayer, Paul	Austin Community College
Thompson, Joyce	Lehigh Carbon Community College
Thompson-Sellers, Ingrid	Georgia Perimeter College
Tomasi, Erik	Baruch College
Toreson, Karen	Shoreline Community College
Townsend, Cynthia	Baker College
Trifiletti, John J.	Florida Community College at Jacksonville
Trivedi, Charulata	Quinsigamond Community College, Woodbridge
Tucker, William	Austin Community College
Turgeon, Cheryl	Asnuntuck Community College
Turpen, Linda	Central New Mexico Community College
Upshaw, Susan	Del Mar College
Unruh, Angela	Central Washington University
Vanderhoof, Dr. Glenna	Missouri State University-Springfield Campus
Vargas, Tony	El Paso Community College
Vicars, Mitzi	Hampton University
Villarreal, Kathleen	Fresno
Vitrano, Mary Ellen	Palm Beach Community College
Vlaich-Lee, Michelle	Greenville Technical College
Volker, Bonita	Tidewater Community College
Waddell, Karen	Butler Community College
Wahila, Lori (Mindy)	Tompkins Cortland Community College
Wallace, Melissa	Lanier Technical College
Walters, Gary B.	Central New Mexico Community College
Waswick, Kim	Southeast Community College, Nebraska
Wavle, Sharon M.	Tompkins Cortland Community College
Webb, Nancy	City College of San Francisco
Webb, Rebecca	Northwest Arkansas Community College
Weber, Sandy	Gateway Technical College
Weissman, Jonathan	Finger Lakes Community College
Wells, Barbara E.	Central Carolina Technical College
Wells, Lorna	Salt Lake Community College
Welsh, Jean	Lansing Community College Nebraska
White, Bruce	Quinnipiac University
Willer, Ann	Solano Community College
Williams, Mark	Lane Community College
Williams, Ronald D.	Central Piedmont Community College
Wilms, Dr. G. Jan	Union University
Wilson, Kit	Red River College
Wilson, MaryLou	Piedmont Technical College
Wilson, Roger	Fairmont State University
Wimberly, Leanne	International Academy of Design and Technology

Winters, Floyd	Manatee Community College	Yip, Thomas	Passaic Community College
Worthington, Paula	Northern Virginia Community College	Zavala, Ben	Webster Tech
		Zaboski, Maureen	University of Scranton
Wright, Darrell	Shelton State Community College	Zlotow, Mary Ann	College of DuPage
Wright, Julie	Baker College	Zudeck, Steve	Broward Community College, North
Yauney, Annette	Herkimer County Community College	Zullo, Matthew D.	Wake Technical Community College

About the Author

Shelley Gaskin, author and Series Editor for the GO! Series, is a Professor of Business and Computer technology at Pasadena City College in Pasadena, California. She holds a master's degree in Business Education from Northern Illinois University and a doctorate in Adult and Community education from Ball State University. Dr. Gaskin has 15 years of experience in the computer industry with several Fortune 500 companies and has developed and written training materials for custom systems applications in both the public and private sector. She is also the author of books on Microsoft Outlook, Microsoft Excel, Microsoft Publisher, and word processing.

GO! Instructor Materials

The following instructor materials are available on either the Instructor Resource CD or from www.pearsonhighered.com/go

Annotated Solution Files
Coupled with the scorecards, these create a grading and scoring system that makes grading fast and easy

Assignment Sheets
Lists all the assignments for the chapter, you just add in the course information, due dates and points. Providing these to students ensures they will know what is due and when

Point-Counted Production Tests
Exams for each project and chapter

Power Point Lectures
PowerPoint presentations for each chapter

Scorecards
Can be used either by students to check their work or by you as a quick check-off for the items that need to be corrected

Solution Files
Answers to the projects in the book

Scripted Lectures
Classroom lectures prepared for you

Test Bank
Includes a variety of test questions for each chapter

Companion Web Site
Online content such as the Online Study Guide, Glossary, and Student Data Files are all at www.pearsonhighered.com/go

Getting Started with Windows 7

OUTCOMES
At the end of this chapter you will be able to:

PROJECT 1A
Create a folder, save a file, and manage your user account.

OBJECTIVES
Mastering these objectives will enable you to:

1. Create a New Folder and Save a File on a Removable Storage Device (p. 3)
2. Identify the Functions of an Operating System (p. 18)
3. Use the Getting Started Information and Windows Help and Support (p. 19)
4. Log Off, Turn Off Your Computer, and View Power Options (p. 23)
5. Manage Your User Account (p. 25)

PROJECT 1B
Manage windows and open files and programs.

6. Display Libraries, Folders, and Files in a Window (p. 31)
7. Start Programs and Open Data Files (p. 45)
8. Manage the Display of Individual and Multiple Windows (p. 52)

Soundsnaps/Shutterstock

In This Chapter

In this chapter you will use Microsoft Windows 7, which is software that manages your computer's hardware, software, and data files. Compared to previous versions of Windows, you will find that Windows 7 is faster and less complex. In this chapter you will log on to your computer, explore the features of Windows 7, create folders and save files, manage multiple windows, log off of your computer, and examine user accounts.

The projects in this chapter relate to the **Bell Orchid Hotels**, headquartered in Boston, and which own and operate resorts and business-oriented hotels. Resort properties are located in popular destinations, including Honolulu, Orlando, San Diego, and Santa Barbara. The resorts offer deluxe accommodations and a wide array of dining options. Other Bell Orchid hotels are located in major business centers and offer the latest technology in their meeting facilities. The company plans to open new properties and update existing properties over the next ten years.

Project 1A Using Windows 7

Project Activities

In Activities 1.01 through 1.08, you will participate in training along with Steven Ramos and Barbara Hewitt, both of whom work for the Information Technology Department at the Boston headquarters office of the Bell Orchid Hotels. After completing this part of the training, you will be able to log on to and log off of your computer, create folders and save files on a removable storage device, and distinguish among types of users of the computer. You will capture two screens that will look similar to Figure 1.1.

Project Files

For Project 1A, you will need the following files:

Two new Snip files

You will save your files as:

Lastname_Firstname_1A_USB_Snip
Lastname_Firstname_1A_Modem_Snip

Project Results

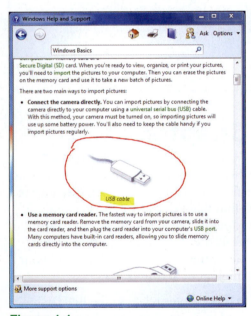
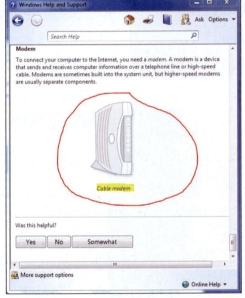

Figure 1.1
Project 1A Using Windows 7

Objective 1 | Create a New Folder and Save a File on a Removable Storage Device

A *program* is a set of instructions that a computer uses to accomplish a task, such as word processing, accounting, or data management. A program is also referred to as an *application*.

Windows 7 is an *operating system* developed by Microsoft Corporation. An operating system is a computer program that manages all the other programs on your computer, stores files in an organized manner, allows you to use software programs, and coordinates the use of computer hardware such as the keyboard and mouse.

A *file* is a collection of information that is stored on a computer under a single name, for example a text document, a picture, or a program.

Every file is stored in a *folder*—a container in which you store files—or a *subfolder*, which is a folder within a folder. Windows 7 stores and organizes your files and folders, which is the primary task of an operating system.

Alert! | Variations in Screen Organization, Colors, and Functionality are Common in Windows 7

Individuals and organizations can determine how Windows 7 displays; thus, the colors and the organization of various elements on the screen can vary. Your college or organization may customize Windows 7 to display a college picture or logo, or restrict access to certain features. The basic functions and structure of Windows 7 are not changed by such variations. You can be confident that the skills you will practice in this textbook apply to Windows 7 regardless of available functionality or differences between the pictures in the book and your screen.

Activity 1.01 | Turning On Your Computer, Logging On to a Windows 7 User Account, and Exploring the Windows 7 Environment

Before you begin any computer activity, you must, if necessary, turn on your computer and its monitor. This process is commonly referred to as *booting the computer*. Because Windows 7 does not require you to completely shut down your computer except to install or repair a hardware device, in most instances moving the mouse or pressing a key will wake your computer in a few seconds. Thus, most of the time you will skip the lengthier boot process.

In those instances where you must press the power button and initiate the boot process, the *BIOS (Basic Input/Output System)* program will run, which checks your hardware devices. The BIOS is installed by your computer's manufacturer and is part of the hardware of your system; it is *not* part of Windows 7. As its final process, the BIOS program loads Windows 7.

In this activity, you will turn on your computer and log on to Windows 7. If you are the only user of your own computer, you can disable the logon process if you want to do so. In most organizations, you will be required to log on in some manner.

Note | Comparing Your Screen with the Figures in This Textbook

Your screen will more closely match the figures shown in this textbook if you set your screen resolution to 1024 × 768. At other resolutions, your screen will closely resemble, but not match, the figures shown. To view your screen's resolution, on the desktop, right-click in a blank area, click Screen resolution, and then click the Resolution arrow. To adjust the resolution, move the slider to the desired setting, and then click OK.

---

1 If necessary, turn on your computer and monitor, and then compare your screen with Figure 1.2. If no password is required, move to Step 3.

The Windows 7 screen displays and indicates the names and pictures associated with all active user accounts. In this figure, only two users display. If you are able to set up your own user account, you can select a picture of your choice.

Your organization might have a custom logon screen with a logo or logon instructions, and thus will differ from the one shown.

There are several editions of Windows 7. The editions you might see commonly in the United States are Home Premium, Professional, Ultimate, and Enterprise. For the tasks you complete day to day, all of the functionality exists in all of these editions. Only larger organizations require the functions in Professional, Ultimate, and Enterprise.

Figure 1.2

Your screen color and background may vary

Name and picture of active user accounts

Bell Orchid Offices account (your user names will vary)

YourName account (your user names will vary)

Displays shutdown options

Edition of Windows 7 indicated (your edition may differ)

Displays the Ease of Access options

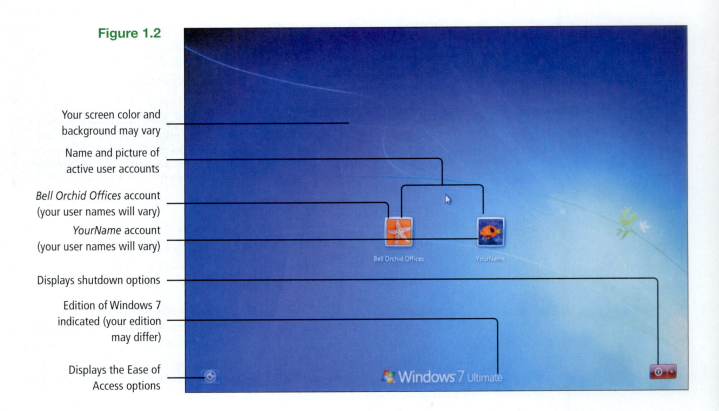

2 If there are two or more users on the computer you are using, point to your user account name to display a glow effect, and then click your user account name or its associated picture. If necessary, type your password in the Password box, and then click the circled arrow to the right of the Password box—or press Enter.

Note | Differing Logon Procedures and Passwords

Depending on whether you are working on your own computer, in a college lab, or in an organization, your logon process may differ. If you have a different logon screen, log on as directed and move to Step 3 of this activity. If you are working in a classroom or lab, ask your instructor or lab assistant about the user account name and password to use. On your own computer, use your own user account name and password. If no passwords are set on your computer and you do not need to log on, you are ready to begin Step 3.

---

3 Take a moment to compare your screen with Figure 1.3 and study the table in Figure 1.4.

Figure 1.3

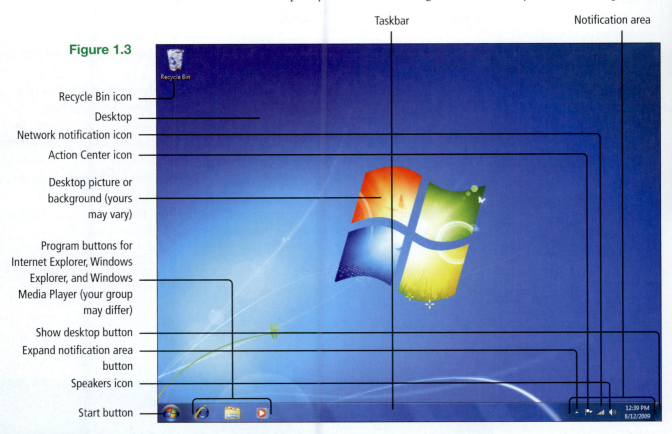

Taskbar

Notification area

Recycle Bin icon

Desktop

Network notification icon

Action Center icon

Desktop picture or background (yours may vary)

Program buttons for Internet Explorer, Windows Explorer, and Windows Media Player (your group may differ)

Show desktop button

Expand notification area button

Speakers icon

Start button

Parts of the Windows 7 Desktop

Action Center icon in the notification area	Displays the Action Center, which is a central place to view alerts and take actions related to things that need your attention.
Desktop	Serves as a surface for your work, like the top of an actual desk, and is the main screen area that you see after you turn on your computer; here you can arrange *icons*—small pictures that represent a file, folder, program, or other object—on the desktop such as shortcuts to programs, files, folders, and various types of documents in the same manner you would arrange physical objects on top of a desk.
Desktop background	Displays the colors and graphics of your desktop; you can change the desktop background to look the way you want it such as using a picture or a solid color. Also called *wallpaper*.
Network notification icon	Displays the status of your network.
Notification area	Displays notification icons and the system clock and calendar; sometimes referred to as the *system tray*.
Program buttons	Launch Internet Explorer, the Web browser program developed by Microsoft that is included with Windows 7; Windows Explorer, the program that displays the files and folders on your computer; and Windows Media Player, the program that plays and organizes your digital media files.
Recycle Bin	Contains files and folders that you delete. When you delete a file or folder, it is not actually deleted; it stays in the Recycle Bin if you want it back, until you take action to empty the Recycle Bin.
Show desktop button	Displays the desktop by making any open windows transparent (when pointed to) or minimized (when clicked).
Speakers icon	Displays the status of your speakers (if any).
Start button	Displays the *Start menu*—a list of choices that provides access to your computer's programs, folders, and settings.
Taskbar	Contains the Start button, optional program buttons, and buttons for all open programs; by default, it is located at the bottom of the desktop, but you can move it.

Figure 1.4

Another Way

Alternatively, press the Windows logo key located in the lower left corner of most keyboards.

4 In the lower left corner of your screen, move the mouse pointer over—*point* to—the **Start** button 🪟, and then *click*—press the left button on your mouse pointing device—to display the **Start** menu.

The *mouse pointer* is any symbol that displays on your screen in response to moving your mouse.

The Start menu has three parts: The left pane, the Search box at the bottom, and the right pane. The panes might be divided by menu separators into separate sections.

The large left pane displays a list of some installed programs, which might be customized by your computer manufacturer, and the All Programs button.

The Search box enables you to look for programs and files on your computer by typing search words in the box.

The right pane provides access to commonly used folders, files, settings, and features, and an area where you can log off from Windows or shut down (turn off) your computer.

5 Compare your screen with Figure 1.5 and take a moment to study the parts of the **Start** menu described in the table in Figure 1.6.

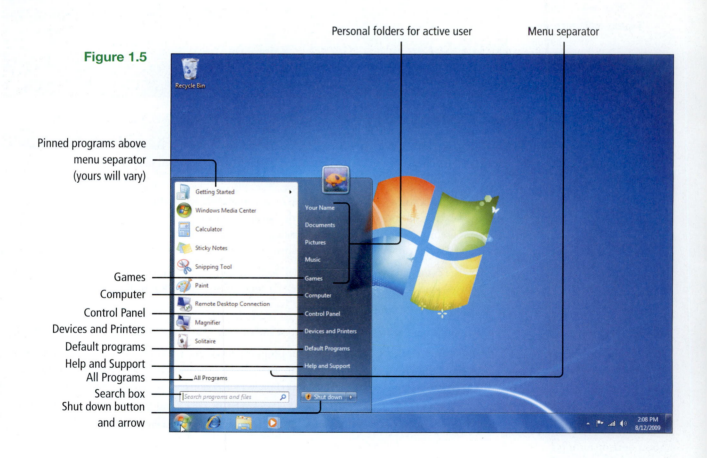

Figure 1.5

Parts of the Start Menu

All Programs	Displays all the programs on your computer system that are available to you; some groups of programs display in a folder.
Computer	Opens a window from which you can access disk drives, cameras, printers, scanners and other hardware connected to your computer.
Control Panel	Opens the Control Panel, where you can customize the appearance and functionality of your computer, install or uninstall programs, set up network connections, and manage user accounts.
Default Programs	Opens a window where you can choose which program you want Windows 7 to use for activities such as Web browsing or photo viewing.
Devices and Printers	Displays a window where you can view information about the printer, mouse, and other devices installed on your computer.
Games	Opens the Games folder, from which you can access all of the games on your computer.
Help and Support	Opens Windows Help and Support, where you can browse and search Help topics about how to use Windows and your computer.
Personal folders	Displays, for the user currently logged on, the user account picture, personal folder, and the user's Documents, Music, Pictures, and Videos folders, the locations in which the user logged on would most likely store files.
Pinned programs	Displays programs, at the top above the menu separator, that you have *pinned*—placed in a manner that remains until you remove it—to the Start menu because they are programs you use frequently. Below the menu separator, Windows displays recently used programs or programs that Windows detects as those that you use frequently.
Search box	Searches your programs, personal folder, e-mail messages, saved instant messages, appointments, and contacts by typing search terms.
Shut down button and arrow	Turns off the computer; clicking the arrow displays a menu with additional options for switching users, logging off, restarting, or shutting down.

Figure 1.6

6 Be sure the Start menu 🌀 is still displayed, and then compare your screen with Figure 1.7.

In Figure 1.7, portions of the Start menu are transparent; for example, you can see parts of the desktop design behind the right pane of the Start menu. If your version of Windows 7 has this capability and it is enabled, and if your computer system's graphics hardware supports transparency, you might also notice this transparent effect.

Figure 1.7

Right pane of
Start menu transparent
(yours may differ)

More Knowledge | Get Information About Your Computer's Ability to Display Transparency

In the Control Panel, click Appearance and Personalization, click Personalization, click Window Color, and then if necessary, click to put a checkmark in the box next to Enable transparency. Or, in Windows Help and Support, in the Search box type *transparency*. There you will find information about the system requirements for displaying transparency.

Activity 1.02 | Creating a New Folder on a Removable Storage Device

Recall that a file is a collection of information stored on a computer under a single name. Examples of a file include a Word document, an Excel workbook, a picture, a song, or a program. Recall also that a folder is a container in which you can store files. You probably store paper documents (files) in folders on your desk or in a file drawer. In the same manner, Windows 7 organizes and keeps track of your electronic files by letting you create and label electronic folders into which you can place your files.

In this activity, you will create a new folder on a *removable storage device*. Removable storage devices, such as a USB flash drive or a flash memory card, are commonly used to transfer information from one computer to another. Such devices are also useful when you want to work with your files on different computers. For example, you probably have files that you work with at your college, at home, and possibly at your workplace.

A *drive* is an area of storage that is formatted with a file system compatible with your operating system and is identified by a drive letter. For example, your computer's **hard disk drive**—the primary storage device located inside your computer where most of your files and programs are typically stored—is usually designated as drive C. Removable storage devices that you insert into your computer will be designated with a drive letter—the letter designation varies from one computer to another.

> **Alert!** | **Locate Your USB Flash Drive**
>
> You will need a USB flash drive to complete this activity.

1 Insert a USB flash drive into your computer. If this is the first time you have used this device in the computer, you may see one or more messages in your notification area indicating that device software is being installed and that your device is ready to use.

2 In the upper right corner of the **AutoPlay** window, **Close** the **AutoPlay** window, and click the small x in the upper right corner of any displayed message in the notification area.

AutoPlay is a Windows 7 feature that lets you choose which program to use to start different kinds of media, such as music CDs, or CDs and DVDs containing photos. It displays when you plug in or insert media or storage devices.

A *window* is a rectangular area on your screen that displays programs and content, and which can be moved, resized, minimized, or closed; the content of every window is different, but all windows display on the desktop.

3 Display the **Start** menu, and then on the right side, click **Computer**. Compare your screen with Figure 1.8.

The *folder window* for *Computer* displays. A folder window displays the contents of the current folder, library, or device, and contains helpful parts so that you can *navigate*—explore within the organizing structure of Windows.

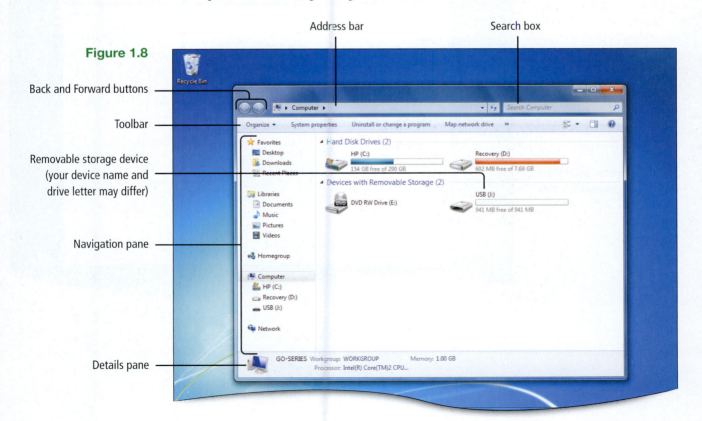

Figure 1.8

Address bar

Search box

Back and Forward buttons

Toolbar

Removable storage device (your device name and drive letter may differ)

Navigation pane

Details pane

A *library* is a collection of items, such as files and folders, assembled from various locations. A *location* is any disk drive, folder, or other place in which you can store files and folders.

In the Computer window, you have access to all the storage areas inside and connected to your computer such as your hard disk drive, DVD or CD drives, removable storage devices, and network drive locations if you are connected to a network and have storage space there.

4 Under **Devices with Removable Storage**, locate the removable storage device you inserted in Step 1, move your mouse over—point to—the device name to display the ⬚ pointer, and then click the *right* mouse button one time—referred to as *right-click*—to display a *shortcut menu*.

A shortcut menu is a context-sensitive menu that displays commands and options relevant to the selected object.

Another Way

Point to the device name and double-click to display the file list for the device.

5 On the displayed shortcut menu, click **Open** to display the file list for this device. Notice that in the **navigation pane**, *Computer* expands to display all of the drives that you can access, and the commands on the **toolbar** change. Compare your screen with Figure 1.9.

The *navigation pane* is the area on the left side of a folder window; it displays Favorites, Libraries, and an expandable list of drives and folders. If you are connected to a network, the name of the network, such as *Homegroup*, displays.

A *toolbar* is a row, column, or block of buttons or icons, usually displayed across the top of a window, which contains commands for tasks you can perform with a single click or buttons that display a menu of commands. The toolbar contains commands for common tasks that are relevant to the displayed folder window.

Figure 1.9

Toolbar displays commands

Computer expanded in navigation pane

6 On the toolbar, click **New folder**, and notice in the file list, a folder icon displays with *New folder* highlighted in blue, as shown in Figure 1.10.

Figure 1.10

New folder command
on toolbar

New folder on your device,
the contents of your
file list may vary

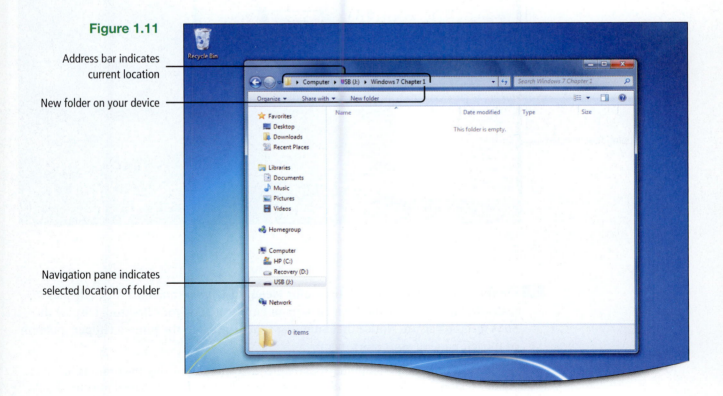

7 With the text *New folder* highlighted in blue, type **Windows 7 Chapter 1** and press (Enter) to confirm the folder name and select—highlight in blue—the new folder. With the folder selected, press (Enter) again to open the folder window. Compare your screen with Figure 1.11.

To *select* means to specify, by highlighting, a block of data or text on the screen with the intent of performing some action on the selection.

A new folder is created on your removable storage device. In the ***address bar***, the ***path*** from Computer to your device to your folder is indicated. The address bar displays your current location in the folder structure as a series of links separated by arrows. A path is a sequence of folders (directories) that leads to a specific file or folder.

Figure 1.11

Address bar indicates
current location

New folder on your device

Navigation pane indicates
selected location of folder

8 In the upper right corner of the window, click the Close 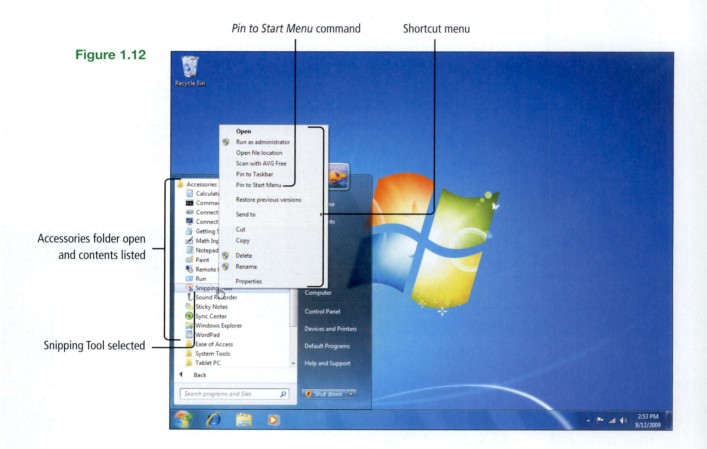 button to close the window.

Activity 1.03 | Using Snipping Tool to Create a File

Snipping Tool is a program that captures an image of all or part of a computer screen. A *snip*, as the captured image is called, can be annotated, saved, copied, or shared via e-mail. This is also referred to as a *screen capture* or a *screenshot*.

1 Be sure the removable storage device on which you created your folder is still inserted in the computer. Display the **Start** menu 🔵, and then click **All Programs**.

2 On the list of programs, click the **Accessories** folder to display a list of Accessories. *Point* to Snipping Tool, and then right-click. Compare your screen with Figure 1.12.

Pin to Start Menu command   Shortcut menu

Figure 1.12

Accessories folder open
and contents listed

Snipping Tool selected

3 On the shortcut menu, click **Pin to Start Menu**, (if *Unpin from Start Menu* displays instead, skip this step) and then click in an empty area of your desktop. Display the **Start** menu 🔵 again. Notice that **Snipping Tool** displays in the pinned (upper) portion of the left pane of your **Start** menu.

Because you will use Snipping Tool frequently while completing the projects in this textbook, it is recommended that you leave Snipping Tool pinned to your Start menu.

Another Way

If it displays, in the middle of the Windows Help and Support window, click Learn about Windows Basics.

4 From the displayed **Start** menu, at the bottom of the right pane, click **Help and Support**. In the **Windows Help and Support** window, in the **Search Help** box, type **Windows Basics** and then press Enter. On the displayed list, click **Windows Basics: all topics**. Compare your screen with Figure 1.13.

A vertical *scroll bar* displays on the right side of this window. A scroll bar displays when the contents of a window are not completely visible; you can use it to move the window up, down, left, or right to bring the contents into view. A scroll bar can be vertical as shown or horizontal and displayed at the bottom of a window.

Within the scroll bar, you can move the *scroll box* to move the window up, down, left, or right to bring the contents of the window into view. The position of the scroll box within the scroll bar indicates your relative position within the window's contents. You can click the *scroll arrow* at either end of the scroll bar to move within the window in small increments.

Each computer manufacturer has some control over the Help and Support opening screen. At the top of this screen, the manufacturer may place links to its own support and information about your computer's hardware.

Windows Help and Support window

Figure 1.13

Up scroll arrow

Windows Basics: all topics

Scroll box

Scroll bar

Down scroll arrow

Horizontal scroll bar/box

Taskbar button for Help program

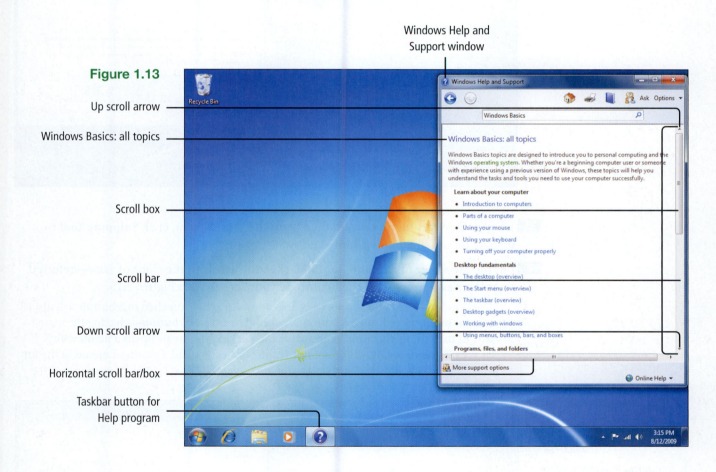

5 Click the down scroll arrow as necessary to bring the heading **Pictures and games** into view—or move the wheel on your mouse if you have one—and then click **Working with digital pictures**. Scroll down, if necessary, until you can see the illustration of a **USB cable**, as shown in Figure 1.14.

Figure 1.14

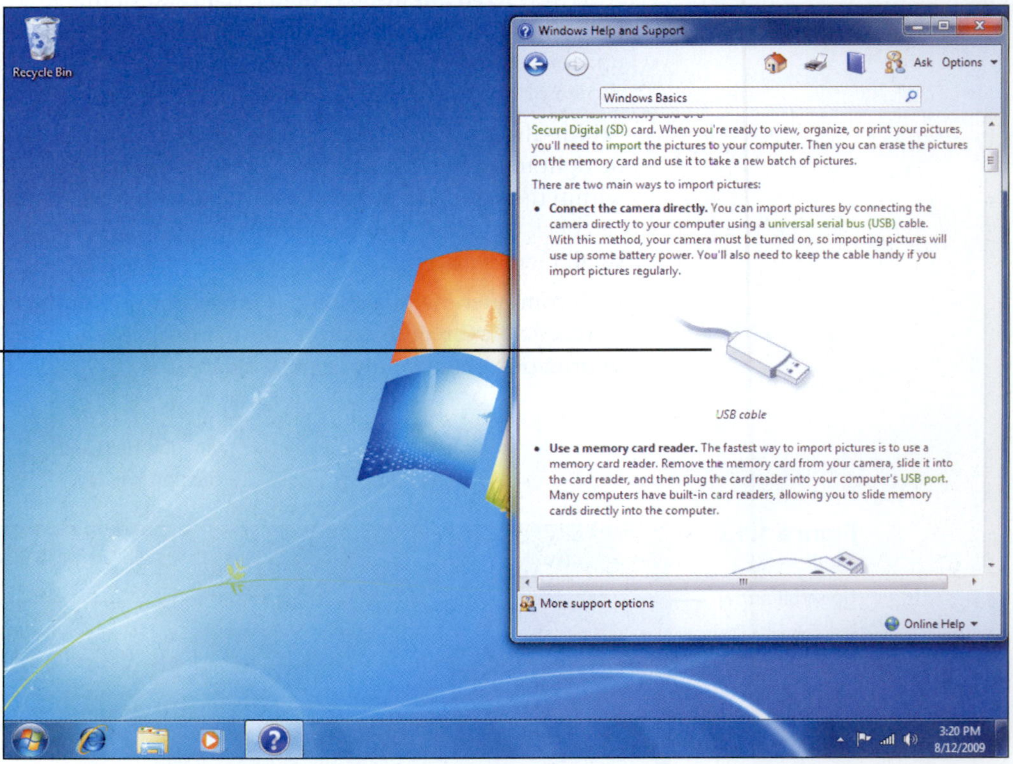

USB cable illustration —

6 Display the **Start** menu 🔵, and then from the pinned area, click **Snipping Tool** to display the small **Snipping Tool** window.

7 On the **menu bar** of the **Snipping Tool**, click the **arrow** to the right of *New*—referred to as the **New arrow**—and then compare your screen with Figure 1.15.

The Windows Help and Support window dims. An arrow attached to a button will display a menu when clicked. Such a button is referred to as a ***split button***—clicking the main part of the button performs a command and clicking the arrow opens a menu with choices. A ***menu*** is a list of commands within a category, and a group of menus at the top of a program window is referred to as the ***menu bar***.

Figure 1.15

Menu bar —
Arrow indicates a menu will display when clicked —
Snipping Tool window —

New menu —

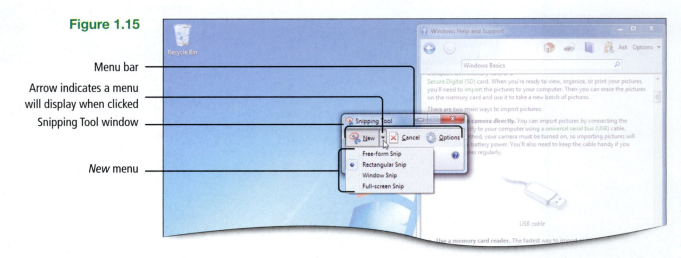

8 On the displayed menu, notice that there are four types of snips.

A *free-form snip* lets you draw an irregular line, such as a circle, around an area of the screen. A *rectangular snip* lets you draw a precise box by dragging the mouse pointer around an area of the screen to form a rectangle. A *window snip* captures the entire displayed window—such as the Help window. A *full-screen snip* captures the entire screen.

To *drag* is to move something from one location on the screen to another location while holding down the left mouse button; the action of dragging includes releasing the mouse button at the desired time or location.

9 From the displayed menu, click **Window Snip**. Then, move your mouse pointer over the open **Windows Help and Support** window, and notice that a red rectangle surrounds the window; the remainder of your screen dims.

10 With the pointer positioned anywhere over the surrounded window, click the left mouse button one time. Drag the scroll box to position the snip near the top of the window, and then compare your screen with Figure 1.16.

Your snip is copied to the Snipping Tool mark-up window. Here you can annotate—mark or make notes on—save, copy, or share the snip.

Snipping Tool mark-up window

Figure 1.16

Pen button arrow (arrow indicates a menu will display when clicked)

Scroll box

Your captured window snip

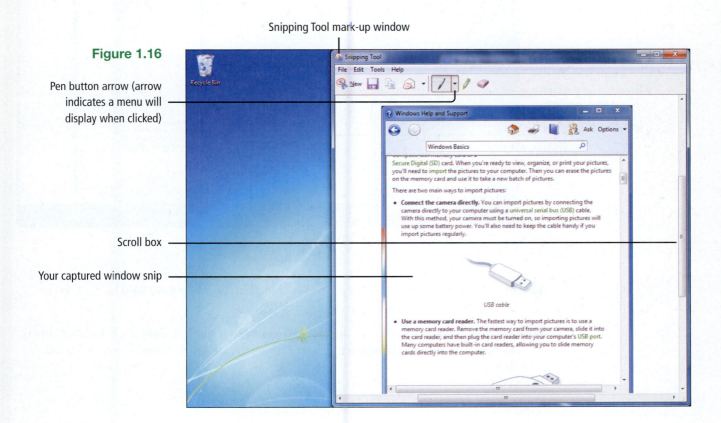

11 On the toolbar of the **Snipping Tool** mark-up window, click the **Pen button arrow**, and then click **Red Pen**. Notice that your mouse pointer displays as a red dot.

12 In the illustration of the USB cable, point to the end of the cable in the upper left portion of the picture, and then while holding down the left mouse button, draw a red free-form circle around the illustration of the USB cable as shown in Figure 1.17. If you are not satisfied with your circle, on the toolbar, click the Eraser button, point anywhere on the red circle, click to erase, and then begin again.

13 On the toolbar of the **Snipping Tool** mark-up window, click the **Highlighter** [/] button. Notice that your mouse pointer displays as a small yellow rectangle.

14 Under the illustration of the USB cable, point to the caption text *USB cable*, hold down the left mouse button, and then drag over the text to highlight it in yellow. If you are not satisfied with your yellow highlight, on the toolbar, click the Eraser button [⬦], point anywhere on the yellow highlight, click to erase, and then begin again. Compare your screen with Figure 1.17.

Figure 1.17

Highlighter button ————

Eraser button ————

Free-form red circle
around illustration
Mouse pointer displays
as yellow rectangle ————

USB cable highlighted
in yellow ————

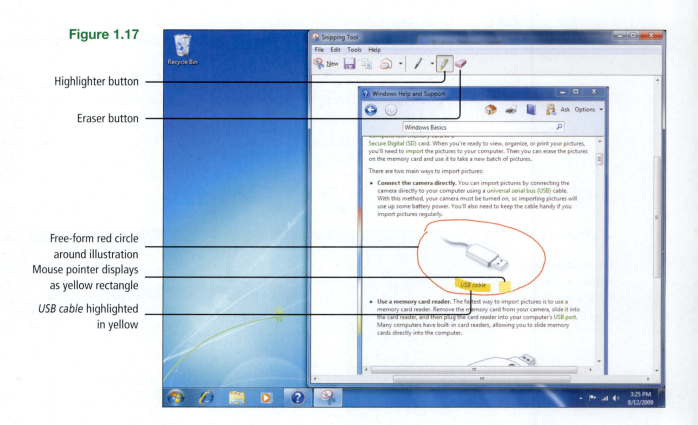

15 On the **Snipping Tool** mark-up window's toolbar, click the **Save Snip** button [💾] to display the **Save As** dialog box.

16 In the **Save As** dialog box, in the **navigation pane** on the left, drag the scroll box down as necessary to view **Computer**. Under **Computer**, click the name of your USB flash drive.

Another Way

Right-click the folder name and click Open.

17 In the **file list**, scroll as necessary, locate and *double-click*—press the left mouse button two times in rapid succession while holding the mouse still—your **Windows 7 Chapter 1** folder. Compare your screen with Figure 1.18.

Figure 1.18
Address bar indicates path to folder

Computer in navigation pane

File name box

Save as type box

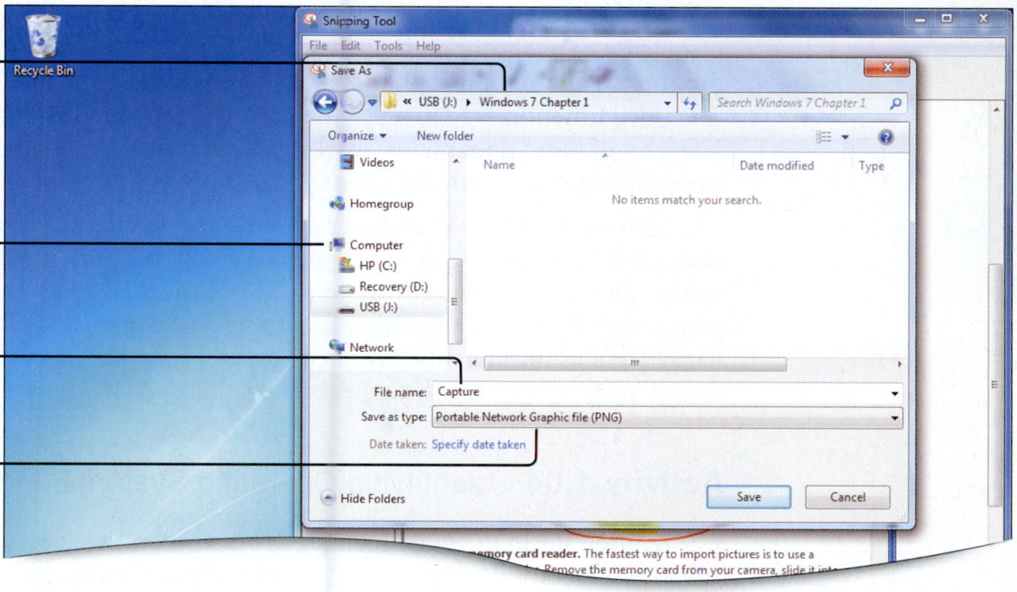

Note | Successful Double-Clicking Requires a Steady Hand

Double-clicking needs a steady hand. The speed of the two clicks is not so important as holding the mouse still between the two clicks. If you are not satisfied with your result, try again.

18 At the bottom of the **Save As** dialog box, locate the **Save as type** box, click anywhere in the box to display a list, and then from the displayed list click **JPEG file**.

JPEG, which is commonly pronounced *JAY-peg*, and stands for Joint Photographic Experts Group, is a common file type used by digital cameras and computers to store digital pictures. JPEG is popular because it can store a high-quality picture in a relatively small file.

19 At the bottom of the **Save As** dialog box, click in the **File name** box to select the text *Capture*, and then using your own name, type **Lastname_Firstname_1A_USB_Snip**

Within any Windows-based program, text highlighted in blue—selected—in this manner will be replaced by your typing.

Note | File Naming in This Textbook

Windows 7 recognizes file names with spaces. However, some older Internet file transfer programs do not. To facilitate sending your files over the Internet, in this textbook you will be instructed to save files using an underscore instead of a space. The underscore key is the shift of the - key—on most keyboards located two keys to the left of Bksp.

20 In the lower right corner of the window, click the **Save** button.

21 Close [X] the **Snipping Tool** mark-up window and the **Windows Help and Support** window. Hold this file until you finish Project 1A, and then submit as directed by your instructor.

You have successfully created a folder on a removable storage device and saved a file within that folder.

Objective 2 | Identify the Functions of an Operating System

Operating system software has three major functions. The first function is to manage your computer's hardware—the printers, scanners, disk drives, monitors, and other hardware attached to it. The second function is to manage the application software installed on your computer—programs like those in Microsoft Office 2010 and other programs you might install to manage your money, edit photos, play games, and so on. The third function is to manage the *data* generated from your application software. Data refers to all those documents, worksheets, pictures, songs, and so on that you create and store during the day-to-day use of your computer.

In most instances, when you purchase a computer, the operating system software is already installed. The operating system consists of many smaller programs, stored as system files, which transfer data to and from the disk and transfer data in and out of your computer's memory. Other functions performed by the operating system include hardware-specific tasks such as checking to see if a key has been pressed on the keyboard and, if it has, displaying the appropriate letter or character on the screen.

Activity 1.04 | Identifying Operating System Functions

Windows 7, in the same manner as other operating systems and earlier versions of the Windows operating system, uses a *graphical user interface*—abbreviated as *GUI* and pronounced GOO-ee. A graphical user interface uses graphics such as an image of a file folder or wastebasket that you click or double-click to activate the item represented. A GUI commonly incorporates the following:

A *pointer*—any symbol that displays on your screen in response to moving your mouse and with which you can select objects and commands.

A *pointing device*, such as a mouse or touchpad, to control the pointer.

Icons—small images that represent commands, files, or other windows. By selecting an icon and pressing a mouse button, you can start a program or move objects to different locations on your screen.

A *desktop*—a simulation of a real desk that represents your work area; here you can arrange icons such as shortcuts to programs, files, folders, and various types of documents in the same manner you would arrange physical objects on top of a desk.

The parts of your computer such as the central processing unit (CPU), memory, and any attached devices such as a printer, are collectively known as *resources*. The operating system keeps track of the status of each resource and decides when a resource needs attention and for how long. Fortunately, you need not be concerned about these operations; Windows 7 performs these tasks with no effort on your part.

There will be times when you want and need to interact with the functions of the operating system; for example, when you want to install a new hardware device like a color printer. Windows 7 provides tools such as Devices and Printers with which you can interact with the operating system about new hardware that you attach to your computer.

Software application programs are the programs that enable you to do work on, and be entertained by, your computer—programs such as Word and Excel found in the Microsoft Office suite of products, Adobe Photoshop, and computer games. An application program, however, cannot run on its own—it must run under the direction of the operating system.

For the everyday use of your computer, the most important and most often used function of the operating system is managing your files and folders—referred to as *data management*. In the same manner that you strive to keep your paper documents and file folders organized so that you can find information when you need it, your goal when organizing your computer files and folders is to group your files so that you can find information easily. Managing your data files so that you can find your information when you need it is an important computing skill. Fortunately, the organization of Windows 7's filing system makes doing so a logical and straightforward process.

To check how well you can identify operating system functions, take a moment to answer the following questions:

1 Of the three major functions of the operating system, the first is to manage your computer's _____ such as disk drives, monitors, and printers.

2 The second major function of the operating system is to manage the application _____ such as Microsoft Word, Microsoft Excel, and video games.

3 The third major function of the operating system is to manage the _____ generated from your applications—the files such as Word documents, Excel worksheets, pictures, and songs.

4 Windows 7 uses graphics such as images of a file folder or a wastebasket that you click to interact with the operating system; such a system is referred to as a _____ _____ _____

5 One of the most important computing skills you can learn is how to manage your _____ _____ so that you can find your information quickly.

Objective 3 | Use the Getting Started Information and Windows Help and Support

The Windows 7 *Getting Started* feature is a task-centered grouping of links to tools that can help you get started with and add new features to your computer. Additionally, when you need information about the basic setup and operation of your computer or about how to do something, you can rely on *Windows Help and Support*. Windows Help and Support is the built-in help system for Windows 7.

Another Way

Getting Started may
display on the Start
menu; or, on the Start
menu, click Help and
Support, and then click
the link *How to get
started with your
computer.* Then point
to and click *Click to
open Getting Started.*

Activity 1.05 | Using the Getting Started Information and Windows
Help and Support

1 On the taskbar, click the **Start** button ⊙, and then on the right, click **Control
Panel**. Notice that in the upper right corner of the window, the insertion point
is blinking in the search box. Type **get** and then compare your screen with
Figure 1.19.

Windows 7 searches using a lookup method known as ***word wheel***, in which each new
character that you type into a search box further refines a search. In this instance, typing
only *get* refines the search of Control Panel enough so that the Getting Started link
displays at the top of the screen.

The ***insertion point*** is a blinking vertical line that indicates where text or graphics will be
inserted.

The settings in the Control Panel control nearly everything about how Windows 7 looks
and performs. For example, this is where you can change the color of your desktop. Some
of the most common reasons to go to the Control Panel are to install new software
programs, to uninstall software programs you no longer want, to connect to new
networks, and to back up your computer.

Figure 1.19

Control Panel window

get typed in Search box

Getting Started displays

2 At the top of the **Control Panel** window, click **Getting Started**, and then compare your screen with Figure 1.20.

Here you can link to online resources or to information about basic tasks such as backing up your files or adding new users to your computer.

Figure 1.20

Getting Started window —

3 In the **Getting Started** window, click **Personalize Windows**, notice the description at the top of the window, and then in the center right of the window, click **Personalize Windows**.

The Personalization window displays. As you progress in your study of Windows 7, you will practice many distinctive ways to personalize your computer.

4 On the taskbar, click the **Start** button 🔵, and then on the right, click **Help and Support**. Locate and then display **Windows Basics: all topics**. Compare your screen with Figure 1.21.

> The Windows Help and Support window displays a list of basic help topics. In this manner, you can have more than one window open on your desktop, and in fact it is common to have multiple windows open at one time.

Figure 1.21

Windows Help and Support window

List of Windows Basics topics

Taskbar buttons for open windows

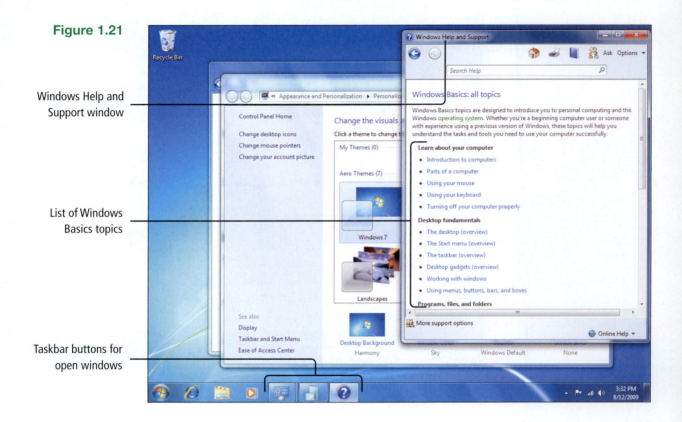

5 In the **Windows Help and Support** window, under **Learn about your computer**, click **Parts of a computer**. Under **In this article** click **Modem**, and then read the information about modems.

6 From the **Start** menu 🔵, click **Snipping Tool**, click the **New arrow**, click **Window Snip**, point to the modem picture, and then click one time. Using the red pen, draw a circle around the modem, and then highlight the text *Cable modem* in yellow.

7 Click the **Save Snip** button 💾. Be sure the folder window for your chapter folder displays, be sure the type is **JPEG**, and then in the **File name** box, using your own name type **Lastname_Firstname_1A_Modem_Snip**

8 In the lower right corner, click the **Save** button or press [Enter]. Hold this file until the end of this project, and then submit as directed by your instructor.

9 **Close** ❌ the **Snipping Tool** window. In the upper left corner of the **Windows Help and Support** window, click the **Back** button ⬅. Under **Desktop fundamentals**, click **The desktop (overview)** and examine the available information.

> You can see that Windows Help and Support offers useful information that is attractively presented and logically arranged.

10 At the top of the **Windows Help and Support** window, click in the box that indicates *Search Help*, type **security** and then press ⌷Enter⌷.

> You can also search the entire Windows Help and Support database by typing one or more words in the Search box.

11 In the displayed list, click **Security checklist for Windows 7**. At the top of the **Windows Help and Support** window, click the **Browse Help** button 📘.

> *Contents* is a list of information arranged by topic, similar to a table of contents in a book.

12 In the upper right corner of each open window, click the **Close** ❎ button until all windows are closed and only your desktop displays.

Objective 4 | Log Off, Turn Off Your Computer, and View Power Options

On your own computer, when you are done working, log off from Windows 7 if necessary, and then set your computer properly so that your data is saved, you save energy, and your computer remains secure.

When you turn off your computer by using the *Sleep* command, Windows 7 automatically saves your work, the screen goes dark, the computer's fan stops, and your computer goes to sleep. A light on your computer's case may blink or turn yellow to indicate the sleep mode. You need not close your programs or files because your work is saved. When you wake up your computer by pressing a key or moving the mouse, you need only to enter your password (if required); your screen will display exactly like it did when you turned off your computer. Your computer uses a small amount of power in sleep mode.

Activity 1.06 | Logging Off and Turning Off Your Computer

In an organization, there might be a specific process for logging off from Windows 7 and turning off the computer. The policy at Bell Orchid Hotels requires an employee to log off or lock the computer when away from his or her desk and to activate Sleep mode when leaving the building.

1 Display the **Start** menu 🟦, and then in the lower right corner, point to the **Shut down arrow** [Shut down ▷] to display the submenu. Compare your screen with Figure 1.22, and then take a moment to study the table in Figure 1.23.

Figure 1.22
Shut down
button submenu

Shut down button

Options for Logging On To and Off From Windows 7 and Turning Off Your Computer Properly	
Switch user	Logs the active user account off of Windows, and then displays the Windows 7 welcome screen with all user accounts so that another user can log on to Windows.
Log off	Logs the active user account off of Windows, and then displays the Windows 7 welcome screen. From this point, you or another user can log on to Windows.
Lock	Locks the computer so that a password (if applicable) is required to log back on to your desktop. Others can log on to their own desktops while your desktop is locked by clicking the Switch User button. Use this feature if you are leaving your desk for a short time so that others cannot view your work and to prevent those who do not have a user account on your computer from using it.
Restart	Restarts the computer and clears the *system cache*—an area of the computer's memory where Windows 7 stores information it needs to access quickly. Use this feature if your computer is operating slowly or having technical problems, or after installing new software or software updates.
Sleep	Saves your work, turns off the screen display, stops the computer's fan, and puts the computer to sleep; uses a small amount of power to keep your work in memory. After sleeping for several hours, everything in memory is saved on the hard disk.
Hibernate	Displays as an option on some laptop computers and is similar to Sleep.
Shut down	Closes all programs and network connections and stops the hard disk. No power is used. Shut down only to install or repair hardware inside the computer or attach hardware that does not connect with a USB cable.

Figure 1.23

2 On the right side of the **Start** menu 🟦, click **Control Panel**, and then click **Hardware and Sound**. Click **Power Options**.

Here you can change your power plan or make other changes to the manner in which your computer uses power. These options are set by your computer's manufacturer, and are usually optimized for the best use of power on your system. Consult the user manual for your computer before adjusting these settings.

3 On the left, click **Change when the computer sleeps**.

Here you can change the amount of time that elapses before your computer *automatically* turns off the display and puts the computer to sleep, which happens if you leave your computer unattended.

4 Close [❌] the **Edit Plan Settings** window.

Objective 5 | Manage Your User Account

On your own computer, you can elect to use no user accounts and disable the password on the first administrator account. If you do that, when you start or wake your computer, the desktop will display and no logon or password is required. The administrator will be the only user. Because Windows 7 supports multiple users, however, there is always at least one user—the initial administrator that was established when the system was purchased or when Windows 7 was installed.

As the administrator of your own computer, you can restrict access to your computer so that only people you authorize can use your computer or view its files. This access is managed through a user account, which is a collection of information that tells Windows 7 what files and folders the account holder can access, what changes the account holder can make to the computer system, and what the account holder's personal preferences are. Each person accesses his or her user account with a user name and password, and each user has his or her own desktop, files, and folders.

User accounts are useful because you can share a computer with other people in your family or organization while maintaining your own desktop and files that others cannot see and settings that others cannot change. For example, you may prefer that your screen displays with a light background, however another person using the same computer may prefer a screen with a dark background.

Windows 7 provides three types of user accounts—administrator, standard, and guest—and each one provides a different level of computer control. When upgrading a computer to Windows 7, you will be asked to create a user account. On a new computer with Windows 7 already installed, follow the steps provided by the computer manufacturer or those in the following activities to add a password to the administrator account if you want to do so.

An **administrator account** allows complete access to the computer. Administrators can make changes that affect other users, change security settings, install software and hardware, access all files on the computer, and make changes to other user accounts. It is the most powerful type of account, because it permits the most control over the computer.

Even if you are the only person using your computer, after you have finished setting up your computer, Microsoft recommends that you create and use a **standard user account** for your day-to-day computing. A standard user account enables you to use most of the capabilities of the computer, install some software, and change systems settings that do not affect other users or the security of the computer. While using a standard user account, you can do almost anything that you can do with an administrator account, but you might be prompted for the administrator password before you can perform certain tasks such as installing some software or changing security settings.

If you are the only person using your computer, you can use a single administrator account as your user account and even remove the password from the administrator account so that no logon or password is required. However, Windows 7 recommends that you set up a standard user account for most of your work and use the administrator account only when you need to perform tasks that affect the entire computer system. By doing so, you protect your computer by preventing anyone else from making changes to your computer.

A **guest account** allows people to have temporary access to your computer. People using the guest account cannot install software or hardware, change settings, or create a password. To use the guest account, you must turn it on. Because the guest account allows a user to log on to your network, if you have one, browse the Internet, and shut down the computer, it is a good idea to disable the guest account when it is not being used. A **network** refers to a group of computers or other devices, such as printers and scanners, which communicate either wirelessly or by using a physical connection. Small home networks of two or more computers and printers are becoming increasingly common.

Activity 1.07 | Managing Your Own User Account

If necessary, wake your computer by pressing any key or moving the mouse, and then if necessary, log on to Windows or use your organization's logon process.

1 Display the **Start** menu 🌐. On the right, click **Control Panel**, and then click **User Accounts and Family Safety** (or User Accounts)—this varies depending on your edition of Windows 7.

2 Under **User Accounts**, click **Change your account picture**. In the displayed **Change Your Picture** window, click the **soccer ball picture**, and then compare your screen with Figure 1.24.

You can use one of your own photos as the user picture by clicking *Browse for more pictures* and then navigating to a stored image.

Figure 1.24

Change Your
Picture window

Status of the current
user (yours will differ)

Soccer ball picture selected

Change Picture button

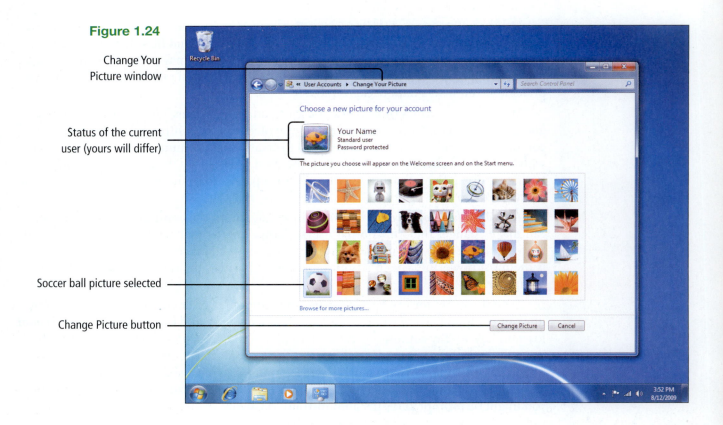

3 In the lower right corner, click the **Change Picture** button, and then at the top of the **Control Panel** window, click **Change your Windows password**. Notice that your new picture displays.

Here you can *change* your Windows 7 logon password, or, if you want to do so, you can *remove* your password completely so that no password is required to log on. If you do not want to have to enter a password each time you use your computer, and if you are confident that no one else will use your computer in an unauthorized manner, you can remove your password completely.

Here you can also change your account name. If you are logged on with an Administrator account, you can also manage the accounts of other users.

On this screen, you can also create a password reset disk, which you can insert if you forget your password. To do so, follow the instructions on the screen after starting the *Create a password reset disk* command.

4 **Close** the **User Accounts** window.

> **More Knowledge** | Using a Reset Disk if You Forget Your Password
>
> If you use a password on your computer, it is a good idea to create a password reset disk. Then, if you forget your password when logging on, click OK in the displayed error message. Windows 7 will display the password hint you entered when you created the password, which might remind you of your password. If you still cannot remember your password, insert the flash drive on which you created your reset disk, click Reset password, and then follow the steps in the displayed Password Reset Wizard. Reserve a flash drive for this purpose and use it only if necessary to reset.

Activity 1.08 | Creating and Deleting User Accounts

> **Alert!** | This is an Optional Activity
>
> This activity is optional; you can complete this activity if you are logged on with an administrator account, or if you know the administrator password.

Some Windows 7 features are available only to users who are logged on with an administrator account; for example, only an administrator can add new user accounts or delete user accounts. If you are logged on with administrator rights, you can complete the steps in this activity. If you do not have an administrator account or do not know the administrator password, you can read through the steps for information.

1 From the **Start** menu, display **Control Panel**, and then under **User Accounts and Family Safety** (or User Accounts), click **Add or remove user accounts**—enter the password if prompted.

2 In the lower portion of the screen, click **Create a new account**.

The Create New Account window displays. Here you create the name for the new user account. The new user account name will display on the Windows 7 welcome screen. It will also display in the Start menu when this account holder is logged on. The default user account type is a standard user, as indicated by the selected option button.

When creating user names, consider developing a *naming convention*—a plan that provides a consistent pattern for names.

3 In the **New account name** box, type **B Hewitt** and then in the lower right corner, click the **Create Account** button.

Windows 7 creates the new standard user account and applies one of the pictures. You may not see the user pictures if you are logged on as a standard user and accessed this screen by typing the administrator password.

4 In the **Manage Accounts** window, click **B Hewitt**. Then, in the **Change an Account** window, click **Create a password**.

Although not required, it is good practice to have a password for each user. Passwords prevent unauthorized access to that user's desktop and files. Effective passwords are at least eight characters in length and are not obvious to others. For example, using your pet's name is not a good password because it could be easily guessed by others. Passwords are also *case sensitive*, that is, capitalization must match each time the characters are typed.

5 In the **New password** box, type **gowindows7** and press Tab. In the **Confirm new password** box, type **gowindows7** Notice that instead of your typing, a series of black circles displays to prevent others from seeing your password as you create it.

6 Point to and then click the link **How to create a strong password**, and then compare your screen with Figure 1.25.

> The Windows Help and Support window displays. Here you can read valuable information about creating strong passwords. Use Windows 7's Help and Support system in this manner to enhance your learning and understanding of Windows 7.

Figure 1.25

Windows Help and Support window

Close button

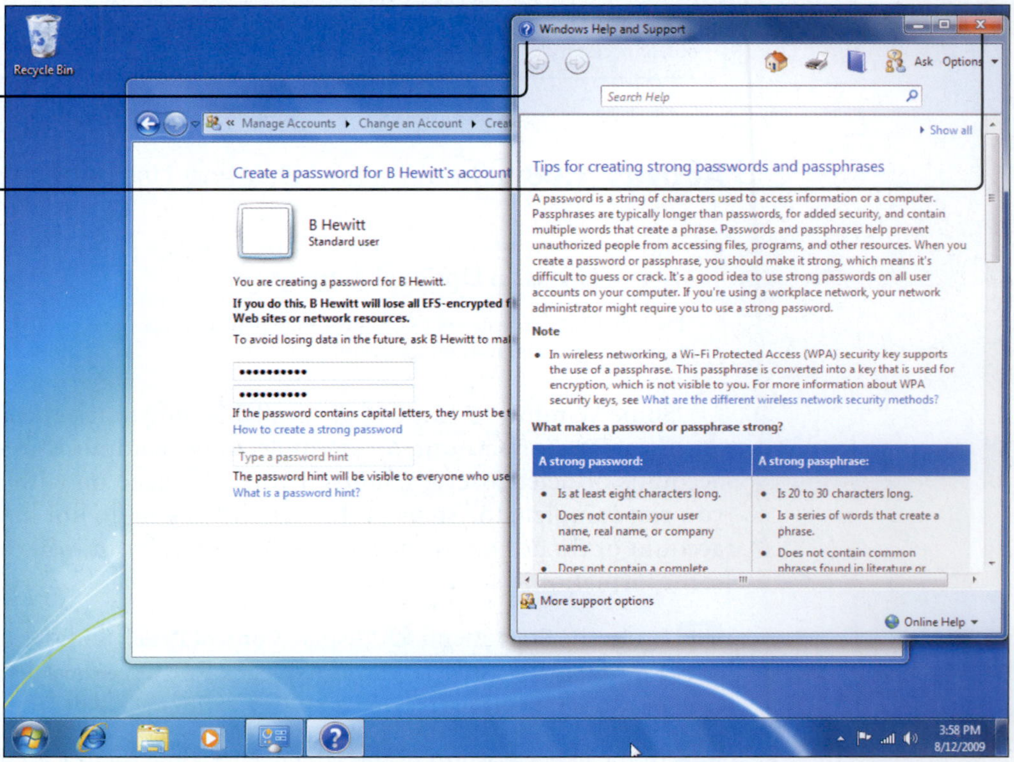

7 **Close** ☒ the **Windows Help and Support** window. Click in the **Type a password hint** box and type **textbook name**

8 In the lower right corner, click the **Create password** button, and then **Close** ☒ the **Change an Account** window.

9 On the **Start** menu 🏁, point to the **Shut down arrow**, and then click **Switch user**. Wait a moment for the Welcome screen to display, and then notice the new account for *B Hewitt*. Notice also that your name is indicated as *Logged on*.

10 Click your user name and type your password if necessary.

11 From the **Start** menu 🏁, display **Control Panel**, and then under **User Accounts and Family Safety** (or User Accounts), click **Add or remove user accounts**. Type your administrator password if necessary.

12 Click the **B Hewitt** account name to display the **Change an Account** window, and then under **Make changes to B Hewitt's account**, click **Delete the account**.

> In the displayed Delete Account window, you have the option to keep the files and settings of the user you are about to delete. In those instances where you want to save these files, you can click Keep Files.

13 Click **Delete Files**, and then in the displayed **Confirm Deletion** window, click **Delete Account**.

14 Close the **Manage Accounts** window.

15 Submit the two snip files that are the results of this project as directed by your instructor.

More Knowledge | Logging on the First Time with a New User Account

When a new account user logs on the first time, Windows indicates that a new desktop is being prepared. Recall that each user account has its own desktop and set of personal folders.

End **You have completed Project 1A** ——————————————

Project 1B Working With Windows, Programs, and Files

In Activities 1.09 through 1.18, you will train with Steven Ramos and Barbara Hewitt, employees in the Information Technology Department at the Boston corporate office of the Bell Orchid Hotels, so that you will be able to open and use application programs, open data files, manage multiple windows on your desktop, and locate files and folders on your computer system. You will capture four screens that look similar to Figure 1.26.

Project Files

For Project 1B, you will need the following files:

Student Resource CD or a flash drive containing the student data files
New snip files

You will save your files as:

Lastname_Firstname_1B_Grouped_Snip
Lastname_Firstname_1B_WordPad_Snip
Lastname_Firstname_1B_SideBySide_Snip
Lastname_Firstname_1B_Snap_Snip

Project Results

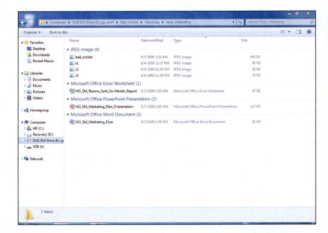
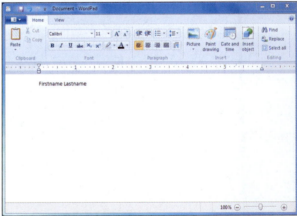
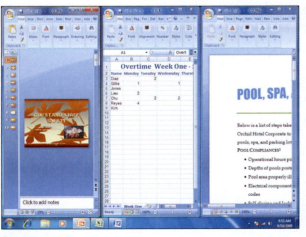
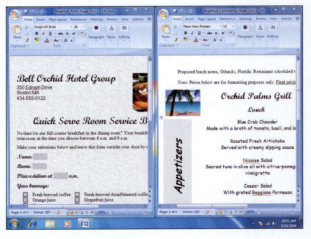

Figure 1.26
Project 1B Working With Windows, Programs, and Files

Objective 6 | Display Libraries, Folders, and Files in a Window

A file is the fundamental unit of storage that enables Windows 7 to distinguish one set of information from another. Recall that a file is a collection of information stored on a computer under a single name such as a Word document, an Excel workbook, a picture, a song, or a program.

A folder is the basic organizing tool for files. Recall that a folder is a container in which you store files. In a folder, you can store files that are related to one another. You can also put a folder inside of another folder, which is referred to as a subfolder. You can create any number of subfolders, and each can hold any number of files and additional subfolders.

Windows 7 arranges folders in a structure that resembles a *hierarchy*—an arrangement where items are ranked and where each level is lower in rank than the item above it. In this manner, a hierarchy gives a visual representation of related files and folders. The hierarchy of folders is referred to as the *folder structure*. A sequence of folders in the folder structure that leads to a specific file or folder is a path.

A library is a collection of items, such as files and folders, assembled from various locations; the locations might be on your computer, on an external hard drive connected to your computer, or on another computer in your network. A library does not actually store your items; rather, a library provides a single access point from which you can open folders and files from different locations.

Activity 1.09 | Displaying Libraries, Folders, and Files in a Folder Window

When you open a folder or library, a folder window displays. The folder window is the one feature you will use most often in Windows 7. A folder window shows you the contents of a folder or library. The design of the folder window helps you navigate—explore within the folder structure for the purpose of finding files and folders—Windows 7 so that you can save and locate your files and folders efficiently.

In this activity, you will open a folder window and examine its parts.

1 Log on to your computer to display your Windows 7 desktop, and then click the **Start** button. At the top of the right section, locate your user account name under the picture, point to the name to display the **ScreenTip** *Open your personal folder*, and then compare your screen with Figure 1.27.

A *ScreenTip* displays useful information when you perform various mouse actions, such as pointing to screen elements.

For each user account, Windows 7 creates a desktop and a *personal folder*, and for the logged on user, the folder is always located at the top of the Start menu in this manner. Within the personal folder for each user account, Windows 7 creates a number of subfolders, some of which also display on the Start menu for your convenience; for example, *Documents*, *Pictures*, *Music*, and *Games*.

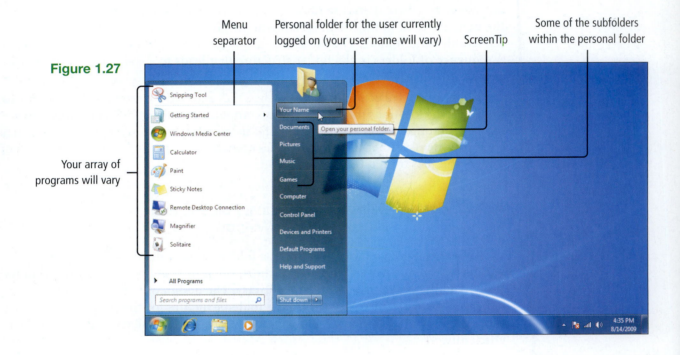

Figure 1.27

2 Click your user name, and then compare your screen with Figure 1.28.

For each user account, Windows 7 creates this group of folders. If you have set up other users on your system with passwords, they cannot access your set of folders when they are logged in.

Close button

Figure 1.28

All of the subfolders in your personal folder—created by Windows 7

Windows Explorer button on the taskbar

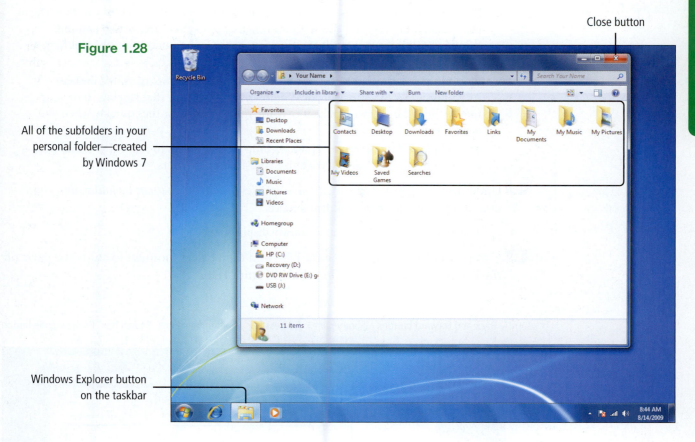

3 In the upper right corner of the window, click the **Close** ✕ button to close the window.

4 On the taskbar, click the **Windows Explorer** button 📁 to display the **Libraries** window.

Windows Explorer is the program within Windows 7 that displays the contents of libraries, folders, and files on your computer, and which also enables you to perform tasks related to your files and folders such as copying, moving, and renaming. Windows Explorer is at work any time you are viewing the contents of a library, a folder, or a file.

By default, the Windows Explorer button on the taskbar opens your Libraries. As you progress in your study of Windows 7, you will see that storing all of your files within a library will make it easy for you to find your files quickly when you need them.

The Windows Explorer icon shows a group of file folders to remind you that this program helps you find and organize your files and folders.

Another Way

Point to Documents, right-click to display a shortcut menu, and then click Open.

5 Under the text *Open a library to see your files and arrange them by folder, date, and other properties*, double-click **Documents**.

The window for the Documents library displays.

6 Compare your screen with Figure 1.29, and then take a moment to study the parts of the window as described in the table in Figure 1.30.

Back and Forward buttons   Library pane   Address bar   Column headings   Search box   Preview pane button

Figure 1.29

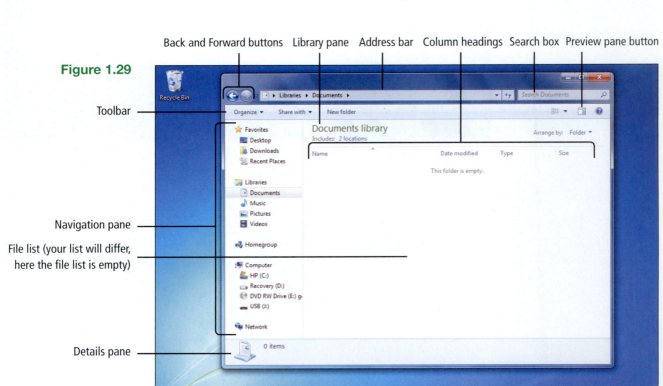

Toolbar

Navigation pane

File list (your list will differ, here the file list is empty)

Details pane

Parts of the Documents Library Window

Window Part	Function
Address bar	Displays your current location in the file structure as a series of links separated by arrows.
Back and Forward buttons	Provides the ability to navigate to other folders you have already opened without closing the current folder window. These buttons work with the address bar; that is, after you use the address bar to change folders, you can use the Back button to return to the previous folder.
Column headings	Identify the columns. By clicking on the column heading, you can change how the files in the file list are organized; by clicking on the arrow on the right, you can sort items in the file list.
Details pane	Displays the most common properties associated with the selected file.
File list	Displays the contents of the current folder or library. If you type text into the Search box, only the folders and files that match your search will display here—including files in subfolders.
Library pane	Enables you to customize the library or arrange files by different *file properties*—information about the files, such as the author, the date the file was last changed, and any descriptive *tags* (a property that you create to help you find and organize your files) you might have added to the file. This pane displays only when you are in a library, such as the Documents library.
Navigation pane	Displays Favorites, Libraries, a Homegroup if you have one, and an expandable list of drives and folders in an area on the left side of a folder window. Use Favorites to open your most commonly used folders and searches; use Libraries to access your libraries. If you have a folder that you use frequently, you can drag it to the Favorites area so that it is always available.
Preview pane button	Opens an additional pane on the right side of the file list to display a preview of a file (not a folder) that you select in the file list.
Search box	Enables you to type a word or phrase and then searches for a file or subfolder stored in the current folder that contains matching text. The search begins as soon as you begin typing, so for example, if you type *G*, all the files that start with the letter *G* will display in the file list.
Toolbar	Provides buttons with which you can perform common tasks, such as changing the appearance of your files and folders, copying files to a CD, or starting a digital picture slide show. The buttons change in context with the type of file selected; for example, if a picture file is selected, different buttons display than if a music file is selected.

Figure 1.30

7 With the **Documents** folder window displayed, insert the **Student Resource CD** that came with this book—or a USB flash drive containing the files. Wait a few moments, and then **Close** [x] the **AutoPlay** window that displays when removable media is inserted. In the **navigation pane**, under **Computer**, scroll down as necessary, and notice that your DVD or other inserted device displays.

Alert! | If you are not using the Student Resource CD

If your student data files are on a USB flash drive instead of a CD, insert the USB flash drive, and then in the following steps, select the appropriate USB flash drive instead of the CD.

---

8 Move your [cursor] pointer anywhere into the **navigation pane**, and notice that a **black arrow** ◢ displays to the left of *Favorites, Libraries*, and *Computer*, to indicate that these items are expanded, and a **white arrow** ▷ displays to the right of items that are collapsed (hidden).

You can click these arrows to collapse and expand areas in the navigation pane.

9 In the **navigation pane**, under **Computer**, click your **CD/DVD** (or USB device) one time to display its contents in the **file list**. Compare your screen with Figure 1.31.

In the navigation pane, *Computer* displays all of the drive letter locations attached to your computer, including the internal hard drives, CD or DVD drives, and any connected devices such as USB flash drive.

Figure 1.31

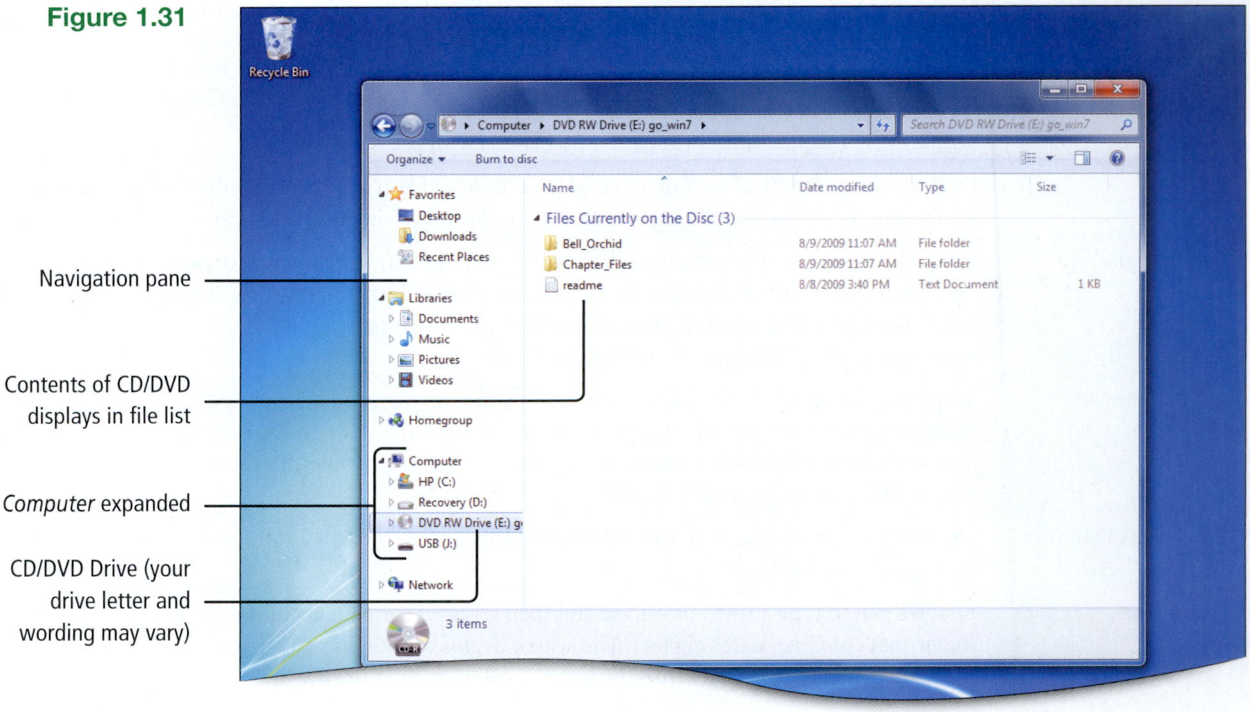

Navigation pane

Contents of CD/DVD displays in file list

Computer expanded

CD/DVD Drive (your drive letter and wording may vary)

Another Way

Right-click the folder, and then click Open.

10 In the **file list**, double-click **Bell_Orchid** to display the subfolders.

Recall that the corporate office of the Bell Orchid Hotels is in Boston. The corporate office maintains subfolders labeled for each of its large hotels in Honolulu, Orlando, San Diego, and Santa Barbara.

11 In the **file list**, double-click **Orlando** to display the subfolders, and then look at the **address bar** to view the path. Compare your screen with Figure 1.32.

> Within each city's subfolder, there is a structure of subfolders for the Accounting, Engineering, Food and Beverage, Human Resources, Operations, and Sales and Marketing departments.
>
> Because folders can be placed inside of other folders, such an arrangement is common when organizing files on a computer.
>
> In the address bar, the path from your CD/DVD (or flash drive) to the Bell_Orchid folder to the Orlando folder displays as a series of links.

Figure 1.32

Address bar displays path as links

Department subfolders in the Orlando folder

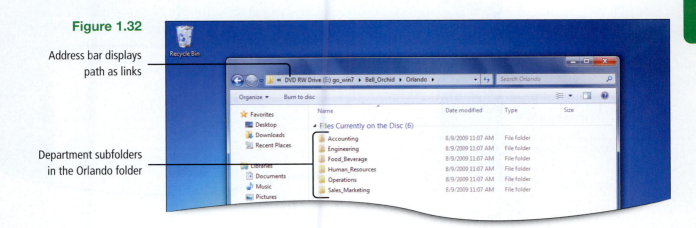

12 In the **address bar**, to the right of **Bell_Orchid**, click the ▶ arrow to display a list of the subfolders in the **Bell_Orchid** folder. On the list that displays, notice that **Orlando** displays in bold indicating it is open in the file list. Then, on the list, click **Honolulu**.

> The subfolders within the Honolulu folder display.

13 In the **address bar**, to the right of **Bell_Orchid**, click the ▶ arrow again to display the subfolders in the **Bell_Orchid** folder. Then, on the **address bar** (not on the list), point to **Honolulu** and notice that the list of subfolders in the **Honolulu** folder displays.

> After you display one set of subfolders in the address bar, all of the links are active and you need only point to them to display the list of subfolders.
>
> Clicking an arrow to the right of a folder name in the address bar displays a list of the subfolders in that folder. You can click a subfolder name to display its contents. In this manner, the address bar is not only a path, but it is also an active control with which you can step from the current folder directly to any other folder above it in the folder structure just by clicking on a folder name.

Another Way

In the file list, double-click the Sales_Marketing folder.

14 On the list of subfolders for **Honolulu**, click **Sales_Marketing** to display its contents in the file list. Compare your screen with Figure 1.33.

The files in the Sales_Marketing folder for Honolulu display. To the left of each file name, an icon indicates the program used to create each file. Here, there is one PowerPoint file, one Excel file, one Word file, and four JPEG images.

Your dates will differ

Figure 1.33

Address bar displays path

Files in the Sales_ Marketing folder

Word program icon

PowerPoint program icon

Excel program icon

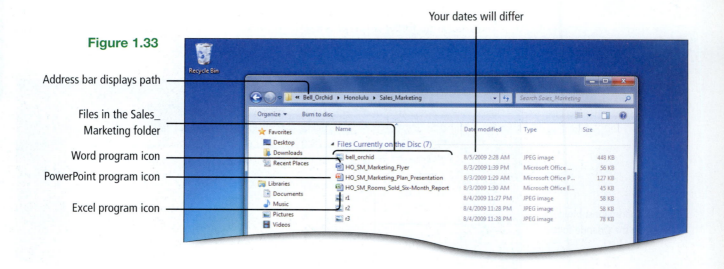

15 In the upper left corner of the folder window, click the **Back** button ⊙.

The Back button retraces each of your clicks in the same manner as clicking the Back button when you are browsing the Internet.

Another Way

Point to the folder, right-click, and then click Open.

16 In the **file list**, point to the **Human_Resources** folder, and double-click to open the folder.

17 In the **file list**, click one time to select the PowerPoint file **HO_HR_New_Employee_Presentation**. At the bottom of the window, notice the **details pane**, which displays information about the selected file.

18 In the upper right corner of the window, click the **Preview Pane** button ▣ to display the first slide of the PowerPoint file in the **preview pane**. Compare your screen with Figure 1.34.

In the preview pane that displays on the right, you can use the scroll bar to scroll through the slides in the presentation; or, you can click the up or down scroll arrow to view the slides.

Figure 1.34

Preview pane button

Preview pane

PowerPoint file selected

First slide of PowerPoint presentation displays in preview pane

Details pane displays file properties

Scroll bar in preview pane

19 In the upper right corner, click the **Preview Pane** button again ▣ to close the preview pane.

Use the preview pane when you want to look at a file quickly without actually opening it.

Activity 1.10 | Using the Navigation Pane to Display the Folder Structure

When it is useful to do so, you can use the navigation pane on the left side of a folder window to navigate files and folders and to display the folder structure.

1 On the left side of the window, in the lower portion of the **navigation pane**, point to your **CD/DVD** drive or USB device containing the student files, and then click the white expand arrow ▷ to display the two subfolders immediately below the name of your CD/DVD drive.

2 To the left of **Bell_Orchid**, click the expand arrow ▷ to display the subfolders. Scroll down if necessary, and then to the left of **San_Diego**, click the expand arrow ▷ to display the subfolders. Compare your screen with Figure 1.35.

In the navigation pane, the folder structure is shown in a visual hierarchy.

Figure 1.35

Folder structure displays

Navigation pane

3 In the **navigation pane**, under **San_Diego**, click **Accounting** to display the files in the Accounting subfolder in the file list.

Optionally, you can hide the display of the navigation pane, but it is recommended that you leave the navigation pane displayed because of its usefulness in displaying the drives on your computer and the folder structure when you want to see the structure in a hierarchical view.

4 In the upper right corner of the window, click the **Close** button ☒.

Activity 1.11 | Changing Views, Sorting, Grouping, and Filtering in a Folder Window

When looking at a list of files and folders in a folder window, there are a variety of useful arrangements in which you can view your data.

1 Be sure the device that contains the student files that accompany this textbook is inserted in your computer—either the Student Resource CD or a USB flash drive. Also, be sure that the removable storage device you are using to store files is inserted—this can be the same device on which the student files are located.

2 On the taskbar, click the **Windows Explorer** button 🗂. In the **navigation pane**, click **Computer** to display in the **file list** all the disk drives and removable devices attached to your computer.

3 In the upper right corner of the **Computer** window, on the toolbar, click the **View button arrow** . Compare your screen with Figure 1.36.

By default, the Computer window displays in Tiles view—small icons arranged in two columns. Seeing the icons helps you distinguish what type of devices are attached. For example, a CD or DVD displays a disc icon.

The Computer window is divided into the Hard Disk Drives section and the Devices with Removable Storage section.

Figure 1.36

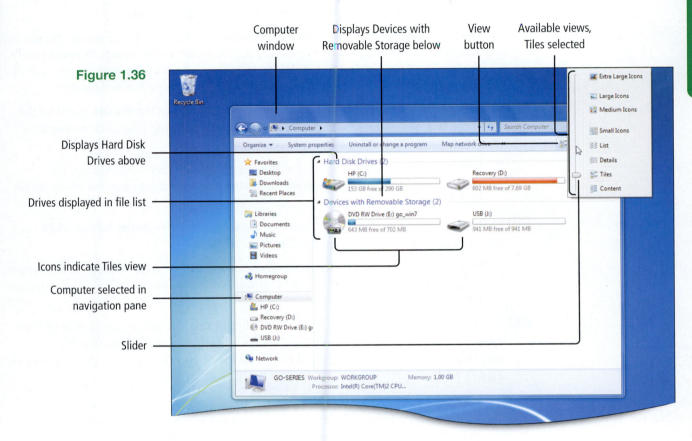

4 In the list of available views, drag the slider to the **Details** view, release the mouse button, and then notice the columnar arrangement in the **file list**. Click the **View button arrow** again, and this time, drag the slider up slowly, but do not release the left mouse button—instead, pause at each view and notice how the view in the **file list** changes as you move from one to the next.

5 Set the view to **Large Icons**, and then determine if you see the Windows logo on one of the hard disk drives.

On your own computer, you might see the Windows logo on the hard drive, which indicates the drive on which the Windows 7 operating system is installed. In a college lab, this may not display. In this manner, some views are convenient for different purposes.

6 Return the view to the Computer window's default **Tiles** view. In the **file list**, double-click the **CD/DVD drive** to display its contents. In the **file list**, double-click the **Bell_Orchid** folder to open it. Open the **Honolulu** folder to display its subfolders. In the list of **Honolulu** subfolders, open the **Sales_Marketing** folder.

7 Click the **View button arrow** [icon], and notice that the default view for a list of files is the **Details** view. Slowly drag the slider up, pausing to examine each view in the file list, and then set the view to **Large Icons**.

> The near-photographic quality of Windows 7 enables you to actually read the first slide in the PowerPoint file HO_SM_Marketing_Plan_Presentation. These are *Live Icons*—for some applications, they display a small picture of the actual contents of each file or folder.

8 Click the **View button arrow** [icon], and then set the view to **Content**.

> *Content view* displays a vertical list that includes the program icon, the date the file was last modified, the file size, and other properties such as author names or tags. Information like this is referred to as *metadata*, which is the data that describes other data; for example, the collective group of a file's properties, such as its title, subject, author, and file size.

9 Click the **View button arrow** [icon], and then click **Details**. In the **file list**, point to the Excel file **HO_SM_Rooms_Sold_Six-Month_Report** and then right-click to display a shortcut menu.

> From the shortcut menu, you can perform various tasks with the selected file. For example, you can open it—which will simultaneously start the program in which the file was created— print it, or copy it.

10 In the upper right corner of the folder window, click the **Maximize** button [icon], and then notice that the folder window fills the screen.

> When you are working with folder windows, enlarge or maximize windows as necessary to make it easier to view your work. The Maximize command optimizes your workspace for a single window.

11 In the column headings area, point to the light gray line on the right side of the **Type** column until the [icon] pointer displays, hold down the left mouse button, and then drag to the right until all of the text in this column displays, as shown in Figure 1.37.

Address bar indicates path and folder that is active in folder window

Column widened to display all text in Type column

Mouse pointer

Figure 1.37

Column headings

Window maximized to fill the screen

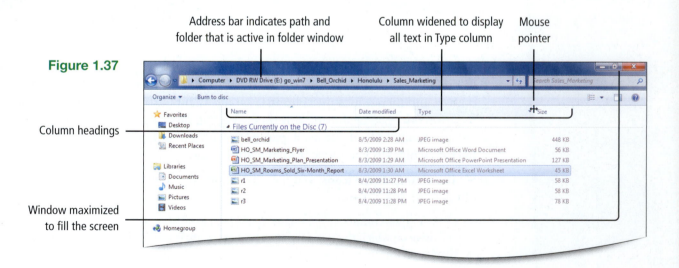

12 Point to the **Name** column heading and right-click. On the displayed shortcut menu, click **Size All Columns to Fit**.

The width of all columns adjusts to fit the contents.

13 Click the **Name** column heading to select it and notice the pale arrow near the upper edge. Click the column heading **Name** several times and notice how the alphabetical order of the file names changes each time you click, as indicated by the arrow.

When a column heading is selected, a small up or down arrow displays at the top of the heading. Each time you click the column heading, you will alternate between sorting that column in ascending or descending order.

For text, ascending order is from A to Z and descending order is from Z to A. For numbers, ascending order is from smallest to largest, and descending order is from largest to smallest.

14 Be sure the **Name** column is sorted in ascending order—the pale arrow at the top of the column points upward. Point to the **Type** column heading, and then at the right end of the heading, click the **black arrow** ▼. Click the check box to the left of **Microsoft Excel Worksheet**, click in a blank area of the **file list** to close the menu, and then compare your screen with Figure 1.38.

The list is *filtered* by Excel files—only files that meet the criteria of being an Excel file display. When you filter the contents of a folder by a file property such as *Type*, only the files with that property display. If you have a long list of files, this is a useful tool to narrow the list of files that you are looking at.

When you see a check mark at the right end of a column heading in this manner, you will know that the list is filtered.

Figure 1.38

Check mark indicates that the list is filtered

Only an Excel file displays

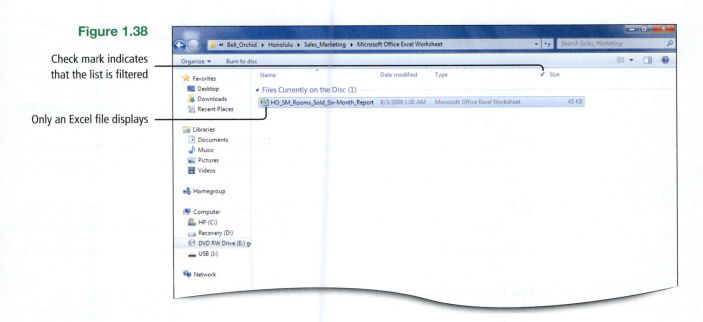

15 Point to the column heading **Type**, click the check mark that displays at the right, and then click to clear the check box to the left of **Microsoft Excel Worksheet** to redisplay all the files in the folder.

16 Click anywhere in a blank area of the file list, and then right-click. On the shortcut menu, point to **Group by**, and then on the submenu, click **Type**. If necessary, click the **Type** column heading to sort it in ascending order. Compare your screen with Figure 1.39.

> The files are grouped by type, and the types are in alphabetical order. That is, JPEG is first, followed by Microsoft Excel, and so on. When you group files by a file property such as *Type*, a separate group will display for each file type, and a heading identifies each group and indicates the number of files in the group.

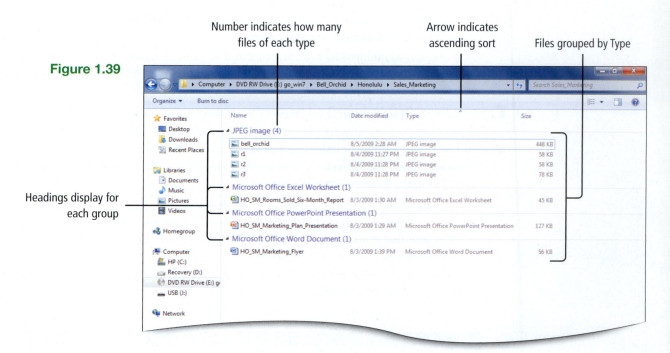

Figure 1.39

Number indicates how many files of each type

Arrow indicates ascending sort

Files grouped by Type

Headings display for each group

17 Display the **Start** menu, and then either from the pinned programs area, or by clicking All Programs, Accessories, and then Snipping Tool, display the **Snipping Tool window**.

18 Click the **New arrow**, click **Window Snip**, click anywhere in the **Sales_Marketing** folder window to select the window, and then on the **Snipping Tool** mark-up window's toolbar, click the **Save Snip** button.

19 In the **Save As** dialog box, in the **navigation pane** on the left, drag the scroll bar down as necessary to view **Computer**. Under **Computer**, click the name of your USB flash drive.

20 In the **file list**, scroll as necessary, locate and double-click your **Windows 7 Chapter 1** folder.

21 In the **File name** box and using your own name, type **Lastname_Firstname_1B_ Grouped_Snip** Be sure the file type is **JPEG**. Click the **Save** button, and then **Close** the **Snipping Tool** window. Hold this file until you finish Project 1B, and then submit this file as directed by your instructor.

22 Right-click in a blank area of the **file list**, point to **Group by**, and then click (**None**) to ungroup the files.

23 In the upper right corner, click the **Restore Down** button, and then **Close** all open windows.

> Restore Down returns the window to the size it was before you maximized it.

Objective 7 | Start Programs and Open Data Files

When you are using the software programs installed on your computer, you create and save data files—the documents, worksheets, databases, songs, pictures, and so on that you need for your job or personal use. Thus, most of your work with Windows 7 is concerned with locating and starting your programs and locating and opening your files.

You can start programs from the Start menu or from the desktop by creating a shortcut to the program there. You can open your data files from within the program in which they were created, or you can open a data file from a folder window, which will simultaneously start the program and open your file.

Activity 1.12 | Starting Programs and Opening Data Files

One way to start a program is from one of the three areas of the Start menu: the upper left, which displays the programs you have pinned there for easy access; the bottom left, which displays programs that you have recently used; or the All Programs list.

1 Be sure the Student Resource CD or flash drive containing the student data files is inserted in your computer. From the **Start** menu ⊞, point to **All Programs**, locate and click the **Accessories** folder, and then on the displayed list, click **Paint**. Compare your screen with Figure 1.40.

> *Paint* is a program that comes with Windows 7 with which you can create and edit drawings and display and edit stored photos.
>
> Recall that *All Programs* lists all of the programs available on your computer. If your list of programs is larger than the window, a scroll bar displays so that you can scroll the list. Names that display a file folder icon to the left will open to display the programs within the folder.

Figure 1.40

Paint program window ——

Ribbon of commands to use the Paint program ——

Tools group on the Home tab ——

2 On the **Ribbon** across the top of the window, with the **Home tab** active, in the **Tools group**, click the **Pencil** icon. Move your mouse pointer into the white drawing area, hold down the left mouse button, and then try writing your first name in the white area of the window.

3 In the upper left corner, to the left of the **Home tab**, click the blue tab—the **Paint** tab— to display a menu of commands of things you can do with your picture.

4 On the **Paint** menu, click **Exit**. In the displayed message, click **Don't Save**.

> Messages like this display in most programs to prevent you from forgetting to save your work. A file saved in the Paint program creates a graphic file in the JPEG format.

5 Display the **Start** menu 🪟, and then at the bottom of the menu, notice that your insertion point is blinking in the box labeled *Search programs and files*. Type **wordpad** When the program name displays in the list above, click the name to open the program. Notice that this program window has characteristics similar to the Paint program window; for example, it has a Ribbon of commands.

> If you do not immediately see a program on the All Programs list, type all or part of the name in the Search box in this manner. WordPad is another program included with Windows 7; it is a convenient program for simple word processing tasks.

6 With the insertion point blinking in the document window, type your first and last name.

7 From the **Start** menu 🪟, start **Snipping Tool** and create a **Window Snip**. Click anywhere in the WordPad window to display the **Snipping Tool** mark-up window. Save the snip in the chapter folder you created on your flash drive as **Lastname_Firstname_1B_WordPad_Snip** Hold this file until you finish Project 1B, and then submit this file as directed by your instructor.

8 **Close** ❎ the **Snipping Tool** window. In the upper right corner of the **WordPad** window, click the **Close** button ❎, and then click **Don't Save**.

9 From the **Start** menu 🪟, point to **All Programs**, click the **Microsoft Office** folder, and then from the displayed list, click **Microsoft Word**. Compare your screen with Figure 1.41.

Note | Version of Microsoft Office

You can use either Microsoft Word 2007 or Microsoft Word 2010.

The Word program window has features that are common to other programs you have opened; for example, commands are arranged on tabs. When you create and save data in Word, you create a Word document file.

Figure 1.41

Commands arranged on tabs

Word program window (Word 2007 shown here, Word 2010 has a similar arrangement)

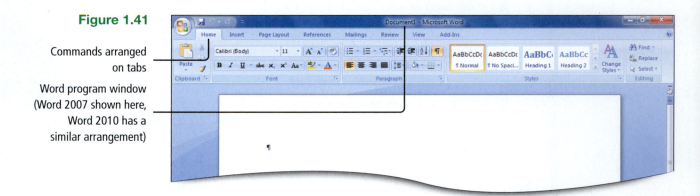

10 Press Ctrl + F12 to display the **Open** dialog box. Compare your screen with Figure 1.42, and then take a moment to study the table in Figure 1.43.

Recall that a dialog box is a window containing options for completing a task; its layout is similar to that of a folder window. When you are working in a program, use the Open dialog box to locate and open existing files that were created in the program.

By default, the Open dialog box displays the path to the *Documents* library of the user logged on. On your own computer, you can create a folder structure within the Documents library to store your documents. Alternatively, you can use the skills you have practiced to navigate to other locations on your computer, such as your removable USB flash drive.

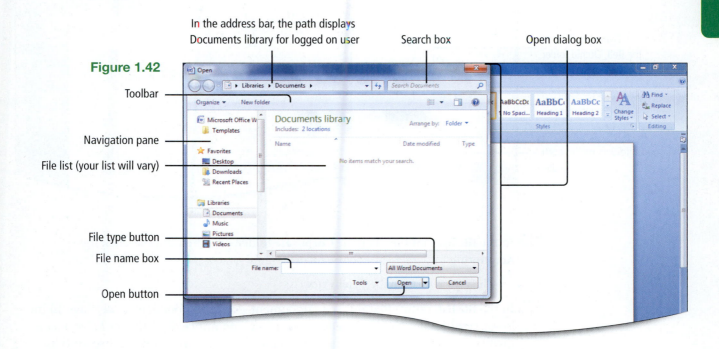

Figure 1.42

Figure 1.43

Dialog Box Element	Function
Address bar	Displays the path in the library or folder structure; by default, the path displays the Documents library for the active user.
File list	Displays the list of files and folders that are available in the library or folder indicated in the address bar.
File name box	Enables you to type the name of a specific file to locate it.
File type button	Enables you to restrict the type of files displayed in the file list, for example the default, All Word Documents, restricts the type of files displayed to only Word documents. You can click the arrow and adjust the restrictions to a narrower or wider group of files.
Navigation pane	Enables access to Favorites, Libraries, and Computer.
Search box	Filters the file list based on text that you type; the search is based on text in the file name and in the file itself, and on other properties that you can specify. The search takes place in the current folder or library, as displayed in the address bar, and in any subfolders within that folder.
Toolbar	Displays relevant tasks; for example, creating a new folder.

11 In the **navigation pane**, scroll down as necessary, and then under **Computer**, click your **CD/DVD Drive**. In the **file list**, double-click the **Bell_Orchid** folder to open it and display its contents in the file list. Click the **View button arrow** ⊞ ▾, and then set the view to **Large Icons**. Compare your screen with Figure 1.44.

Notice that the Live Icons feature indicates that each folder contains additional subfolders.

Figure 1.44

Five subfolders in the Bell_Orchid folder

CD/DVD Drive selected in navigation pane

Live Icons indicate subfolders within each folder.

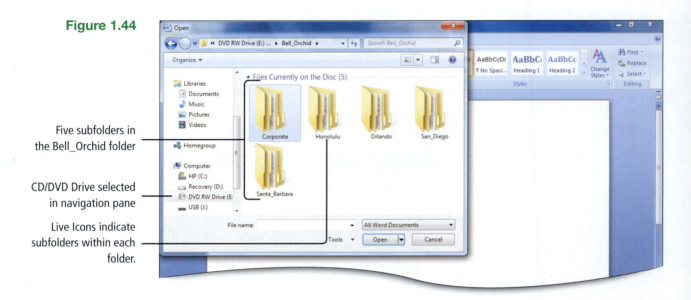

12 In the **file list**, double-click the **Corporate** folder, and then double-click the **Accounting** folder.

The view returns to the Details view.

13 In the **file list**, notice that only one document—a Word document—displays. In the lower right corner, locate the **File type** button, and notice that *All Word Documents* displays as the file type. Click the **File type arrow**, and then from the displayed list, click **All Files**. Compare your screen with Figure 1.45.

When you change the file type to *All Files*, you can see that the Word file is not the only file in this folder. By default, the Open dialog box displays only the files created in the active program; however, you can display variations of file types in this manner.

Figure 1.45

Excel file type icon

PowerPoint file type icon
Word file type icon

Folder displays all types of files

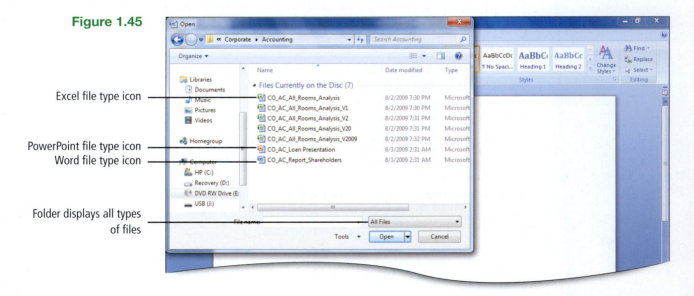

Microsoft Office file types are identified by small icons, which is a convenient way to differentiate one type of file from another. Although you can view all the files in the folder, you can open only the files that were created in the active program, which in this instance is Microsoft Word.

14 Change the file type back to **All Word Documents**. Then in the **file list**, double-click the **CO_AC_Report_Shareholders** Word file to open the document. Take a moment to scroll through the document.

15 **Close** [×] the Word window. On the taskbar at the bottom of your screen, click the **Windows Explorer** button 📁. In the **navigation pane**, under **Computer**, click your **CD/DVD Drive** to display its contents in the file list.

16 In the **file list**, open the **Bell_Orchid** folder, then open the **Corporate** folder, and then open the **Accounting** folder.

17 In the **file list**, double-click the **CO_AC_Loan_Presentation** file. When the **PowerPoint** window displays, if necessary **Maximize** [□] the program window. Compare your screen with Figure 1.46.

Figure 1.46

PowerPoint program window

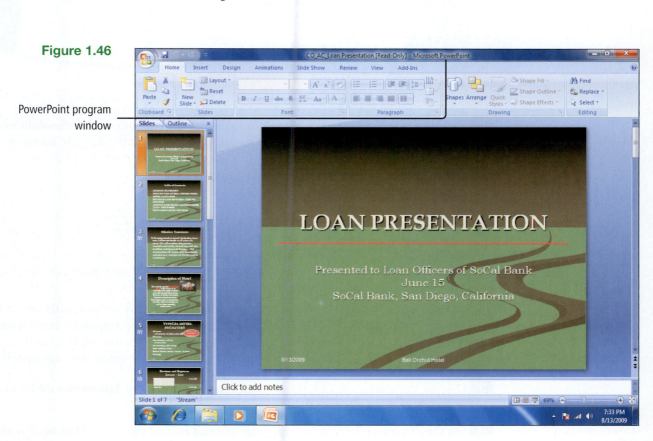

18 **Close** [×] the PowerPoint program window.

Another Way

Expand each folder level in the navigation pane.

19 In the **address bar**, to the right of **Bell_Orchid**, click ▶, and then compare your screen ----► with Figure 1.47.

Recall that the address bar is not just a path; rather, it contains active links from which you can click a folder name in the path, and then navigate directly to any displayed subfolders.

Figure 1.47

Path in address bar

Active links to subfolders

20 From the displayed list, click **Honolulu** to display the contents of the **Honolulu** folder in the **file list**. Open the **Food_Beverage** folder, and then open the **HO_FB_Banquet_Contract** file. Take a moment to view this document in the open Word program. **Close** ❌ Word, and then **Close** ❌ the folder window.

Activity 1.13 | Adding and Removing Desktop Icons

On your desktop, you can add or remove *shortcuts*, which are desktop icons that link to any item accessible on your computer or on a network, such as a program, file, folder, disk drive, printer, or another computer.

You may already have some shortcuts on your desktop. By default, only one desktop icon displays in Windows 7—the Recycle Bin; however, your computer manufacturer or organization may have placed other icons, representing shortcuts, on your desktop. Many programs automatically create a desktop icon shortcut when they are installed.

1 Display the **Start** menu 🪟, point to **All Programs**, click the **Accessories** folder to open it, and then *right-click* the **Paint** program.

2 On the displayed shortcut menu, point to **Send to**, and then click **Desktop (create shortcut)**. Click anywhere on the desktop to close the Start menu, and then notice that an icon for the **Paint** program displays on the desktop.

If you want easy access from your desktop to a program, create a shortcut to the program by using this technique.

3 On the right side of the **Start** menu 🪟, *right-click* **Control Panel**. On the shortcut menu, click **Show on Desktop**. Click anywhere on the desktop to close the Start menu.

When creating desktop shortcuts, the command *Desktop (create shortcut)* creates an icon containing a small arrow like the Paint program shortcut. The command *Show on Desktop* displays an icon with no arrow like the Control Panel shortcut. Regardless, the icon will link you to the program, object, or location indicated.

4 On the taskbar, click the **Windows Explorer** button . In the **navigation pane**, click your **CD/DVD Drive**, and then in the **file list**, *right-click* the **Bell_Orchid** folder. On the shortcut menu, point to **Send to**, and then click **Desktop (create shortcut)**. **Close** the **Computer** window, and then compare your screen with Figure 1.48.

> If you want easy access *from your desktop* to a folder or file that you use often, create shortcuts in this manner.

Figure 1.48

Desktop icon representing shortcut to Recycle Bin

Desktop icon representing shortcut to Control Panel

Desktop icon representing shortcut to Paint program

Desktop icon representing shortcut to Bell_Orchid folder on CD

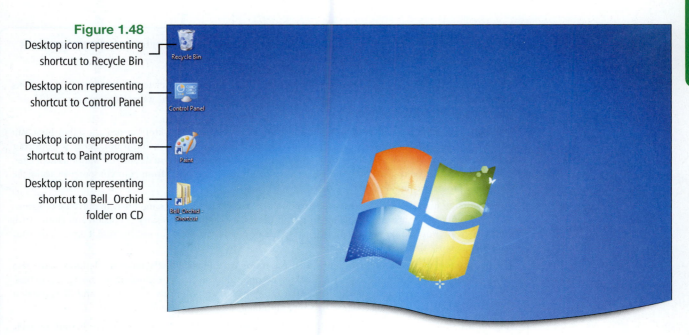

5 Double-click the **Paint** desktop icon on your desktop, **Close** the **Paint** program, and then in a similar manner, test the other desktop icons that you created.

> Because most of your work with Windows 7 is concerned with locating and opening your programs and files, you can see that using techniques like creating shortcuts on the desktop will speed your everyday computer work.

6 **Close** any open windows. On the desktop, point to the shortcut you created for the **Bell_Orchid** folder, right-click, and then on the shortcut menu, click **Delete**. Read the message that displays, and then click **Yes**.

> When you delete shortcuts from the desktop, you are deleting only the shortcut icon; you are not deleting the actual programs or files associated with the icon. The shortcut icon serves only as a *pointer* to the actual location.

Note | If you *save* a file or folder directly to the desktop, deleting it from the desktop will delete the folder or file

If you *save* a file or create a folder directly on the desktop, it is stored there. The icon that displays is not a shortcut—it displays no arrow. If you delete that icon, you will delete the actual file or folder. The file or folder is still recoverable from the Recycle Bin until the Recycle Bin is emptied. The best organizing structure is to store all of your files in the appropriate library—Documents in the Documents library, and so on—and not clutter your desktop with individual files and folders. Likewise, avoid cluttering your desktop with too many program shortcut icons. As you progress in your study of Windows 7, you will see that the taskbar is a better place to create shortcuts to programs.

7 Point to the icon you created for the **Paint** program, hold down the left mouse button, drag the icon into the **Recycle Bin**, and then release the mouse button.

> The *Recycle Bin* stores anything that you delete from your computer. Anything stored there can be retrieved, including the shortcuts that you just created, until the contents are permanently deleted by activating the Empty Recycle Bin command.

8 Using one of the techniques you have just practiced, remove the **Control Panel icon** from your desktop—do *not* remove the Recycle Bin icon.

More Knowledge | **When is it a good idea to have desktop shortcuts for a program or a folder?**

You have seen that removing shortcut icons from your desktop does not delete the actual files or programs associated with the icon. Rather, removing a shortcut deletes the pointer to the item. Thus, you can confidently remove from your desktop any shortcuts that are not useful to you.

For example, computer manufacturers commonly place shortcuts on the desktop for programs they hope you will purchase or use. Double-click each shortcut to see if it is of value to you, and if not, delete it from your desktop. Removing the shortcut does not remove the program or item, so if you decide you want this item later, it will still be available. If it is a program you will never use, also uninstall it from your computer by using the Uninstall a program command on the Control Panel.

Some computer manufacturers have started to reduce the number of shortcuts and offers to purchase programs on new computers because of complaints from consumers about the unnecessary confusion and clutter such shortcuts create. You should never feel obligated to use or purchase a program just because it appears on your computer. Remove those you do not want.

Placing desktop shortcuts for frequently used programs or folders directly on your desktop may seem convenient, but as you add more icons, your desktop becomes cluttered and the shortcuts are not as easy to find. A better organizing method is to use the taskbar for shortcuts to programs. For folders and files, the best organizing structure is to create a logical structure of folders within your Documents library.

You can also drag frequently-used folders to the Favorites area in the navigation pane so that they are available any time you open Windows Explorer. As you progress in your study of Windows 7 in this textbook, you will practice techniques for using the taskbar and the Favorites area of the navigation pane to streamline your work, instead of cluttering your desktop.

Objective 8 | Manage the Display of Individual and Multiple Windows

Activity 1.14 | Moving, Sizing, Hiding, Closing, and Switching Between Windows

When you start a program or open a folder, it displays in a window. A window is the screen element you work with most often in Windows 7. You can move, resize, maximize, minimize (hide from view), and close windows. You can also freely arrange and overlap multiple open windows on your screen, with the window currently in use on top.

1 From the **Start** menu 🪟, open the **WordPad** program—either from the recently used programs area on the left side, or by opening the Accessories folder from the All Programs menu.

2 Notice that in the taskbar, a button displays representing the open program, and the button displays a glass frame, indicating the program is open.

3 Point to the **WordPad** window's *title bar*—the bar across the top of the window that displays the program name—to display the 🔾 pointer, and then if necessary, drag the window until its position is approximately in the center of the desktop.

> Use this technique to reposition any open window.

4 Point to the window's lower right corner until the ⬉ pointer displays, and then drag up and to the left about 1 inch—the measurement need not be precise. Compare your screen with Figure 1.49.

When you drag the corner of a window in this manner, the window resizes both vertically and horizontally. You can resize a window by pointing to any of the window's borders or corners to display a two-headed arrow, and then drag the border or corner to shrink or enlarge the window.

Figure 1.49

Title bar with program name *WordPad*

Minimize button

Maximize button

Close button

Diagonal resize pointer

Program button in the taskbar displays in a glass frame to indicate an open program

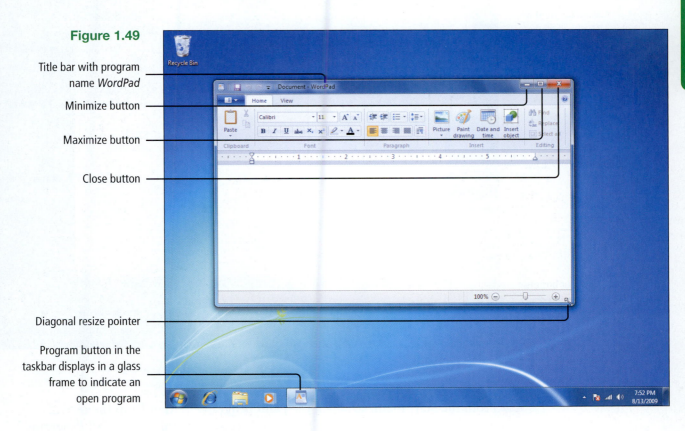

5 In the upper right corner, click the **Maximize** button 🔲 so that the WordPad program fills the entire screen. Then, in the upper right corner, click the **Restore Down** button 🔲 to return the window to its previous size.

The Restore Down button restores the window to the size it was before it was maximized.

6 From the **Start** menu ⊞, point to **All Programs**, click the **Accessories** folder, and then click **Calculator**. If necessary, drag the title bar of the **Calculator** window so that it overlaps an area of the **WordPad** window.

7 On the taskbar, notice that both programs—**WordPad** and **Calculator**—display a glass frame indicating the programs are both open; however, the **Calculator** program's button is slightly brighter, because it is the active window.

The most recently opened window is the active window.

8 Click anywhere in the **WordPad** window, and notice that it becomes the active window and moves in front of the **Calculator** window, as shown in Figure 1.50.

> Additionally, the WordPad button on the taskbar becomes the brighter of the two open programs.

Figure 1.50

Calculator window behind WordPad window (yours may be blocked entirely from view)

WordPad window active

Taskbar buttons representing open programs, WordPad slightly brighter

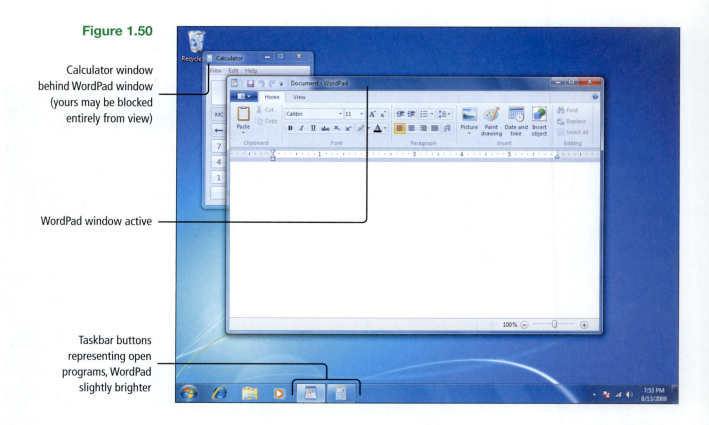

9 From the **Start** menu ⊞, open the **Paint** program—either from the recently used list on the Start menu or from the Accessories folder in the All Programs area. Notice that in the taskbar, three buttons, each representing an open program, display.

> All open programs display an icon on the taskbar with a glass frame. The active program has the brightest frame.

10 In the upper right corner of the **Paint** window, click the **Minimize** button. Then, in the taskbar, click the **WordPad** button to minimize the window.

> You can use either of these techniques to minimize a window without closing it.

11 Using either of the techniques you just practiced, minimize the **Calculator** window.

> Minimizing a window hides the window and gets it out of the way, but it does not close the window. The window remains open—visible only as a button on the taskbar.
>
> The taskbar is your tool to switch between open windows. To open or switch to another window, just click its taskbar button.

12 Move your mouse pointer into the desktop area, and then on the taskbar, point to the **Calculator** button to display a thumbnail representation of the program window. Then point to the **Paint** button to display its thumbnail.

> A *thumbnail* is a reduced image of a graphic.

13 On the taskbar, click the **Paint** button, and notice that the window looks exactly as it did before you minimized it. **Close** ❎ the **Paint** window. Notice that the button is removed from the taskbar, because the window is closed.

> **Note** | Buttons Pinned to the Taskbar
>
> If the button remains on the taskbar but does not display a glass frame, it means the program has been pinned to the taskbar. As you progress in your study of Windows 7, you will practice pinning a program to the taskbar.

14 On the taskbar, point to the **WordPad** button, right-click, and then on the displayed **Jump List**, click **Close window**.

A *Jump List* displays destinations and tasks from a program's taskbar button.

15 Point to the **Calculator** button, and then move your mouse pointer into the thumbnail. Notice that the window opens and in the thumbnail, a **Close** ❎ button displays. In the thumbnail, click the small **Close** ❎ button.

Activity 1.15 | Using Aero Peek and Displaying Multiple Windows in the Cascade, Stack, and Side by Side Arrangements

You have seen that you can have multiple windows open and move among them by clicking the buttons on the taskbar. There are several different arrangements by which you can *display* multiple open windows on the desktop.

1 On the taskbar, click the **Windows Explorer** button 📁, and then in the **navigation pane**, click your **CD/DVD Drive**. In the **file list**, open **Bell_Orchid**, then open **Corporate**, and then open **Engineering**.

2 With the files from the **Engineering** folder displayed in the **file list**, open the Word file **CO_EN_Pool_Report**, and notice that the **Word** program—the program in which the file was created—opens and displays the file. If necessary, **Maximize** 🔲 the Word window so it fills the screen.

On the taskbar, both the Windows Explorer and Word program icons display with a glass frame.

3 On the taskbar, click the **Windows Explorer** button 📁, and notice that the folder window for the **Engineering** folder displays.

4 From the **file list**, open the Excel file **CO_EN_Architect_Overtime**. If necessary, **Maximize** 🔲 the Excel window.

5 On the taskbar, click the **Windows Explorer** button again to redisplay the **Engineering** folder window, and then open the PowerPoint file **CO_EN_April_Safety_Presentation**. If necessary, **Maximize** the PowerPoint window. Compare your screen with Figure 1.51.

Figure 1.51

PowerPoint file displays (PowerPoint 2007 displays here; you might have PowerPoint 2010)

Show desktop button

Buttons on taskbar indicate four windows open— Windows Explorer, Word, Excel, PowerPoint

6 In the taskbar, point to the **Word** icon, and then move your mouse pointer into the thumbnail that displays. Notice that the Word document fills the screen. Then, move your pointer back into the taskbar, and notice that the Word document no longer fills the screen.

This full-screen window preview is provided by *Aero Peek*, a technology that assists you when you have multiple windows open by allowing you to *peek* at either the desktop that is behind open windows (*Preview Desktop*) or at a window that is hidden from view by other windows (*Full-Screen Window Preview*). Then, you can move the mouse pointer back into the taskbar to close the peek.

7 In the lower right corner of your screen, on the extreme right edge of the taskbar, point to the glass rectangle—the **Show desktop** button— to display the ScreenTip *Show desktop*, and then notice that you can peek at the desktop behind all the open windows—the open windows are hidden; windows that are not maximized display window outlines.

8 Click the **Show desktop** button to minimize, rather than hide, all of the open windows, and notice that no window outlines display.

9 Click the **Show desktop** button again to maximize all of the open windows. Notice that the PowerPoint window is still the active window.

By using Aero Peek, you can minimize all open windows, or just peek at the desktop. Aero Peek is useful if you need to locate a program shortcut or view other information items on your desktop.

10 On the taskbar, point to an open area—an area where no buttons display—and right-click. On the displayed shortcut menu, click **Cascade windows**. Compare your screen with Figure 1.52

In the *cascade* arrangement, the open windows display in a single stack, fanned out so that each title bar is visible. From the cascaded arrangement, you can click the title bar of any of the windows to make it the active window.

Figure 1.52

Four windows display in a cascaded arrangement (Office 2007 displays here; you might have Office 2010)

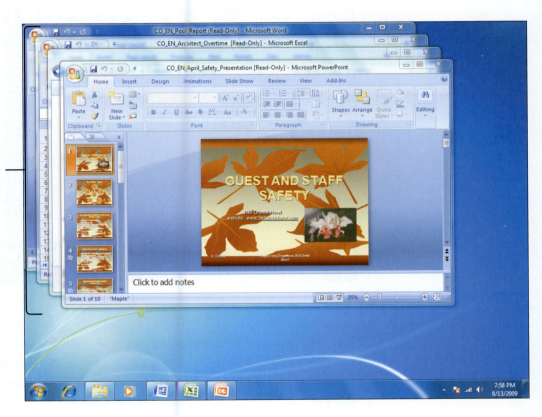

Another Way

Right-click the Windows Explorer button, and then on the Jump List, click Close window.

11 On the taskbar, point to the **Windows Explorer** button, move your mouse pointer into the thumbnail, and then click the small red **Close** button in the thumbnail.

12 Point to an open area of the taskbar, right-click, and then click **Show windows stacked**.

In the *stacked* arrangement, the three open windows display across the width of the screen in a vertical stack.

13 Display the taskbar menu again, and then click **Show windows side by side**. Compare your screen with Figure 1.53.

> In the *side by side* arrangement, the open windows display side by side. You can work in any of the files. Clicking in a window makes it the active window until you click in another window.

Figure 1.53

Three windows displayed side by side (your screens may display in a different order; Office 2007 shown here, you might have Office 2010)

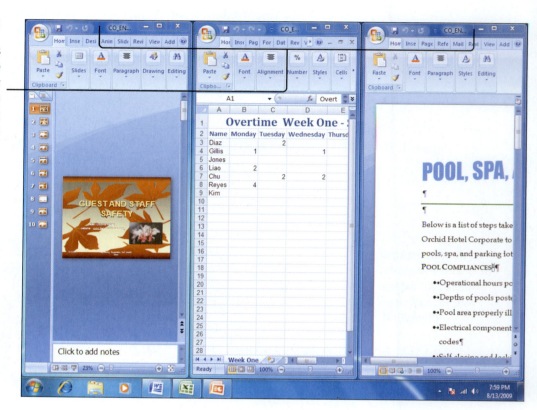

14 From the **Start** menu 🟢, open **Snipping Tool**, click the **New arrow**, and then click **Full-screen Snip**. Click the **Save Snip** button 🔲. In the **Save As** dialog box in the **navigation pane** on the left, scroll down as necessary to view **Computer**. Under **Computer**, click the name of your USB flash drive.

15 In the **file list**, scroll as necessary, locate and double-click your **Windows 7 Chapter 1** folder.

16 In the **File name** box and using your own name, type **Lastname_Firstname_1B_ SideBySide_Snip** Be sure the file type is **JPEG**. Click the **Save** button, and then **Close** ❎ the **Snipping Tool** window. Hold this file until you finish Project 1B, and then submit this file as directed by your instructor.

17 Right-click in an open area of the taskbar to display the taskbar menu again, and then click **Undo Show side by side**.

18 When the display returns to the stacked arrangement, in the upper right corner of *each* window, first click the **Maximize** button 🔲 so that the program fills the entire screen, and then click the **Minimize** button 🔲 to leave the window open but not displayed. Leave the three windows open on the taskbar for the next activity.

> Maximizing the windows assures that the next time the program is opened, it will be maximized; otherwise, the program may display in its most recently used size.

Activity 1.16 | Switching Windows by Using Aero Flip 3D

Aero Flip 3D arranges your open windows in a three-dimensional stack that you can flip through quickly without having to click buttons on the taskbar.

Alert! | Versions of Windows 7 With Aero Flip 3D

Aero Flip 3D is available in Windows 7 Home Premium, Professional, Ultimate, and Enterprise editions.

---

1 Be sure the three files from the previous activity are open and minimized to display only as glass-framed buttons on the taskbar. On your keyboard, locate the ⊞ key, which is typically in the lower left corner of your keyboard between Ctrl and Alt.

2 Hold down ⊞ and then press the Tab key repeatedly to flip through the open windows as shown in Figure 1.54, and then release both keys to display the document at the top of the stack.

Your desktop is considered to be one of the open windows.

Figure 1.54

Open documents and the desktop display in a stack (your order may differ)

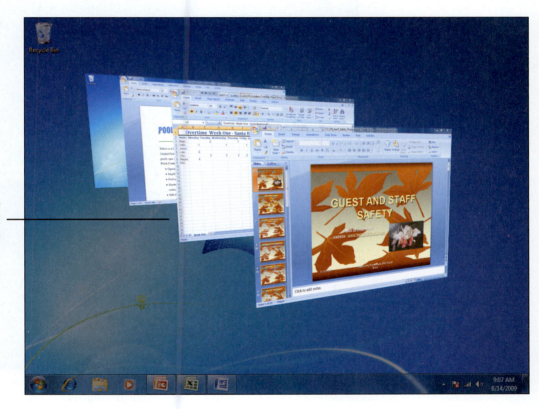

3 Repeat the technique you just practiced, and then flip through the stack until the PowerPoint presentation with the maple leaves is on top. Release the keys to maximize and make the PowerPoint document the active window.

4 **Close** the PowerPoint window.

5 In the taskbar, point to the **Excel** icon, right-click, and then on the displayed **Jump List**, click **Close window**.

6 In the taskbar, point to the **Word icon**, move your mouse pointer into the thumbnail, and then click the small red **Close** [×] button.

You can use any of these techniques to close an open window.

Activity 1.17 | Using Snap to Display Windows

Snap is a Windows 7 feature that automatically resizes windows when you move—*snap*—them to the edge of the screen. You can use Snap to arrange windows side by side, expand windows vertically, or maximize a window.

You will find Snap useful to compare two documents, copy or move files between two windows, maximize a window by dragging instead of clicking the Maximize button, and to expand long documents to reduce the amount of scrolling.

1 Close any open windows, and then start the **Paint** program. If the window is maximized—fills the entire screen—click the **Restore Down** button [□].

2 Point to the **title bar**, and then drag to the left until your [↖] pointer reaches the edge of the screen and an outline of the window displays, as shown in Figure 1.55.

Figure 1.55

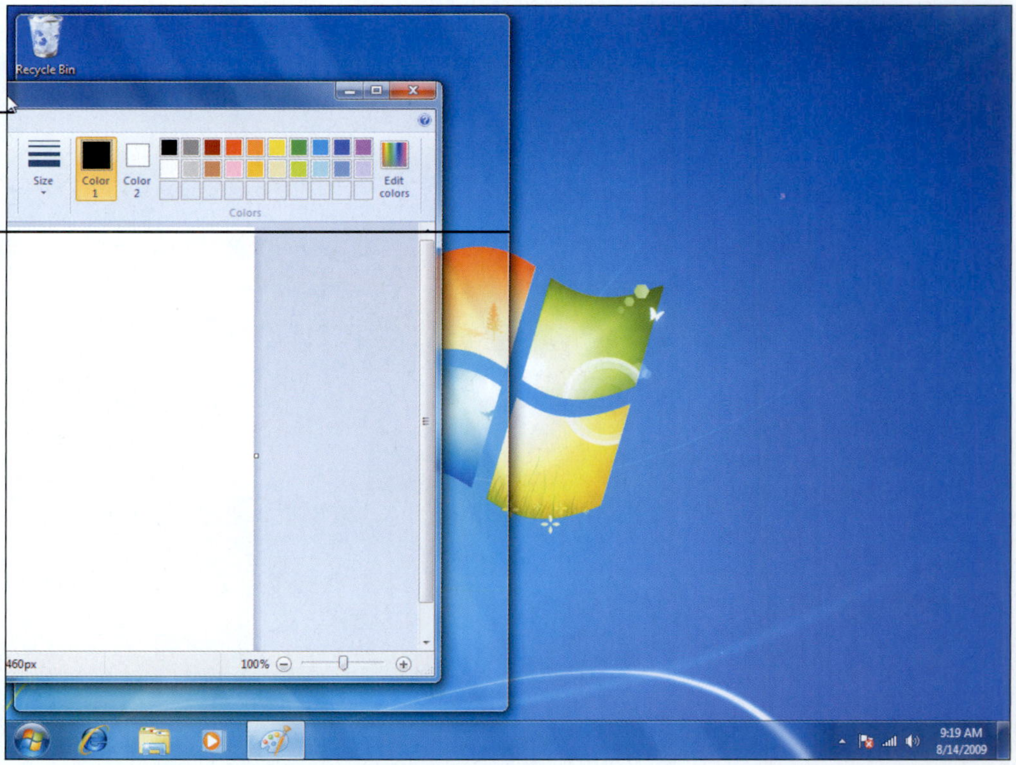

Mouse pointer at edge of screen

Outline of window

3 Release the mouse button, and notice that the window expands to half of the left side of the screen and extends fully from top to bottom.

4 Drag the title bar into the center of the screen, and notice that the window reverts to its former size.

5 To maximize vertically, but not horizontally, point to the bottom edge of the screen until the ⬍ pointer displays, and then drag to the bottom of the screen.

The window maximizes vertically but not horizontally. You can also drag the upper edge of a window with the ⬍ pointer for the same result.

6 Drag the title bar into the center of the screen so that the window reverts to its former size.

7 Drag the title bar upward until the ⬉ pointer reaches the top of the screen and the window maximizes. Release the mouse button.

8 Drag the title bar into the center of the screen to restore the window to its former size, and then **Close** ▣ the **Paint** window.

> **More Knowledge** | Aero Shake
>
> If you have several unmaximized windows open, for example your Documents library window and your Music library window, you can point to the title bar of the active window, hold down the left mouse button, and then move your mouse back and forth vigorously in a shaking motion; all other windows will minimize. This feature is **Aero Shake**. Shake the window again, and all the minimized windows will be visible again. Use Aero Shake when you want to focus on a single window without minimizing all your other open windows one by one.

Activity 1.18 | Using Snap to Display Two Windows Side by Side

1 From **Windows Explorer** 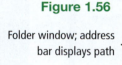, open your **CD/DVD** drive, open the **Bell_Orchid** folder, and then navigate to **Corporate ▶ Food_Beverage ▶ Restaurants**. Compare your screen with Figure 1.56.

Figure 1.56

Folder window; address bar displays path

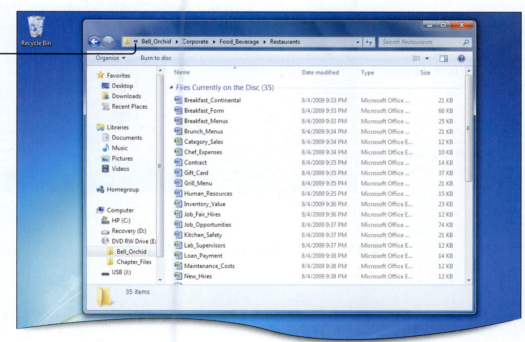

2 Open the Word file **Breakfast_Continental**. If necessary, **Maximize** the Word window. Click the **Windows Explorer** button ![icon] again, and then open the Word file **Breakfast_Form**. In the taskbar, right-click the **Windows Explorer** button ![icon], and then click **Close window**.

3 In the taskbar, point to the **Word icon**, and notice that two stacked tiles display, indicating that two windows are open in Word. Notice also that the icon lights up in a color compatible with the Word icon. Compare your screen with Figure 1.57.

> A program's taskbar icon will display stacked tiles in this manner for each open file, which provides a visual cue to indicate the number of open files. Additionally, when you point to an icon on the taskbar, the icon will light up in a color compatible with the icon color.
>
> When you point to a program icon that has more than one file open, a thumbnail for each open file displays in a thumbnail grouping. To switch to a different file, simply click its thumbnail.

Figure 1.57

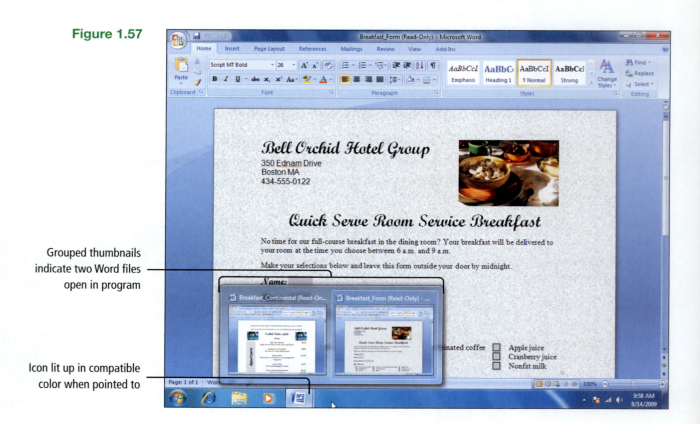

Grouped thumbnails indicate two Word files open in program

Icon lit up in compatible color when pointed to

4 Move your mouse pointer away from the Word icons to cancel the thumbnail display.

5 Point anywhere in the **title bar** of the displayed file, drag to the left until your pointer reaches the left edge of the screen, and then release the mouse button. Compare your screen with Figure 1.58.

The window for the Breakfast_Form file *snaps* to occupy the left half of the screen.

Figure 1.58

Breakfast_Form file occupies left half of screen

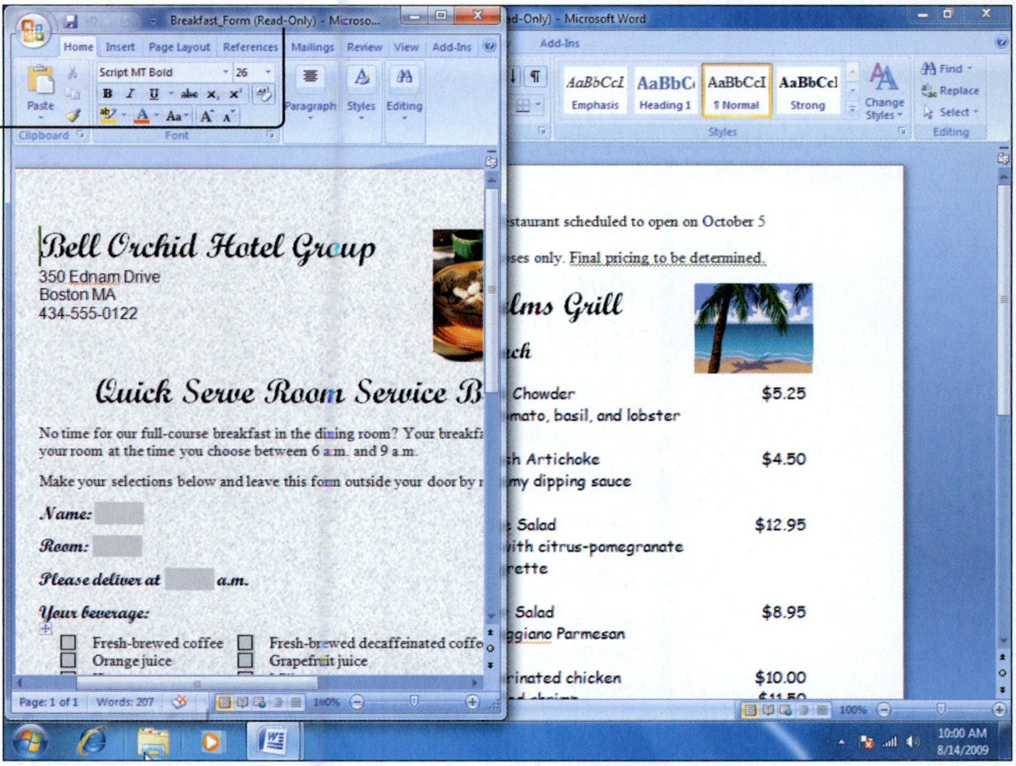

6 On the right side of the screen, point anywhere in the visible title bar of the **Breakfast_Continental** file, and then drag the ⬉ pointer to the right side of the screen and release the mouse button. Notice that the window *snaps* to occupy the right half of the screen. Compare your screen with Figure 1.59.

Use this technique when you want to compare two files. As you progress in your study of Windows 7, you will also practice this technique for the purpose of copying files.

Figure 1.59

Breakfast_Continental
file occupies left
half of screen

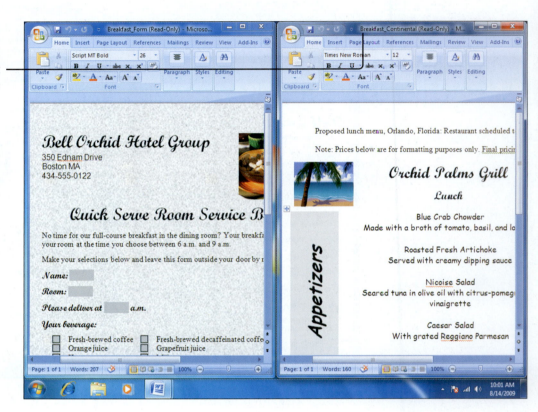

7 From the **Start** menu 🟦, open **Snipping Tool**, click the **New arrow**, and then click **Full-screen Snip**. Click the **Save Snip** button 🖫. In the **Save As** dialog box, in the **navigation pane** on the left, drag the scroll box down as necessary to view **Computer**. Under **Computer**, click the name of your USB flash drive.

8 In the **file list**, scroll as necessary, locate and double-click your **Windows 7 Chapter 1** folder.

9 In the **File name** box and using your own name, type **Lastname_Firstname_1B_Snap_Snip** Be sure the file type is **JPEG**. Click the **Save** button, and then **Close** ❎ the **Snipping Tool** window.

10 **Close** ❎ both Word files. Remove your Student Resource CD and any other removable storage devices. Submit the four snip files from this project to your instructor as directed.

End **You have completed Project 1B** ──────────────────────────────

Content-Based Assessments

Summary

Windows 7 is an operating system program that manages your hardware, manages your software programs, and stores and manages your data. In this chapter, you used Snipping Tool to capture screen shots, created a folder on a removable device and saved files, and used Windows 7 Help and Support.

Key Terms

Matching

Match each term in the second column with its correct definition in the first column by writing the letter of the term on the blank line in front of the correct definition.

_____ 1.   A set of instructions that a computer uses to accomplish a task, such as word processing, accounting, or data management; also referred to as an *application*.

_____ 2.   A computer program that manages all the other programs on your computer, stores files in an organized manner, and coordinates the use of computer hardware such as the keyboard and mouse.

_____ 3.   An operating system developed by Microsoft Corporation.

_____ 4.   A collection of information that is stored on a computer under a single name, for example a text document, a picture, or a program.

_____ 5.   A container in which you store files.

_____ 6.   A folder within a folder.

_____ 7.   The area that serves as a surface for your work, like the top of an actual desk, and which is the main screen area that you see after you turn on your computer.

_____ 8.   The button that displays the Start menu.

_____ 9.   The screen area that contains the Start button, optional program buttons, and buttons for all open programs; by default, it is located at the bottom of the desktop, but you can move it.

_____ 10.   A window from which you can customize the look and functionality of your computer, add or remove programs, set up networks, and manage user accounts.

_____ 11.   A portable device on which you can store files, such as a USB flash drive, a flash memory card, or an external hard drive.

_____ 12.   An area of storage that is formatted with a file system compatible with your operating system and is identified by a drive letter.

_____ 13.   Displays the contents of the current folder, library, or device, and contains helpful parts so that you can navigate.

_____ 14.   A collection of items, such as files and folders, assembled from various locations.

_____ 15.   The area on the left side of a folder window, which displays favorites, libraries, and an expandable list of drives and folders.

A Control panel

B Desktop

C Drive

D File

E Folder

F Folder window

G Library

H Navigation pane

I Operating system

J Program

K Removable storage device

L Start button

M Subfolder

N Taskbar

O Windows 7

Multiple Choice

Circle the correct answer.

1. A row of buttons across the top of a window that contains commands for tasks is a:
    A. taskbar
    B. toolbar
    C. menu bar

2. The area that displays your current location in the folder structure as a series of links separated by arrows is the:
    A. file list
    B. taskbar
    C. address bar

3. A program included with Windows 7 with which you can capture an image of all or part of a computer screen, and then annotate, save, copy, or share the image via e-mail is:
    A. print screen
    B. capture
    C. Snipping Tool

4. The box in a scroll bar that you drag to reposition a document on the screen is the:
    A. scroll box
    B. text box
    C. search box

5. The system by which you interact with your computer and which uses graphics such as an image of a file folder or wastebasket that you click to activate the item represented is a graphical:
    A. user interface
    B. language
    C. program

6. Turning off your computer in a manner that closes all open programs and files, closes your network connections, stops the hard disk, and discontinues the use of electrical power is called:
    A. sleep
    B. shut down
    C. hibernate

7. The user account type that lets you make changes that will affect other users of the computer and permits the most control over the computer is the:
    A. administrator account
    B. guest account
    C. standard user account

8. A folder created for each user account labeled with the account holder's name, and which displays at the top of the Start menu and contains subfolders such as Documents, is the:
    A. Personal folder
    B. Contacts folder
    C. Videos folder

9. The program within Windows 7 that displays the contents of libraries, folders, and files on your computer, and which also enables you to perform tasks related to your files and folders such as copying, moving, and renaming is:
    A. Snipping Tool
    B. Windows Explorer
    C. Internet Explorer

10. The area that displays the contents of the current folder or library is the:
    A. details pane
    B. preview pane
    C. file list

Content-Based Assessments

Apply 1A skills from these Objectives:

1. Create a New Folder and Save a File on a Removable Storage Device
2. Identify the Functions of an Operating System
3. Use the Getting Started Information and Windows Help and Support
4. Log Off, Turn Off Your Computer, and View Power Options
5. Manage Your User Account

Skills Review | Project 1C Exploring Windows

Project Files

For Project 1C, you will need the following files:

Student Resource CD or a USB flash drive containing the student data files
win01_1C_Answer_Sheet (Word document)

You will save your file as:

Lastname_Firstname_1C_Answer_Sheet

1 **Close** [✕] all open windows. On the taskbar, click the **Windows Explorer** button. In the **navigation pane**, click the drive that contains the student files for this textbook, and then navigate to **Chapter_Files ▶ Chapter_01**. Double-click the Word file **win01_1C_Answer_Sheet** to open Word and display the document. Press F12 to display the **Save As** dialog box in Word, navigate to your **Windows 7 Chapter 1** folder, and then using your own name, save the document as **Lastname_Firstname_1C_Answer_Sheet** Click OK if you see a message regarding file formats.

On the taskbar, click the **Word** button to minimize the window and leave your Word document accessible from the taskbar. **Close** the **Chapter_01** folder window. As you complete each step in this project, click the Word button on the taskbar to open the document, type your one-letter answer in the appropriate cell of the Word table, and then on the taskbar, click the button again to minimize the window for the next step.

From the **Start menu**, display the **Control Panel**, and then with the insertion point blinking in the search box, type **get** In the list that displays, click **Getting Started**. Which of the following is true?

A. From this screen, you can create a new folder.

B. Several links on this screen will take you to online sources of information.

C. From this screen, you can shut down your computer.

2 Close [✕] the Getting Started window. What is your result?

A. All windows close and the desktop displays.

B. The Control Panel window remains open.

C. The Create Password window displays.

3 **Close** [✕] the **Control Panel** window. Display the **Start menu**, and then at the top of the right side of the menu, under the picture, click your user name. In the displayed window, where does your user name display?

A. In the address bar

B. In the details pane

C. In the file list

4 In the **navigation pane**, under **Libraries**, click **Documents**. What is your result?

A. The first document in the library opens in its application.

B. The contents of the Documents library displays in the file list.

C. The contents of the Documents library displays in the address bar.

(Project 1C Exploring Windows continues on the next page)

Skills Review | Project **1C** Exploring Windows (continued)

5 In the **navigation pane**, click **Computer**. What is your result?

A. The storage devices attached to your computer display in the file list.

B. All of the files on the hard drive display in the file list.

C. Your computer restarts.

6 According to the toolbar in this window, which of the following is true?

A. From this window you can restart your computer.

B. From this window you can open the PowerPoint application.

C. From this window you can uninstall or change a program.

7 **Close** the **Computer** window. From the **Start** menu, display the **Control Panel**, and then click **User Accounts and Family Safety** (or User Accounts). Which of the following is true?

A. Both B. and C. are true.

B. From this screen, you can change your Windows password.

C. From this screen, you can change your account picture.

8 Click **Change your account picture**. According to this screen, where does your picture appear.

A. On the Start menu.

B. On the Welcome screen.

C. On both the Welcome screen and the Start menu.

9 **Close** the **Change Your Picture** window. From the **Start** menu, click **Help and Support**. In the **Search** box, type **shortcuts** and then press Enter. Click **Keyboard shortcuts**, scroll down as necessary, and then click **Windows logo key keyboard shortcuts**. Scroll as necessary to view the table. According to this information, to open the **Start** menu using the keyboard, you can press:

A. ⊞

B. ⊞ + 1

C. Alt + F4

10 **Close** **Help and Support**. Display the **Start** menu, click **Control Panel**, click **Hardware and Sound**, and then click **Power Options**. In the introduction, click **Tell me more about power plans**. Based on the information in the Windows Help and Support window, which of the following is *not* true?

A. Power plans can reduce the amount of power your computer uses.

B. Power plans can maximize your system's performance.

C. A power plan is a collection of software settings.

Be sure you have typed all of your answers in your Word document. Save and close your Word document, and submit as directed by your instructor. **Close** all open windows.

End **You have completed Project 1C** ————————————————

Content-Based Assessments

Apply 1B skills from these Objectives:

- **6** Display Libraries, Folders, and Files in a Window
- **7** Start Programs and Open Data Files
- **8** Manage the Display of Individual and Multiple Windows

Skills Review | Project **1D** Working with Windows, Programs, and Files

Project Files

For Project 1D, you will need the following files:

> **Student Resource CD or a flash drive containing the student data files**
> **win01_1D_Answer_Sheet (Word document)**

You will save your file as:

> **Lastname_Firstname_1D_Answer_Sheet**

1 Close [✕] all open windows. On the taskbar, click the **Windows Explorer** button. In the **navigation pane**, click the drive that contains the student files for this textbook, and then navigate to **Chapter_Files ▶ Chapter_01**. Double-click the Word file **win01_1D_Answer_Sheet** to open Word and display the document. Press F12 to display the **Save As** dialog box in Word, navigate to your **Windows 7 Chapter 1** folder, and then using your own name, save the document as **Lastname_Firstname_1D_Answer_Sheet** If necessary, click OK regarding file formats.

On the taskbar, click the **Word** button to minimize the window and leave your Word document accessible from the taskbar. **Close** the **Chapter_01** folder window. As you complete each step in this project, click the Word button on the taskbar to open the document, type your one-letter answer in the appropriate cell of the Word table, and then on the taskbar, click the button again to minimize the window for the next step.

On the taskbar, click the **Windows Explorer** button. In the **navigation pane**, click the CD/DVD Drive or flash drive that contains the student files. In the file list on the right, how many *folders* display?

- **A.** None
- **B.** One
- **C.** Two

2 In the file list on the right, double-click the **Bell_Orchid** folder to open it, and then double-click the **Corporate** folder to open it. Which of the following best describes the contents of the Corporate folder?

- **A.** Only individual files display.
- **B.** Only folders display.
- **C.** Both individual files and folders display.

3 In the **address bar**, to the right of **Bell_Orchid**, click ▶. What is the result?

- **A.** The file list no longer displays folders.
- **B.** A small list drops down to display the names of the subfolders within the Bell_Orchid folder.
- **C.** The navigation pane closes.

(Project 1D Working with Windows, Programs, and Files continues on the next page)

Skills Review | Project **1D** Working with Windows, Programs, and Files (continued)

4 If necessary, click in an open area of the file list to close the list, and then in the **file list**, double-click the **Engineering** folder to open it. In an open area, right-click. On the displayed shortcut menu, point to **Group by**, and then on the displayed submenu, click **Type**. How many different groups of file types display?

A. Three

B. Four

C. Five

5 Be sure the **Engineering** folder is still grouped by type. How many Excel worksheets are in this folder?

A. One

B. Two

C. Three

6 Which file type group has the most number of files?

A. Microsoft Word Document

B. Microsoft PowerPoint Presentation

C. JPEG image

7 Right-click anywhere in the file list, point to **Group by**, and then click (**None**). Click the **Name** column heading as necessary so that the files in the folder are sorted in alphabetical order—recall that clicking a column heading sorts the column alternately in ascending and descending order and that the pale arrow at the top of the column heading indicates how the column is sorted. Open the file **CO_EN_Meeting_Room_Construction**. What happens?

A. The file displays only as a button on the taskbar.

B. The file opens in the application program in which it was created—PowerPoint.

C. A message displays asking you what program to open for this file.

8 Close [✕] the **PowerPoint** window and the **Windows Explorer** window. Display the **Start** menu, click **All Programs**, click the **Accessories** folder, and then point to **Snipping Tool**. Right-click, point to **Send to**, and then click **Desktop (create shortcut)**. Click outside of the Start menu to close it. Which of the following is true?

A. A shortcut icon with an arrow, which when clicked will open the program, displays on the desktop.

B. The Snipping Tool program opens.

C. All of the snips that you created in Projects 1A and 1B display on the desktop.

9 Drag the **Snipping Tool** shortcut to the **Recycle Bin** to delete the shortcut from the desktop. Recall that deleting a shortcut deletes only the shortcut icon on the desktop. It does not delete the program. On the taskbar, click your Word Answer Sheet document to display it. From the **Start** menu, open **Microsoft Excel**. Point to an open area of the taskbar, right-click, and then click **Show windows side by side**. Which of the following is *not* true?

A. Two windows, one for Word and one for Excel, display—one on the left and one on the right.

B. The Excel window is larger than the Word window.

C. Both the Word and Excel buttons display on the taskbar.

(Project 1D Working with Windows, Programs, and Files continues on the next page)

Skills Review | Project **1D** Working with Windows, Programs, and Files (continued)

10 In an empty area of the taskbar, right-click, and then click **Undo Show side by side**. Close ▣ the **Excel** window, and minimize the **Word** window. On the **Start** menu, click **All Programs**, click **Accessories**, and then click **Notepad** to start the program. Using the same technique, start the **Paint** program, and then the **Calculator** program. On the taskbar, which program button is shown as active—the glass frame is brighter and less translucent than the other two?

A. Notepad

B. Paint

C. Calculator

Be sure you have typed all of your answers in your Word document. Save and close your Word document, and submit as directed by your instructor. Close ▣ all open windows.

End **You have completed Project 1D** ——————————————

Apply **1A** skills from these Objectives:

1. Create a New Folder and Save a File on a Removable Storage Device
2. Identify the Functions of an Operating System
3. Use the Getting Started Information and Windows Help and Support
4. Log Off, Turn Off Your Computer, and View Power Options
5. Manage Your User Account

Mastering Windows 7 | Project **1E** Windows Help and Support

In the following Mastering Windows 7 project, you will capture and save a snip that will look similar to Figure 1.60.

Project Files

For Project 1E, you will need the following file:

New Snip file

You will save your file as:

Lastname_Firstname_1E_Smartphone_Snip

Project Results

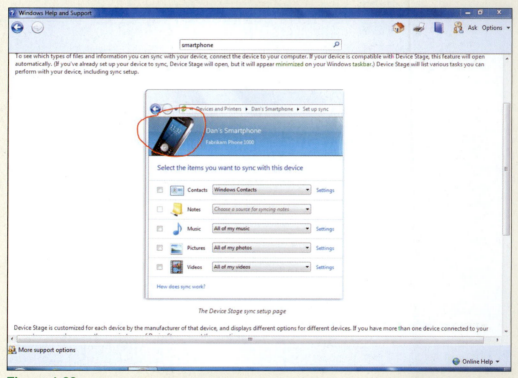

Figure 1.60

(Project 1E Windows Help and Support continues on the next page)

Mastering Windows 7 | Project 1E Windows Help and Support (continued)

1 Display the **Windows Help and Support** window, and then search for **smartphone** Click **Sync music, pictures, contacts, and calendars with a mobile device**. Maximize the window.

2 In the first paragraph, click the green word *sync* and read the definition. Then, scroll down as necessary to position the figure in the middle of your screen.

3 Start **Snipping Tool**, click the **New button arrow**, and then click **Window Snip**. Click anywhere in the **Windows Help and Support** window to capture it.

4 On the toolbar of the **Snipping Tool** mark-up window, click the **Pen button arrow** and then click **Red Pen**.

Draw a circle around the picture of the phone, and then click the **Save Snip** button.

5 In the displayed **Save As** dialog box, in the **navigation pane**, scroll down, and then under **Computer**, click your USB flash drive. In the file list, open your **Windows 7 Chapter 1** folder so that its name displays in the address bar, and then as the **File name**, and using your own name, type **Lastname_Firstname_1E_ Smartphone_Snip**

6 Be sure the file type is **JPEG**. **Save** the snip, **Close** Snipping Tool, and then **Close** the **Windows Help and Support** window.

Submit your snip file as directed by your instructor.

End **You have completed Project 1E** ────────────────────

Apply **1B** skills from these Objectives:

6 Display Libraries, Folders, and Files in a Window

7 Start Programs and Open Data Files

8 Manage the Display of Individual and Multiple Windows

Mastering Windows 7 | Project **1F** Cascade Screens

In the following Mastering Windows 7 project, you will navigate the Bell_Orchid folder structure, start a program by opening a file, open a file in a program, manage multiple windows, cascade multiple windows, and capture and save a screen that will look similar to Figure 1.61.

Project Files

For Project 1F, you will need the following file:

> New Snip file

You will save your file as:

> Lastname_Firstname_1F_Cascade_Snip

Project Results

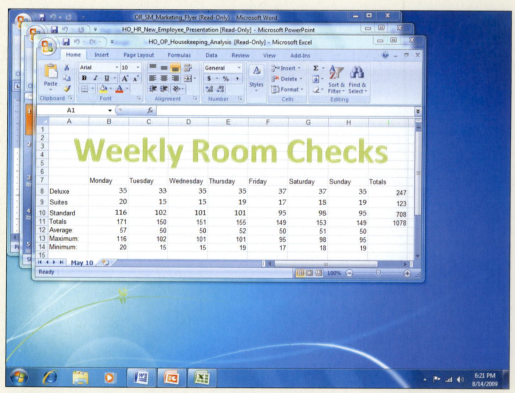

Figure 1.61

(Project 1F Cascade Screens continues on the next page)

Content-Based Assessments

Mastering Windows 7 | Project **1F** Cascade Screens (continued)

1 From the **Start** menu, locate and open **Microsoft Word**. Press Ctrl + O to display the **Open** dialog box, in the **navigation pane** click the device that contains your student files, and then from the **Bell_Orchid** folder, locate and open the **Marketing Flyer** document for the **Orlando** hotel. If necessary, maximize the Word window.

2 With the **Word** document displayed on your screen, on the taskbar, click the **Windows Explorer** button, and then in the **navigation pane**, click the device that contains your student files. Open the **Bell_Orchid** folder, and then in the **Honolulu** folder, open the **HO_HR_New_Employee_Presentation** from the **Human_Resources** folder. If necessary, maximize the PowerPoint window.

3 On the taskbar, click the **Windows Explorer** button to redisplay the folder window. On the **address bar**, to the right of **Honolulu**, click ▶, and then click **Operations**. Open the Excel file **HO_OP_Housekeeping_Analysis**.

4 On the taskbar, right-click the **Windows Explorer** button, and then on the **Jump List**, click **Close window**. Display the three open windows in the **Cascade** arrangement.

5 Create a **Full-screen Snip** of your screen with the three cascaded windows, and then save it in your chapter folder as **Lastname_Firstname_1F_Cascade_Snip**

6 Close ▣ the **Snipping Tool** window. **Maximize** ▣ and then **Close** ▣ each window. Submit your snip file as directed by your instructor.

 You have completed Project 1F

Outcomes-Based Assessments

Rubric

The following outcomes-based assessments are *open-ended assessments*. That is, there is no specific correct result; your result will depend on your approach to the information provided. Make *Professional Quality* your goal. Use the following scoring rubric to guide you in *how* to approach the problem, and then to evaluate *how well* your approach solves the problem.

The *criteria*—Software Mastery, Content, Format and Layout, and Process—represent the knowledge and skills you have gained that you can apply to solving the problem. The *levels of performance*—Professional Quality, Approaching Professional Quality, or Needs Quality Improvements—help you and your instructor evaluate your result.

	Your completed project is of Professional Quality if you:	Your completed project is Approaching Professional Quality if you:	Your completed project Needs Quality Improvements if you:
1-Software Mastery	Choose and apply the most appropriate skills, tools, and features and identify efficient methods to solve the problem.	Choose and apply some appropriate skills, tools, and features, but not in the most efficient manner.	Choose inappropriate skills, tools, or features, or are inefficient in solving the problem.
2-Content	Construct a solution that is clear and well organized, contains content that is accurate, appropriate to the audience and purpose, and is complete. Provide a solution that contains no errors in spelling, grammar, or style.	Construct a solution in which some components are unclear, poorly organized, inconsistent, or incomplete. Misjudge the needs of the audience. Have some errors in spelling, grammar, or style, but the errors do not detract from comprehension.	Construct a solution that is unclear, incomplete, or poorly organized; contains some inaccurate or inappropriate content; and contains many errors in spelling, grammar, or style. Do not solve the problem.
3-Format and Layout	Format and arrange all elements to communicate information and ideas, clarify function, illustrate relationships, and indicate relative importance.	Apply appropriate format and layout features to some elements, but not others. Overuse features, causing minor distraction.	Apply format and layout that does not communicate information or ideas clearly. Do not use format and layout features to clarify function, illustrate relationships, or indicate relative importance. Use available features excessively, causing distraction.
4-Process	Use an organized approach that integrates planning, development, self-assessment, revision, and reflection.	Demonstrate an organized approach in some areas, but not others; or, use an insufficient process of organization throughout.	Do not use an organized approach to solve the problem.

Outcomes-Based Assessments

Apply a combination of the **1A** and **1B** skills.

Problem Solving | Project **1G** Help Desk

Project Files

For Project 1G, you will need the following file:

win01_1G_Help_Desk

You will save your file as:

Lastname_Firstname_1G_Help_Desk

From the student files that accompany this textbook, open the **Chapter_Files** folder, and then in the **Chapter_01** folder, locate and open the Word document **win01_1G_Help_Desk**. Save the document in your chapter folder as **Lastname_Firstname_1G_Help_Desk**

The following e-mail question has arrived at the Help Desk from an employee at the Bell Orchid Hotel's corporate office. In the Word document, construct a response based on your knowledge of Windows 7. Although an e-mail response is not as formal as a letter, you should still use good grammar, good sentence structure, professional language, and a polite tone. Save your document and submit the response as directed by your instructor.

To: Help Desk

We have a new employee in our department, and as her user picture, she wants to use a picture of her dog. I know that Corporate Policy says it is ok to use an acceptable personal picture on a user account. Can she change the picture herself within her standard user account, or does she need an administrator account to do that?

End **You have completed Project 1G** ——————————————————

Outcomes-Based Assessments

Apply a combination of the **1A** and **1B** skills.

Problem Solving | Project **1H** Help Desk

Project Files

For Project 1H, you will need the following file:

> **win01_1H_Help_Desk**

You will save your file as:

> **Lastname_Firstname_1H_Help_Desk**

From the student files that accompany this textbook, open the **Chapter_Files** folder, and then in the **Chapter_01** folder, locate and open **win01_1H_Help_Desk**. Save the document in your chapter folder as **Lastname_Firstname_1H_Help_Desk**

The following e-mail question has arrived at the Help Desk from an employee at the Bell Orchid Hotel's corporate office. In the Word document, construct a response based on your knowledge of Windows 7. Although an e-mail response is not as formal as a letter, you should still use good grammar, good sentence structure, professional language, and a polite tone. Save your document and submit the response as directed by your instructor.

To: Help Desk

When I'm done using my computer at the end of the day, should I use the Sleep option or the Shut Down option, and what's the difference between the two?

End **You have completed Project 1H** ————————————————————

Outcomes-Based Assessments

Apply a combination of the 1A and 1B skills.

Problem Solving | Project 1I Help Desk

Project Files

For Project 1I, you will need the following file:

win01_1I_Help_Desk

You will save your document as:

Lastname_Firstname_1I_Help_Desk

From the student files that accompany this textbook, open the **Chapter_Files** folder, and then in **Chapter_01** folder, locate and open **win01_1I_Help_Desk**. Save the document in your chapter folder as **Lastname_Firstname_1I_Help_Desk**

The following e-mail question has arrived at the Help Desk from an employee at the Bell Orchid Hotel's corporate office. In the Word document, construct a response based on your knowledge of Windows 7. Although an e-mail response is not as formal as a letter, you should still use good grammar, good sentence structure, professional language, and a polite tone. Save your document and submit the response as directed by your instructor.

To: Help Desk

In my department, we are setting up a new folder structure to store documents related to the marketing campaign for the new theme park being built at the Orlando facility. Because I will use these folders frequently, can you suggest a good place to set up the folder structure? I think the desktop is the best place to store folders that I will be using frequently, right?

End **You have completed Project 1I**

Managing Libraries, Folders, Files, and Using Search

OUTCOMES

At the end of this chapter you will be able to:

PROJECT 2A

Navigate in Windows 7 using Windows Explorer; create, copy, move, and delete files and folders to create an organized computer file structure.

PROJECT 2B

Use Search to find programs, controls, files, and folders on a computer.

OBJECTIVES

Mastering these objectives will enable you to:

1. Copy Files From a Removable Storage Device to the Hard Disk Drive (p. 85)
2. Navigate by Using Windows Explorer (p. 88)
3. Create, Name, and Save Files (p. 91)
4. Create Folders and Rename Folders and Files (p. 96)
5. Select, Copy, and Move Files and Folders (p. 100)
6. Delete Files and Folders and Use the Recycle Bin (p. 118)

7. Search From the Start Menu (p. 123)
8. Search From a Folder Window (p. 127)
9. Save, Reuse, and Delete a Search (p. 130)
10. Search From the Control Panel Window and the Computer Window (p. 132)
11. Add Tags to Improve a Search (p. 134)

Laura Gangi Pond/Shutterstock

In This Chapter

In this chapter, you will practice the most useful computing skills you can acquire—managing your data so that you can find your files and folders easily. Many of the frustrations that computer users experience result from not being able to locate their desired information quickly and efficiently, or not understanding where a program saves new files. In this chapter, you will practice techniques that include creating and naming files and folders in a consistent format, organizing your files into folders, arranging folders into a logical folder structure, and searching for files when you are not certain where they are located. You will also practice navigating within a folder structure by using the navigational tools in the Windows Explorer program.

The projects in this chapter relate to the **Bell Orchid Hotels**, headquartered in Boston, and which own and operate resorts and business-oriented hotels. Resort properties are located in popular destinations, including Honolulu, Orlando, San Diego, and Santa Barbara. The resorts offer deluxe accommodations and a wide array of dining options. Other Bell Orchid hotels are located in major business centers and offer the latest technology in their meeting facilities. The company plans to open new properties and update existing properties over the next ten years.

Project 2A Managing Files and Folders

Project Activities

In Activities 2.01 through 2.13, you will assist Barbara Hewitt and Steven Ramos, who work for the Information Technology Department at the Boston headquarters office of the Bell Orchid Hotels. Barbara and Steven have been asked to organize some of the files and folders that comprise the corporation's computer data. You will capture screens that look similar to Figure 2.1.

Project Files

For Project 2A, you will need the following files:

Student Resource CD or a flash drive containing the student data files

You will save your files as:

Lastname_Firstname_2A_Europe_Folders_Snip
Lastname_Firstname_2A_HR_Snip
Lastname_Firstname_2A_Compressed_Snip

Project Results

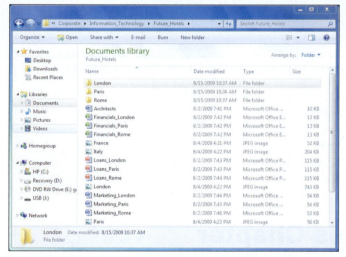

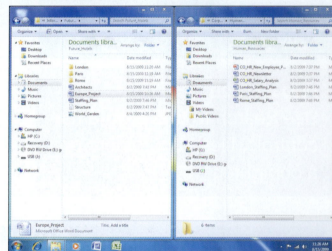

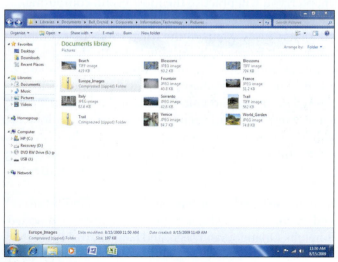

Figure 2.1

Project 2A Managing Files and Folders

> **Alert! | If you are working on a computer that is not your own, for example in a college lab, plan your time to complete Project 2A in one working session.**
>
> Because you will need to store and then delete files on the hard disk drive of the computer at which you are working, it is recommended that you complete this project in one working session—*unless you are working on your own computer or you know that the files will be retained.* In your college lab, it is possible that files you store will not be retained after you log off. Allow approximately 45 to 60 minutes to complete Project 2A.

Objective 1 | Copy Files From a Removable Storage Device to the Hard Disk Drive

A *program* is a set of instructions that a computer uses to accomplish a task, such as word processing, accounting, or data management. A program is also referred to as an *application*.

Windows 7 is an *operating system* developed by Microsoft Corporation. An operating system is a computer program that manages all the other programs on your computer, stores files in an organized manner, allows you to use software programs, and coordinates the use of computer hardware such as the keyboard and mouse.

A *file* is a collection of information that is stored on a computer under a single name, for example a text document, a picture, or a program.

Every file is stored in a *folder*—a container in which you store files—or a *subfolder*, which is a folder within a folder. Windows 7 stores and organizes your files and folders, which is the primary task of an operating system.

Activity 2.01 | Copying Files From a Removable Storage Device to the Documents Library on the Hard Disk Drive

Barbara and Steven have the assignment to transfer and then organize some of the corporation's files to a computer that will be connected to the corporate network. Data on such a computer can be accessed by employees at any of the hotel locations through the use of sharing technologies. For example, *SharePoint* is a Microsoft technology that enables employees in an organization to access information across organizational and geographic boundaries.

1 Log on to your computer and display your Windows 7 desktop. Insert the Student Resource CD that accompanies this textbook into the **CD/DVD Drive**—or insert the USB flash drive that contains these files if you obtained them from a different source. Wait a moment for your computer to recognize the removable media, and then if necessary, **Close** ⊠ the **AutoPlay** dialog box.

Recall that the AutoPlay dialog box displays when you insert removable storage devices into your computer.

2 On the taskbar, click the **Windows Explorer** button 📁 to display the **Libraries** window.

Recall that *Windows Explorer* is the program in Windows 7 that displays the contents of libraries, folders, and files on your computer, and which also enables you to perform tasks related to your files and folders such as copying, moving, and renaming. Windows Explorer is at work any time you are viewing the contents of a library, a folder, or a file.

3 In the **navigation pane**, under **Computer**, click your **CD/DVD** drive to display the contents in the **file list**. Compare your screen with Figure 2.2.

Recall that in the navigation pane, under Computer, you have access to all the storage areas inside your computer, such as your hard disk drives, and to any devices with removable storage, such as CDs or DVDs and USB flash drives.

Figure 2.2

Bell_Orchid folder
in file list

Contents of CD
display in file list

CD/DVD drive selected
in navigation pane

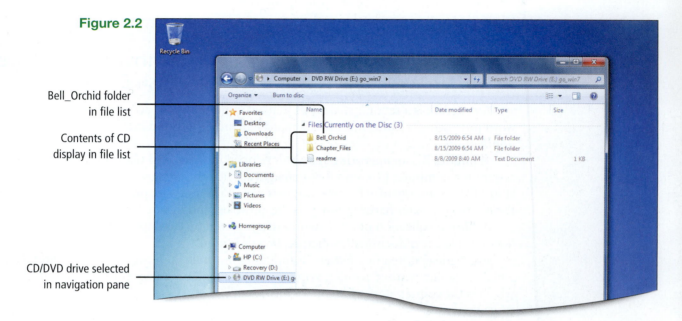

4 In the **file list**, point to the **Bell_Orchid** folder and right-click. On the displayed shortcut menu, point to **Send to**. Compare your screen with Figure 2.3.

From the Send to submenu, you can copy the selected file or folder to a variety of places. From this menu you can also create a desktop shortcut to the selected file or folder.

Figure 2.3

Documents on submenu

Shortcut menu
(yours may vary)

Send to submenu (your list
of commands may vary)

5 On the **Send to** submenu, click **Documents**, and then wait a few moments while Windows 7 copies the Bell_Orchid folder from your device to your Documents library on the hard disk drive.

A *progress bar* displays in a dialog box, and also displays on the Windows Explorer taskbar button with green shading. A progress bar indicates visually the progress of a task such as a download or file transfer.

Recall that the Documents library is one of several libraries within your personal folder stored on the hard disk drive. For each user account—even if there is only one user on the computer—Windows 7 creates a personal folder labeled with the account holder's name.

6 When the copy is complete, **Close** [X] the CD/DVD window.

More Knowledge | Deciding Where to Store Your Files

Where should you store your files? In the libraries created by Windows 7 (Documents, Pictures, and so on)? On a removable device like a flash drive or external hard drive?

The design of Windows 7 makes it easy to find your files, especially if you use the libraries. Regardless of where you save a file, Windows 7 will make it easy to find the file again, even if you are not certain where it might be.

The location in which you store your files and folders depends on how you use your computer and how you do your work. The knowledge you gain as you progress in your study of Windows 7 will enable you to decide the best folder structure and storage locations to meet your personal needs. This knowledge will also enable you to work easily with the folder structures in the organizations with which you might be employed.

In Windows 7, you will see that storing all of your files within a *library* will make it easy for you to find your files quickly when you need them. If you perform most of your work on your desktop system or your laptop that travels with you, you can store your files in the libraries created by Windows 7 for your user account—Documents, Pictures, Music, and so on. Within these libraries, you can create folders and subfolders to organize your data. There are several reasons why these libraries are a good choice for storing your files:

- From the Windows Explorer button on the taskbar, your libraries are always just one click away.
- The libraries are designed for their contents; for example, the Pictures folder displays small images of your digital photos.
- You can add new locations to a library; for example, an external hard drive, or a network drive on another computer or network. Locations added to a library behave just like they are on your hard drive.
- Other users of your computer cannot access your libraries.
- The libraries are the default location for opening and saving files within an application, so you will find that you can open and save files with fewer navigation clicks.

Although the libraries are named *Documents* and *Pictures* and so on, you are *not* restricted to storing only one type of file in a particular folder. You have already seen in the Bell_Orchid structure that folders can contain a combination of pictures and documents. However, if you like to store all of your photos together, for example all of the photos you have taken on various vacations, you might choose to store them in the Pictures library.

A storage device such as a USB flash drive is a good choice for storing files when you need to carry your files from one place to another; for example, between your own computer and computers in your campus labs. When you return to your computer, you can copy or move the files from your removable device to the appropriate folders within your user account.

An external hard drive, many of which are pocket sized, is a good choice because it can be included in a library, and thus is easily searchable when you need to find something.

In an organization or in your home, you might be connected to a network on which you have storage space on another computer or server. These can also be part of a library. And increasingly, storage is available on servers on which you can acquire space, such as Microsoft's Windows Live SkyDrive.

Objective 2 | Navigate by Using Windows Explorer

Managing your data—the files and the folders that contain your files—is the single most useful computing skill you can acquire. Become familiar with two important features in Windows 7 if you want to manage your data easily and efficiently—the Windows Explorer program and the *folder window*.

Windows Explorer is the program within Windows 7 that displays windows such as Control Panel and displays the files and folders on your computer in a folder window. A folder window shows you the contents of a folder. Windows Explorer is at work whenever you are viewing the contents of files and folders in a folder window or viewing the features in a window such as Control Panel.

Activity 2.02 | Pinning a Location to a Jump List

There are numerous ways to *navigate*—explore within the folder structure for the purpose of finding files and folders. *Navigation* refers to the actions you perform when you display a window to locate a command, or when you display the folder window for a folder whose contents you want to view.

In this activity, you will practice various ways in which you can navigate by using Windows Explorer. To do so, you will work with the Bell Orchid corporate data that you just copied to your hard disk drive.

1 On the taskbar, click the **Windows Explorer** button 📁.

2 In the **file list**, double-click **Documents** to display the contents of the Documents library in the file list.

3 In the **file list**, locate and double-click the **Bell_Orchid** folder that you just copied to the Documents library to display its contents in the file list. Compare your screen with Figure 2.4.

Figure 2.4

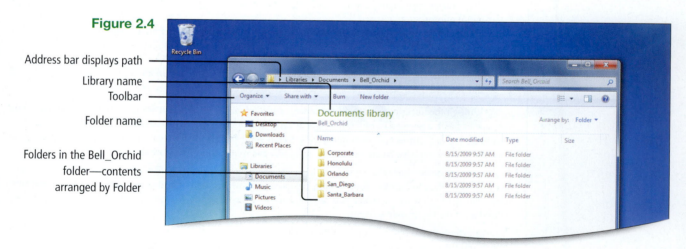

Address bar displays path

Library name

Toolbar

Folder name

Folders in the Bell_Orchid folder—contents arranged by Folder

4 In the **file list**, double-click the **Corporate** folder to display its contents. *Point* to the **Accounting** folder, right-click, and then click **Open**.

Use either technique to open a folder and display its contents. Most computer users use the double-click technique.

5 At the top of the window, in the **address bar**, click **Documents** to redisplay the contents of the Documents library in the file list. Compare your screen with Figure 2.5.

Recall that you can navigate by using the address bar.

Figure 2.5

Address bar displays path

Contents of Documents library displays in file list (your list may include other items)

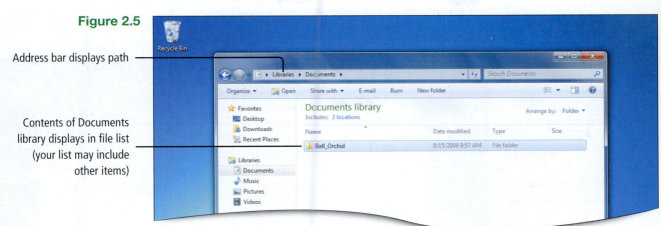

6 In the **file list**, *point* to the **Bell_Orchid** folder, hold down the left mouse button, and then as shown in Figure 2.6, drag the selected folder down to the **Windows Explorer** button until the ScreenTip *Pin to Windows Explorer* displays. Release the mouse button.

Figure 2.6

Bell_Orchid folder in file list

ScreenTip *Pin to Windows Explorer*

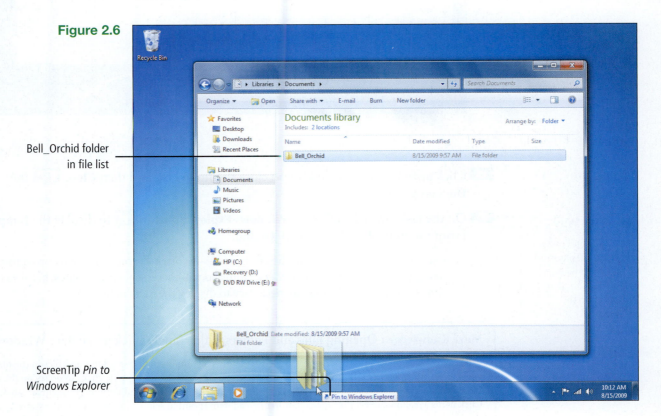

7 Notice the displayed **Jump List**, and then compare your screen with Figure 2.7.

Think of a *Jump List* as a mini start menu for a program; it displays locations in the upper portion and tasks in the lower portion.

Now that you have pinned Bell_Orchid to the Jump List, the locations portion of the list displays both Pinned and Frequent locations.

Figure 2.7

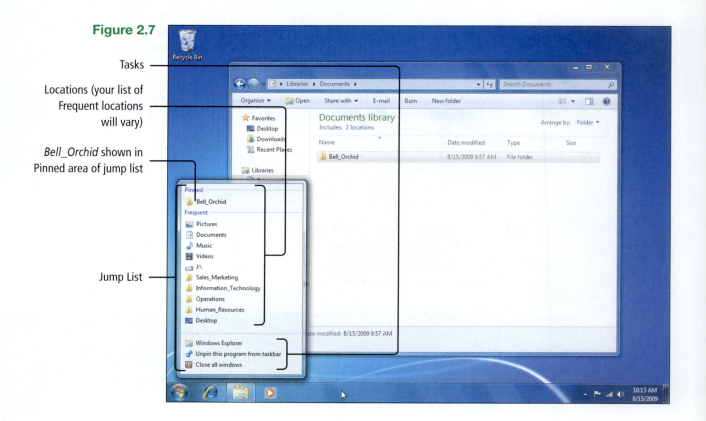

Tasks

Locations (your list of Frequent locations will vary)

Bell_Orchid shown in Pinned area of jump list

Jump List

8 Click anywhere on the desktop to close the **Jump List**, and then **Close** the **Documents** window.

Another Way

Open a Jump List by dragging a taskbar button with your left mouse button slightly upward into the desktop.

9 On the taskbar, right-click the **Windows Explorer** button to display the **Jump List**. From the **Pinned** area, click **Bell_Orchid**.

Use the taskbar—rather than the Start menu—as often as you can to start programs and navigate to specific files and folders. Doing so will increase your efficiency, because it eliminates extra clicks that are necessary to display the Start menu.

More Knowledge | Opening Files and Folders with a Single Click in a Folder Window

When navigating in a folder window, if you prefer a single-click motion to open folders and files in the file list, you can set Windows Explorer to open items with a single click instead of a double click. To do so, on the toolbar of any folder window, click Organize, click Folder and search options, and then on the General tab, under Click items as follows, select the Single-click to open an item (point to select) option button. Alternatively, from the Start menu, display the Control Panel, click Appearance and Personalization, and then under Folder Options, click Specify single- or double-click to open; this will display the Folder Options dialog box.

Objective 3 | Create, Name, and Save Files

In many programs, for example in Paint and the programs in Microsoft Office, the program opens and displays a new unnamed and unsaved file. As you begin creating your file in the program, your work is temporarily stored in the computer's memory until you initiate a Save command, at which time you must choose a file name and a location that is reachable from your computer in which to save your file. Recall that a location is any disk drive, folder, or other place in which you can store files and folders.

For saving files or opening existing files, Windows-based programs use a set of *common dialog boxes*. These are dialog boxes provided by the Windows programming interface that enable programs to have a consistent appearance and behavior. This means that in such dialog boxes, you will find navigation tools that are essentially the same as those in a Windows 7 folder window. For example, in a common dialog box, you will find a navigation pane, toolbar, address bar, Search box, and column headings in which you can sort, group, and filter.

Activity 2.03 | Pinning a Program to the Taskbar

For programs that you use frequently, it is useful to pin the program to the taskbar. The more you perform tasks from the taskbar, the more efficient you will become. Performing tasks from the taskbar reduces the number of times you must display the Start menu. Additionally, placing programs on the taskbar, instead of placing shortcuts to programs on your desktop, keeps your desktop free of clutter.

1 **Close** ☒ the **Bell_Orchid** folder window. From the **Start** menu 🪟, locate the **Microsoft Word** program on your system; the program might already be displayed on your Start menu, or you might need to locate it by displaying the All Programs menu and opening the Microsoft Office folder.

2 Point to the program name, and then as shown in Figure 2.8, drag the program to the taskbar. Release the mouse button when the ScreenTip *Pin to Taskbar* displays. (If the Word program is already pinned to the taskbar on your system, skip this step.)

For programs you use frequently, pin them to the taskbar in this manner.

Figure 2.8

Word program on Start menu (you might have Word 2010)

ScreenTip indicates *Pin to Taskbar*

3 Using the technique you just practiced, pin the **Excel** program to the taskbar, and then click anywhere on the desktop to close the Start menu. Compare your screen with Figure 2.9.

Figure 2.9

Excel program
pinned to taskbar

Word program
pinned to taskbar

Activity 2.04 | Naming and Saving Files in Word and Excel

Various managers at the Bell Orchid Hotels have been placing files related to the new European hotels in the Future_Hotels folder. Barbara and Steven have been asked to create some additional files in the Future_Hotels folder, and then managers will continue to add more information to the files as they gather more data about the new hotels.

1 On the taskbar, click the **Word** icon 📄 to start the program. If necessary, on the **Home tab**, in the **Paragraph group**, click the **Show/Hide** button ¶ to display formatting marks. Then, on the **View tab**, in the **Show group**, be sure the **Ruler** check box is selected. Compare your screen with Figure 2.10.

On the taskbar, the Word icon displays a glass frame to indicate that the program is open.

Figure 2.10

Ruler checkbox selected
in Show group on View
tab (Office 2007 shown;
Office 2010 is similar
in appearance)

Rulers display

Formatting marks display

Word icon framed in
glass to indicate that
the program is running

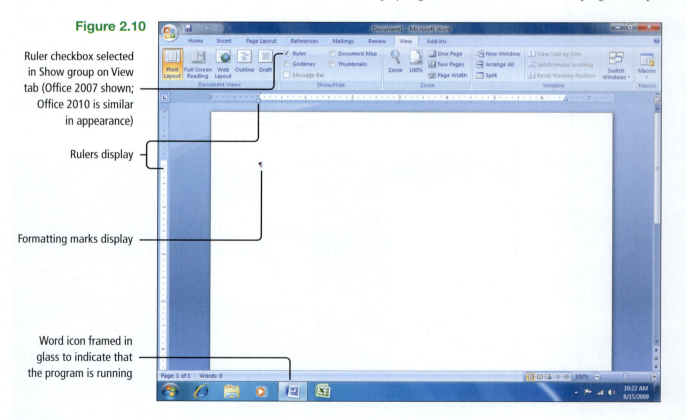

2 In the Word window, at the insertion point, type **The data for this overview of the Europe project will be provided at a later date by the Chief Operations Manager.**

3 Across the top of your keyboard, locate the function keys numbered F1 to F12, and then press F12 to display the **Save As** dialog box. Compare your screen with Figure 2.11.

In the Microsoft Office programs, F12 displays the Save As dialog box.

The Save As dialog box is an example of a common dialog box; that is, this dialog box looks the same in Excel and in PowerPoint and in most other Windows-based programs.

In the Save As dialog box, you must indicate the name you want for the file and the location where you want to save the file. Programs like Microsoft Word commonly ask you to choose a name and location when you save a file.

When working with your own data, it is good practice to pause at this point and determine the logical name and location for your file.

Figure 2.11

Save As dialog box

Address bar indicates path

Navigation pane

File name box, first characters typed become default file name

Save as type defaults to *Word Document*

Default save location is *Documents library* (yours may differ)

Alert! | Do you have a different default location?

If Documents is not your default storage location, in the navigation pane, under Libraries, click Documents. For most programs that you install on your computer, the default location for storing files will be one of the folders in your personal folder—based on the type of file. The default location for storing Word documents will be the Documents folder, the default location for storing pictures will be the Pictures folder, and so on.

Within a specific program, however, there is usually a method whereby you can change the default save location that displays in the Save As dialog box. You can change the default location to any storage area and folder accessible from your computer; to do so, refer to the documentation for the specific program.

4 In the **Save as type box**, notice that the default file type is a **Word Document**. In the **File name** box, notice that Word selects the first characters of the document as the default name.

Recall that many programs use the Documents library as the default storage location; however, you can navigate to other storage locations from this dialog box.

5 Be sure the text in the **File name** box is selected—highlighted in blue; if it is not, click one time with your mouse to select it. Type **Europe_Project** as the **File name**. Then in the lower right corner of the dialog box, click **Save** to save the file in the **Documents** folder.

> In any Windows-based application, such as Microsoft Word, text highlighted in blue will be replaced by your typing.

> The Word document is saved and the file name displays in the title bar of the Word window.

6 On the taskbar, click the **Excel** button [icon] to start the Excel program.

7 Be sure that cell **A1** is the active cell—it is outlined in black—and then type **An overview of the financial plan for the Europe project will be provided at a later date by the Chief Financial Officer.** and then press Enter.

8 Press F12 to display the **Save As** dialog box.

9 In the **address bar**, be sure the path is **Libraries ▶Documents ▶**; if necessary, in the navigation pane, under Libraries, click Documents.

10 In the **file list**, scroll if necessary to view the **Bell_Orchid** folder. Compare your screen to Figure 2.12.

> To save in a location other than the default location, which in this instance is your *Documents* folder, you must navigate to open the folder window for the folder in which you want to save your file.

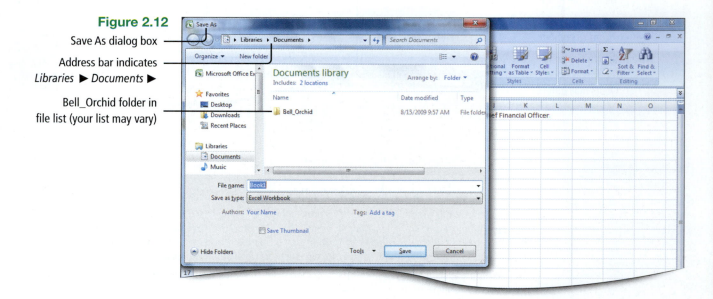

Figure 2.12

Save As dialog box

Address bar indicates
Libraries ▶ Documents ▶

Bell_Orchid folder in
file list (your list may vary)

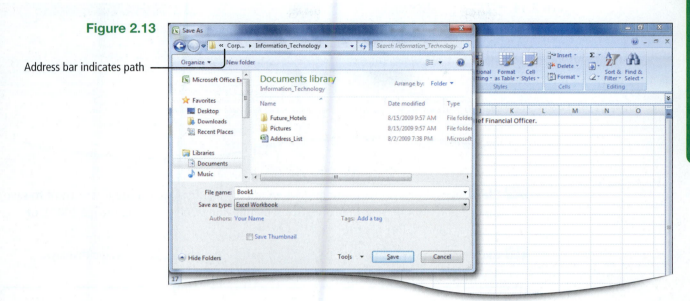

11 In the **file list**, double-click the **Bell_Orchid** folder to open it. Double-click **Corporate**, and then double-click **Information_Technology**. Compare your screen with Figure 2.13.

Figure 2.13

Address bar indicates path —

12 With the **Information_Technology** folder window displayed in the **Save As** dialog box, click in the **File name** box to select the default text *Book1*, type **Europe_Financials** and then in the lower right corner, click the **Save** button—or press Enter—to save the file and close the **Save As** dialog box.

The Excel workbook is saved and the file name displays in the title bar of the Excel window.

13 Press F12 to display the **Save As** dialog box again.

14 In the **address bar**, notice that the **Information_Technology** folder where you stored the previous Excel workbook displays—instead of the Documents folder.

Until you close Excel or change the storage location, Excel will continue to suggest the most recent location as the storage location. Most programs behave in this manner.

15 In the **File name** box, with the text *Europe_Financials* selected—highlighted in blue— type **Europe_Investment_Charts** and then press Enter or click **Save**.

Windows 7 saves and closes the Europe_Financials workbook, and then creates a new workbook, with the name you just typed, based on the old one. Use the Save As command in this manner when you want to create a new document that uses information from an existing document.

Note | The Difference Between Save and Save As

When you are saving something for the first time, for example a new unnamed Excel workbook, the Save and Save As commands are identical. That is, the Save As dialog box will display if you click Save or if you click Save As.

After you have named a file and stored it somewhere, the Save command saves any changes you make to the file without displaying any dialog box. The Save As command will display the Save As dialog box and let you name and save a new document based on the old one. After you name and save the new document, the original document closes, and the new document—based on the old one—displays.

---

16 In cell **A2**, type **A group of charts depicting the investment plan for the Europe project will be provided at a later date by the Chief Financial Officer.** Press Enter. Compare your screen with Figure 2.14.

Figure 2.14

New file name displays in Excel window title bar

Text added in cell A2

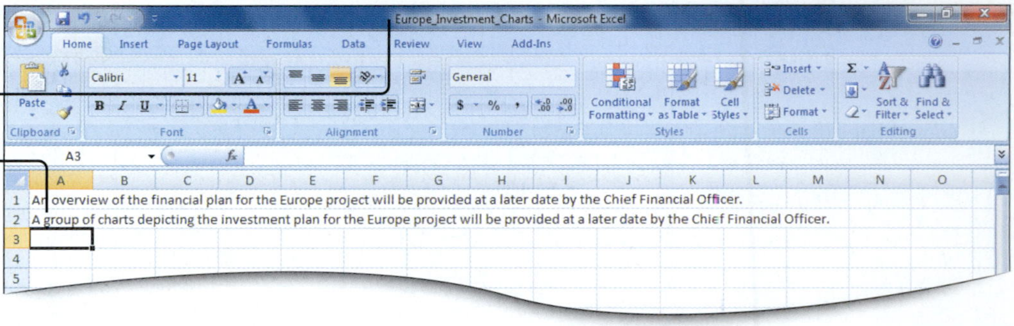

17 **Close** ✖ the Excel window, and when a message displays asking if you want to save the changes you made to **Europe_Investment_Charts**, click **Yes** (in Office 2007), or click **Save** (in Office 2010).

18 **Close** ✖ the Word window; this file was already saved, so no message displays.

More Knowledge | **Rules for Naming Files**

There are three rules to consider when naming files:

- File names usually cannot be longer than 255 characters.
- You cannot use any of the following characters in a file name:
  \ / ? : * " > < |
- File names must be unique in a folder; that is, two files of the same type—for example two Excel files—cannot have the exact same name. Likewise, two subfolders within a folder cannot have the exact same name.

You might also consider this guideline:

- You can use spaces in file names; however, some individuals and organizations prefer not to use spaces. There are some programs, especially when transferring files over the Internet, that may not work well with spaces in file names. In general, however, unless you encounter a problem, it is okay to use spaces. In this textbook, underscores are used instead of spaces in the names of files.

Objective 4 | Create Folders and Rename Folders and Files

As you create files, you will also want to create folders so that you can organize your files into a logical folder structure. It is common to rename files and folders so that the names reflect the content.

Activity 2.05 | Creating Folders and Renaming Folders and Files

Barbara and Steven can see that various managers have been placing files related to the new European hotels in the *Future_Hotels* folder. They can also see that the files have not been organized into a logical structure. For example, files that are related to each other are not in separate folders; instead, they are mixed in with other files that are not related to the topic.

In this activity, you will create, name, and rename folders to begin a logical structure of folders in which to organize the files related to the European hotels project.

1 If necessary, insert the USB flash drive on which you are storing your work for this chapter, and close the AutoPlay dialog box if it displays.

Another Way

If you were not able to pin the folder to the Jump List, click the Windows Explorer button, and then in the Documents library, navigate to the Bell_Orchid folder.

2 On the taskbar, right-click the **Windows Explorer** button 📁 to display the **Jump List**, and then under **Pinned**, click **Bell_Orchid**.

3 In the **address bar**, to the right of **Bell_Orchid**, click ▶, and then on the list click **Corporate**. To the right of **Corporate**, click ▶, and then click **Information_Technology**. To the right of **Information_Technology**, click ▶, and then click **Future_Hotels**.

Some computer users prefer to navigate a folder structure using the address bar in this manner. Use whichever method you prefer—double-clicking in the file list or clicking in the address bar. You can also expand folders in the navigation pane, although the viewing space there is smaller.

Another Way

Right-click in a blank area of the file list, point to View, and then click Details.

4 Be sure the items are in alphabetical order by **Name**. At the right end of the toolbar, click the **View button arrow** ▾, and if necessary, set the view to **Details**. Compare your screen with Figure 2.15.

The *Details view* displays a list of files or folders and their most common *properties*. Properties are descriptive pieces of information about a folder or file such as the name, the date modified, the type, and the size. These are the most common properties and the ones you see in the Details pane when a folder or file is selected.

This view is useful when you are organizing files and folders.

Figure 2.15

Column headings in the file list

Items in alphabetical order by name

Details pane

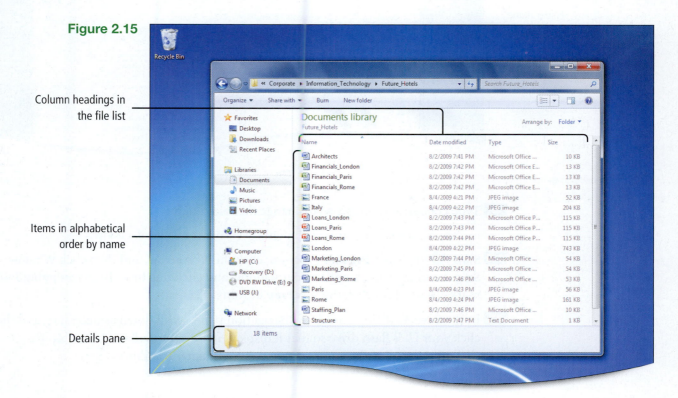

Note | Date Modified and Other Details May Vary

The Date modified and some other details shown in the Figures may differ from what displays on your screen.

5 On the toolbar, click the **New folder** button. With the text *New folder* selected, type **Paris** and press Enter. Click the **New folder** button again, and then type **Venice** and press Enter.

6 Notice how the folders automatically move into alphabetical order. Notice also that when you have both files and folders in a folder, the folders are listed first.

The default organization of a file list in Windows 7 is to list folders first, in alphabetical order, and then files in alphabetical order.

7 Create a new folder named **Essex** and press Enter. Point to the **Venice** folder and right-click. From the displayed menu, click **Rename**, and then notice that the text *Venice* is selected. Type **Rome** and press Enter.

8 Click the **Essex** folder one time to select it. Point to the selected **Essex** folder, and then click one time again. Compare your screen with Figure 2.16.

Recall that any time text like this is selected, your typing replaces the existing text.

Figure 2.16

Folder name
Essex selected

Subfolders display
before files

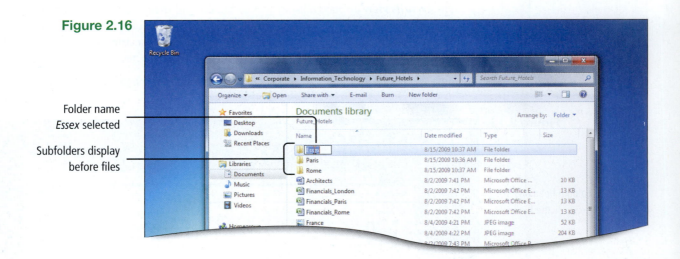

9 Type **London** and press Enter to change the folder name.

You can use either of these techniques to change the name of a folder.

10 Start ● the **Snipping Tool** program, click the **New arrow**, and then click **Window Snip**. Point anywhere in the folder window and click one time. In the **Snipping Tool** mark-up window, click the **Save Snip** button 🖫.

11 In the **Save As** dialog box, in the navigation pane, scroll down as necessary, and then click your USB flash drive so that it displays in the **address bar**. On the toolbar, click the **New folder** button, type **Windows 7 Chapter 2** and press Enter.

12 In the **file list**, double-click your **Windows 7 Chapter 2** folder to open it. Click in the **File name** box, and then replace the selected text by typing **Lastname_Firstname_ 2A_Europe_Folders_Snip** Compare your screen with Figure 2.17.

Figure 2.17

New folder name displays in address bar

Your flash drive selected in the navigation pane

File name

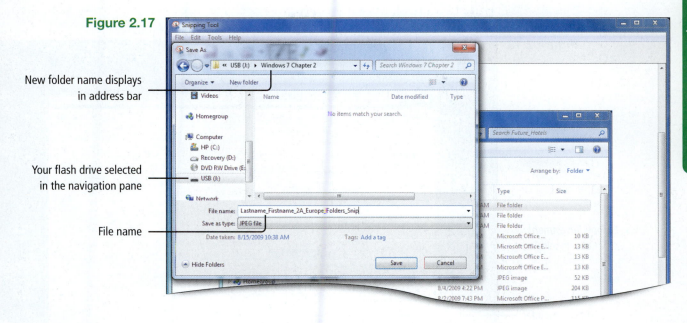

13 Be sure the file type is **JPEG**. Click **Save** or press Enter. **Close** the **Snipping Tool** window. Hold this file until you finish Project 2A.

14 In the **address bar**, click **Information_Technology** to move up one level in the folder structure.

Recall that you can move up by one or more levels by clicking the folder name on the address bar, and you can move to a subfolder in any folder on the address bar by clicking the ▶ arrow and displaying the list of subfolders.

15 In the **column headings area**, point to *Name*, right-click, and then click **Size Column to Fit**.

16 Point to the file **Europe_Investment_Charts** and click one time to select it. Click the file one time again to select the text. Position your mouse pointer anywhere over the selected text and notice that the I pointer displays. Compare your screen with Figure 2.18.

Figure 2.18

Text *Europe_Investment_ Charts* selected

I-beam pointer

17 Position the I pointer slightly to the left of the word *Investment* and click one time to position the insertion point within the file name. By using Del or the arrow keys or any other keys on your keyboard, edit the file name to **Europe_Charts** and press Enter.

You can use any of these techniques to change the name of a file or folder.

18 **Close** ❌ the window.

Objective 5 | Select, Copy, and Move Files and Folders

To **select** is to highlight, by clicking or dragging with the mouse, one or more file or folder names in the file list. Selecting in this manner is commonly done for the purpose of copying, moving, renaming, or deleting the selected files or folders.

Activity 2.06 | Selecting Groups of Files or Folders in the File List

There are several ways to select multiple items in a file list—use whatever method you prefer or that is convenient. The techniques you will practice in this activity apply not only to Windows 7, but also to lists of files that display in other applications.

1 On the taskbar, right-click the **Windows Explorer** button 📁 to display the **Jump List**, and then under **Pinned**, click **Bell_Orchid**. In the upper right corner of the window, click the **Maximize** 🔲 button so that the window fills the entire screen.

Recall that starting from the taskbar is usually the fastest and most efficient way to navigate in Windows 7, so use the Jump Lists whenever it is practical to do so. Think of a Jump List as a mini start menu for a program.

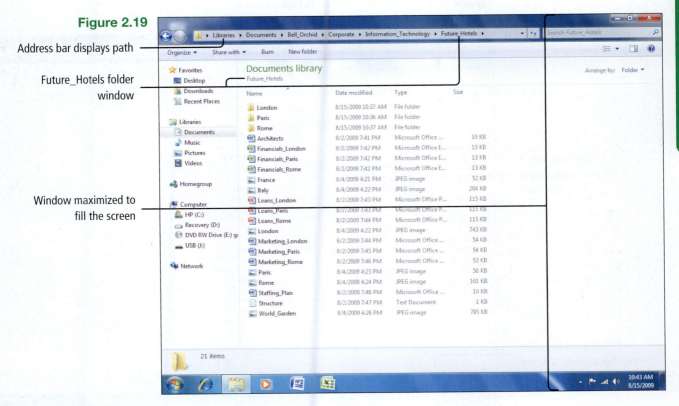

2 With the **Bell_Orchid** folder window displayed, by double-clicking in the file list—or by clicking the links in the address bar—navigate to **Corporate** ▶ **Information_ Technology** ▶ **Future_Hotels**. Compare your screen with Figure 2.19.

Figure 2.19

Address bar displays path

Future_Hotels folder window

Window maximized to fill the screen

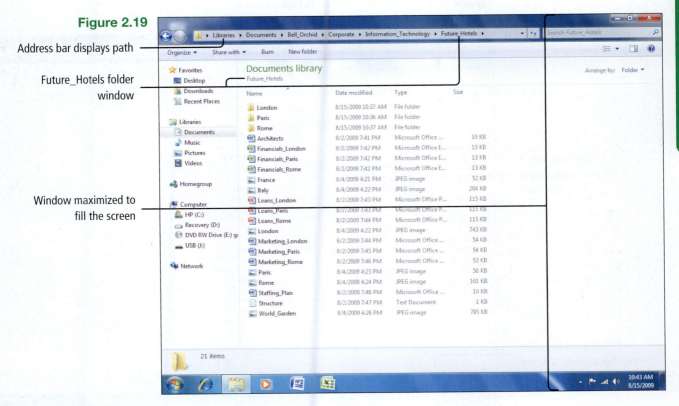

3 In the **file list**, click the Excel file **Financials_London** one time to select it. With the file name selected, hold down Shift, and then click the Word file **Staffing_Plan**.

This technique, commonly referred to as *Shift Click*, selects a consecutive group of files or folders. To select all the items in a consecutive group, you need only to click the first item, hold down Shift, and then click the last item in the group.

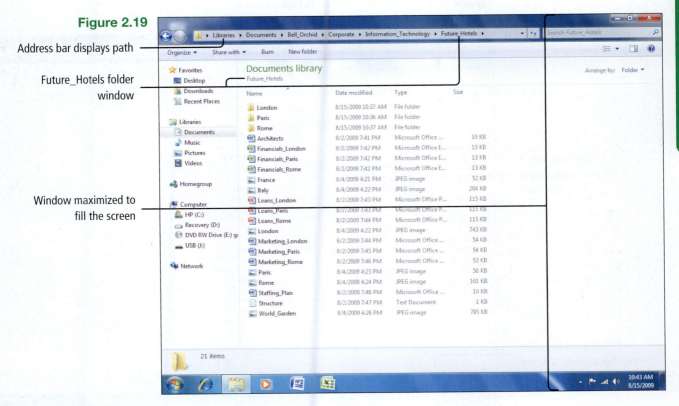

4 Click in a blank area of the **file list** to cancel the selection—also referred to as *deselect*. Point to, but do *not* click in, the empty space immediately to the right of the file name **Financials_London**, hold down the left mouse button, and then drag to the left side of the column and down to the **Financials_Rome** folder, creating a small square as you drag, as shown in Figure 2.20.

Figure 2.20

Dragging creates a selection area around the items

Details pane indicates number of items selected

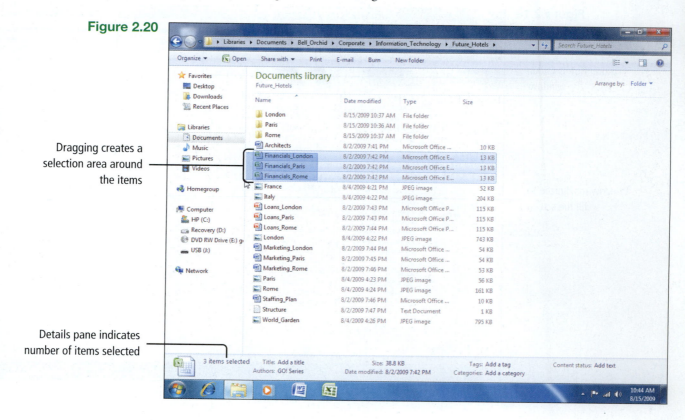

5 Release the left mouse button, and notice that the three files are selected. If you are not satisfied with your result, click in a blank area of the file list to deselect, and then begin again.

In this manner, you can use only the mouse to create a selection around the outside of all the items you want to include in the selection.

6 Deselect by clicking in a blank area of the **file list**. Select the file **Financials_London**, hold down Ctrl, and then click **Marketing_London**. Notice that only the two files are selected. With the two files selected, hold down Ctrl, and then click **Financials_Rome** and **Marketing_Rome**. Release Ctrl.

Four files are selected. Use this Ctrl key technique when you want to select a group of *nonconsecutive* items.

7 With the four files still selected, hold down Ctrl, and then click the selected files **Marketing_Rome** and **Financials_Rome**. Release the key.

To cancel the selection of individual items within a selected group, hold down Ctrl, and then click the items you do *not* want to include.

Another Way

On the toolbar, click Organize, and then on the menu, click Select All.

8 Deselect by clicking in a blank area of the file list. Click any single file or folder in the list, and then hold down Ctrl and press A. Release the two keys.

Use this technique to select all of the files or folders in the file list.

9 Click anywhere in the file list to deselect. In the upper right corner, click the **Restore Down** button 🔲 to restore the window to its previous size, and then **Close** ❎ the **Future_Hotels** folder window.

Activity 2.07 | Copying Files

When you *copy* a file or a folder, you make a duplicate of the original item and then store the duplicate in another location. In this activity, you will assist Barbara and Steven in making copies of the Staffing_Plan file, and then placing a copy in each of the three folders you created—London, Paris, and Rome.

1 In the taskbar, point to the **Windows Explorer** button 📁, hold down the left mouse button, and then drag upward slightly into the desktop to display the **Jump List**. Then, on the **Jump List**, under **Pinned**, click **Bell_Orchid**.

You will increase your efficiency if you make it a habit to work mostly from the taskbar and to display Jump Lists using this technique. After the Jump List displays, you need only move your mouse pointer upward a little more to select the action that you want.

2 With the **Bell_Orchid** folder window displayed, by double-clicking in the file list or following the links in the address bar, navigate to **Corporate ▶ Information_ Technology ▶ Future_Hotels**.

3 **Maximize** 🔲 the folder window and if necessary, set the **View button arrow** 📋 ▾ to **Details**.

Another Way

To perform the Copy command and the Paste command, you can use the keyboard shortcut Ctrl + C to activate the Copy command and the keyboard shortcut Ctrl + V to activate the Paste command. Also, the Copy and Paste commands are available on the Organize menu on the toolbar.

4 In the **file list**, point to the file **Staffing_Plan** and right-click. On the displayed menu, click **Copy**.

The Copy command places a copy of your selected file or folder on the *Clipboard* where it will be stored until you replace it with another Copy command. The Clipboard is a temporary storage area for information that you have copied or moved from one place and plan to use somewhere else.

In Windows 7, the Clipboard can hold only one piece of information at a time. Whenever something is copied to the Clipboard, it replaces whatever was there before. In Windows 7, you cannot view the contents of the Clipboard nor place multiple items there in the manner that you can in Microsoft Word.

5 At the top of the **file list**, point to the **London folder**, right-click, and then click **Paste**. Then double-click the **London** folder to open it. Notice that the copy of the **Staffing_Plan** file displays. Compare your screen with Figure 2.21.

Figure 2.21

London folder window

Staffing_Plan file copied to folder

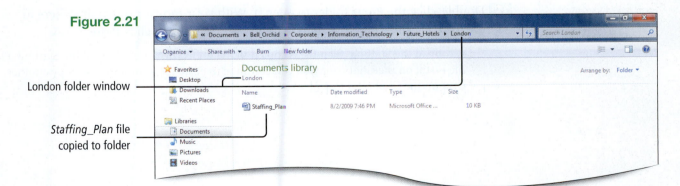

Another Way

On the left end of the address bar, you can press the Back button to retrace your clicks as necessary to display the window you want. Or, click in a blank area of the file list to deselect anything that is selected, and then press Bksp to move up one level in the folder structure.

6 With the **London** folder open, by using any of the techniques you have practiced, rename this copy of the **Staffing_Plan** file to **London_Staffing_Plan** (Hint: The most efficient way to rename this file is to click the file name three times—but not so rapidly that you actually open the file—to display the insertion point in the file name, and then edit the name as necessary.)

7 In the **address bar**, click **Future_Hotels** to redisplay this folder window and move up one level in the folder structure.

8 Select and then point to the **Staffing_Plan** file, hold down Ctrl, drag upward over the **Paris** folder until the ScreenTip + *Copy to Paris* displays as shown in Figure 2.22, and then release the mouse button and release Ctrl.

When dragging a file into a folder, holding down Ctrl engages the Copy command and places a copy of the file at the location where you release the mouse button. This is another way to copy a file or copy a folder.

Figure 2.22

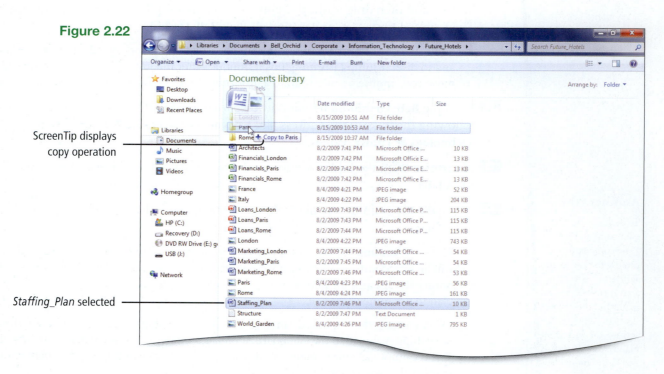

ScreenTip displays copy operation

Staffing_Plan selected

Another Way

To rename a file, click the file name one time to select it, press F2 to select the file name; then type the new name.

9 Open the **Paris** folder window, and then rename the **Staffing_Plan** file **Paris_Staffing_Plan** Then, move up one level in the folder structure to display the **Future_Hotels** folder window.

10 Double-click the **Rome** folder to open it. With your mouse pointer anywhere in the file list, right-click, and then from the shortcut menu click **Paste**.

A copy of the Staffing_Plan file is copied to the folder. Because a copy of the Staffing_Plan file is still on the Clipboard, you can continue to paste the item until you copy another item on the Clipboard to replace it.

11 Rename the file **Rome_Staffing_Plan** and then compare your screen with Figure 2.23.

Figure 2.23

Address bar displays path —

Rome folder active —

Copied file renamed —

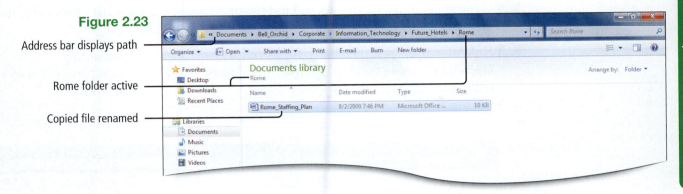

12 On the **address bar**, click **Future_Hotels** to move up one level and open the **Future_Hotels** folder window. Leave this folder open for the next activity.

Activity 2.08 | Moving Files

When you *move* a file or folder, you remove it from the original location and store it in a new location. In this activity, you will move items from the Future_Hotels folder into their appropriate folders.

Another Way

To initiate the Cut command, press Ctrl + X.

---

1 With the **Future_Hotels** folder open, in the **file list**, point to the Excel file **Financials_London** and right-click. On the displayed shortcut menu, click **Cut**.

The file's Excel icon is dimmed on the screen. This action places the item on the Clipboard.

Another Way

To initiate the Paste command, press Ctrl + V.

---

2 Point to the **London** folder, right-click, and then click **Paste**. Notice that the file is removed from the file list. Then open the **London** folder, and notice that the file was pasted into the folder.

3 On the **address bar**, click **Future_Hotels** to move up a level. In the **file list**, point to **Financials_Paris**, hold down the left mouse button, and then drag the file upward over the **Paris** folder until the ScreenTip →*Move to Paris* displays, as shown in Figure 2.24. Release the mouse button.

Figure 2.24

Future_Hotels folder active

ScreenTip indicates → *Move to Paris*

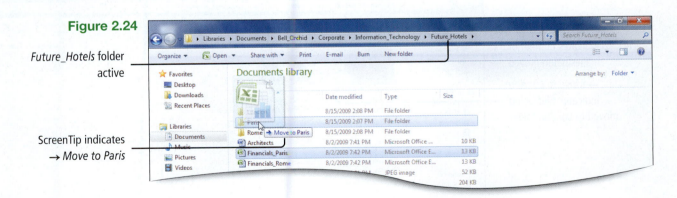

4 Open the **Paris** folder, and notice that the file was moved to this folder. On the **address bar**, click **Future_Hotels** to return to that folder.

5 Using either of the techniques you just practiced, move the **Financials_Rome** file into the **Rome** folder.

6 Hold down Ctrl, and then in the file list, click **Loans_London**, **London**, and **Marketing_London** to select the three files. Release the Ctrl key. Compare your screen with Figure 2.25.

Figure 2.25

Future_Hotels folder active

Three files selected

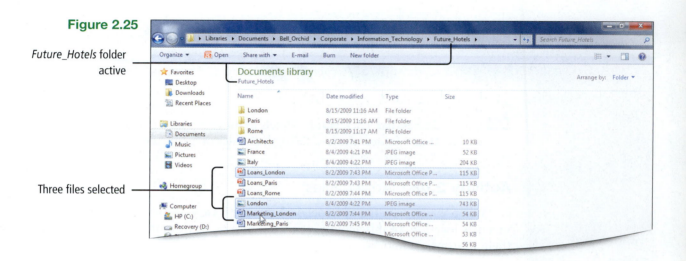

Another Way

Right-click over any of the selected files, click Cut, right-click over the London folder, and then click Paste.

7 Point to any of the selected files, hold down the left mouse button, and then drag upward over the **London** folder until the ScreenTip →*Move to London* displays and *3* displays over the files being moved, as shown in Figure 2.26. Release the mouse button.

The three files are moved to the London folder.

Figure 2.26

Future_Hotels folder active

3 indicates number of files being moved

→ *Move to London* indicates files being moved to London folder

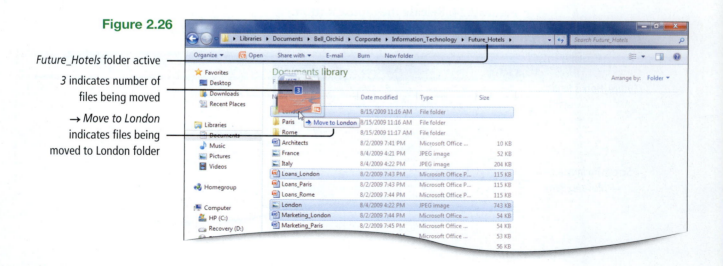

8 Using either the select and drag method, or the select and then Cut and Paste method, select the files **France**, **Loans_Paris**, **Marketing_Paris**, and **Paris**, and move these four files into the **Paris** folder.

9 Select the four files **Italy**, **Loans_Rome**, **Marketing_Rome**, and **Rome**, and move them into the **Rome** folder.

You can see that by keeping related files together, for example, all the files that relate to the Rome hotel, in folders that have an appropriately descriptive name, it will be easier to locate information later.

10 Move the **Architects** file into the **London** folder.

11 In an empty area of the file list, right-click, and then click **Undo Move**. Leave the window open for the next activity.

Another Way
Press Ctrl + Z to undo an action in the file list.

Any action that you make in a file list can be undone in this manner.

Activity 2.09 | Copying and Moving Files by Using Two Windows

Sometimes you will want to open, in a second window, another instance of a program that you are using; that is, two copies of the program will be running simultaneously. This capability is especially useful in the Windows Explorer program, because you are frequently moving or copying files from one location to another.

In this activity, you will open two instances of Windows Explorer, and then use the Snap feature to display both instances on your screen.

To copy or move files or folders into a different level of a folder structure, or to a different drive location, the most efficient method is to display two windows side by side and then use drag and drop; or use copy (or cut) and paste commands.

In this activity, you will assist Barbara and Steven in making copies of the Staffing_ Plan files for the corporate office. You will also place the Europe_Project file, which is still in the Documents folder, in its proper location.

1 In the upper right corner, click the **Restore Down** button 🔲 to restore the **Future_Hotels** folder window to its previous size and not maximized on the screen.

2 Point to the upper edge of the **Future_Hotels** folder window to display the pointer, and then drag the window to the left until the pointer reaches the left edge of the screen and the window snaps into place and occupies the left half of the screen.

Another Way
On the Jump List, click Windows Explorer to open a second copy of the program.

3 On the taskbar, point to the **Windows Explorer** button 📒, drag upward slightly into the desktop to display the **Jump List**, and then click **Bell_Orchid** to open a new folder window. Snap this window to the right side of the screen.

4 In the folder window on the right, navigate to **Corporate ▶ Human_Resources**. Compare your screen with Figure 2.27.

Figure 2.27

Future_Hotels folder window snapped to left side of screen

Corporate ▶ Human_ Resources folder window snapped to right side of screen

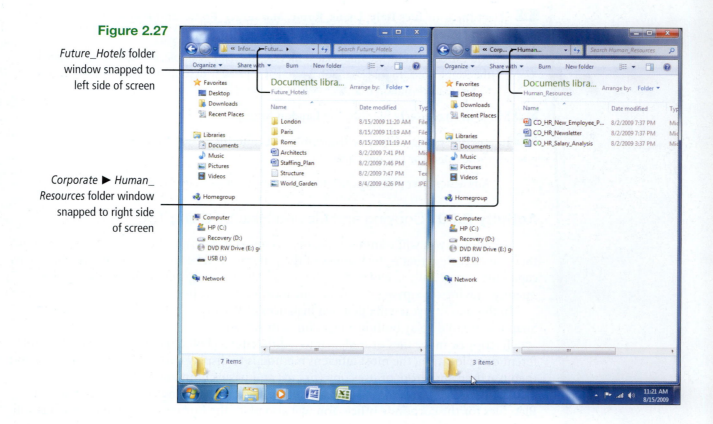

5 In the left window, open the **Rome** folder, and then select the file **Rome_Staffing_Plan**.

6 Hold down Ctrl, and then drag the file into the right window, into an empty area of the **Human_Resources file list**, until the ScreenTip + *Copy to Human Resources* displays, as shown in Figure 2.28, and then release the mouse button and the Ctrl key.

Figure 2.28

ScreenTip + *Copy to Human Resources*

7 In the left window, on the **address bar**, click **Future_Hotels** to redisplay that folder window. Open the **Paris** folder, point to **Paris_Staffing_Plan** and right-click, and then click **Copy**.

8 In the right window, point anywhere in the **file list**, right-click, and then click **Paste**.

You can use either the Copy and Paste commands, or the Ctrl + drag technique, to copy files across two windows.

9 Using either of the techniques you have practiced, in the left window, navigate to the **London** folder, and then copy the **London_Staffing_Plan** file to the **Human_Resources** folder on the right. Compare your screen with Figure 2.29.

Copies of the three files regarding staffing plans for the three European locations display.

Figure 2.29

Three copied files

Navigation pane in right window

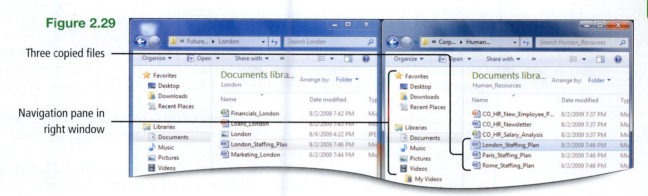

10 In the right window, in the **navigation pane**, click **Documents**. If necessary, scroll to view the file **Europe_Project** that was placed in the Documents folder.

11 In the left window, in the **address bar**, click **Future_Hotels** to redisplay that folder window. In the right window, in the **file list**, point to the **Europe_Project** file, and then drag it into the left window until the ScreenTip → *Move to Future_Hotels* displays, as shown in Figure 2.30, and then release the mouse button.

When dragging and dropping across two locations, to move an item, drag it. To copy an item, hold down Ctrl and then drag it.

This technique works in most Windows-based programs. For example, to copy a selection of text in Word, select it, hold down Ctrl, drag to another location in the document, and release the mouse button. To move a selection of text, simply drag it to the new location.

Figure 2.30

File list shows contents of Documents (your list will vary)

ScreenTip indicates → *Move to Future_Hotels*

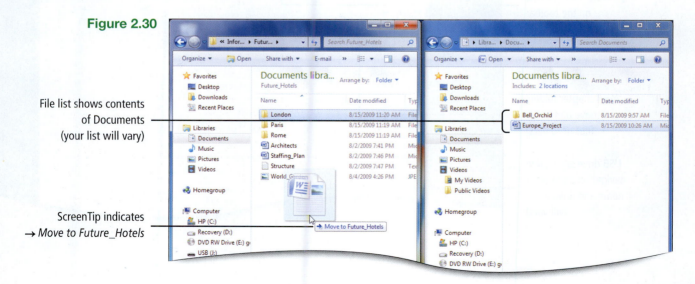

12 In the right window, navigate to **Bell_Orchid ▶ Corporate ▶ Human_Resources**. In the left window, be sure the **Future_Hotels** folder window displays.

13 **Start** 🪟 the **Snipping Tool** program, click the **New arrow**, and then click **Full-screen Snip**. In the **Snipping Tool** mark-up window, click the **Save Snip** button 💾.

14 In the displayed **Save As** dialog box, notice the path in the **address bar**. If necessary, in the navigation pane, under **Computer**, click your USB flash drive, and then display the folder window for your **Windows 7 Chapter 2** folder.

15 Be sure the file type is **JPEG**. Using your own name, name the file **Lastname_Firstname_2A_HR_Snip** and press Enter. Hold this file until you finish Project 2A.

16 **Close** ❌ all open windows.

Activity 2.10 | Copying and Moving Files Among Different Drives

You can copy and move files and folders among different drives; for example from the Documents library on your hard disk drive to your USB flash drive. When copying and moving between drives, dragging files or folders will always result in a copy, regardless of whether you hold down Ctrl.

To *move* files between drives, you can use one of three techniques: 1) right-drag—drag while holding down the *right* mouse button; 2) hold down the Shift key while dragging; 3) use the Cut and Copy commands.

In this activity, you will assist Barbara in moving some of her personal files from the corporate Information_Technology folder to a new folder on a USB flash drive. Additionally, Barbara has a Resume Guide in her personal files, which her colleagues in the Human Resources department would like to have a copy of to share with employees.

1 Be sure your USB flash drive is inserted in your computer. On the taskbar, click the **Windows Explorer** button 📁, and then in the **navigation pane**, under **Computer**, click your USB flash drive to open its folder window. Compare your screen with Figure 2.31.

Figure 2.31

Folder window for USB flash drive (your name and drive letter will vary)

New folder button on the toolbar

Your chapter folders (you may have additional files or folders)

USB drive selected in navigation pane (your name and drive letter will vary)

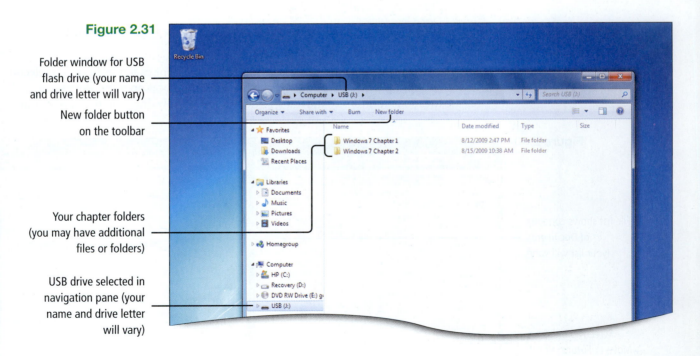

2 On the toolbar, click the **New folder** button, and then with the text *New folder* selected, type **BHewitt_Files** and press Enter to name the folder.

3 Snap the folder window to the *right* side of the screen.

4 On the taskbar, right-click the **Windows Explorer** button 🗂, click **Bell_Orchid**, and then snap the window to the left side of the screen.

Note | Snap to the Left or to the Right?

When using two windows to copy and move files, it does not matter to which side of the screen you snap the window. You can move and copy files in either direction.

---

5 In the left window, navigate to **Bell_Orchid ▶ Corporate ▶ Information Technology**. Compare your screen with Figure 2.32.

In the taskbar, two overlapping glass-framed Windows Explorer icons display to indicate that two windows are open.

Figure 2.32

Left window displays
Information_Technology
folder window

Right window displays
folder window for your
USB flash drive

New folder created on
your USB flash drive

Taskbar icon indicates
two Windows Explorer
windows open

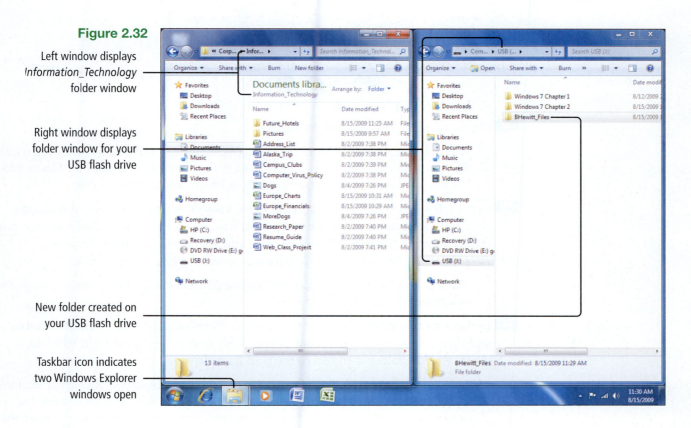

6 Hold down Ctrl, and then in the left window, select the files **Alaska_Trip**, **Campus_Clubs**, **Dogs**, **MoreDogs**, **Research_Paper**, and **Resume_Guide**.

7 Release Ctrl, point to any of the selected files, hold down the *right* mouse button, drag across into the right window until the mouse pointer is over the **BHewitt_Files** folder, and then when you see the ScreenTip + *Copy to BHewitt_Files*, release the right mouse button to display a shortcut menu. Compare your screen with Figure 2.33.

Figure 2.33

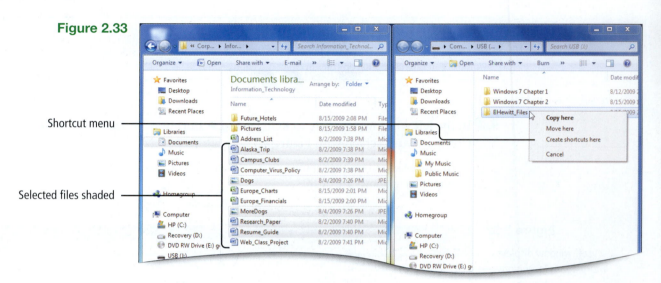

Shortcut menu

Selected files shaded

8 On the displayed menu, click **Move here**.

When *moving* among drives, this right-drag technique is useful, because when you release the right mouse button, you will always have the option to move *or* copy the files or folder. Use this technique to move a group of files or folders among different drives.

9 In the left window, select the file **Web_Class_Project**, which is another of Barbara's personal files that should move to the USB flash drive. Hold down Shift and then drag the file into the **BHewitt_Files** folder until you see the ScreenTip → *Move to BHewitt_Files*. Release the mouse button and release Shift.

This is another technique to move files among different drives; use it to move a single file or a group of consecutive files.

10 In the window on the left, point to the folder **Pictures**, right-click, point to **Send to**, and then click the drive and letter of your USB flash drive. In the right window, notice that the folder is copied to the USB flash drive.

A message indicates that the files are being copied to the destination. Recall that Send to is a *copy* command. You can copy files and folders directly to another drive by using the Send to command. You cannot, however, use this command to send the files to a specific folder on the drive; rather, the files are copied directly to the drive.

11 In the right window, double-click the **BHewitt_Files** folder to open it. Point to the **Resume_Guide** file and right-click, and then click **Copy** to place a copy of the file on the Clipboard.

12 In the left window, on the **address bar**, to the right of **Corporate**, click the ▶, and then compare your screen with Figure 2.34.

Figure 2.34

List of subfolders within the Corporate folder

Resume_Guide selected

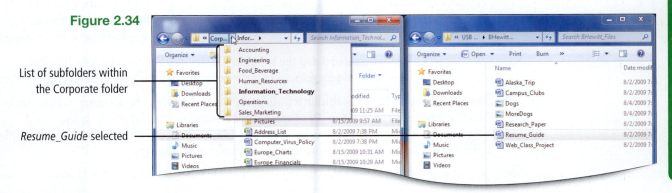

13 On the displayed list of subfolders, click **Human_Resources** to display this folder window.

Recall that the address bar is a convenient way to navigate up or down one or more levels in the folder structure.

Another method is to click the Back arrow as necessary to display the folder that you want. Recall that you can click the Back button to the left of the address bar to navigate through locations you have already visited, in the same manner you use your browser software when displaying sites and pages on the Internet.

14 In the **Human_Resources file list**, right-click in a blank area, and then click **Paste**. Notice that the copy of the file displays in the file list.

15 In the *right* window, in the **BHewitt_Files** folder window, point to the **Resume_Guide** file, and right-click. Compare your screen with Figure 2.35.

Figure 2.35

Resume_Guide in BHewitt_Files folder

Resume_Guide copied to Human_Resources folder

Shortcut menu

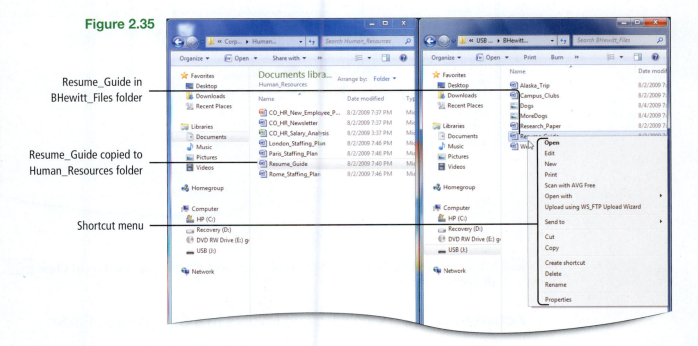

16 On the displayed shortcut menu, click **Open** to open the file in the Word program.

17 At the top to the Word window, click the **Insert tab**, and then on the **Ribbon**, in the **Header & Footer group**, click the **Header** button. At the top of the displayed list, click **Blank**, and then type **Provided to the Human Resources Department by Barbara Hewitt Close** ❎ the Word window, and then click **Yes** or **Save** to save the changes.

Now that Barbara has updated the Resume_Guide file, she wants to copy it to the Human_Resources folder again, so that the copy they have is this updated copy.

18 From the **BHewitt_Files** folder window on the right, drag the **Resume_Guide** file to the left, into the **Human_Resources** folder window, and then when the ScreenTip + *Copy to Human_Resources* displays, release the mouse button to display the **Copy File** dialog box. Compare your screen with Figure 2.36.

Windows 7 recognizes that there is already a file with this name in the Human_Resources folder, although it is not the *most recent* copy now that Barbara has updated the original by adding a header. Within a folder, two files of the same type—a Word document in this instance—cannot have the same name. Likewise, within a folder, two subfolders cannot have the same name.

There are three actions you can take from this dialog box. You can click Copy and Replace, which will replace the old copy with your new copy. Or, you can abandon the copy operation by clicking *Don't copy*. Or, you can complete the copy operation by keeping both files, but Windows 7 will add *(2)* to the name of the new copy so that it will not have the same name.

Figure 2.36

Copy File dialog box ———

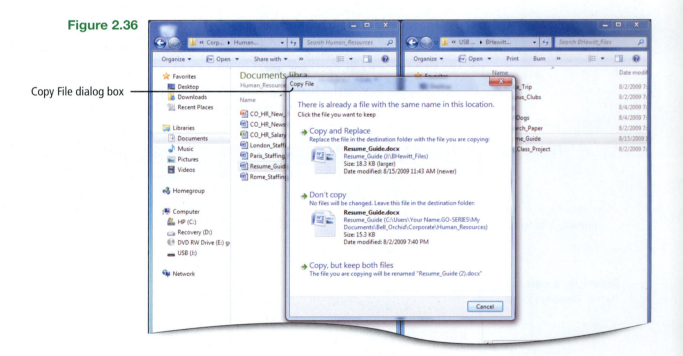

19 Click **Copy and Replace** to replace the old copy with the new updated copy. **Close** ❎ all open windows.

Activity 2.11 | Copying Files and Folders to a Compressed Folder

To *compress* is to reduce the size of a file. Compressed files take up less storage space and can be transferred to other computers, for example in an e-mail message, more quickly than uncompressed files. Because pictures are typically large files, it is common to compress graphic files like pictures. When the picture is expanded, there will be no loss of visual quality.

1 In the taskbar, drag the **Windows Explorer** button 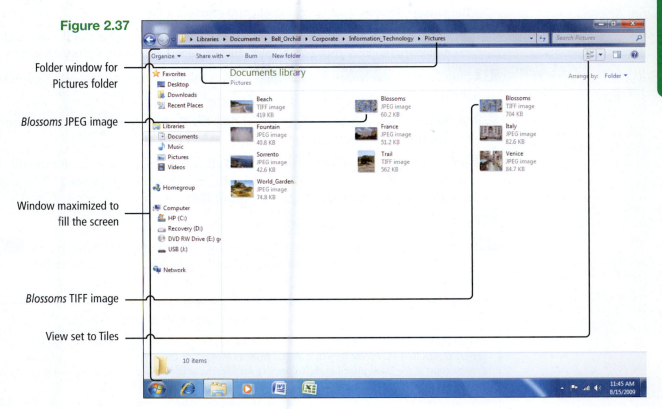 upward slightly into the desktop to display the **Jump List**. Then, on the **Jump List**, under **Pinned**, click **Bell_Orchid**. Navigate to **Bell_Orchid ▶ Corporate ▶ Information_Technology ▶ Pictures**.

2 In the upper right corner, click the **Maximize** button so that the folder window fills the screen. On the toolbar, click the **View button arrow**, and then set the view to **Tiles**. Compare your screen with Figure 2.37.

Figure 2.37

Folder window for Pictures folder

Blossoms JPEG image

Window maximized to fill the screen

Blossoms TIFF image

View set to Tiles

3 Locate the picture **Blossoms** that is a **JPEG** image and notice that its size is **60.2 KB**. Then locate the picture **Blossoms** that is a **TIFF** image and notice that its size is **704 KB**.

Within a folder, two files can have the same name so long as they are of different file types—in this instance a *JPEG* file type and a *TIFF* file type.

JPEG, which stands for *Joint Photographic Experts Group*, is a common file type used by digital cameras and computers to store digital pictures—it is a popular file type because it can store a high-quality picture in a relatively small file.

TIFF, which stands for *Tagged Image File Format*, is a file type used when a very high level of visual quality is needed; for example, if the file will be used to print 8-by-10-inch enlargements.

4 Hold down Ctrl, and then select the files **Beach**, **Fountain**, and **Trail**. Release Ctrl, point to *any* of the selected files, right-click, point to **Send to**, and then click **Compressed (zipped) folder.**

A compressed folder is created containing the three files and is stored in the existing folder—the Pictures folder. The new compressed folder will display the name of the file to which you were pointing when you right-clicked. You can change the name if you want to do so by using any renaming technique.

5 Point to a white area of the **file list** (do not be concerned if another file is framed), right-click, point to **New**, and then click **Compressed (zipped) Folder**. Type **Europe_Images** as the name of the compressed folder, and then press `Enter`.

6 Point to the **France** picture, and then drag it into the **Europe_Images** compressed folder, releasing the mouse button when you see the ScreenTip + *Copy*.

7 Click the **Italy** picture to select it, hold down `Ctrl`, and then select the **Venice** picture. Release `Ctrl`. Right-click over either of the selected files, and then click **Copy**. Point to the **Europe_Images** folder, right-click, and then click **Paste**.

> In this manner you can create a compressed folder, and then use any of the copy techniques that you have practiced to place files or folders into the compressed folder.

8 Double-click the compressed **Europe_Images** folder to view its contents, and notice the three pictures you copied there—*France, Italy,* and *Venice*.

9 In the upper left corner of the window, click the **Back** button to move up one level in the folder structure.

10 Start the **Snipping Tool** program, create a **Full-screen Snip**, and then save the file in the JPEG format on your USB flash drive in your **Windows 7 Chapter 2** folder with the name **Lastname_Firstname_2A_Compressed_Snip**

11 **Close** the **Snipping Tool** window.

12 In the upper right corner of the folder window, click the **Restore Down** button to restore the window to its smaller size, and then **Close** the folder window.

More Knowledge | To Extract Files or Folders From a Compressed Folder

To extract files or folders from a compressed folder, locate the compressed folder that you want to extract. To extract means to decompress, or pull out, files from a compressed form. When you extract a file, an uncompressed copy of the file is placed in the folder you specify. The original file remains in the compressed folder. Compressed files typically have a .zip file name extension.

To extract a single file or folder, double-click the compressed folder to open it. Then, drag the file or folder from the compressed folder to a new location. To extract the entire contents of the compressed folder, right-click the folder, click Extract All, and then follow the instructions.

Activity 2.12 | Copying Files and Folders to a CD/DVD

If your computer includes a CD or DVD recorder, you can copy files to a *writable disc*, which is a CD or DVD disc onto which files can be copied. This process is called *burning a disc*.

Alert! | This is an Optional Activity

This activity is optional. You can complete this activity if the computer at which you are working has a writable CD or DVD drive and you have a blank CD or DVD.

For this activity, you will need a writable CD or DVD drive in your computer and a blank CD or DVD. If you do not have this equipment, you can read through this activity, and then move to Activity 2.13.

---

1 **Close** [×] all open windows. On your computer's case, open your **CD/DVD Drive**, remove the Student Resource CD if it is in the drive, and then depending on your particular computer hardware, place a blank recordable or writable CD or DVD in the drive and close the drive. When the **AutoPlay** dialog box displays, click **Burn files to disc using Windows Explorer**.

2 In the **Disc title** box, replace the highlighted text by typing **Restaurant_Files** and then compare your screen with Figure 2.38.

The first option, *Like a USB flash drive*, will use the **Live File System**. Discs formatted with Live File System enable you to copy files to the disc at any time, instead of copying (burning) them all at once.

The second option, *With a CD/DVD player*, will use the **Mastered** system. Discs created using the Mastered format are more likely to be compatible with older computers, but an additional step is required to burn the collection of files to the disc.

You can use the Live File System or choose to burn discs in the Mastered format, especially if you think the disc will be read on an older computer that does not use the Windows XP, Windows Vista, or the Windows 7 operating system.

Figure 2.38

Burn a Disc dialog box ————

Disc title typed ————

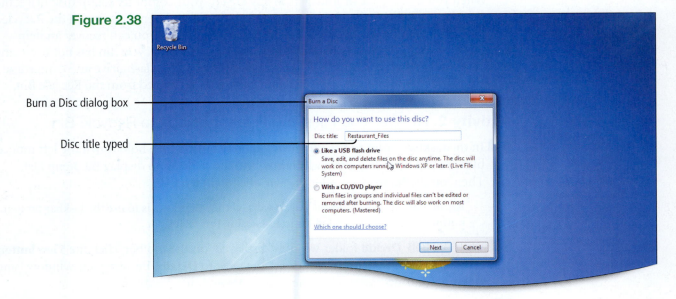

Note | Which CD or DVD Format?

For complete information on the formats for burning music and video discs, in the Windows Help and Support window type *Which CD or DVD format should I use?*

3 Click **Like a USB flash drive**, and then in the lower right corner, click **Next**; wait a few moments until the disc is formatted. Then, click **Open folder to view files**.

4 Snap this empty disc folder window to the right side of the screen.

5 On the taskbar, drag the **Windows Explorer** button [icon] slightly into the desktop, and then at the top of the **Jump List**, click **Bell_Orchid**. Snap this window to the left side of the screen, on the toolbar, click the **View button arrow** [icon], and then set the view back to **Details**.

6 In the left window, navigate to **Bell_Orchid ▶ Corporate ▶ Food_Beverage**. Hold down [Ctrl], and then in the **file list**, select the three files **CO_FB_Banquet_Contract**, **CO_FB_Menu_Analysis**, **CO_FB_Menu_Presentation**.

7 Drag the selected files into the right window. Release the mouse button when the ScreenTip + *Copy to Drive Restaurant_Files* (your exact text will vary). Wait a few moments for the copy to complete.

> The files are copied to the CD.

8 **Close** ❎ both windows.

> Later, you can continue to open files from and copy other files to this CD as needed.

9 Open your **CD/DVD Drive**, if necessary wait for it to eject, and then remove the disc and close your **CD/DVD Drive**.

Objective 6 | Delete Files and Folders and Use the Recycle Bin

It is good practice to delete files and folders that you no longer need from your hard disk drive and removable storage devices. Doing so frees up storage space on your devices and makes it easier to keep your data organized.

When you delete a file or folder from any area of your computer's hard disk drive, the file or folder is not immediately deleted. Instead, the deleted item is stored in the Recycle Bin and remains there until the Recycle Bin is emptied. Thus, you can recover an item deleted from your computer's hard disk drive so long as the Recycle Bin has not been emptied. Items deleted from removable storage devices like a USB flash drive and from some network drives are immediately deleted and cannot be recovered from the Recycle Bin.

Activity 2.13 | Deleting Files and Folders Using the Recycle Bin

1 In the taskbar, point to the **Windows Explorer** button 📁, hold down the left mouse button, and then drag upward slightly into the desktop to display the **Jump List**. Then, on the **Jump List**, under **Pinned**, click **Bell_Orchid**.

> Recall that the most efficient way to work within Windows is to use the taskbar program buttons and their associated Jump Lists using this technique.

2 With the **Bell_Orchid** folder window displayed, on the toolbar, click the **View button arrow** , and then, if necessary, set the view to **Details**. Be sure your window is not maximized. If necessary, click the **Restore Down** button .

3 Navigate to **Bell_Orchid ▶ Corporate ▶ Information_Technology**.

4 Point to the **Computer_Virus_Policy** file, right-click, and then from the shortcut menu, click **Delete**. In the displayed **Delete File** dialog box, notice that the message asks if you want to *move this file to the Recycle Bin*. Click **Yes**.

5 In the **file list**, hold down Ctrl, and then select the Excel files **Europe_Charts** and **Europe_Financials**. Release Ctrl, and then press Del. In the displayed **Delete Multiple Items** dialog box, click **Yes** to move the selected items to the **Recycle Bin**. Compare your screen with Figure 2.39.

> You can delete a group of items in this manner.

Figure 2.39

Information_Technology folder window

Recycle Bin on desktop

Only two folders and one file remain in the folder

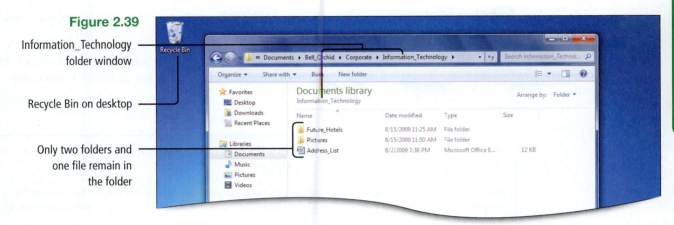

6 Snap the **Information_Technology** window to the right side of your screen. On the **Desktop**, double-click the **Recycle Bin** icon to open its folder window. Set the **View** to **Details**, and then snap the **Recycle Bin** folder to the left side of the screen. Notice that the items in the Recycle Bin are in alphabetic order.

7 In the upper right corner of the **Recycle Bin** window, click in the **Search** box, and then type **virus** Compare your screen with Figure 2.40.

> You can scroll the list to try to find the deleted file you are looking for instead of using the Search box. Commonly, however, you might not remember the exact name of the file. In this instance, Barbara and Steven remembered that the deleted file contained something about *virus* policy, and thus using the Search box was a quick way to find the file.

Figure 2.40 Recycle Bin window snapped to left side of screen

Information_Technology window snapped to right side of screen

Deleted file displays in file list of Recycle Bin window

Search box indicates *virus*

Another Way

Right-click over an item, and then click Restore.

8 In the **Recycle Bin** window, click the **Computer_Virus_Policy** file to select it, and then on the toolbar, click **Restore this item**. In the **Information_Technology** folder window, notice that the file is restored.

9 On the left, in the **Search** box of the **Recycle Bin** window, click ⊠ to cancel the search.

10 In the **Recycle Bin file list**, scroll down to locate and then select the **Europe_Charts** file and the **Europe_Financials** file. With the two files selected, on the toolbar, if necessary click >> to display additional commands, and then click **Restore the selected items**.

11 **Close** ⊠ the **Recycle Bin** window. In the **Information_Technology** folder window, notice the restored files.

12 Using one of the techniques you just practiced, delete the **Address_List** file—click **Yes** to move it to the Recycle Bin. Then, right-click in the **file list** and click **Undo Delete**.

> You can undo a delete in this manner.

More Knowledge | Using the Recycle Bin Icon, Permanently Deleting an Item, and Restoring by Dragging

You can delete items by dragging them from the file list directly into the Recycle Bin icon on the Desktop. If you drag items into the Recycle Bin, you will see the ScreenTip →*Move to Recycle Bin*, but no confirmation message will display.

To permanently delete a file without first moving it to the Recycle Bin, click the item, hold down Shift, and then press Del.

You can restore items by dragging them from the file list of the Recycle Bin window to the file list of the folder window in which you want to restore.

---

13 In the **navigation pane**, under **Computer**, click your USB flash drive. Right-click the folder **BHewitt_Files**, click **Delete**, and then compare your screen with Figure 2.41.

> A message indicates *Are you sure you want to permanently delete this folder?* and a red X displays on the folder icon.

> The Recycle Bin only saves items deleted from your computer's hard disk drive. Anything that you delete from a removable storage device, for example a USB flash drive, a floppy disk, a memory card, an MP3 player, or a digital camera, will be permanently deleted.

Figure 2.41

Message indicates that the folder will be *permanently* deleted

Red X on folder icon

14 Click **Yes** to delete this folder from your USB flash drive. Delete the **Pictures** folder from your USB flash drive.

15 In the **navigation pane** under **Libraries**, click **Documents**. **Delete** the **Bell_Orchid** folder from your **Documents** folder.

> For some of the projects in this textbook, like this one, you will copy files to the Documents folder of the computer at which you are working. At the end of the project, you can remove the files in this manner so that your own computer is not cluttered with extra files. In a college lab, it is possible that logging off automatically deletes files from the Documents folder.

16 On the taskbar, drag the **Windows Explorer** button 📁 slightly up into the desktop, and then on the **Jump List**, notice that the **Bell_Orchid** folder is still pinned there. Click **Bell_Orchid**, and then compare your screen with Figure 2.42.

> Because the folder is now deleted from your hard disk drive, the Problem with Shortcut dialog box displays. Here you can restore the item to your Documents library or delete the shortcut from the Pinned area of the Jump List.

Figure 2.42

Problem with Shortcut dialog box

Another Way

On the Jump List, point to the pinned item, and then click the pin button on the right; or, right-click, and click Unpin from this list.

17 Click **Delete it**, and then **Close** all open windows. If you want to do so on your own computer and are permitted to do so on a college lab computer, empty the Recycle Bin as follows: Point to the **Recycle Bin** icon, right-click, click **Empty Recycle Bin**, and then click **Yes**.

18 Submit your three snip files from this project as directed by your instructor.

End **You have completed Project 2A** ─────────────

Project 2B Searching Your Computer

Project Activities

In Activities 2.14 through 2.18, you will practice with Steven Ramos and Barbara Hewitt, employees in the Information Technology Department at the corporate office of the Bell Orchid Hotels, searching the hotel's files to find data quickly and efficiently. You will capture screens that look similar to Figure 2.43.

Project Files

For Project 2B, you will need the following files:

> New Snip files

You will save your files as:

> Lastname_Firstname_2B_Orlando_Snip
> Lastname_Firstname_2B_Europe_Menus_Snip
> Lastname_Firstname_2B_Tag_Snip

Project Results

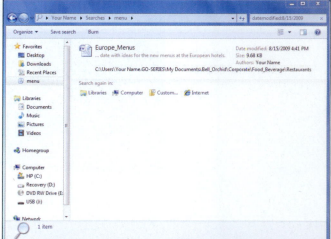
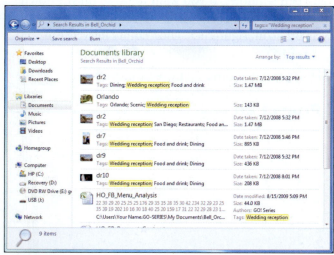

Figure 2.43
Project 2B Searching Your Computer

Objective 7 | Search From the Start Menu

Even if you have arranged your folders and files in a logical way, it is still sometimes challenging and time consuming to locate a specific file when you need it. The hierarchical nature of any filing system means that you often have to navigate downward through multiple levels of your folder structure to find what you are looking for. This navigation task is commonly referred to as *drilling down*.

In Windows 7, you can search your PC in the same easy way that you search on the Internet. Instead of navigating within a folder window, rely on the capability of Windows 7 to conduct a search of your data. Searching for a file—rather than navigating a file structure—is the quick and modern way to locate files.

By using the Windows 7 search capabilities, you will eliminate the tedium of drilling down into your folders. Windows 7 can search for programs and files by using a name, a property, or even text contained within a file.

Activity 2.14 | Searching From the Start Menu

By typing in the search box located at the bottom of the Start menu, you can find installed programs, Web sites in your History or Favorites area, messages in your e-mail, contacts in your Contacts folder, as well as files and folders on your system.

In this activity, you will work with Barbara and Steven to search for information from the search box on the Start menu.

> **Alert! | For Convenience, Plan Your Time to Complete Project 2B in One Working Session**
>
> Because you will need to store and then delete files on the hard disk drive of the computer at which you are working, it is recommended that you complete this project in one working session—*unless you are working on your own computer or you know that the files will be retained.* In your college lab, it is possible that files you store will not be retained after you log off. Allow approximately 30 to 45 minutes to complete Project 2B.

1 If necessary, delete the **Bell_Orchid** folder from your **Documents** folder—for this project you will need a new copy of the files. Insert the Student Resource CD or other device that contains the student files that accompany this textbook. Using the **Send to** command that you practiced in Activity 2.1 of this chapter, copy the **Bell_Orchid** folder from the Student Resource CD to your **Documents** folder.

2 **Close** 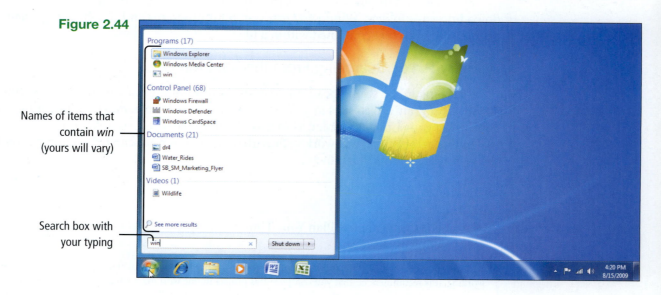 any open windows, and then display the **Start menu** . At the bottom of the Start menu, with your insertion point blinking in the search box, type **win** Compare your screen with Figure 2.44.

> You need not *click* in the search box; as soon as you display the Start menu and begin to type, your typing displays there.

> Your screen will not match the figure exactly, but you can see that Windows 7 instantly begins searching your computer for various categories of items that begin with *win*. Categories that might display include *Programs, Control Panel, Documents, Videos, Files,* and *Communications* (for e-mail messages, contacts, and items from Outlook such as events and tasks).

Figure 2.44

Names of items that contain *win* (yours will vary)

Search box with your typing

Another Way

Press Esc to clear the search box.

3 At the right end of the search box, click ☒ to clear the search box and cancel the list. With the insertion point blinking in the search box, type **word** In the results listed above the search box, under **Programs**, click **Microsoft Word**. When the program displays, **Close** 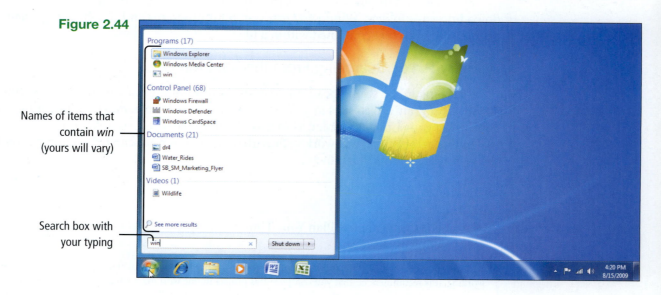 the Word window.

> You can start a program directly from the search results list. If you have numerous programs on your computer, this is a fast way to find and start a program instead of navigating the All Programs menu.

4 Display the **Start** menu , and then type **b** Notice the results listed, and then type **e**

> After typing *e*, your list of results changes to reflect items that begin with *be*. The search box is a *word wheel*, which is a lookup method in which each new character that you type into the search box further refines the search.

5 Type **ll orchid**

> Any item containing *bell orchid* is found. Because the list of results is too long for the display area, *See more results* displays just above the search box. In the displayed list under *Documents,* both file names and folder names are listed.

> Search is not case sensitive; you can type all lowercase letters as a search term.

6 Click **See more results**, and then compare your screen with Figure 2.45.

A folder window displays the results of the search in the indexed locations, and applies yellow highlight to the search term in each folder or file found.

Windows 7 produces search results almost instantly because it employs an *index*, which is a collection of detailed information about the files on your computer. As you work, Windows 7 constantly keeps track of information about your files—for example, words in titles and in the file itself, dates, file types, and so on—and stores that information in the index. When you search for something, Windows searches this summary information in the index instead of searching your entire hard disk drive each time you start a search.

It is this index feature that provides almost instant search results. The Windows 7 libraries—Documents, Pictures, Music, and so on—are always indexed on your system. This is why you should always begin with a library when you plan to save a file.

Figure 2.45

Bell_Orchid in path name highlighted

Search results in the Documents library, an indexed location

Bell Orchid in the document text highlighted

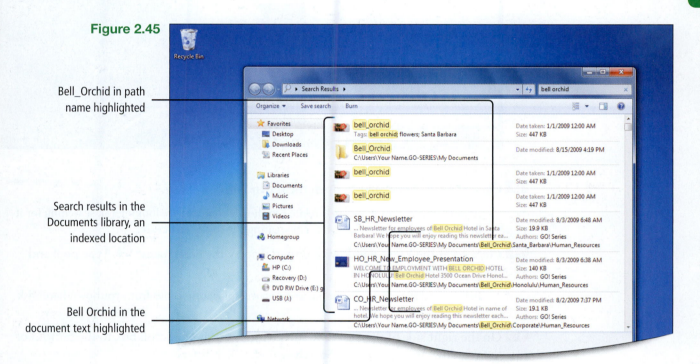

7 **Close** ⊠ the window, and then display the **Start** menu 🟦 . Type **newsletter** and then in the list of results, point to the file **SD_HR_Newsletter**. Compare your screen with Figure 2.46.

The ScreenTip displays information about the file.

Figure 2.46

Files containing the word *newsletter* (your list may vary) ———

ScreenTip for file SD_HR_Newsletter ———

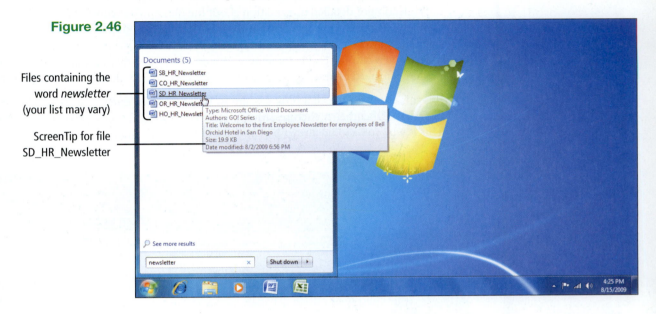

8 Click **SD_HR_Newsletter** to open the file in Word.

If you know one or two words related to the file that you are looking for, searching for it in this manner will be faster than navigating the folder structure.

9 **Close** ⊠ the Word window, and then display the **Start menu** 🟦 . Type **pool** and then click **See more results**.

Bell Orchid files that contain the word *pool* display; other files from your own hard disk drive might also display.

10 On the right side of the **Search Results** window, drag the scroll box to the bottom of the window, and then under **Search again in**, click **Internet**.

The default search engine displays information about pools. In this manner, you can begin an Internet search without first opening your Internet browser. In Windows 7, the default search engine is *Bing*, unless you have changed the default. Bing is Microsoft's search engine.

11 **Close** ⊠ all open windows.

More Knowledge | What Files Are In the Windows 7 Index?

You cannot view the index, but it is used by Windows 7 to perform very fast searches on the most common files on your computer.

Indexed locations include all of the files in your libraries—Documents, Pictures, Music, and so on—e-mail, and *offline files*. Offline files are files from a network that have been copied to your hard disk drive for easy access when you are not connected to the network.

By default, program and system files are not indexed. You rarely need to search for those files, so not including them in the index makes your searches run faster.

Files stored directly on the C drive are not indexed, nor are files on a removable storage device such as a flash drive or CD. You can still search for files and folders stored in these locations. However, the search might not be quite as fast because the search is conducted on the device itself, not on the index.

Objective 8 | Search From a Folder Window

A search box displays in all windows. If you know approximately where a file or folder is, search from the folder window instead of the Start menu. Starting a search from a folder window searches only the files and subfolders in that folder, so your list of results will *not* include items that you know you are *not* looking for, such as an e-mail message or a Web site or a program.

Activity 2.15 | Searching From a Folder Window and Applying a Filter to Search Results

The results of a search in a folder window can be arranged by using any of the sorting, grouping, and filtering techniques that you have practiced. Similarly, you can also change the view of the search results.

1 On the taskbar, click the **Windows Explorer** button 📁, and then in the **file list**, double-click **Documents** to display your Documents library window. In the **file list**, right-click the **Bell_Orchid** folder, and then on the shortcut menu, click **Properties**.

2 In the **Bell_Orchid Properties** dialog box, click the **General tab**. In the center of the tab, to the right of *Contains*, notice the number of files and folders contained in the Bell_Orchid folder.

> A search that you conduct in this folder window will be limited to searching the files and folders in this folder. Recall that the search is conducted on the index, not by searching file by file on the hard disk drive.

3 Close ❌ the **Bell_Orchid Properties** dialog box. In the **file list**, double-click the **Bell_Orchid** folder to display its folder window. In the upper right corner of the folder window, click in the **search** box, type **em** and then at the bottom of the window, in the **Details pane**, notice the number of items that are indicated.

4 Continue typing **ployee** Compare your screen with Figure 2.47.

> Recall that the word wheel technology filters the results of your search with each letter you type, eliminating any results that do not exactly match what you are typing. Within your documents folder, 37 items contain *employee* in the title, in the text, or in a property associated with the file. (Your number could vary if there are undeleted files from previous projects.)

Figure 2.47

Address bar indicates *Search Results* in *Bell_Orchid*

Small box displays and then fades

Details pane, items in *Bell_Orchid* that match search (yours could vary)

5 Click in the **search** box to display suggested filters. Under **Add a search filter**, click **Type:**, and notice that you can filter on either the file extensions for Excel, PowerPoint, and Word, or on the program name itself.

> Based on the search results, Windows 7 will suggest some search filters (in blue text), or you can create your own filter.
>
> Only the file types that are present in the search results will display. In this instance, the results include only Excel, PowerPoint, and Word files.

6 Click **Microsoft PowerPoint Presentation**, and then in the **Details pane** at the bottom of the window, notice that 11 items (your number could vary) are PowerPoint presentations that contain the word *employee* as a property.

7 On the toolbar, click the **View button arrow** ⊞ ▾ , notice that the search results are arranged by **Content**, and then click **Extra Large Icons**.

> By default, search results display in the Content view, because this view contains the most information about the file. You can change the view, however, to whatever is convenient for you. For example, here, seeing the first slide of all the presentations, might assist you in finding the exact file that you want.

8 Point in the white area between the two columns of icons, right-click to display a shortcut menu, point to **Sort by**, and then click **Name**. Display this menu again, point to **Sort by**, and then at the bottom, if necessary, click **Ascending** to sort the list alphabetically. Compare your screen with Figure 2.48.

> The 11 items are alphabetized by name. You can arrange the results of a search by using any of the sorting, grouping, and filtering techniques that you have practiced.

Figure 2.48

View changed to Extra Large Icons

9 On the toolbar, click the **View button arrow** ⊟ ▾, and then return the view to **Content**. At the right end of the search box, click ☒ to clear the search. Notice that recent filters you applied remain available for reuse.

10 With the **Bell_Orchid** folder window redisplayed, in the **search** box, type **seminar**

The Details pane indicates that 6 items in the Bell_Orchid folder have the word *seminar* in the text or as one of the properties associated with the item. (Your number could vary.)

Text that you type in the search box to conduct a search specifies the conditions that identify the specific files you are looking for. Such text is commonly referred to as **criteria**. In this search, the criteria is *seminar*; that is, only files that contain the word *seminar* meet the condition.

11 With the insertion point blinking in the **search** box, press Spacebar, and then type **sales**

The number of items that meet the search criteria is reduced to 5 and the word *sales* is highlighted in yellow in the list of files that meet the criteria. (Your number could vary.)

12 Clear ☒ the **search** box, and then type **honolulu**

Both files and folders contain the search term *Honolulu*—34 items in all. (Your number could vary.)

13 Clear ☒ the **search** box, and then type **pool** In the **Details pane**, notice the number of items that meet the search term. Then, with the insertion point blinking in the **search** box, press Spacebar. Using all uppercase letters by holding down Shift, type **AND** release Shift, press the Spacebar, and then type **orlando** Compare your screen with Figure 2.49.

When you include the word *AND* in this manner—in all uppercase letters—Windows 7 searches for files or folders that contain *pool* and *Orlando*. Only items containing both words display in the search results. As you progress in your study of Windows 7, you will practice using more search techniques of this type.

Figure 2.49

Search term includes
pool AND orlando

Details pane

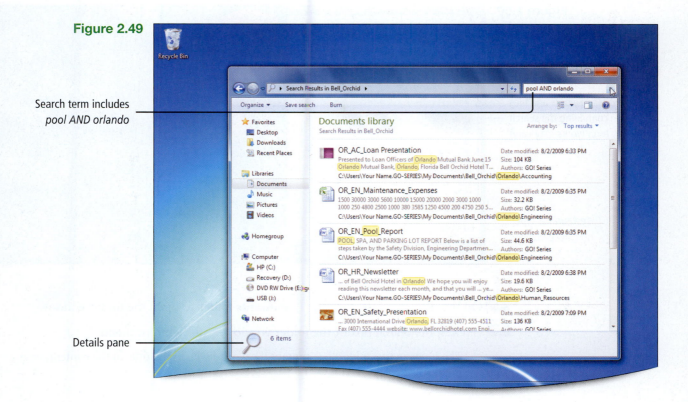

14 Create a **Window Snip**, click in the folder window to capture the window, and then on your USB flash drive, save the snip file in **JPEG** format in your **Windows 7 Chapter 2** folder as **Lastname_Firstname_2B_Orlando_Snip**

15 **Close** 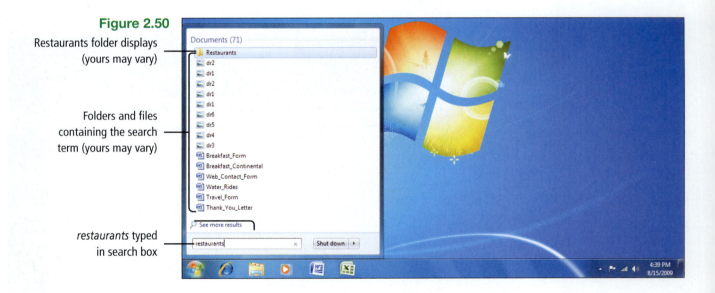 all open windows.

Objective 9 | Save, Reuse, and Delete a Search

If you find yourself searching for the same information repeatedly, you can save time by saving your search. After a search is saved, Windows 7 keeps the search current by automatically adding any newly created items that match the search criteria.

Activity 2.16 | Saving, Reusing, and Deleting a Search

At the Corporate office, the Food and Beverage Director tracks the menus for all of the hotel restaurants. In this activity, you will conduct a search that this Director uses frequently, and then save it for future use.

1 Display the **Start** menu. In the upper right corner, click your user name to open your personal folder. Notice that one of the folders that Windows 7 creates for each user is a **Searches** folder.

> Any searches that you save will be saved in your Searches folder.

2 **Close** the window for your personal folder.

3 Redisplay the **Start** menu, in the **search** box, type **restaurants** and then compare your screen with Figure 2.50.

> If you know the name, or even part of the name, of a folder on your system, this is a quick way to find a folder.

Figure 2.50

Restaurants folder displays (yours may vary)

Folders and files containing the search term (yours may vary)

restaurants typed in search box

4 On the displayed list, click the **Restaurants** folder to open the folder window.

5 Click in the **search** box of the folder window, and then type **menu**

> The items in this folder that contain the word *menu* in the title, in the content, or as a property, display.

6 On the toolbar, click the **Save search** button, and then compare your screen with Figure 2.51.

The Save As dialog box displays, in which you can save your search. The default save location is in the Searches folder and the default file name is the search term *menu*.

Figure 2.51

Save As dialog box ——

Path to the Searches folder in your personal folder ——

File name defaults to search term ——

Type indicates *Saved Search* ——

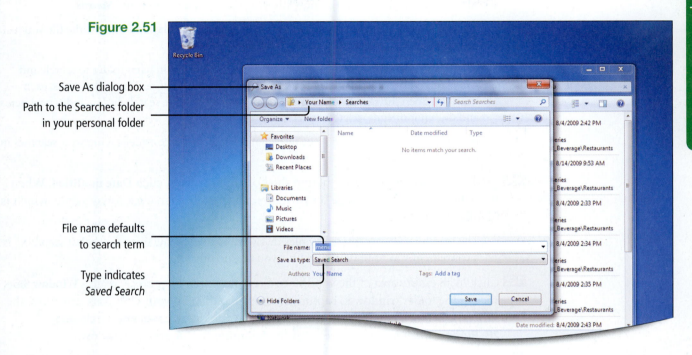

7 Click the **Save** button to save the *menu* search for future use.

8 Close [✕] the **menu** search window. Start **Word**, and then in the new blank document type **The research staff will complete this document at a later date with ideas for the new menus at the European hotels.** Press [F12] to display the **Save As** dialog box. Navigate to **Bell_Orchid ▶ Corporate ▶ Food_Beverage ▶ Restaurants**. Compare your screen with Figure 2.52.

Figure 2.52

Save As dialog box ——

Restaurants folder window ——

File name defaults to first characters in document ——

New Word document ——

9 Click one time in the **File name** box to select the default text, and then type **Europe_Menus** Click **Save**, and then **Close** [x] the Word window.

10 Display your **Documents** folder window. On the left, in the **navigation pane**, under **Favorites**, locate and then click your saved search **menu**. In the displayed results, scroll if necessary to locate the new file you just created—**Europe_Menus**.

> Windows 7 executes the search; the new search results display and include the file you just created.
>
> When you save a search, you are saving its specifications—in what folder to search and what search criteria to match—you are *not* saving the actual search results. Thus, each time you open the search folder, Windows 7 re-executes the search and includes new items and does not include deleted items.
>
> If you search for the same type of information frequently, consider saving your searches in this manner.

11 Click in the **search** box, and then in the box that displays, click **Date modified**. When the **Select a date or date range** box displays, on the calendar, click today's date, which is highlighted in blue.

> The search results are filtered by files that were created today. You can see that searching is a convenient way to find the exact file you are looking for.

12 Click in an empty area of the window to close the search filter box. Create a **Window Snip**, click in the folder window to capture the snip, and then on your USB flash drive, save the snip in JPEG format in your **Windows 7 Chapter 2** folder as **Lastname_Firstname_ 2B_Europe_Menus_Snip** **Close** [x] the **Snipping Tool** mark-up window.

13 In the **navigation pane**, under **Favorites**, point to **menu**, right-click, and then click **Remove**.

> The saved search is removed from the navigation pane, but the search is still saved in your Searches folder, and will display in the search filter box for this window.

14 **Close** [x] all open windows.

Objective 10 | Search From the Control Panel Window and the Computer Window

Most of your searching will involve searching your data—the files and folders that you create in the day-to-day use of your computer.

You can also search from the Control Panel window and the Computer window. Recall that from the Control Panel, you can change settings for Windows 7. These settings control nearly everything about how Windows 7 looks and works, so it is useful to be able to search for a command instead of trying to decide under which area of the Control Panel it might be found.

Activity 2.17 | Searching From the Control Panel and Computer Windows

1 From the **Start** menu , display the **Control Panel**. Notice that the insertion point is blinking in the **search** box, and thus you can begin to type immediately. Type **mouse** and notice that mouse commands display. Press Spacebar, type **pointer** and notice that different commands display. Press Spacebar, type **speed** and then compare your screen with Figure 2.53.

> The Control Panel displays the commands related to the speed of the mouse pointer. Recall that the word wheel technology narrows down your search with each character and word that you type.

Figure 2.53

Search box in Control Panel window

Command related to mouse pointer speed

2 Under **Mouse**, click **Change the mouse pointer display or speed**.

> In the Mouse Properties dialog box, you can change the speed of your mouse.

3 **Close** the **Mouse Properties** dialog box. In the **search** box, click × to clear the search, and then search for **printer**

> Various commands related to printers display.

4 **Close** the **Control Panel** window. Be sure your USB flash drive with your chapter folder is inserted. On the taskbar, click the **Windows Explorer** button , and then in the **navigation pane**, under **Computer**, click your USB flash drive.

5 Click in the **search** box and type **compressed** and wait for the search to complete; notice that a green progress bar displays in the **address bar**.

> When the search is complete, the file you created in Project A, *Lastname_Firstname_2A_Compressed_Snip* displays in the search results. Other files on your flash drive might also display.

> A search conducted from the Computer window searches the devices that you select. Recall that only the libraries associated with your personal folder are indexed, and no removable devices are indexed. Thus, searching outside of the personal folders may take a little longer.

6 **Close** the Search Results window.

Objective 11 | Add Tags to Improve a Search

When you type in the search box, Windows 7 *filters* the items in the folder that you are searching. By filtering, the search displays only those files and folders that meet the criteria specified in the search box. If the search criteria matches text in the item's name, in the item's content, or in one of the item's properties, then the item will display in the search results.

Recall that *properties* are descriptive pieces of information about a folder or file such as the title, the date modified, the size, the author, or the type of file. These are the most common properties and the ones you see in the Details pane when a folder or file is selected. You can search for specific properties in the search box. Recall that the *group* of properties associated with a file or folder is referred to as **metadata**—the data that describes other data; for example, the collective group of a file's properties, such as its title, subject, author, and file size.

Activity 2.18 | Adding and Searching for a Tag

By default, Microsoft Office documents contain standard properties such as Author and Title for which you can specify your own text. Other programs have similar file properties. You can also create a **tag**, which is a property that *you* create and add to a file to help you find and organize your files. In this activity, you will assist Barbara and Steven in adding the tag *Wedding reception* to some of the corporate files so that hotel managers can locate information that will help them promote wedding receptions in the hotels.

1 On the taskbar, click the **Windows Explorer** button 📁, display your **Documents** library, and then navigate to **Bell_Orchid ▶ Honolulu ▶ Food_Beverage**. Compare your screen with Figure 2.54.

Figure 2.54

Food_Beverage folder window for Honolulu location

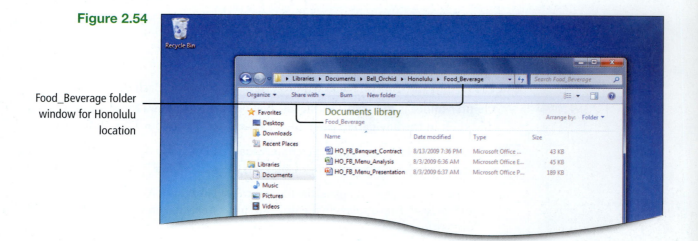

2 Point to one of the column headings, for example *Name* or *Size*, and right-click. Notice that there are numerous properties listed that you can display in the folder window if you want to do so. On the shortcut menu, click **Tags**.

3 Point to the Excel file **HO_FB_Menu_Analysis**, right-click, and then on the shortcut menu, click **Properties**. In the displayed dialog box, click the **Details tab**, under **Description**, click **Tags**, and then type **W** Compare your screen with Figure 2.55.

A list of existing tags that begin with *W* in the Bell_Orchid folder displays. Some files in this folder already have the tag *Wedding reception* and thus, it displays on the list of tags. This tag is helpful to hotel managers when they want to find files that contain information about promoting the sale of wedding receptions.

After a tag is created, it is easily added to other files without having to type the entire tag. The other tags on the list were created for other files within the Bell_Orchid folder structure.

For some file types, for example picture and music files, you can add a tag directly in the Details pane of the folder window.

Figure 2.55

Tags column added to file list window

Properties dialog box for HO_FB_Menu_Analysis

Details tab

Existing tags that begin with W (your list may vary)

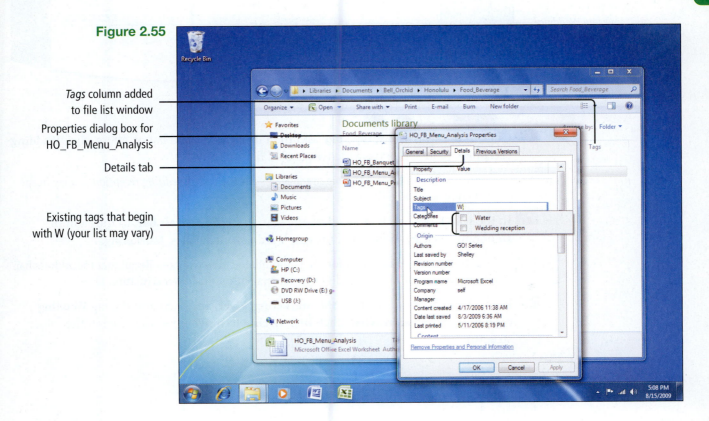

4 In the displayed list, scroll down if necessary, click the **Wedding reception** checkbox, and then at the bottom of the dialog box, click **OK**. In the **Tags column**, notice that *Wedding reception* displays.

5 In the **file list**, right-click the Word file **HO_FB_Banquet_Contract**. Display the **Properties** dialog box, click the **Details tab**, and then click **Tags**. Type **W** and then add the *Wedding reception* tag. Click **OK**, and then compare your screen with Figure 2.56.

In the Tags column, two files indicate Wedding reception.

Figure 2.56

Tags column ———

Two files in this folder indicate *Wedding reception* as a tag ———

6 Click in the **search** box, type **tag:** and then in the displayed list of filters, click **Wedding reception**. Notice that only the two tagged files display.

Only the files in this folder that are tagged with the term *Wedding reception* display in the search results.

7 In the **search** box, click ⌧ to clear the search. In the **address bar**, to the right of **Honolulu**, click ▶, and then in the displayed list, click **Sales_Marketing**.

The Sales_Marketing folder for the Honolulu location displays. Recall that the address bar is convenient for moving to different folders within the folder structure.

8 Right-click the Word file **HO_SM_Marketing_Flyer**, and then add the tag **Wedding reception**. In the **address bar**, click **Bell_Orchid** to move up to this level in the folder structure.

Another Way

Click tags:= "Wedding reception" if it displays.

9 In the **search box**, type **tag:** In the displayed list of search filters, scroll to the bottom of the list, and then locate and click **Wedding reception**. Compare your screen with Figure 2.57.

> The three files in the Bell_Orchid folder structure that you tagged with *Wedding reception* display, in addition to some photos that already contained the tag *Wedding reception*.

Figure 2.57

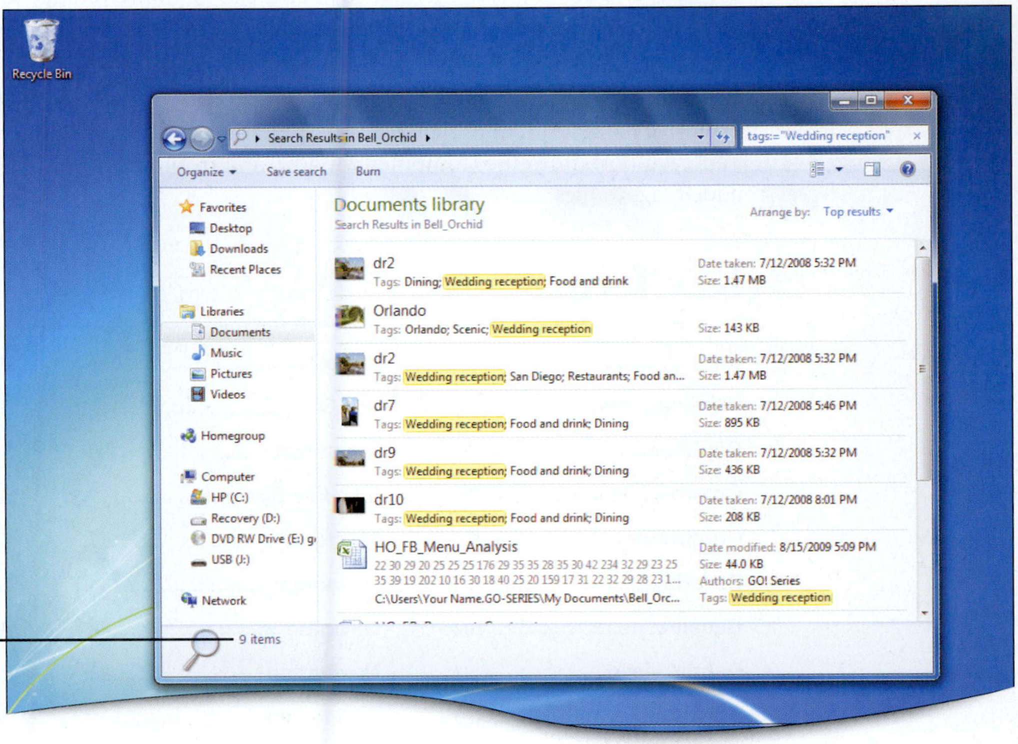

9 files have the tag *Wedding Reception*

10 Create a **Window Snip**, click anywhere in the window to capture, and then on your USB flash drive, save the snip in JPEG format in your **Windows 7 Chapter 2** folder as **Lastname_Firstname_2B_Tag_Snip Close** [×] the **Snipping Tool** markup window.

11 In the **file list**, select the first file, and then in the **Details pane**, click the **Tags** box. Point to the text *Wedding reception* and click to select the text. Press Bksp to delete this tag, and then click the **Save** button.

> You can add and delete tags as you need them.

12 In the **search** box, click [×] to clear the search and redisplay the **file list** for the **Bell_Orchid** folder.

13 Point to the **Tags** column heading, right-click, and then click to deselect **Tags** and remove the column from display. **Close** [×] all open windows.

14 Display your **Documents** folder window, and then delete the **Bell_Orchid** folder from your **Documents** folder. Submit your three snip files from this project as directed by your instructor.

> For some of the projects in this textbook, like this one, you will copy files to the Documents folder of the computer at which you are working. At the end of the project, delete the files in this manner.

End You have completed Project 2B ————————————————————

Summary

In this chapter, you used the Windows Explorer program and folder windows to increase your navigation skills to find your files and folders. Organizing your files and folders in a logical manner that suits your needs will help you to find your data quickly. In this chapter, you practiced naming, renaming, copying, and moving files and folders to create an organized folder structure. Another way to maintain good organization of your data is to delete the files and folders you no longer need. In this chapter, you deleted files and folders, and also restored deleted items from the Recycle Bin.

All of the search features in Windows 7 help you to find files quickly without having to perform extensive navigation. In this chapter, you practiced searching from the Start menu, from the Control Panel window, from the Computer window, and from folder windows. You also saved a search and added tags to files.

Key Terms

Content-Based Assessments

Matching

Match each term in the second column with its correct definition in the first column. Write the letter of the term on the blank line in front of the correct definition.

A Clipboard

B Common dialog boxes

C Deselect

D Details view

E Folder window

F Jump List

G Navigate

H Navigation

I Personal folder

J Progress bar

K Properties

L Select

M SharePoint

N Shift Click

O Windows Explorer

_____ 1. The program within Windows 7 that displays the contents of libraries, folders, and files on your computer, and which also enables you to perform tasks related to your files and folders such as copying, moving, and renaming.

_____ 2. A Microsoft technology that enables employees in an organization to access information across organizational and geographic boundaries.

_____ 3. In a dialog box or taskbar button, a bar that indicates visually the progress of a task such as a download or file transfer.

_____ 4. A folder created for each user account, labeled with the account holder's name, and which contains the subfolders Documents, Pictures, and Music, among others; always located at the top of the Start menu.

_____ 5. A window that displays the contents of the current folder, library, or device, and contains helpful parts so that you can navigate—explore within the organizing structure of Windows.

_____ 6. To explore within the folder structure of Windows 7 for the purpose of finding files and folders.

_____ 7. The actions you perform to display a window to locate a command or display the folder window for a folder whose contents you want to view.

_____ 8. A list that displays when you right-click a button on the taskbar, and which displays locations (in the upper portion) and tasks (in the lower portion) from a program's taskbar button; functions as a mini start menu for a program.

_____ 9. The dialog boxes, such as Save and Save As, provided by the Windows programming interface that enable programs to have a consistent appearance and behavior.

_____ 10. A file list view that displays a list of files or folders and their most common properties.

_____ 11. Descriptive pieces of information about a folder or file such as the name, the date modified, the author, the type, and the size.

_____ 12. To specify, by highlighting, a block of data or text on the screen with the intent of performing some action on the selection.

_____ 13. A technique in which the SHIFT key is held down to select all the items in a consecutive group; you need only click the first item, hold down SHIFT, and then click the last item in the group.

_____ 14. The term that refers to canceling the selection of one or more selected items.

_____ 15. A temporary storage area for information that you have copied or moved from one place and plan to use somewhere else.

Multiple Choice

Circle the correct answer.

1. The action that reduces the size of a file, and which is especially useful for pictures, is:
   - **A.** compress
   - **B.** compact
   - **C.** copy

2. A common file type used by digital cameras and computers to store digital pictures is a :
   - **A.** TIFF
   - **B.** JPEG
   - C   snip

3. A graphic image file type used when a very high level of visual quality is needed is a:
   - **A.** TIFF
   - **B.** JPEG
   - **C.** snip

4. The action of decompressing (pulling out) files from a compressed form is:
   - **A.** copying
   - **B.** deselecting
   - **C.** extracting

5. A CD or DVD disc onto which files can be copied is referred to as being:
   - **A.** writable
   - **B.** readable
   - **C.** selected

6. The process of writing files on a CD or DVD is:
   - **A.** drilling
   - **B.** burning
   - **C.** writing

7. A file storage system for creating CDs and DVDs that allows you to copy files to the disc at any time, instead of copying them all at once, is:
   - **A.** Live File System
   - **B.** Mastered
   - **C.** Compressed

8. A file system for creating CDs and DVDs that is useful if the files will be read on an older computer is:
   - **A.** Live File System
   - **B.** Mastered
   - **C.** Compressed

9. The process of navigating downward through multiple levels of your folder structure to find what you are looking for is called:
   - **A.** deselecting
   - **B.** selecting
   - **C.** drilling down

10. A lookup method in which each new character that you type into the search box further refines the search is the:
    - **A.** tag
    - **B.** word wheel
    - **C.** progress bar

Content-Based Assessments

Apply 2A skills from these Objectives:

1. Copy Files From a Removable Storage Device to the Hard Disk Drive
2. Navigate by Using Windows Explorer
3. Create, Name, and Save Files
4. Create Folders and Rename Folders and Files
5. Select, Copy, and Move Files and Folders
6. Delete Files and Folders and Use the Recycle Bin

Skills Review | Project 2C Managing Files and Folders

Project Files

For Project 2C, you will need the following files:

Student Resource CD or a flash drive containing the student data files
win02_2C_Answer_Sheet (Word document)

You will save your file as:

Lastname_Firstname_2C_Answer_Sheet

1 **Close** ❎ all open windows. On the taskbar, click the **Windows Explorer** button. In the **navigation pane**, click the drive that contains the student files for this textbook, and then navigate to **Chapter_Files** ▶ **Chapter_02**. Double-click the Word file **win02_2C_Answer_Sheet** to open Word and display the document. Press F12 to display the **Save As** dialog box in Word, navigate to your **Windows 7 Chapter 2** folder, and then using your own name, save the document as **Lastname_Firstname_2C_Answer_Sheet** If necessary, click OK regarding new formats.

On the taskbar, click the **Word** button to minimize the window and leave your Word document accessible from the taskbar. **Close** the **Chapter_02** folder window. As you complete each step in this project, click the Word button on the taskbar to open the document, type your one-letter answer in the appropriate cell of the Word table, and then on the taskbar, click the button again to minimize the window for the next step.

If necessary, insert the Student Resource CD in the appropriate drive, and then by using the **Send to** command, copy the **Bell_Orchid** folder to your **Documents** library—you will need a new copy of the files for this project. On your USB flash drive, create a folder named **Europe** By which of the following methods can you create a new folder:

A. In the file list, right-click, point to New, and then click Folder.

B. On the toolbar, click the New folder button.

C. Either A. or B.

2 Display the **Documents** file list, and then navigate to **Bell_Orchid** ▶ **Corporate** ▶ **Food_Beverage** ▶ **Restaurants**. The *quickest* way to select the **Breakfast_Continental**, **Breakfast_Form**, **Breakfast_Menus**, and **Brunch_Menus** files is:

A. Hold down Ctrl and click each file.

B. Hold down Ctrl and press A.

C. Draw a selection area around the four contiguous files.

3 **Maximize** 🔲 the **Restaurants** window. Select the files **Breakfast_Continental**, **Breakfast_Form**, **Breakfast_Menus**, and **Brunch_Menus**, and then copy these files to your USB flash drive. Which of the following are methods you could use to perform this copy:

A. Create a compressed folder.

B. Use the Send to command.

C. Drag the selected files to the Desktop.

(Project 2C Managing Files and Folders continues on the next page)

Skills Review | Project 2C Managing Files and Folders (continued)

4 Be sure the **Restaurants** window displays. In the **file list**, the quickest way to select the noncontiguous files **Grill_Menu** and **Refreshments** is to:

A. Hold down [Ctrl] and then click each file name.

B. Hold down [Tab] and then click each file name.

C. Hold down [Shift] and then click each file name.

5 Select **Grill_Menu** and **Refreshments** and send them to your USB flash drive. Then display your USB flash drive window. Rename the folder **Europe** to **Menus** Rename the file **Refreshments** to **Pool_Menu** Which of the following is true:

A. Your USB flash drive now contains a folder named Europe and a folder named Menus.

B. You can use the same technique to rename a file and to rename a folder.

C. You must have permission to rename a folder or a file.

6 In your USB flash drive folder window, in the **file list**, select the files **Breakfast_Continental**, **Breakfast_Form**, **Breakfast_Menus**, **Brunch_Menus**, **Grill_Menu** and **Pool_Menu** and then drag them into the **Menus** folder. The result of this action is:

A. The files were copied to the Menus folder.

B. The files were moved to the Menus folder.

C. The files were deleted.

7 Open the **Menus** folder on your USB flash drive. Right-click the **Pool_Menu** file, and then from the displayed menu, click **Copy**. Right-click in an empty area of the **file list**, and then click **Paste**. Your result is:

A. A file named *Pool_Menu – Copy* displays in the file list.

B. A file named *Second_Pool_Menu* displays in the file list.

C. An error message indicates *Duplicate File Name, Cannot Copy.*

8 In the **Menus** folder, create a compressed folder and name it **Breakfast** Drag the files **Breakfast_Continental**, **Breakfast_Form**, and **Breakfast_Menus** into the compressed folder. The result of this action is:

A. The three files no longer display in the file list.

B. The three files remain displayed in the file list.

C. The three files display but are renamed as *Compressed_Breakfast_Continental, Compressed_Breakfast_Form*, and *Compressed_Breakfast_Menus.*

9 In the **navigation pane**, click to select your USB flash drive. Delete the **Menus** folder. In the **Delete Folder** dialog box, the following message displays:

A. Are you sure you want to permanently delete this folder?

B. Are you sure you want to copy this folder to the Recycle Bin?

C. Are you sure you want to move this folder to the Recycle Bin?

(Project 2C Managing Files and Folders continues on the next page)

Skills Review | Project **2C** Managing Files and Folders (continued)

10 In the **Delete Folder** dialog box, click **Yes**. In the navigation pane, click **Documents**, and then delete the **Bell_Orchid** folder. In the **Delete Folder** dialog box, the following message displays:

A. Are you sure you want to permanently delete this folder?

B. Are you sure you want to copy this folder to the Recycle Bin?

C. Are you sure you want to move this folder to the Recycle Bin?

Click **Yes**. In the upper right corner of the folder window, click the **Restore Down** button . Be sure you have typed all of your answers in your Word document. **Save** and **Close** your Word document, and submit as directed by your instructor. **Close** ❌ all open windows.

End **You have completed Project 2C** ——————————————————

Apply **2B** skills from these Objectives:

- 7 Search From the Start Menu
- 8 Search From a Folder Window
- 9 Save, Reuse, and Delete a Search
- 10 Search From the Control Panel Window and the Computer Window
- 11 Add Tags to Improve a Search

Skills Review | Project **2D** Searching Your Computer

Project Files

For Project 2D, you will need the following files:

Student Resource CD or a flash drive containing the student data files
win02_2D_Answer_Sheet (Word document)

You will save your file as:

Lastname_Firstname_2D_Answer_Sheet

1 **Close** [x] all open windows, and then open Windows Explorer. From the student files that accompany this textbook, locate and open the **Chapter_Files** folder. In the **Chapter_02** folder, locate and open the Word document **win02_2D_Answer_Sheet**. Display the **Save As** dialog box, and then using your own name, save the document in your **Windows 7 Chapter 2** folder that you created on your removable storage device—or another location of your choice—as **Lastname_Firstname_2D_Answer_Sheet** If necessary, click OK regarding new formats.

On the taskbar, click the **Word** button to minimize the window and leave your Word document accessible from the taskbar. As you complete each step in this project, click the Word button on the taskbar to open the document, type your one-letter answer in the appropriate cell of the Word table, and then on the taskbar, click the button again to minimize the window for the next step. **Close** the **Chapter_02** folder window.

Insert the Student Resource CD, and then by using the **Send to** command, copy the **Bell_Orchid** folder to your **Documents** folder. Display your **Documents** folder, and then display the **Bell_Orchid** folder window. In the **search** box, type **beverage** What is your result?

A. Only folders containing the word *beverage* display.

B. Only files containing the word *beverage* display.

C. Both files and folders containing the word *beverage* display.

2 In the Details pane, notice the number of files that display, and then with *beverage* displayed in the **search** box, type **s** to form the word *beverages*. What is your result?

A. Both B and C are correct.

B. The number of items displayed decreases.

C. Only files display—no folder names contain the word *beverages*.

3 **Clear** [x] the **search** box, and then search for **shareholders** What is your result?

A. Five Excel files display.

B. Three Word files display.

C. Five Word files display.

4 Open the **SD_AC_Report_Shareholders** file. In what year was the Bell Orchid Hotel in San Diego acquired?

A. 2005

B. 2006

C. 2007

(Project 2D Searching Your Computer continues on the next page)

Content-Based Assessments

Skills Review | Project **2D** Searching Your Computer (continued)

5 **Close** the Word document that you just opened. **Clear** ⊠ the **search** box, and then search for **guests** Be sure the View is set to Details, and then filter the **Type** column by **Microsoft PowerPoint Presentation**. How many presentations display in the file list?

A. 2

B. 10

C. 1

6 In the **Type** column, remove the **PowerPoint** filter, and then apply the **Word** filter. How many Word documents display?

A. 26

B. 15

C. 10

7 **Clear** ⊠ the **search** box, and then begin a new search using the criteria **clerk AND newsletter** How many files display that contain both *clerk* and *newsletter*?

A. 3

B. 5

C. 7

8 Begin a new search using the criteria **housekeeping** and then filter the results in the **Type** column by **Microsoft Excel**. How many files display?

A. 2

B. 5

C. 10

9 **Close** the search window. From the **Start** menu, open **Control Panel**. In the **search** box, type **autoplay** Which of the following topics are listed?

A. Remove the Autoplay feature

B. Change default settings for media or devices

C. Both A and B

10 **Close** the **Control Panel** window. Display the **Start** menu, and then type **tag:flower** Which of the following is included in the displayed list?

A. Blossoms

B. bell_orchid

C. Both A and B

Delete the **Bell_Orchid** folder in the **Documents** window. Be sure you have typed all of your answers in your Word document. **Save** and **Close** your Word document, and submit as directed by your instructor. **Close** all open windows.

End **You have completed Project 2D**

Apply **2A** skills from these Objectives:

1. Copy Files From a Removable Storage Device to the Hard Disk Drive
2. Navigate by Using Windows Explorer
3. Create, Name, and Save Files
4. Create Folders and Rename Folders and Files
5. Select, Copy, and Move Files and Folders
6. Delete Files and Folders and Use the Recycle Bin

Mastering Windows 7 | Project **2E** Managing Files and Folders

In the following Mastering Windows 7 project, you will move, copy, rename, and organize files and folders. You will capture and save a screen that will look similar to Figure 2.58.

Project Files

For Project 2E, you will need the following file:

> New Snip file

You will save your file as:

> Lastname_Firstname_2E_Rooms_Snip

Project Results

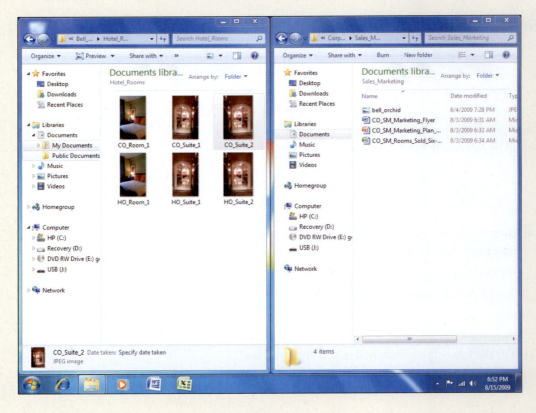

Figure 2.58

(Project 2E Managing Files and Folders continues on the next page)

Content-Based Assessments

Mastering Windows 7 | Project 2E Managing Files and Folders (continued)

1 Insert the Student Resource CD in the appropriate drive, and then by using the **Send to** command, copy the **Bell_Orchid** folder from the CD to your **Documents** library. Then, display the **Documents** folder window and open the **Bell_Orchid** folder window. In the **Bell_Orchid** folder, create a new folder named **Hotel_Rooms** and then open the **Hotel_Rooms** folder window. Snap this window to the left side of your screen.

2 On the taskbar, right-click the **Windows Explorer** button, and then on the **Jump List**, click **Windows Explorer** to open a second window. In the new window, navigate to **Documents ▶ Bell_Orchid ▶ Honolulu ▶ Sales_Marketing** to display this folder window, and then snap the window to the right side of your screen. Select the files **r1**, **r2**, and **r3**, and then *copy* them to the **Hotel_Rooms** folder. In the **Hotel_Rooms** folder, rename **r1** as **HO_Suite_1** Rename **r2** as **HO_Room_1** and rename **r3** to **HO_Suite_2**

3 In the right window, click the **Back arrow** as necessary, and then navigate to **Corporate ▶ Sales_Marketing** to display its folder window. Select the files **r1**, **r2**, and **r3**, and *move* them to the **Hotel_Rooms** folder. In the **Hotel_Rooms** folder, rename **r1** as **CO_Suite_1** Then rename **r2** as **CO_Room_1** and rename **r3** as **CO_Suite_2** In the left window, change the **View** to **Large Icons**.

4 Insert the USB flash drive on which you created your chapter folder. Create a **Full-screen Snip**, and then **Save** the snip in your **Windows 7 Chapter 2** folder as **Lastname_Firstname_2E_Rooms_Snip** and submit it as directed by your instructor.

5 **Close** the mark-up window. **Close** the **Hotel_Rooms** window. In the remaining window, display your **Documents** library, and then delete the **Bell_Orchid** folder. **Close** the window.

End **You have completed Project 2E**

Content-Based Assessments

Apply **2B** skills from these Objectives:

7 Search From the Start Menu

8 Search From a Folder Window

9 Save, Reuse, and Delete a Search

10 Search From the Control Panel Window and the Computer Window

11 Add Tags to Improve a Search

Mastering Windows 7 | Project **2F** Searching Your Computer

In the following Mastering Windows 7 project, you will conduct a search, add tags, and then search for tagged files. You will capture and save a screen that will look similar to Figure 2.59.

Project Files

For Project 2F, you will need the following file:

New Snip file

You will save your file as:

Lastname_Firstname_2F_Umbrella_Tables

Project Results

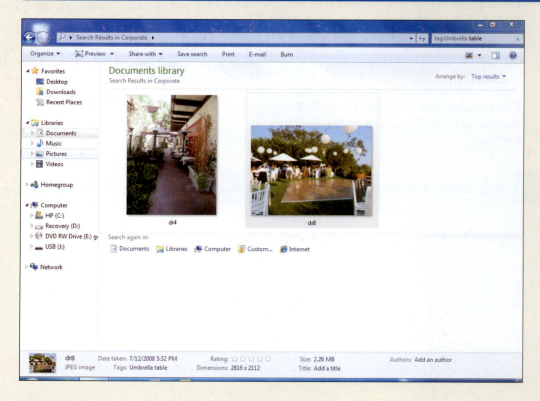

Figure 2.59

(Project 2F Searching Your Computer continues on the next page)

Mastering Windows 7 | Project **2F** Searching Your Computer (continued)

1 Insert the Student Resource CD in the appropriate drive, and then by using the **Send to** command, copy the **Bell_Orchid** folder from the CD to your **Documents** folder. Then, open your **Documents** folder and navigate to **Bell_Orchid ▶ Corporate** to display this folder window. **Maximize** 🔳 the window.

2 Search the folder using the criteria **dr** If necessary, set the view to **Details**. Point to the **Type** column heading, click the **arrow** that displays, and then filter the results by **JPEG Image**.

3 Select the file named **dr4**. At the bottom of the window, in the **Details pane**, click the **Tags** box, and then type **Umbrella table** to add this tag. At the right end of the **Details pane**, click **Save**. Add the same tag to the file **dr8** and click **Save**. Then, in

the **Type** column, clear the filter from the search results.

4 Clear ⊠ the **search** box, and then search for files using the criteria **tag:Umbrella table** Change the view to **Extra Large Icons**. Select the **dr8** file so that it displays in the **Details pane**.

5 Insert the USB flash drive on which you created your chapter folder. Create a **Window Snip**, and then click in the window to capture. **Save** the snip in your **Windows 7 Chapter 2** folder as **Lastname_Firstname_2F_Umbrella_Tables_Snip** and submit it as directed by your instructor.

6 **Close** all open windows. Then, display your **Documents** folder, delete the **Bell_Orchid** folder, in the upper right corner, click the **Restore Down** button, and then close the window.

End **You have completed Project 2F**

Outcomes-Based Assessments

Rubric

The following outcomes-based assessments are open-ended assessments. That is, there is no specific correct result; your result will depend on your approach to the information provided. Make Professional Quality your goal. Use the following scoring rubric to guide you in how to approach the problem, and then to evaluate how well your approach solves the problem.

The criteria—Software Mastery, Content, Format and Layout, and Process—represent the knowledge and skills you have gained that you can apply to solving the problem. The levels of performance—Professional Quality, Approaching Professional Quality, or Needs Quality Improvements—help you and your instructor evaluate your result.

	Your completed project is of **Professional Quality** if you:	Your completed project is **Approaching Professional Quality** if you:	Your completed project **Needs Quality Improvements** if you:
1-Software Mastery	Choose and apply the most appropriate skills, tools, and features and identify efficient methods to solve the problem.	Choose and apply some appropriate skills, tools, and features, but not in the most efficient manner.	Choose inappropriate skills, tools, or features, or are inefficient in solving the problem.
2-Content	Construct a solution that is clear and well organized, contains content that is accurate, appropriate to the audience and purpose, and is complete. Provide a solution that contains no errors in spelling, grammar, or style.	Construct a solution in which some components are unclear, poorly organized, inconsistent, or incomplete. Misjudge the needs of the audience. Have some errors in spelling, grammar, or style, but the errors do not detract from comprehension.	Construct a solution that is unclear, incomplete, or poorly organized; contains some inaccurate or inappropriate content; and contains many errors in spelling, grammar, or style. Do not solve the problem.
3-Format and Layout	Format and arrange all elements to communicate information and ideas, clarify function, illustrate relationships, and indicate relative importance.	Apply appropriate format and layout features to some elements, but not others. Overuse features, causing minor distraction.	Apply format and layout that does not communicate information or ideas clearly. Do not use format and layout features to clarify function, illustrate relationships, or indicate relative importance. Use available features excessively, causing distraction.
4-Process	Use an organized approach that integrates planning, development, self-assessment, revision, and reflection.	Demonstrate an organized approach in some areas, but not others; or, use an insufficient process of organization throughout.	Do not use an organized approach to solve the problem.

Outcomes-Based Assessments

Apply a combination of the 2A and 2B skills.

Problem Solving | Project 2G Help Desk

Project Files

For Project 2G, you will need the following files:

> win02_2G_Help_Desk

You will save your file as:

> Lastname_Firstname_2G_Help_Desk

From the student files that accompany this textbook, open the **Chapter_Files** folder, and then in **Chapter_02** folder, locate and open the Word document **win02_2G_Help_Desk**. Save the document in your chapter folder as **Lastname_Firstname_2G_Help_Desk**

The following e-mail question has arrived at the Help Desk from an employee at the Bell Orchid Hotel's corporate office. In the Word form, construct a response based on your knowledge of Windows 7. Although an e-mail response is not as formal as a letter, you should still use good grammar, good sentence structure, professional language, and a polite tone. Save your document and submit the response as directed by your instructor.

To: Help Desk

I am not sure about the differences between copying and moving files and folders. When is it best to copy a file or a folder and when is it best to move a file or folder? Can you also describe some techniques that I can use for copying or moving files and folders? Which do you think is the easiest way to copy or move files and folders?

End **You have completed Project 2G** ————————————————

Apply a combination of the **2A** and **2B** skills.

Problem Solving | Project **2H** Help Desk

Project Files

For Project 2H, you will need the following files:

> win02_2H_Help_Desk

You will save your file as:

> Lastname_Firstname_2H_Help_Desk

From the student files that accompany this textbook, open the **Chapter_Files** folder, and then in **Chapter_02** folder, locate and open **win02_2H_Help_Desk**. Save the document in your chapter folder as **Lastname_Firstname_2H_Help_Desk**

The following e-mail question has arrived at the Help Desk from an employee at the Bell Orchid Hotel's corporate office. In the Word form, construct a response based on your knowledge of Windows 7. Although an e-mail response is not as formal as a letter, you should still use good grammar, good sentence structure, professional language, and a polite tone. Save your document and submit the response as directed by your instructor.

To: Help Desk

My colleague told me that there is a difference between deleting files and folders from my hard disk drive and from my removable media devices like my USB flash drive. What is the difference, if any?

 You have completed Project 2H ——————————

Apply a combination of the **2A** and **2B** skills.

Problem Solving | Project 2I Help Desk

For Project 2I, you will need the following file:

> win02_2I_Help_Desk

You will save your document as:

> Lastname_Firstname_2I_Help_Desk

From the student files that accompany this textbook, open the **Chapter_Files** folder, and then in **Chapter_02** folder, locate and open **win02_2I_Help_Desk**. Save the document in your chapter folder as **Lastname_Firstname_2I_Help_Desk**

The following e-mail question has arrived at the Help Desk from an employee at the Bell Orchid Hotel's corporate office. In the Word document, construct a response based on your knowledge of Windows 7. Although an e-mail response is not as formal as a letter, you should still use good grammar, good sentence structure, professional language, and a polite tone. Save your document and submit the response as directed by your instructor.

To: Help Desk

I am the Banquet Manager at the Orlando hotel. I need to locate all the files that have to do with Banquets. When I search on the term *banquets*, I get all the files specifically relating to Banquets, but other files that are not banquet-related display in the results; for example, marketing materials that mention our banquet facilities. Do you have any suggestions on how I might locate only the files that I am interested in? In addition, I am constantly adding banquet-related files, so I would like to be able to reuse my search. Do you have any suggestions on how I could do that?

End **You have completed Project 2I** ————————————————

Advanced File Management and Advanced Searching

OUTCOMES

At the end of this chapter you will be able to:

PROJECT 3A
Navigate and display your files and folders for maximum ease of use and efficiency in completing tasks.

OBJECTIVES

Mastering these objectives will enable you to:

1. Navigate by Using the Address Bar (p. 157)
2. Create and Navigate Favorites (p. 162)
3. Personalize the Display of Folders and Files (p. 165)
4. Recognize File Types and Associate Files with Programs (p. 179)

PROJECT 3B
Conduct a search of your computer that includes multiple criteria and administer the search engine and index.

5. Filter Searches in the Search Box (p. 187)
6. Search by Using the Search Folder (p. 197)
7. Save a Search, Manage Search Behavior, and Manage the Index (p. 204)

Shutterstock

In This Chapter

In this chapter, you will see that although most of the work with your data occurs inside the program in which the file was created, for example when working on an Excel worksheet, there are still many times when you are outside of the program and using Windows Explorer to find or organize your files and folders.

The address bar is a good way to navigate, and in this chapter, you will use more techniques to take advantage of everything it has to offer. You will also use Favorites to increase your efficiency. The Search feature in Windows 7 is powerful; using it properly can reduce frustration when you are trying to find your data. In this chapter, you will practice additional search techniques so that you will always be able to find your files quickly.

The projects in this chapter relate to the **Bell Orchid Hotels**, headquartered in Boston, and which own and operate resorts and business-oriented hotels. Resort properties are located in popular destinations, including Honolulu, Orlando, San Diego, and Santa Barbara. The resorts offer deluxe accommodations and a wide array of dining options. Other Bell Orchid hotels are located in major business centers and offer the latest technology in their meeting facilities. The company plans to open new properties and update existing properties over the next ten years.

Project 3A Using Advanced File Management Techniques

In Activities 3.01 through 3.07, you will work with Barbara Hewitt and Steven Ramos, employees in the Information Technology department at the headquarters office of Bell Orchid Hotels, as they explore how to navigate and display the files and folders on a computer for maximum efficiency and ease of use. You will capture screens that will look similar to Figure 3.1.

For Project 3A, you will need the following files:

Student Resource CD (or a USB flash drive containing these files)
New Snip files

You will save your files as:

Lastname_Firstname_3A_Bella_Snip
Lastname_Firstname_3A_Checkbox_Snip
Lastname_Firstname_3A_Tag_Arrange_Snip
Lastname_Firstname_3A_Wordcount_Snip
Lastname_Firstname_3A_Extensions_Snip

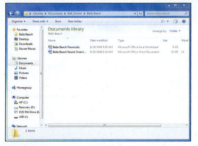
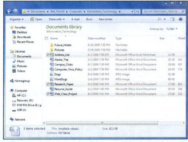

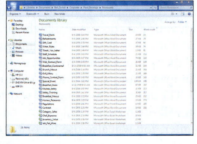
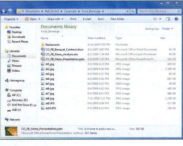

Figure 3.1
Project 3A Using Advanced File Management Techniques

Objective 1 | Navigate by Using the Address Bar

Recall that the address bar displays your current *location* as a series of links separated by arrows. The term *location* is used, rather than the term *folder*, because you can navigate to both folders and to other resources. For example, you can navigate to the Control Panel from the address bar.

Every element of the address bar—the folder names and each arrow—is an active control. That is, you can move from the currently displayed folder directly to any folder above it in the path just by clicking on a folder name. Additionally, you can click the Forward and Back buttons to the left of the address bar to navigate through folders you have already visited, just as if you were surfing the Internet. You can actually surf the Internet by typing a Web address into the address bar, which opens a new Internet Explorer window.

Activity 3.01 | Navigating by Using the Address Bar

A primary function of your operating system is to store and keep track of your files. A file folder on a disk in which you store files is referred to as a **directory**. The location of any file can be described by its **path**. A path is a sequence of folders—*directories*—that leads to a specific file or folder.

1 If necessary, *delete* the Bell_Orchid folder from your **Documents** folder—for this project you will need a new copy of the files. Insert the Student Resource CD or other device that contains the student files that accompany this textbook. By using the **Send to** command, copy the **Bell_Orchid** folder from the Student Resource CD to your **Documents** folder.

2 Insert your USB flash drive, and then **Close** [x] all open windows. On the taskbar, click the **Windows Explorer** button [icon], and then navigate to **Documents ▶ Bell_Orchid ▶ Corporate**. Be sure the **View** [icon] is set to **Details**. In the **address bar**, locate the **location icon**, as shown in Figure 3.2.

The **location icon** depicts the location—library, disk drive, folder, and so on—you are currently accessing. Here, a buff-colored folder displays.

Figure 3.2
Address bar
Location icon for a folder
Folder window for *Corporate* folder

3 In the **address bar**, click the **location icon** one time, and then compare your screen with Figure 3.3.

> The path that describes the folder's location displays and is highlighted. The path begins with the disk, which is indicated by *C:*—the main hard disk drive of your computer.
>
> Following the disk is the sequence of subfolders, each separated by a backslash (\). On the *C:* hard disk drive, the folder *Users* contains your personal folder with your name and the name of your computer. Your personal folder contains the *Documents* library, which contains the *Bell_Orchid* folder that you copied there. The *Bell_Orchid* folder contains the *Corporate* folder.

Figure 3.3
Path describes
folder's location

Location icon

Your personal folder
(your folder's name and
computer name will differ)

Backslashes separate
the parts of the path

C: indicates disk

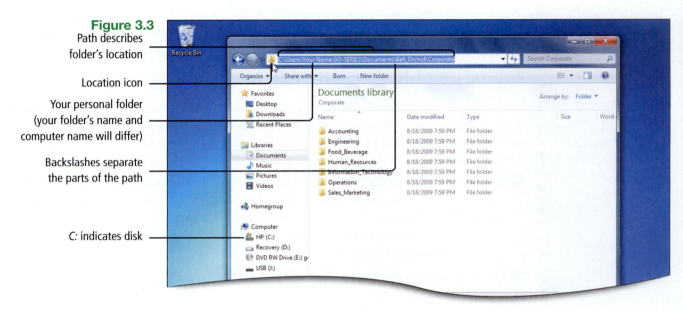

Another Way

Press Esc to cancel the path display.

4 Click in a blank area of the **file list** to cancel the display of the path.

5 In the **navigation pane**, under **Libraries**, click **Documents**, and then compare your screen with Figure 3.4.

> The location icon changes to depict the location being accessed—the Documents library.

Figure 3.4

Location icon displays the
Documents library icon

Documents selected
in navigation pane

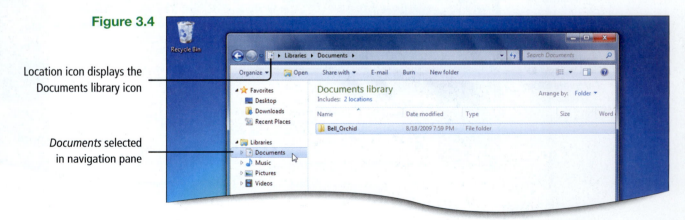

6 In the **navigation pane**, under **Computer**, click your **C:** hard disk drive. In the **address bar**, notice the hard disk drive icon that displays as the **location icon**—a small Windows logo may display there. In the **navigation pane**, click your **USB flash drive**, and notice the **location icon**.

7 If your Student Resource CD is still in the drive, in the **navigation pane**, click it one time. Notice that the **location icon** displays as a CD. Then, under **Libraries**, click **Music.** Compare your screen with Figure 3.5.

Figure 3.5

Location icon for
Music library

8 On the **address bar**, click the **Back** button five times or as many times as necessary to redisplay the **Corporate** folder window.

Recall that the Forward and Back buttons enable you to navigate to locations you have already visited. In a manner similar to when you are browsing the Web, the locations you have visited are stored in a location history, and you can browse that location history by clicking the Back and Forward buttons.

9 To the immediate right of the **Forward** button, locate and click the **Recent Pages** button . Compare your screen with Figure 3.6.

The *Recent Pages* button displays a list of recently accessed locations, and the current location is indicated by a check mark. By clicking an item on this list, you can move to a recently accessed location quickly. The list is limited to the current session; thus, only locations you have accessed since starting Windows Explorer display on the list.

Location icon

Figure 3.6

Recent Pages button

Forward button

List of Recent Pages

Current location indicated
by check mark

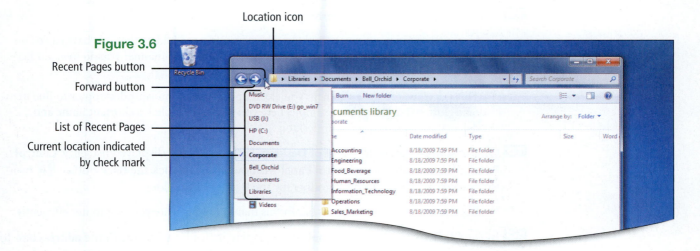

10 On the displayed list, click **Bell_Orchid**. If you do not see Bell_Orchid on the list, click Bell_Orchid in the address bar. To the right of the **location icon**, click ▶ and then compare your screen with Figure 3.7.

> The ▶ to the immediate right of the location icon always displays, *below* the separator line, a list of available *base locations*—locations that you frequently need to access to manage your computer. These include Libraries, your Homegroup if you have one, your personal folder, Computer, Network, Control Panel, and Recycle Bin.
>
> *Above* the separator line, any folders in the path that cannot fit on the address bar will display, along with Desktop.

Figure 3.7

Bell_Orchid folder window

Location icon

List of base locations
below separator line

Separator line

11 On the displayed list, notice the **separator line** below **Desktop**.

> Locations above the separator line are part of the current path. Recall that your desktop is considered the top of your hierarchy; it is created for each user account name and contains your personal folder.

12 On the displayed list, click **Desktop**.

> Here you can view and work with any shortcuts, files, or folders that you have stored on the desktop. In the file list, you can open items in the same manner you do in any other file list.
>
> This is a convenient view to help you clean up any clutter on your desktop or to *find* items on a cluttered desktop. For example, here you could right-click a shortcut name and delete the shortcut from your desktop.

13 On the **address bar**, to the right of **Desktop**, click ▶. On the displayed list, click **Control Panel**, and then after the Control Panel window displays, click the **Back** button 🔙 two times to return to the folder window for the **Bell_Orchid** folder.

> Use the features of the address bar in this manner to navigate your computer efficiently.

14 In the **file list**, double-click **Honolulu** to display its folder window. In the **address bar**, to the right of **Bell_Orchid**, click ▶ and then on the displayed list, click **Orlando**.

> You can access a subfolder of any folder displayed in the address bar by clicking the arrow to the right of the folder and displaying its list of subfolders.

15 In the **address bar**, to the right of **Bell_Orchid**, click ▶ and then on the displayed list, click **Corporate**. In the **file list**, double-click the **Information_Technology** folder to display its folder window, and then compare your screen with Figure 3.8.

On the address bar, to the right of the location icon, double chevrons << replace ▶. Double chevrons indicate that the current path is too long to fit in the address bar. If your window is larger than the one shown in Figure 3.8, you might not see the double chevrons.

Figure 3.8

Double chevrons indicate available space cannot display entire path (yours may differ)

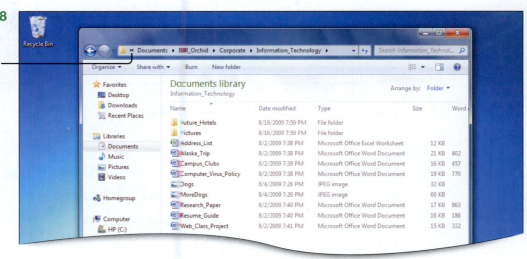

16 If the double chevrons << display in your folder window, click them, and then compare your screen with Figure 3.9. If they do not display, just examine Figure 3.9.

The part of the path that cannot display is shown above the separator line. Below the separator line, the base locations display.

Figure 3.9

Separator line

Parts of the path that cannot display in the available space

Base locations

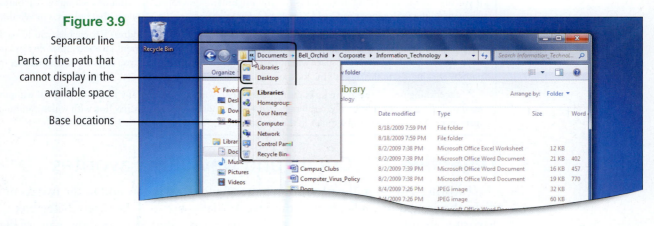

17 Press Esc to close the menu, and then **Maximize** ⬜ the folder window. Notice that the entire path displays, and the double chevrons no longer display.

Even with the folder window maximized, a path that contains numerous subfolders will be forced to display the double chevrons. When you see the double chevrons in this manner, you will know that the entire path is not visible.

18 If your computer is connected to the Internet, in the **address bar**, click the **location icon** to display the path description. With the path selected (highlighted in blue), type **www.bls.gov** and press Enter.

The Web site for the U.S. Department of Labor's Bureau of Labor Statistics displays. In this manner, you can type a Web address directly in the address bar without opening Internet Explorer.

19 **Close** ![x button] the Web page to redisplay your folder window. Compare your screen with Figure 3.10.

> Two additional buttons display at the end of the address bar. The Previous Locations button provides a drop-down list of locations you have accessed.
>
> The Refresh button updates the view and displays any updates to contents in the selected location, which is more likely to occur if you are viewing a network location.

Figure 3.10

Previous Locations button ————

Refresh button ————

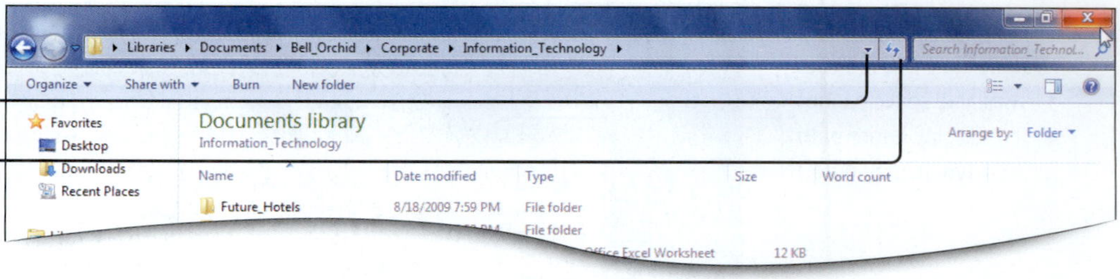

20 In the upper right corner, click the **Restore Down** button ![restore down button] to return the window to its previous size, and then **Close** ![x button] all open windows.

> There is no *correct* way to navigate your computer. You can use any combination of techniques in the navigation pane, the address bar, and in the file list of a folder window to display the location you want.
>
> By using the various active controls in the address bar, you can significantly reduce the number of clicks that you perform when navigating your computer.

More Knowledge | **Are You Looking for the Up Button That Displays in Windows XP?**

If you are used to navigating in Windows XP, you might have developed the habit of clicking the Up button to navigate up the folder structure level by level. And you might be wondering where that button is in Windows 7.

With Windows 7, you have no need for the Up button, because the address bar enables you to navigate your folder structure in a more efficient manner. The entire path of your current location either displays in the address bar or, if the address bar space will not accommodate the entire path, you can view the remainder of the path by clicking << to the right of the location icon as shown in Figure 3.9.

By clicking one of the active links in the address bar, you can jump to any folder in the path without the need to drill upward. Additionally, recall that each ▶ in the address bar is an active link with which you can navigate directly to a subfolder of a folder in the current path.

Objective 2 | Create and Navigate Favorites

Favorites display in the navigation pane of a folder window and in the two common dialog boxes within applications—the Save As dialog box and the Open dialog box. Favorites are folders or locations that Windows 7 has determined as those you are likely to need to reach easily.

You can change the Favorites list any way you want. If you have a folder for a project that you are working on, you can add it to the Favorites area, and then delete it when you no longer need it. For each user account, all Windows Explorer libraries share the same list of Favorites.

Activity 3.02 | Creating and Navigating Favorites

Three items display in the Favorites area by default—Desktop, Downloads, and Recent Places. Recall that searches you save display under Favorites. Saved searches are an example of a *virtual folder*—a folder that does not represent a physical location but rather contains the results of a search.

1 **Close** [x] any open windows. On the taskbar, click the **Windows Explorer** button [icon], double-click **Documents**, and then drag the **Bell_Orchid** folder to the **Windows Explorer** button [icon] on the taskbar to pin it to the **Jump List**. Click on the desktop to close the **Jump List**.

> Recall that it is efficient to pin frequently used folders to the Jump List in this manner.

2 If you want to do so, pin Word and Excel to the taskbar—or leave them on the taskbar if they are still pinned there from your work on the previous chapter.

3 Double-click **Bell_Orchid** to display its folder window, and then on the toolbar, click **New folder**. Type **Bella Beach** and then press Enter to name the new folder.

4 Point to the **Bella Beach** folder, drag it to the left under **Favorites** until a line displays under the text *Favorites* and you see the ScreenTip *Create link in Favorites* as shown in Figure 3.11, and then release the mouse button.

> A link to the *Bella Beach* folder is created in the Favorites area of the navigation pane. The position is determined by where the black line displays as you drag into the Favorites area.

Figure 3.11

Line displays under *Favorites* and indicates position

ScreenTip indicates link being created

Word and Excel programs pinned to taskbar (optional)

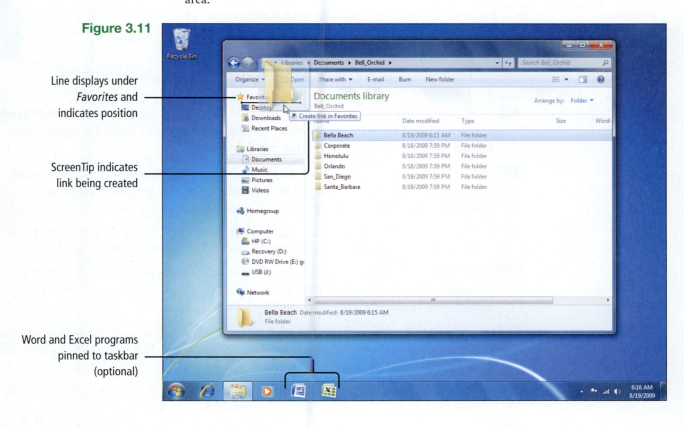

5 **Close** [x] the **Bell_Orchid** folder window, and then start the **Microsoft Word** program. Notice that the program might still be pinned to your taskbar from the activities in the previous chapter, or you might have to locate and start the program from the Start menu or the All Programs menu.

6 In the new blank document, type **Information regarding this new resort near Bella Beach will be added to this document at a later date.**

7 Press F12 to display the **Save As** dialog box. In the **navigation pane**, under **Favorites**, click the link to the **Bella Beach** folder to display its path in the **address bar**. As the **File name** type **Bella Beach Resort Overview** and then compare your screen with Figure 3.12.

Figure 3.12

Save As dialog box

Path displays in address bar

Favorites area

Link to *Bella Beach* folder

File name entered

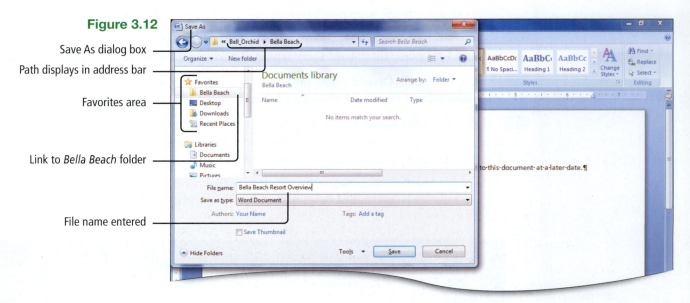

8 In the lower right corner, click **Save**, and then **Close** Word. Start **Microsoft Excel**. In cell **A1** type **Financial information for the new resort in Bella Beach will be added to this document at a later date.** Press Enter.

9 Press F12 to display the **Save As** dialog box. In the **navigation pane**, under **Favorites**, click **Recent Places**. Notice that the **Bella Beach** folder not only displays under **Favorites**, but it also displays in the list of **Recent Places**.

Because you recently accessed the Bella Beach folder, it will display in the list of Recent Places. Finding a recent location here is often easier than navigating within your folder structure.

10 In the list of **Recent Places** on the right, double-click **Bella Beach** to display its path in the **address bar**. Click in the **File name** box to select the default text, and then type **Bella Beach Financials** Click **Save**, and then **Close** Excel.

11 On the taskbar, point to the **Windows Explorer** button, drag it up slightly into the desktop to display the **Jump List**, and then under **Pinned**, click **Bell_Orchid**. Open the **Bella Beach** folder window.

Remember to practice using efficient methods like opening locations from the Jump List and displaying the Jump List by dragging instead of right-clicking.

12 **Start** the **Snipping Tool** program, click the **New arrow**, and then click **Window Snip**. Point anywhere in the folder window and click one time. In the **Snipping Tool** mark-up window, click the **Save Snip** button.

13 In the **Save As** dialog box, in the **navigation pane**, scroll down as necessary, and then click your USB flash drive so that it displays in the **address bar**. On the toolbar, click the **New folder** button, type **Windows 7 Chapter 3** and press Enter.

14 In the **file list**, double-click your **Windows 7 Chapter 3** folder to open it. Click in the **File name** box, and then replace the selected text by typing **Lastname_Firstname_ 3A_Bella_Snip** Be sure the file type is **JPEG**, and press Enter. **Close** the **Snipping Tool** mark-up window. Hold this file until you finish Project 3A, and then submit this file as directed by your instructor.

15 Under **Favorites**, point to **Bella Beach** and right-click. On the displayed shortcut menu, click **Remove**.

This action removes only the *link* to the folder; the folder itself is still contained in the Bell_Orchid folder.

Place folders under Favorites as you need them, and then remove them when you are no longer accessing them frequently.

16 **Close** ❎ the folder window and any other open windows.

By using the Favorites area, you have many ways to navigate quickly.

Objective 3 | Personalize the Display of Folders and Files

Windows 7 includes the word *personalize* prominently in various commands and in the Control Panel. For example, when you right-click on the desktop, the *Personalize* command displays on the shortcut menu. By using the tools available in Windows 7, you can change the way your files and folders function, as well as how the content in your folders displays.

Activity 3.03 | Locating and Identifying Subfolders in the Personal Folders

Recall that when you create a new user account and then log on as that user, Windows 7 creates a desktop and a personal folder. In this activity, you will locate and identify the subfolders in your Personal folder.

1 **Close** ❎ any open windows. On the taskbar, click the **Windows Explorer** button 📁, and then in the **navigation pane**, under **Computer**, click your **C: drive**. Then in the **file list**, locate the **Users** folder and double-click it to display its folder window.

Each user of the system for which a user account has been created has a folder in the Users folder with his or her name.

2 In the **address bar**, to the right of the **location icon**, click ▶. On the displayed list, click your personal folder—the folder with your user name. Compare your screen with Figure 3.13.

Figure 3.13
Your user name in the address bar (your user name will vary)
Location icon

Subfolders created by Windows 7 in your personal folder (yours may vary)

3 Take a moment to study what each folder in your personal folder stores as shown in the table in Figure 3.14.

Subfolders Created by Windows 7 in each User Account's Personal Folder

Contacts	Contains information about contacts that you create—a **contact** is a collection of information about a person or organization, such as the contact's name, e-mail address, phone number, and street address.
Desktop	Contains the icons you place on your desktop; the desktop you see when you start Windows 7 is associated with this folder.
Downloads	Acts as the default location for files downloaded from the Web when using Internet Explorer; anything you download will be stored here unless you navigate to a different location during the download process.
Favorites	Contain folders for your Internet Explorer Favorites.
Links	Stores the shortcuts that appear in the Favorites area of the navigation pane; you can drag folders to which you need quick access into this folder and they will display in the Favorites area.
My Documents	Stores the files in your Documents library such as Word documents and text files, but can contain any type of file; this folder is the default location for the Save As dialog box in many applications.
My Music	Works with and stores digital music and other audio files; if you rip music from an audio CD or purchase music from an online music service such as Apple iTunes Music Store or Zune Store, those files will typically be saved to this folder by default.
My Pictures	Stores digital photographs and other picture files, although picture files can be stored anywhere.
My Videos	Stores digital videos of any kind, including home movies.
Saved Games	Stores game information for Windows 7-compatible game titles.
Searches	Stores search criteria that you have saved and named.

Figure 3.14

4 **Close** [×] the folder window for your personal folder.

Activity 3.04 | Using the Folder Options Dialog Box to Change How Folders Function and Display

You can personalize the way your folders look and behave to suit your needs. For example, if you have difficulty performing a double-click, you can set all your files and folders to open with a single click. Many computer users make this change to their computers.

1 On the taskbar, click the **Windows Explorer** button [icon], and then double-click **Documents** to open its folder window.

2 In the **file list**, point to the **Bell_Orchid** folder and right-click, and then on the displayed shortcut menu, click **Open in new window.** Compare your screen with Figure 3.15.

The Bell_Orchid folder opens in a new window. Open a folder in a new window if you want to keep open all the folders you are working with on the screen at the same time; for example, as another method to drag files from one folder to another.

Figure 3.15

Two windows open

Bell_Orchid opens in a new window

Windows Explorer on taskbar indicates two windows open

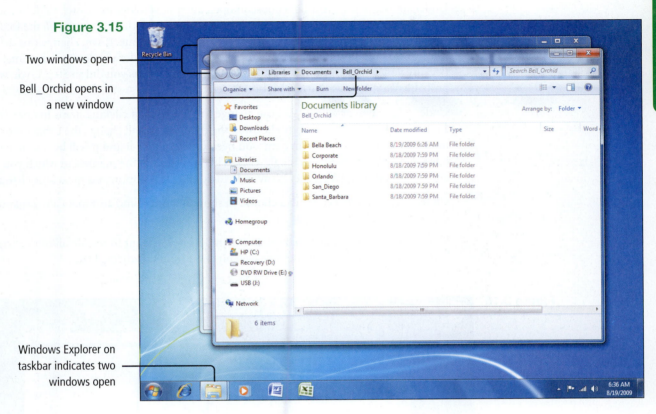

Another Way

Display the Control Panel, click Appearance and Personalization, and then click Folder Options.

3 Close ❌ the **Bell_Orchid** folder window. On the toolbar of the **Documents** window, click the **Organize** button. On the displayed menu, click **Folder and search options**, and then if necessary, click the **General tab**. Compare your screen with Figure 3.16.

Changes that you make in the Folder Options dialog box affect *all* of your folder windows, regardless of what disk drive or folder's content displays. On the General tab, there are three significant changes you can make to the behavior of *all* of your folder windows.

Under *Browse folders*, you can choose to open *every* new folder in its own folder window, in the manner that you did in Step 1 of this activity. Recall that this keeps *all* the folder windows you are working with on the screen at the same time. If you change this default setting, keep in mind that this behavior will apply to *all* folder windows *all* the time. Because you can easily do this on a folder-by-folder basis, as you did in Step 1, you will probably want to leave the default option selected.

Under *Click items as follows*, you can change the behavior of clicking items to open them. Changing the default setting by choosing the first option will change the behavior of your mouse as follows: To select an item, you need only point to it and it will be selected; to open an item, you need only single-click. This is similar to the manner in which you select and open links in a Web page. Many individuals like this option and make this change.

Under *Navigation pane*, you can choose to show all folders and automatically expand to the current folder.

If you select some of these changes and then decide you want to restore all of the original behaviors, you can click the Restore Defaults button in this dialog box.

Figure 3.16

Folder Options dialog box

General tab selected

Browse folders area

Click items as follows area

Navigation pane area

Restore Defaults

More Knowledge | Double-click or Single-click?

In earlier versions of Windows, testing was conducted with computer users on making the *single-click to open behavior* the default. However, the majority of computer users were accustomed to the double-click method, so double-click remains the default. Many computer users opt to change from the *double-click to open behavior* to the *single-click to open behavior*.

If you prefer to have Windows 7 behave more like a Web page, that is, you perform a single-click to activate something and you point to something to select it, you might want to consider making this change on your computer.

4 In the **Folder Options** dialog box, click the **View tab**, and then notice the two buttons under **Folder views**.

Here you can select one of the Windows 7 views, for example *Details* or *Content* or *Small Icons*, to apply to every folder window you open. To accomplish this, open any folder window and change it to the view you want for all folder windows. Then display this dialog box and click the Apply to Folders button.

Because Windows 7 selects a view that is appropriate for the type of data, and because you can change the view easily on a folder-by-folder basis, you will probably not want to adjust this setting. If you make the adjustment and do not like it, display the dialog box and click the Reset Folders button.

5 Under **Advanced settings**, scroll down to view the lower portion of the list, and then click to select the check box to the left of **Use check boxes to select items**. At the bottom of the dialog box, click **OK**. Notice that a check box displays next to Bell_Orchid in the file list and the check box is selected.

6 In your **Documents** folder window, navigate to **Bell_Orchid ▶ Corporate ▶ Information_Technology**. Point to the Excel file **Address_List**, and then compare your screen with Figure 3.17.

A check box displays in the *Name* column heading and in the upper left corner of the file to which you are pointing. By enabling the ***check box feature***, when you point to a file or folder, a check box displays in the upper left corner.

Figure 3.17

Check box in *Name* heading

Check box displays when pointing to file

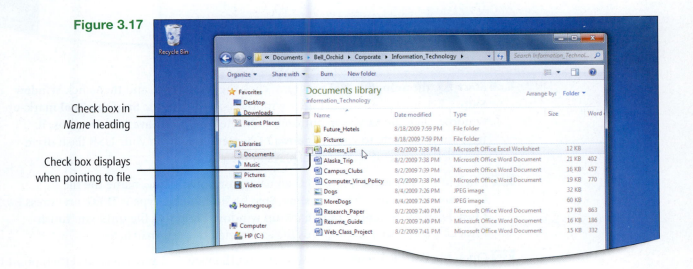

7 Click the **check box** for the **Address_List** file, and notice that a check mark displays in the check box. Point to the left of the file **Research_Paper** and click its check box. Point to the left of the file **Web_Class_Project** and click its check box. Compare your screen with Figure 3.18.

> The files you select by clicking directly in the check box remain selected. Thus, you need not remember to hold down ⌈Ctrl⌉ to select a noncontiguous group of files. This setting also makes it easier to see which files are selected and which files are not selected.

> Many individuals enable this feature to make selecting multiple files easier and visually distinctive. If you like this feature, you might consider enabling it on your own system.

Figure 3.18

Three non-contiguous files selected

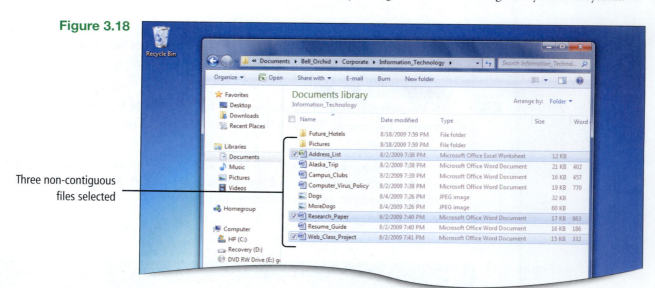

8 **Start** 🪟 the **Snipping Tool** program, click the **New arrow**, and then click **Window Snip**. Click anywhere in the folder window, and then in the **Snipping Tool** mark-up window, click the **Save Snip** button 💾. In the displayed **Save As** dialog box, if necessary, navigate to your **Windows 7 Chapter 3** folder on your USB flash drive and click to select it so that it displays in the address bar.

9 Click in the **File name** box, and then using your own name, name the file **Lastname_Firstname_3A_Checkbox_Snip** be sure the file type is **JPEG**, and press ⌈Enter⌉. **Close** 🞩 the **Snipping Tool** mark-up window. Hold this file until you finish Project 3A, and then submit this file as directed by your instructor.

10 Open the **Future_Hotels** folder window, set the view to **Large Icons**, and then point to various files in this folder. Notice that the check box feature continues to display.

> Recall that any setting you change in the Folder Options dialog box will be applied to *all* files and folders on your computer.

11 On the toolbar, click **Organize**, click **Folder and search options**, click the **View tab**, and then under **Advanced settings**, select the first checkbox—**Always show icons, never thumbnails**. Click **OK**, and then compare your screen with Figure 3.19.

Changing this setting results in the display of a static (unchanging) icon instead of the Live Icon preview of the actual file. Some individuals select this setting to speed the performance of their computer, because it takes a little longer to display the Live Icons.

Unless you have an extremely large number of image files, however, you will probably *not* want to change this setting. Retaining the Live Icon preview is helpful to identify quickly the files for which you are looking.

Figure 3.19

Live Icon previews replaced by a standard image

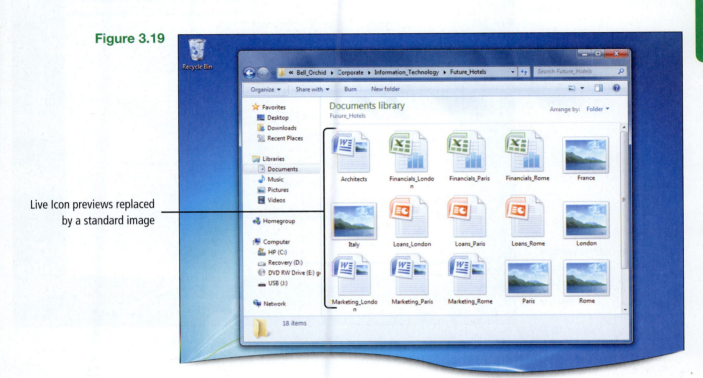

12 Return the **View** [icon] to **Details**, and then **Close** [icon] the folder window and any other open windows. From the **Start menu** [icon], display the **Control Panel**. Click **Appearance and Personalization**, and then click **Folder Options**.

This is another method to display the Folder Options dialog box.

13 In the **Folder Options** dialog box, click the **View tab**. Compare your screen with Figure 3.20. Take a moment to scroll down the list under **Advanced settings** and study the table in Figure 3.21.

Becoming familiar with these settings will enable you to further personalize the manner in which your folders display to suit your own comfort and ease of use.

Figure 3.20

Folder Options dialog box

View tab

Control Panel window

Advanced settings list

Folder Options window icon on taskbar

Control Panel icon on taskbar

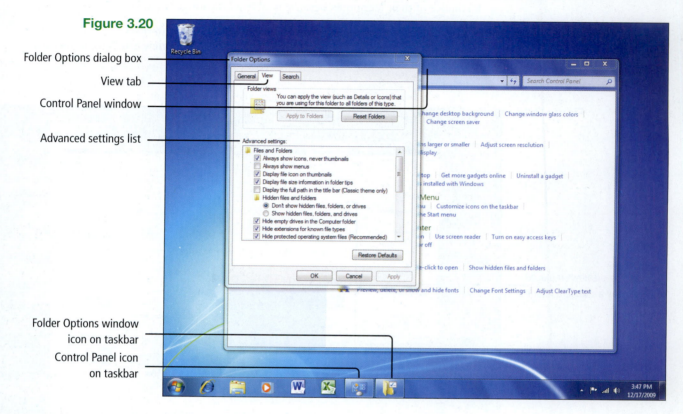

Advanced Settings in the View Tab of the Folder Options Dialog Box

Setting	Description and Default Setting
Always show icons, never thumbnails	Replaces Live Icons with a standard image. Off by default.
Always show menus	Displays a menu bar above the toolbar, which contains a few commands that are not available from the toolbar. Off by default.
Display file icon on thumbnails	Displays a small version of the application icon, for example the green Excel icon, on the file name, which makes it easier to determine which application opens the file. On by default.
Display file size information in folder tips	Displays the size of the file in a ScreenTip when you point to the file. On by default.
Display the full path in the title bar (Classic theme only)	Displays the full path of the file in the title bar of the folder window; however, this applies only to the Classic view of folders. Off by default.
Hidden files and folders	Displays hidden files and displays them as a paler ghost image. Off by default.
Hide empty drives in the Computer folder	Hides the display of drive letters in which there is no device attached. On by default.
Hide extensions for known file types	Hides the display of the file extensions for files, for example *.docx* for a Word 2007 file. On by default (by default, extensions are hidden from view).
Hide protected operating system files (Recommended)	Hides files with the *System* attribute from file listings. On by default.
Launch folder windows in a separate process	Launches each folder window in a separate memory space, increasing stability but decreasing performance. You might try this setting if your computer frequently fails, and you are trying to minimize problems or troubleshoot. Off by default.
Restore previous folder windows at logon	Redisplays, upon restart, any windows that you had open when Windows 7 was shut down. Off by default.
Show drive letters	Displays both the drive letter and the friendly name for a drive. If you clear this setting, only the friendly name will display. On by default.
Show encrypted or compressed NTFS files in color	Changes the text color for any files that use NTFS (New Technology File System) compression or NTFS encryption. On by default.
Show pop-up description for folder and desktop items	Displays a ScreenTip when you point to an item. On by default.
Show preview handlers in preview pane	Displays the contents of a file in the Preview pane when the Preview pane is enabled. On by default. Clearing this option could improve your computer's performance speed.
Use check boxes to select items	Displays a selection check box when you point to an item. Off by default.
Use Sharing Wizard (Recommended)	Limits the capability to assign complex permissions to files, which simplifies the process. On by default.
When typing into list view	Lets you choose between typing the value into the Search field automatically or displaying the results in the view. By default, set to *Select the typed item in the view.*

Figure 3.21

14 In the lower right corner of the **Folder Options** dialog box, click the **Restore Defaults** button to restore any settings that you have changed to the default settings. Click **OK**. **Close** 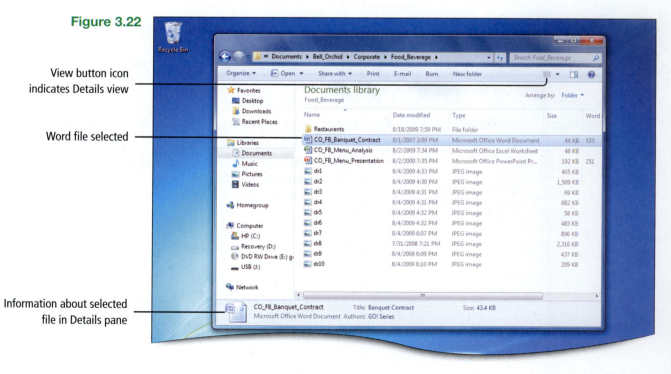 the **Control Panel** window.

Activity 3.05 | Personalizing Views and Using the Arrange By Feature

In the file list of a folder window, in addition to setting the *view*—for example Details view, Large Icons view, and so on—you can also change the *arrangement* of items by using the *Arrange by* feature. In a folder window, the Arrange by feature enables you to arrange the items by Author, Date modified, Tag, Type, or Name. The default arrangement is Folder.

1 **Close** any open windows. On the taskbar, click the **Windows Explorer** button. In the **navigation pane**, click **Computer**. Be sure the **View** is set to **Tiles**.

> The default view for the Computer window is Tiles; for most other windows the default view is Details. Recall, however, that Windows 7 remembers the most recently used view for a folder window, and continues to display that view each time that particular folder window is opened.

> To change this view behavior, you could change the view for *all* of your folders on the General tab in the Folder Options dialog box.

> Because you can change the view easily—recall that you can click the View button repeatedly to cycle through some of the views without actually displaying the View menu—you will probably *not* want to make any permanent changes.

2 In the **navigation pane**, under **Libraries**, click **Documents**, and then navigate to **Bell_Orchid ▶ Corporate ▶ Food_Beverage**. Be sure the **View** is **Details**. Click to select the Word file **CO_FB_Banquet_Contract**. Compare your screen with Figure 3.22.

> Details view is the default view for most folder windows, but of course any window will display in its most recently displayed view. The Details view presents substantial information about each file. When a folder or file in the file list is selected, the Details pane at the bottom of the window displays information about the selected item.

Figure 3.22

View button icon indicates Details view

Word file selected

Information about selected file in Details pane

3 On the toolbar, click the **View** button one time to cycle to the **Tiles** view.

> The Tiles view combines medium-sized icons with some information—file name, file type, and file size.

4 Click the **View** button two times to cycle to **Large Icons**.

> The Large Icons view provides large icons, which make it easy to see the content of files that include the Live Icon preview. For example, here you can see the actual picture files and the first slide of the PowerPoint presentation when a file is selected.

5 Click the **View** button one time to cycle to the **List** view.

> The List view displays only the file icon and the file name. The advantage of the List view is that you can see the full file name without widening the Name column.

6 Click the **View** button one time to cycle to the default **Details** view.

> Repeatedly clicking the View button cycles the view through five of the seven available views—Tiles, Content, Large Icons, List, and Details.

7 At the right side of the **Documents library pane**, locate **Arrange by**, and notice that *Folder* is the current arrangement. Notice also that this **file list** includes the **Restaurants** subfolder and a list of files.

8 To the right of *Folder*, click the **Arrange by arrow**, and then click **Name**.

> When you arrange the folder window by Name, all of the files in the folder *and* in any subfolders display. The subfolders themselves do not display.

> This arrangement is useful when you want to see all the files in a folder without opening each subfolder.

9 Click the **Arrange by** arrow again, and then return the arrangement to **Folder**. In the **file list**, notice that the **Restaurants** subfolder once again displays. Notice also that the **Food_Beverage** folder contains only one PowerPoint file and one Excel file.

10 Set **Arrange by** to **Type**, point to the **Excel** stack, and then on the ScreenTip, notice that **16** Excel files display.

> The Arrange by feature includes all items in the folder, plus any items in any subfolders. This is a useful way to see the number of files of a specific *type* in a folder without opening each subfolder.

11 Set **Arrange by** back to **Folder**, which is the default. Navigate to **Bell_Orchid ▶ Santa_Barbara ▶ Sales_Marketing ▶ Media**. Click the **Arrange by** arrow, and then click **Tag**. Click the stack **Gardens**, and then compare your screen with Figure 3.23.

> Windows 7 sorts the group of files into stacks by tag, and when you select a stack, in the Details pane, the number of files with the tag *Gardens* is indicated.

Figure 3.23

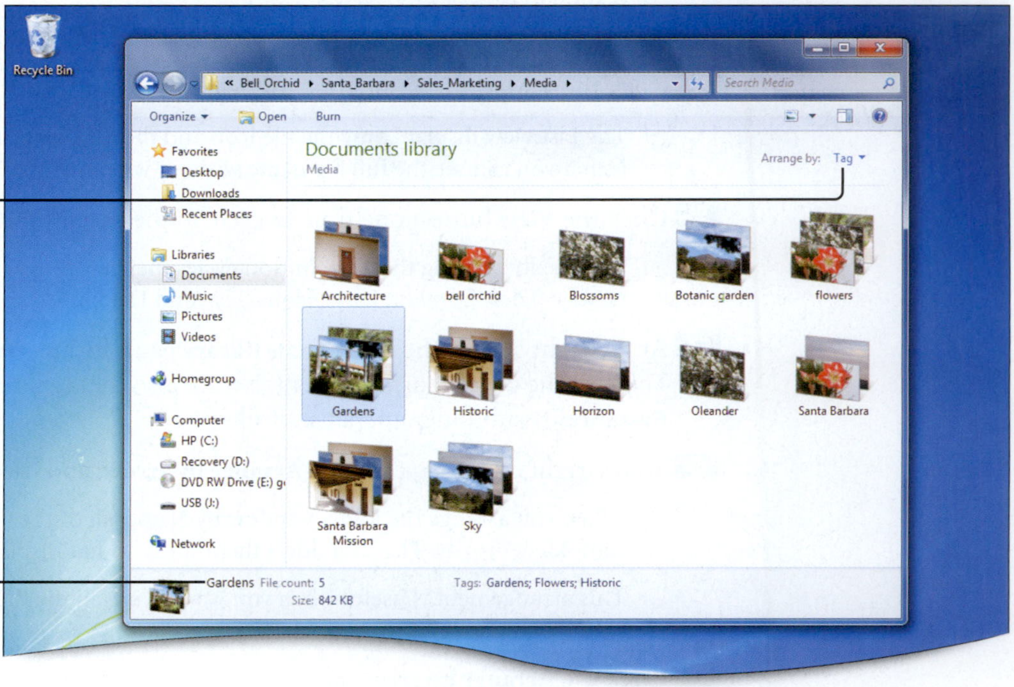

Files arranged by tag ———

Details pane indicates
number of files with ———
the tag *Gardens*

12 **Start** 🪟 the **Snipping Tool** program, click the **New arrow**, and then click **Window Snip**. Click anywhere in the folder window, and then in the **Snipping Tool** mark-up window, click the **Save Snip** button 💾. In the displayed **Save As** dialog box, if necessary navigate to your **Windows 7 Chapter 3** folder on your USB flash drive and click to select it so that it displays in the address bar.

13 Click in the **File name** box, and then using your own name, name the file **Lastname_ Firstname_3A_Tag_Arrange_Snip** be sure the file type is **JPEG**, and press ⏎. **Close** ❎ the **Snipping Tool** mark-up window, but leave the **Media** window open. Hold this file until you finish Project 3A, and then submit this file as directed by your instructor.

Activity 3.06 | Sorting Files by Properties

You can select any property that the file supports, and use it to sort files.

1 Set **Arrange by** back to **Folder**. Navigate to **Bell_Orchid ▶ Corporate ▶ Food_Beverage ▶ Restaurants**. **Maximize** ⬜ the window.

2 In the **file list**, point to any of the column headings, right-click, and then at the bottom of the displayed menu, click **More**.

> The Choose Details dialog box displays. From this dialog box, you can select any property that the file supports, and use it to sort files.

3 In the **Choose Details** dialog box, scroll down to the end of the list, and then select the **Word count** check box. Click **OK**.

4 Point to the **Word count column heading**, and then click two times so that the small arrow at the upper edge of the column heading points downward. Compare your screen with Figure 3.24.

> A Word count column is added to the folder window, and the files that support Word count—Microsoft Word documents—are sorted in descending order. Microsoft Excel files do not contain a word count.

> Properties such as those you can see in the Choose Details dialog box offer many ways to sort and find files.

Figure 3.24

Word count column added to Folder window

Files sorted in descending order by Word count

Restaurants folder window maximized

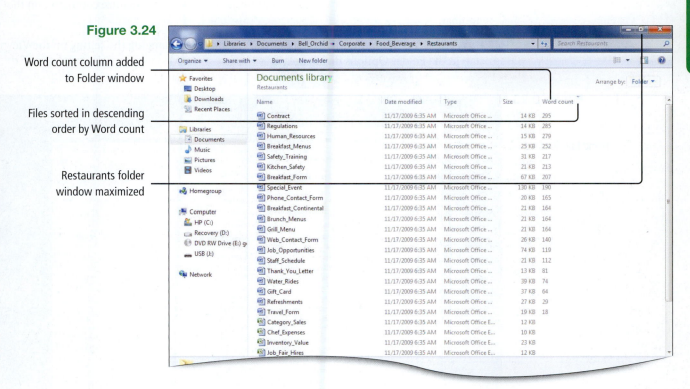

5 Start the **Snipping Tool** program, click the **New arrow**, and then click **Window Snip**. Point anywhere in the folder window and click one time. In the **Snipping Tool** mark-up window, click the **Save Snip** button.

6 Navigate to your chapter folder if necessary. Using your own name, name the file **Lastname_Firstname_3A_Wordcount_Snip** be sure the file type is **JPEG**, and press Enter. **Close** the **Snipping Tool** mark-up window; leave your **Restaurants** folder window displayed. Hold this file until you finish Project 3A, and then submit this file as directed by your instructor.

7 Point to any of the column headings, right-click, click **More**, and then notice that Word count moved to the upper portion of the list, in the group of Details that currently display in this folder window. Click to *clear* the **Word count** check box, and then click **OK**.

> The Word count column no longer displays in the Folder window.

8 In the upper right corner, click the **Restore Down** button. Click *Name* in the **Name column** to resort the items alphabetically.

9 **Close** 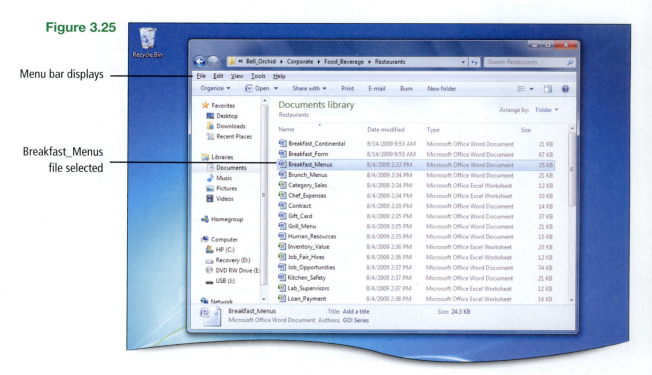 all open windows. On the taskbar, click the **Windows Explorer** button ![icon], double-click **Documents**, and then navigate to **Bell_Orchid ▶ Corporate ▶ Food_Beverage ▶ Restaurants**. If necessary, click the Name column to sort the files in alphabetic order.

10 Click to select the Word file **Breakfast_Menus**, and then press and release [Alt]. Compare your screen with Figure 3.25.

> A menu bar displays above the toolbar. By default, Windows 7 does not show menu bars in Windows Explorer. This menu bar displayed in Windows XP, but is not so commonly used, because most of its offerings are now available from the Organize command on the toolbar.
>
> If you prefer to have this menu display, you can do so by changing the setting on the View tab in the Folder Options dialog box.

Figure 3.25

Menu bar displays

Breakfast_Menus file selected

11 On the displayed menu bar, click **Edit**, and then at the bottom of the displayed menu, click **Invert Selection**.

> In the file list, all of the files *except* the Breakfast_Menus file are selected. This command is not available from the toolbar, although you could, of course, simply select all the files, hold down [Ctrl], and click those that you do not want to include in the selection.
>
> As soon as you perform an action, the menu bar is hidden again and no longer displays.

12 **Close** 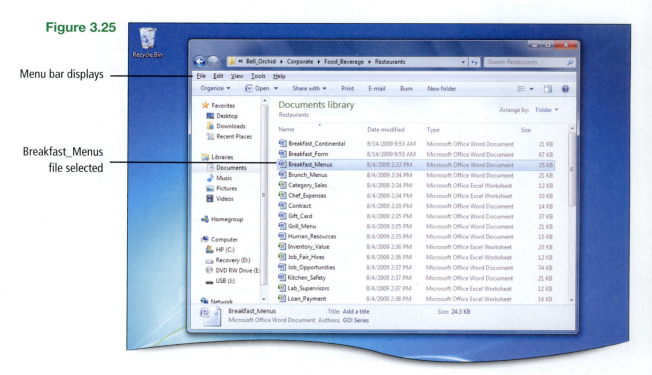 all open windows.

Objective 4 | Recognize File Types and Associate Files with Programs

A *file name extension* is a set of characters that helps Windows 7 understand what kind of information is in a file and what program should open it. A *program* is a set of instructions that a computer uses to perform a specific task, such as word processing, accounting, or data management. A program is also commonly referred to as an *application*.

A file name extension appears at the end of the file name, following a period. In the file name *Address_List.xlsx*, the extension is *xlsx*, which indicates to Windows 7 that this is an Excel 2007 or Excel 2010 file.

Activity 3.07 | Recognizing File Types and Associating Files with Programs

1 From the **Windows Explorer Jump List**, display the **Bell_Orchid** folder, and then navigate to **Bell_Orchid ▶ Corporate ▶ Food_Beverage**.

2 In the file list, click to select the Word file **CO_FB_Banquet_Contract**, and then on the toolbar, notice that the **Open** button displays the Word icon. Compare your screen with Figure 3.26.

Figure 3.26
Path displays in address bar

Open button on toolbar displays Word icon

Word file selected in file list

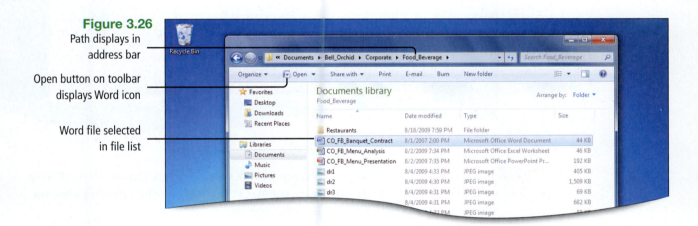

3 On the toolbar, point to the **Open button arrow** to display the ScreenTip *More options*, and then click the arrow.

The Open button is an example of a *split button*; that is, when you point to the button, there are two parts—the arrow that displays a menu, and the part of the button with the command name, which will perform the command.

When you open a file from the file list, Windows 7 uses the file extension of the file to determine which program to use to open the file. For most files, such as a Word document, Windows 7 not only determines which program to use to open the file, but also displays the icon representing the program on the toolbar.

You can see by the icon which program will be used to open the file. If you are unfamiliar with the icon, click the Open button *arrow* to display the name of the program that will open the file.

4 On the displayed menu, click **Choose default program**, and then compare your screen with Figure 3.27.

> The Open with dialog box displays. Here you can view the file extension for a file. For a file created in Microsoft Word 2007 or Word 2010, the file extension is *.docx*. In this dialog box, Windows 7 indicates and selects the recommended program to use.

> For most files, you will probably open the file in the program in which it was created.

Figure 3.27

Open with dialog box

File name with extension

Always use the selected program to open this kind of file check box

5 In the lower right corner of the **Open with** dialog box, click **Cancel**. In the **file list**, select the file **CO_FB_Menu_Presentation**. On the toolbar, click the **Open button arrow**, and then click **Choose default program**.

> Here you can see that the file extension for a file created with Microsoft PowerPoint 2007 or PowerPoint 2010 is *.pptx*.

6 Click **Cancel** to close the dialog box. On the toolbar, click **Organize**, and then click **Folder and search options**. In the displayed **Folder Options** dialog box, click the **View tab**.

7 Under **Advanced settings**, locate the **Hide extensions for known file types** setting, and then click to clear—remove the check mark from—the check box. Click **OK**. In the **Food_Beverage** folder window, in the **file list**, point to the **Name** column heading, right-click, and then click **Size Column to Fit**. Compare your screen with Figure 3.28.

> By default, Windows 7 hides file name extensions to make file names easier to read. If for any reason you need to do so, you can choose to make extensions visible by changing the default setting in the Folder Options dialog box.
>
> On your screen, you can see that displaying the file extensions results in a list of file names that includes the file extensions.

Figure 3.28

Name column widened

File extensions display for each file name

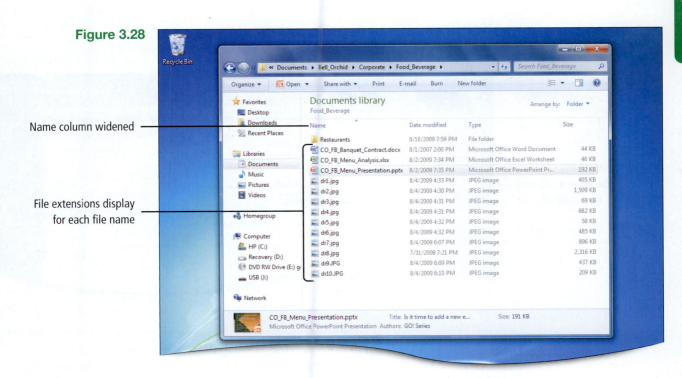

8 Start the **Snipping Tool** program, click the **New arrow**, and then click **Window Snip**. Point anywhere in the folder window and click one time. In the **Snipping Tool** mark-up window, click the **Save Snip** button.

9 Navigate to your chapter folder if necessary. Using your own name, name the file **Lastname_Firstname_3A_Extensions_Snip** be sure the file type is **JPEG**, and press Enter. **Close** the **Snipping Tool** mark-up window; leave your **Food_Beverage** folder window displayed. Hold this file until you finish Project 3A, and then submit this file as directed by your instructor.

10 Open the **Restaurants** folder window. Be sure the **View** is set to **Details** and that the **Name** column is sorted alphabetically. Right-click the **Name** column heading, and then click **Size Column to Fit**. Right-click the **Type** column heading, and then click **Size Column to Fit**.

> Because the Type column displays in a folder window in Details view, and because file names commonly display an identifying icon, for most individuals, there is probably no need to display the file extensions.

11 Click to select the Word file **Brunch_Menus.docx**, and then click the file again to select the file name. Notice that only the file name, and not the file extension is selected. Compare your screen with Figure 3.29.

> Usually, file extensions should *not* be changed, because you might not be able to open or edit the file after doing so. Because Windows 7 keeps track of which file is associated with which program—referred to as the *file association*—you do not have to be concerned about typing a file extension when you name a new file.
>
> Here you can see that even if you choose to display file extensions, Windows 7 will help you avoid changing the file extension by only highlighting the portion of the name that you would normally rename.

Restaurants folder window

Figure 3.29

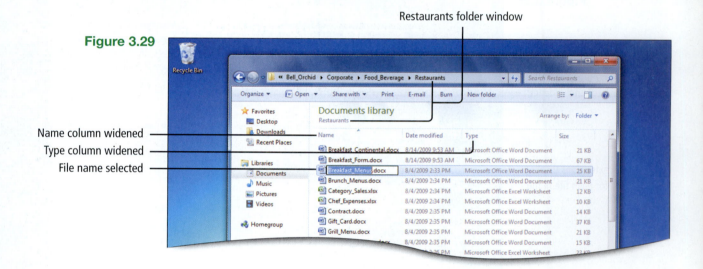

Name column widened

Type column widened

File name selected

Note | Sometimes It Is Useful to Change a File Extension

There are times when it is useful to change a file extension; for example, when you want to change a text file (.txt) to an HTML file (.htm) so that you can view it in a Web browser. Delete the file extension and type the new one. Windows 7 will warn you that changing the file name extension might cause the file to stop working properly. Click Yes if you are certain that the extension you typed is appropriate for your file.

---

12 On the toolbar, click the **Organize** button, and then click **Folder and search options**. In the displayed **Folder Options** dialog box, click the **View tab**, and then in the lower right, click **Restore Defaults** to reselect the **Hide extensions for known file types** check box. Click **OK**.

> In the file list of the Restaurants folder window, the file extensions no longer display; they are hidden.

13 In the **address bar**, to the right of **Corporate**, click ▶, and then from the displayed list, click **Information_Technology**. Display the **Future_Hotels** folder window.

14 Select the JPEG file **Italy**. On the toolbar, click the **Preview button arrow**, and then click **Choose default program**. Compare your screen with Figure 3.30.

> When you select an image file, the Open button might display the word *Open* or *Preview* or *Edit*, depending on the default program.

> Photographs differ from other files because there may be two or more programs on your computer that can display them.

> The default program to view a photo in Windows 7 is Windows Photo Viewer. On the computer at which you are working, this default may have been changed.

File extension *.jpg*   Browse button

Figure 3.30

Future_Hotels folder window

Preview button on toolbar (your icon may vary)

List of programs associated with a JPEG image (yours may vary)

Windows Photo Viewer selected (your selected program may vary)

Always use the selected program to open this kind of file selected

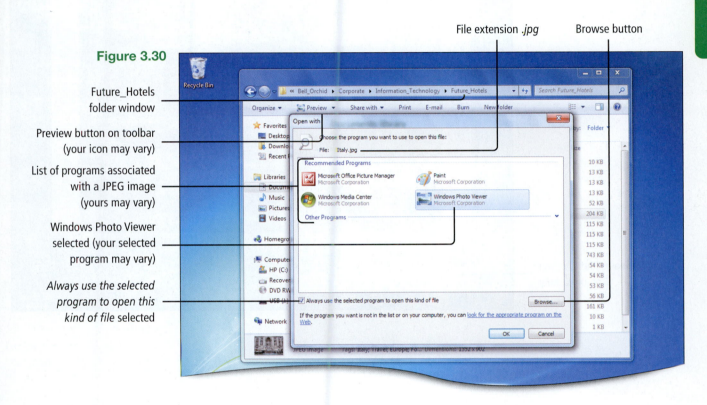

15 Under **Recommended Programs**, click **Paint** (or some other program if Paint is not available) and then click **OK**. Wait for the picture to display. If necessary, on the taskbar, click the **Paint** button to make the window active. **Close** the **Italy - Paint** window.

16 In the **file list**, be sure the **Italy** JPG file is still selected, and then notice on the **toolbar**, that the **Edit** button displays with the **Paint** program icon.

17 On the toolbar, click the **Edit button arrow**, click **Choose default program**, and then at the bottom of the **Open with** dialog box, notice that the check box **Always use the selected program to open this kind of file** is selected. Notice also that a **Browse** button displays in the lower right.

> If this check box is selected, then a program that you select in this dialog box will become the default program to open this file. If you need to select a program that is not listed, you can click the Browse button to open the Program Files folder on your computer and select an appropriate program.

18 Under **Recommended Programs**, click **Windows Photo Viewer** and then click **OK**. Compare your screen with Figure 3.31.

The picture displays in Windows Photo Viewer.

Figure 3.31

Italy picture displays in Windows Photo Viewer

Windows Photo Viewer icon on taskbar

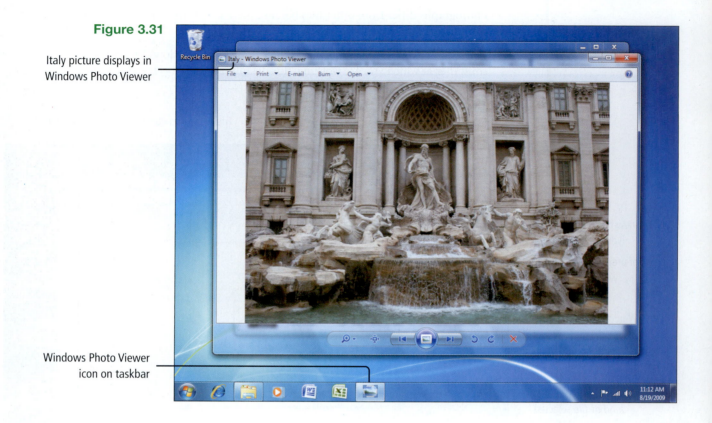

19 **Close** all open windows. Display the **Start** menu 🪟, and then on the right, click **Default Programs**. Click **Associate a file type or protocol with a program**, and then compare your screen with Figure 3.32.

> The Set Associations window displays. From the Start menu, the Default Programs command opens the Default Programs window of the Control Panel. In the Set Associations window, you can scroll to view a list of the many types of files that you might work with on your computer, and you can also change the program associated with a specific type of file.

Figure 3.32

Set Associations window
(your list may vary)

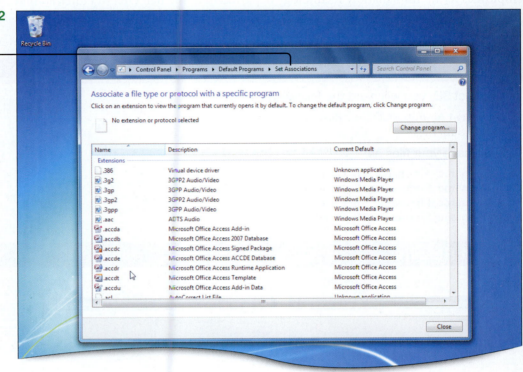

20 Display the **Documents** folder window, and then delete the **Bell_Orchid** folder. Unpin **Bell_Orchid** from the **Windows Explorer Jump List**. **Close** all open windows.

More Knowledge | What if the wrong program loads a file or if no program will open a file?

In most instances, when you open a file from a folder window, Windows 7 automatically knows which program should open the file because of the file extension. If a program other than the one you intended opens your file, close the program, display the folder window, right-click the file, click Open with, and then in the displayed dialog box, use the techniques you have practiced to set a default program for this type of file. Alternatively, change the default in the Set Associations window of the Control Panel.

For example, different brands of media players are sometimes installed on new computers, and when you open a music file, a program that is not your program of choice might be set as the default. If no program will open your file, Windows 7 provides a dialog box from which you can search the Web to find an appropriate program if one is available. If you cannot find a program to open your file, you will have to check with whoever gave you the file and possibly purchase the program with which it is associated. It is not recommended that you try to open any file unless it came from a trusted source or was created on your own computer.

End **You have completed Project 3A**

Project 3B Using Advanced Search Techniques

Project Activities

In Activities 3.08 through 3.13 you will train with Steven Ramos and Barbara Hewitt, employees in the Information Technology department at the Bell Orchid Hotel, so that you will be able to use advanced search techniques. You will capture screens that look similar to Figure 3.33.

Project Files

For Project 3B, you will need the following files:

Student Resource CD (or a flash drive containing these files)
New Snip files

You will save your files as:

Lastname_Firstname_3B_Garden_Snip
Lastname_Firstname_3B_Natural_Snip
Lastname_Firstname_3B_Custom_Snip
Lastname_Firstname_3B_Saved_Search_Snip

Project Results

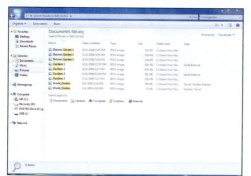
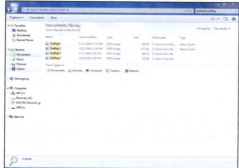
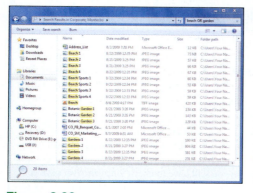
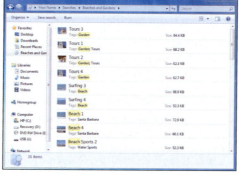

Figure 3.33
Project 3B Advanced Search Techniques

Objective 5 | Filter Searches in the Search Box

Your documents, music, video, photos, and e-mail messages are created, stored, and accessed in electronic form on your computer, resulting in an ever-increasing number of files. Additionally, each year the storage capacity of computer hard drives increases substantially. Thus, it becomes harder to keep track of your computer files, regardless of how careful you are when organizing your files in a folder structure.

Rely on Windows 7's Search features to help you find what you are looking for. If you can remember any detail about a file or a saved e-mail message that you need to access—for example, when it was created or some of its content—Windows 7 can find it for you quickly. Additionally, Windows 7 can help you visualize your files by arranging them in various ways; for example, by date or by author name.

Recall that every Windows Explorer window—folder windows, Control Panel, and so on—contains a search box in which you can enter part of a word, a complete word, or a phrase. The search feature immediately searches file names, *file properties*—also called *metadata*—and text within each file and then returns results instantly. File properties display information about your files, such as the name of the author and the date that the file was last modified. Metadata is the data that describes other data. For example, the collective group of a file's properties, such as its title, subject, author, and file size, comprise that file's metadata.

Three features define the search capabilities in Windows 7:

- *Search is everywhere.* You are never more than a few keystrokes away from what you are looking for, because a search box displays in every window and in the Start menu.

- *Search is fast.* Recall that Windows 7 produces search results almost instantly because it employs an *index*, which is a collection of detailed information about the files on your computer. When you start a search, Windows 7 searches this summary information in the index rather than searching file by file on your hard disk drive.

- *Any search can be saved.* You can save any search that you conduct and then rerun that search. The results will include any new files that meet the search criteria since the last time the search was conducted. In this manner, the search that you rerun is said to be *live*.

Activity 3.08 | Creating and Adding Tags

Recall that a *tag* is a property that you create and add to a file. Tags help you to find and organize your files, because you can include a tag in a search of your files.

1 Copy *two* folders to your **Documents** folder as follows: First, if necessary, *delete* the Bell_Orchid folder from your Documents folder—for this project you will need a new copy of the files. Insert the Student Resource CD or other device that contains the student files that accompany this textbook. By using the **Send to** command that you practiced in Activity 2.1 of Chapter 2, copy the **Bell_Orchid** folder from the Student Resource CD (or other device) to your **Documents** folder. Leave the window open.

2 On your Student Resource CD (or other device) navigate to **Chapter_Files ▶ Chapter_03**. Right-click the **Montecito** folder, point to **Send to**, and then click **Documents**.

3 When the copy operation is complete, in the **navigation pane**, under **Libraries**, click **Documents** to display your **Documents** folder window.

4 Point to the **Montecito** folder and drag it into the **Bell_Orchid** folder; release the mouse button when the ScreenTip *Move to Bell_Orchid* displays, as shown in Figure 3.34.

Alternatively, you could use any other method you have practiced to move this folder into the Bell_Orchid folder.

Figure 3.34

Documents folder window —

Bell_Orchid folder —

ScreenTip indicates *Montecito* folder being moved into *Bell_ Orchid* folder

5 Drag the **Bell_Orchid** folder onto the **Windows Explorer** icon on the taskbar to pin it to the **Jump List**. Compare your screen with Figure 3.35.

Because you will be displaying the Bell_Orchid folder window numerous times in this project, pinning the Bell_Orchid folder to the Jump List will increase your efficiency by reducing the number of clicks necessary to display the folder window.

Recall that pinning locations like this one to the Jump List, and then deleting them when they are no longer useful to you, is one of the methods by which you can personalize your computing environment.

Figure 3.35

Jump List indicates Bell_ Orchid in Pinned area

Your list of locations will vary

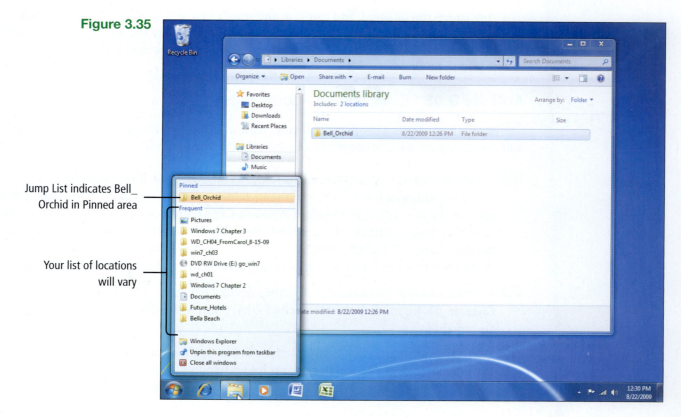

6 Navigate to **Bell_Orchid ▶ Montecito ▶ Activities** and then in the **file list**, right-click the Word file **Fishing**. At the bottom of the shortcut menu, click **Properties**

7 In the **Fishing Properties** dialog box, click the **Details tab**, under **Description**, click **Tags**, and then type **Fishing** Compare your screen with Figure 3.36.

Figure 3.36

Address bar displays path

Fishing Properties dialog box

Details tab

Fishing tag added to file

Tags area

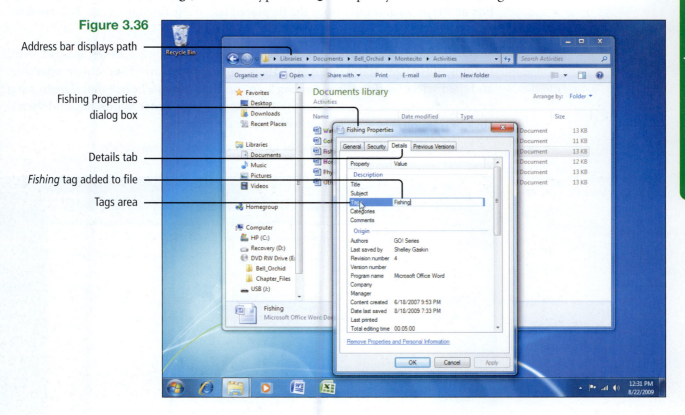

8 Click **OK** to add the tag and close the dialog box. In the **file list**, right-click the Word file **Golf**, and then use the technique you just practiced to add the tag **Golf**

9 Right-click the file **Other_Sports** and add the tag **Volleyball** Right-click the file **Water_Sports** and add the tag **Water Sports**

> **Note** | Adding Tags to Multiple Word Files
>
> You can select a group of Word documents, right-click any of the selected files, click Properties, click the Details tab, and then add the same tag to the selected group.

10 On the **address bar**, to the right of **Montecito**, click ▶, and then from the list click **Photos** to display this folder window. Select the file **Fly Fishing 1**, and then at the bottom of the window, in the **Details pane**, click in the **Tags** box. Begin typing **Fi** and then when the list of possible tags displays, click the **Fishing** check box. On the right end of the **Details pane**, click the **Save** button.

After a tag is created, you can select it from a list in this manner. Recall that for picture files, you can modify tags directly in the Details pane.

> **Alert!** | Tags Can Vary Depending on Recent Use of Your Computer
>
> The list of possible tags that displays can vary depending on previous usage of the computer at which you are working. Pictures on the computer that have been downloaded from other sources might have tags that will display on the list.

11 Using the technique you just practiced, locate the files **Golf 1** and **Golf 2** and add the **Golf** tag to both files—as soon as you begin typing you will be able to select the tag from a list and then click the **Save** button.

12 Scroll up as necessary, select the file **Beach Sports 3**, hold down Ctrl, and then select **Beach Sports 4**. In the **Details pane**, notice that *2 items* are selected. Click in the **Tags** box and type **Vo** and then from the displayed list of existing tags, click **Volleyball** to add this tag to both files—click **Save**.

13 Select the file **Beach Sports 1**, hold down Ctrl and select the file **Beach Sports 2**. While holding down Ctrl, scroll down with the scroll bar so the two files remain selected, and then select **Surfing 1**, and **Surfing 2**. In the **Details pane**, notice that *4 items selected* is indicated. Release Ctrl, click in the **Tags** box, add the **Water Sports** tag, and then click **Save**. Compare your screen with Figure 3.37.

Use the Ctrl key to select a group of files and add the same tag to each.

Figure 3.37

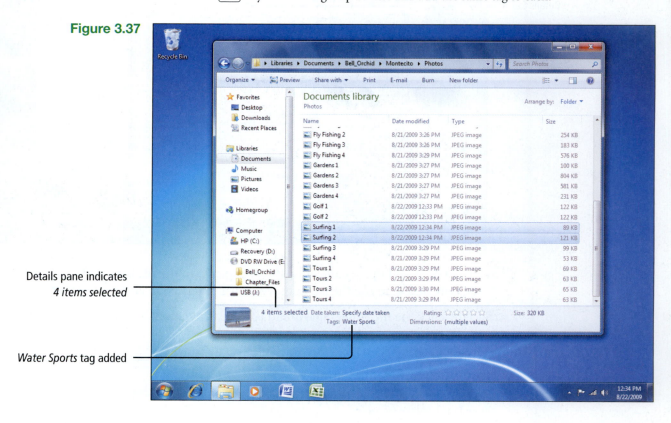

Details pane indicates
4 items selected

Water Sports tag added

14 Select the files **Tours 1** and **Tours 2**. Add the tag **Tours** to these two files—the tag might already exist on other files; if so you will be able to select it from the displayed list. Click **Save**.

15 By using the techniques you have just practiced, add the tag **Santa Barbara** to the following four files: **Beach 1**, **Beach 4**, **Gardens 1** and **Gardens 3** and then click **Save**.

16 Navigate to **Montecito ▶ Tours**. Point to the Word file **Tours** and right-click. From the shortcut menu, click **Properties**, and then on the **Details tab**, add the tag **Tours**

Recall that the list of possible tags that displays will vary depending on previous usage of your computer.

17 Close all open windows.

Activity 3.09 | Filtering a Search by Using Properties

Windows 7 will search all of the files in the current folder window for whatever you type in the search box. In the indexed locations, it will search by looking in the file name, file contents, and file properties—including tags. For example, if you type *April*, Windows 7 will find any file that contains *April* in the file name, in the file contents, in the tag, or authored by someone named *April*.

If you want to search more selectively, you can filter your search in the search box by specifying which file property to search. To filter by a file property, separate the name of the property and the search term with a colon.

1 On the taskbar, drag the **Windows Explorer** button 🔲 up slightly into the desktop to display the **Jump List**, and then under **Pinned**, click **Bell_Orchid**. In the upper right corner, click in the **search** box, and then type **water**

> Recall that Windows 7 can perform fast searches because the search is conducted on the *index*, not on each file on the hard disk drive. The index is a collection of detailed information about the files on your computer, which Windows 7 keeps track of and stores.
>
> In the displayed Search Results window, a large number of files have one or more properties that match the criteria *water*. Your Documents folder is included in the ***Indexed locations***, which includes *all* of the folders in your personal folder (Documents, Pictures, and so on), e-mail, and offline files if any.
>
> In indexed locations, Windows 7 searches file names and contents; that is, it will look for matches to your search term in file names, folder names, file properties including tags, folder properties, and in the actual text content of files.
>
> In non-indexed locations, Windows 7 searches only file names and folder names.

2 Be sure the **View** 🔳 is **Details** and the **Name** column is sorted alphabetically.

3 In the **search** box, click ✕ to clear the search. **Maximize** 🔲 the window.

4 In the **search** box, type **tag:water**

5 In the **file list**, point to any of the column headings, right-click, and then click **Tags** to add this column to the **file list**. Right-click the **Tags** column heading, and then click **Size Column to Fit**. Compare your screen with Figure 3.38.

You can filter a search by searching only on the tags attached to files by typing *tag:* in the search box followed by your search criteria. Within all the subfolders in the Bell_Orchid folder, eight items have *water* as part of their tag, and in the Tags column, *water* is highlighted.

Details view, sorted alphabetically by Name column   Property *Tags* displays the search criteria in yellow   Tags column displayed and sized to fit   Filtered search criteria

Figure 3.38

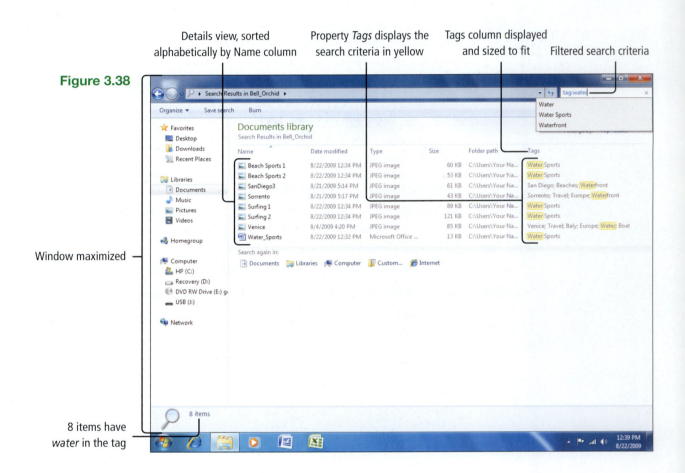

Window maximized

8 items have *water* in the tag

6 In the list of files that matched the search criteria, look at the tag for the files **SanDiego3** and **Sorrento**. Notice that *Waterfront* is among the tags attached to these two files, and thus this file is considered a match.

By default, Windows 7 uses *partial matching*—matching to part of a word or phrase rather than to whole words. Thus, *waterfront* is a match for the criteria *water*. If you prefer to search by whole words only, you can change this option.

7 In the **search** box, click ☒ to clear the search, and then type **tag:water sports**

Five items display in the Search Results folder window. The files that match the criteria are narrowed to those in the Bell_Orchid folder that have the exact tag *water sports*. Additionally, the word *Sports* is highlighted in yellow in the file names where it occurs.

8 Clear ☒ the **search** box, and then type **tag:golf** Compare your screen with Figure 3.39. Three files display.

Figure 3.39

Figure 3.39

Search criteria

Three items display

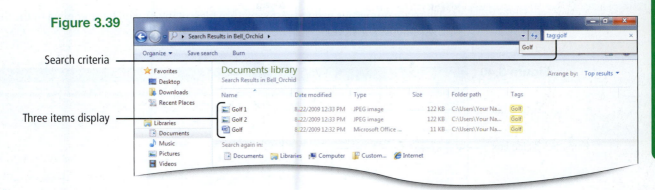

9 Clear ☒ the **search** box, type **name:surfing**

Four files that contain *surfing* in the file name display. *Name* is a property that you can use as criteria in a filtered search. The Name filter searches only the file names.

10 Clear ☒ the **search** box, type **name:garden**

Nine files contain *garden* somewhere in the file name.

11 Start 🪟 the **Snipping Tool** program, click the **New arrow**, and then click **Window Snip**. Click anywhere in the folder window, and then in the **Snipping Tool** mark-up window, click the **Save Snip** button 💾. In the displayed **Save As** dialog box, if necessary navigate to your **Windows 7 Chapter 3** folder on your USB flash drive and click to select it so that it displays in the address bar.

12 Using your own name, name the file **Lastname_Firstname_3B_Garden_Snip** be sure the file type is **JPEG**, and press Enter. **Close** ❌ the **Snipping Tool** mark-up window. Hold this file until you finish Project 3B, and then submit this file as directed by your instructor.

13 Clear ☒ the **search** box, and then type **beach** Notice the number of files that display (27), and then **Clear** ☒ the **search** box. Type **name:beach** and notice that only *9 items* contain the word *beach* in the file name.

When searching for files, keep in mind that when searching in indexed locations, typing a search term will search file names, folder names, file properties, folder properties, and in the actual text content of files.

To narrow the search for a tag, a file name, or some other property, type the name of the property followed by a colon and then type the search term.

14 Clear ⊠ the **search** box, and then type **camera:canon** In the list of files that match the search criteria, right-click the file **Gardens 3**, and then on the shortcut menu, click **Properties**. Click the **Details tab**, drag the scroll box down about half way, and then compare your screen with Figure 3.40.

> There are numerous properties for picture files, many of which are applied to the file by the camera's software.

Figure 3.40

Details tab

Properties dialog box

Scroll box

Camera maker indicates *Canon*

Camera properties

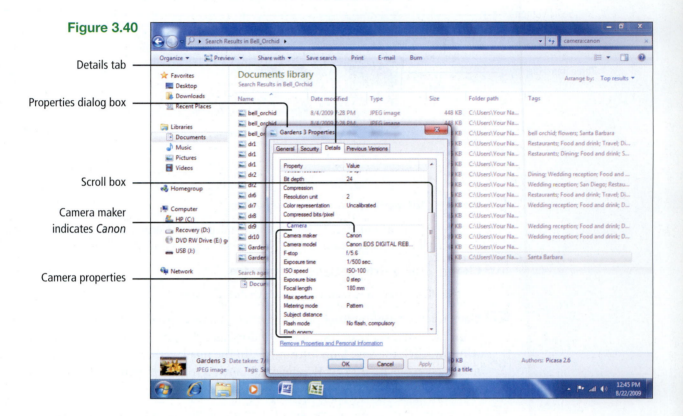

15 At the bottom of the **Gardens 3 Properties** dialog box, click **Cancel**. In the **file list**, point to the column heading **Name**, and then right-click. At the bottom of the shortcut menu, click **More**. Take a moment to scroll down the list and examine the properties that might be assigned to a file by one or more software programs.

> CDs and DVDs usually have various tags so that you can search by Artist or Genre (for example Jazz or Classical). Software programs such as those from a digital camera or a video camera commonly attach numerous properties to a file to make it easy to find the files based on specific technical details such as *F-stop*.

> Likewise, properties such as *Cell phone* and *Business phone* are assigned by contact management programs such as Microsoft Outlook.

16 Close ❌ the **Choose Details** dialog box, and then **Clear** ⊠ the **search** box. Leave the window open.

More Knowledge | What's the Difference Between a Tag and a Property?

A tag is simply another type of property, but one that *you* create and add to a file. Whereas most file properties are added by either Windows 7 or the software that creates the file, a tag is probably the most useful property, because you can add tags that contain words or phrases that are meaningful to you.

In the future, more software programs will enable you to add tags at the time you create and save your file, which will enable you to rely more on tag searches to find what you are looking for.

Activity 3.10 | Filtering a Search by Using Boolean Operators, Quotes, and Natural Language

In addition to filtering by various properties, you can also filter a search by using the *Boolean operators* AND, OR, and NOT. The term Boolean is taken from the name George Boole, who was a 19th century mathematician. Boole developed the mathematics of logic that govern the logical functions—true and false. A statement using Boolean operators expresses a condition that is either true or false.

You can also use quotes to find an exact phrase in a search or enable the *natural language* feature of Windows 7. If you enable a natural language search, you can perform searches in a simpler way, without using colons and without the need to enter any Boolean operators.

1 If necessary Clear ⌧ the **search** box, and then type **shareholders AND orlando**

Boolean filters such as AND must be typed in all uppercase letters. The *AND filter* finds files that contain both the word *shareholders* and the word *orlando*—even if those words are not next to each other.

As you type *shareholders*, Windows 7 begins filtering based on the search term found in file names, folder names, file properties, folder properties, and in the actual text content of files. After you narrow the search by typing *AND orlando*, the search is narrowed down to one file.

You can see that if you know something about the contents or name of the file you are looking for, it might be easier to search for the file than to navigate your folder structure.

Note | Windows 7 Search Ignores Capitalization

You need not capitalize to have Windows 7 find your search term. For example, you can type *orlando* instead of *Orlando*. However, you must use uppercase letters for the Boolean operators.

---

2 Clear ⌧ the **search** box, and then type **shareholders NOT orlando** Be sure the view is **Details** and be sure the list is in alphabetical order by **Name**. Compare your screen with Figure 3.41.

The *NOT filter* finds files that contain the word *shareholders* but that do not contain the word *orlando*.

Figure 3.41

Search criteria

List of files that contain *shareholders* but not *orlando* (7 items display)

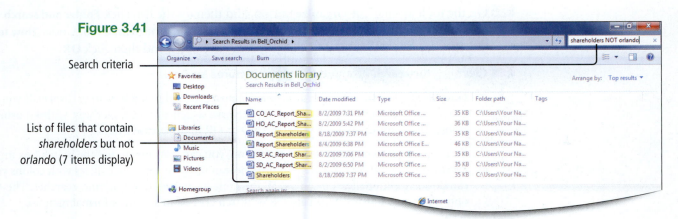

3 Clear ⌧ the **search** box, and then type **shareholders OR orlando**

The *OR filter* finds files that contain either the word *shareholders* or the word *orlando*. Because either of the conditions can be present, OR will result in a larger number of results, but will assist you in narrowing your search nonetheless.

4 **Clear** ☒ the **search** box, and then including the quote marks, type **"teenage restaurant workers"**

One file—*Kitchen_Safety*— displays. The exact phrase *teenage restaurant workers* is contained within the text of this document.

The *quotes filter* finds files that contain the exact phrase placed within the quotes. You can see that if you know just a little about what you are looking for, filtered searches can help you find files quickly without navigating a folder structure.

5 **Clear** ☒ the **search** box, type **type:pptx** and notice that only PowerPoint files display.

File type is one of the properties on which you can search. You can use the file extension associated with a program as the search criteria, or you can type the program name, for example *PowerPoint*.

6 Press Spacebar one time, and then continue typing so that the **search** box criteria indicates **type:pptx AND name:safety** Compare your screen with Figure 3.42.

In this manner, you can combine different property filters with Boolean filters to locate a file. Five files meet this criteria; that is, each file is a PowerPoint file and contains the word *safety* in the file name.

Figure 3.42

Search criteria

PowerPoint presentations containing *safety* in the file name

7 **Clear** ☒ the **search** box, and then type **pictures surfing** Notice that no files matching the search criteria display.

8 On the toolbar, click the **Organize** button, and then on the list, click **Folder and search options**. In the displayed **Folder Options** dialog box, click the **Search tab**. Under **How to search**, select the **Use natural language search** check box, and then click **OK**.

9 **Clear** ☒ the **search** box, and then type **pictures surfing**

Four files that contain the word *surfing* as a property and that are *pictures* display. If you enable natural language search, you can perform searches in a simpler way, without using colons and without the need to enter AND or OR in uppercase letters.

Even with natural language search turned on, you can continue to use the search box in *exactly* the same way. If you want to use Boolean filters or introduce filters with colons you can do so. Additionally, you can use all the same properties to refine your searches. The only difference is that you can also enter search criteria in a more informal manner.

10 **Start** 🪟 the **Snipping Tool** program, click the **New arrow**, and then click **Window Snip**. Click anywhere in the folder window. In the **Snipping Tool** mark-up window, click the **Save Snip** button 💾. In the displayed **Save As** dialog box, if necessary navigate to your **Windows 7 Chapter 3** folder on your USB flash drive and click to select it so that it displays in the address bar.

11 Using your own name, name the file **Lastname_Firstname_3B_Natural_Snip** be sure the file type is **JPEG**, and press ⏎Enter. **Close** ❎ the **Snipping Tool** mark-up window. Hold this file until you finish Project 3B, and then submit this file as directed by your instructor.

12 On the toolbar, click the **Organize** button, click **Folder and search options**, click the **Search tab**, and then in the lower right corner, click **Restore Defaults**. Click **OK** to close the dialog box.

> On your own computer, you might want to leave the natural language feature enabled.

13 In the **file list**, point to any column heading, right-click, and then click to deselect the **Tags** checkbox.

14 In the upper right corner of the window, click the **Restore Down** button 🔳 to redisplay the window in its previous size, and then **Close** ❎ all open windows.

Objective 6 | Search by Using the Search Folder

The search box searches only the current view—the files that are in the current folder, including all the subfolders in that folder. If you search and do not find what you are looking for, it is possible that you began your search in the wrong folder.

For example, if you are looking for a video with the tag *Grand Canyon* that is stored in your Videos library, you will not find it by looking in your Documents library. Instead use the *Search folder*. The Search folder conducts a search in the entire set of indexed locations, which includes your personal folder with all of its libraries and any offline files. The Search folder is a good choice for searches whenever you:

- Do not know where a file or folder is located and you want to look in many locations at once; for example, in Documents and in Pictures.

- Want to search in two or more folders, but not *all* folders, at the same level within a hierarchy; for example, in Orlando and Honolulu but not in the other Bell_Orchid locations.

Activity 3.11 | Searching from the Search Folder

1 Hold down  and press F. Compare your screen with Figure 3.43.

The Search folder displays and the insertion point is blinking in the search box. Here you can apply a filter based on *Kind*—for example a game or an instant message or a music file.

When the Search folder is displayed in this manner—by pressing ⊞ + F—the search will be conducted on the set of locations called *indexed locations*, which includes *all* of the folders in your personal folder (Documents, Pictures, and so on) and offline files if any.

Recall that offline files refer to files from a network that have been copied to your hard disk drive for easy access when you are not connected to that network. This happens more typically in large organizations where you have access to files stored on a network.

Recall that in indexed locations, Windows 7 searches file names and contents; that is, it will look for matches to your search term in file names, folder names, file properties, folder properties, and in the actual text content of files. In non-indexed locations, Windows 7 searches only file names and folder names.

Figure 3.43

Search folder

To begin, type in the search box

2 With the insertion point blinking in the **search** box, type **water** click in the Search box to display the filter box, and then under **Add a search filter**, click **Kind**. Compare your screen with Figure 3.44.

A list of various kinds of items by which you can filter the search displays.

Figure 3.44

List of kinds of items to filter by

Alert! | Your Search Results May Differ From Those Shown

A search conducted in the *indexed locations* may display different results than the figures in this textbook, because you have additional files in your personal folder.

---

3 On the displayed list, scroll down and click **Picture**. Compare your screen with Figure 3.45.

By clicking one of the Kind filters, you can narrow the search results by certain kinds of files, for example pictures or e-mail. Filtering results in this manner makes it easier to find specific files.

Figure 3.45

Picture filter selected

Only pictures that contain the property *water* display (your list may vary)

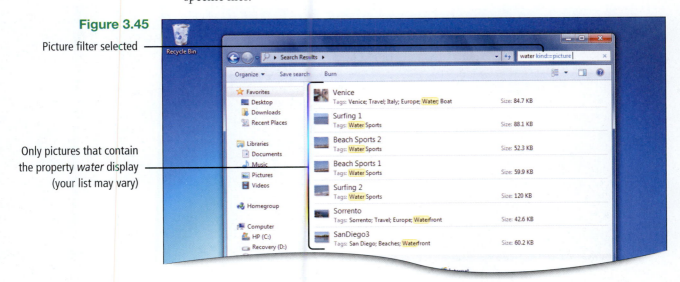

4 **Close** ![close button] the **Search Results** window and any other open windows.

Activity 3.12 | Using Custom Search

To customize a search, use the Custom button in any Search Results folder.

1 On the taskbar, drag the **Windows Explorer** ![icon] icon into the desktop, and then on the **Jump List**, under **Pinned**, click **Bell_Orchid**.

2 Click in the **search** box, and then type **beach OR garden** Drag the scroll box to the bottom of the displayed results, and then compare your screen with Figure 3.46.

A total of 48 items in the Bell_Orchid folder contain the word *beach* or the word *garden* as a property. Recall that in indexed locations, the word might be part of the text of the file.

Figure 3.46

Search criteria

Search criteria in a file name highlighted in yellow

Details pane indicates *48 items* contain the search criteria

Scroll bar at bottom

Custom search button

3 At the bottom of the search results, under **Search again in**, click **Custom**. In the **Choose Search Location** dialog box, under **Change selected locations**, to the left of **Libraries**, click ▷ to expand the folder structure.

Use the *Custom search* to define a specific scope—range of locations—for your search.

4 To the left of **Documents**, click ▷. Expand ▷ **My Documents**, and then expand ▷ **Bell_Orchid**. Compare your screen with Figure 3.47.

Bell_Orchid expanded

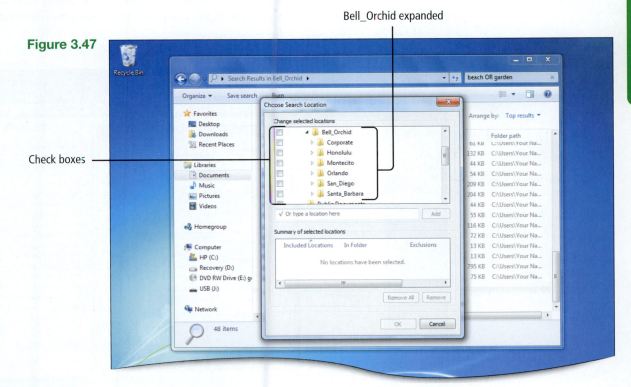

Figure 3.47

Check boxes

5 Under **Change selected locations**, in the column of check boxes along the left edge, click the **check box** for **Corporate**, and then notice that in the lower portion of the dialog box, under **Summary of selected locations**, the Corporate folder displays.

6 Click the **check box** for **Montecito**, and then compare your screen with Figure 3.48.

Under Summary of selected locations, the two folders that you selected display. Here you can select as many locations as you need. This is especially useful if you want to search in two folders at the same level of a hierarchy, for example in Corporate and Montecito but not in the other folders at this level. Or, you can select a number of different folders at various levels.

Figure 3.48

Two folders selected

Two selected folders display

OK button

7 Click **OK** to apply the search criteria to only the two selected folders. In the **Details pane**, notice that *29 items* in the Corporate and Montecito folders have the word *beach* or *garden* as a property. Compare your screen with Figure 3.49.

Figure 3.49

Scope of search results (Corporate and Montecito) indicated in address bar

Search criteria in a file name highlighted

Search criteria

8 Start <img> the **Snipping Tool** program, click the **New arrow**, and then click **Window Snip**. Click anywhere in the **Search Results** window. In the **Snipping Tool** mark-up window, click the **Save Snip** button. In the displayed **Save As** dialog box, if necessary navigate to your **Windows 7 Chapter 3** folder on your USB flash drive and click to select it so that it displays in the address bar.

9 Using your own name, name the file **Lastname_Firstname_3B_Custom_Snip** be sure the file type is **JPEG**, and press Enter. **Close** the **Snipping Tool** mark-up window. Hold this file until you finish Project 3B, and then submit this file as directed by your instructor.

10 *Do not close the Search Results window;* leave the **Search Results in Corporate; Montecito** search folder window open for the next activity.

More Knowledge | **Indexing an External Hard Drive Attached to Your Computer**

You have seen that searching locations that are *indexed* results in a fast search result. You can include folders from an external hard drive in a library, which means they will become one of the indexed locations. Connect the external hard drive to your computer, and be sure that it is recognized in the Computer window under Hard Disk Drives. If the device displays there, folders on the drive can be included in a library and indexed. Some USB flash drives also have this capability. Just plug the device in, and if it displays in the Computer window under Hard Disk Drives, its data can be included in a library. Navigate to and select the folder or folders on the external drive that you want to include in the library. On the toolbar, click Include in library, and then click the library name, for example Documents.

Objective 7 | Save a Search, Manage Search Behavior, and Manage the Index

After you have built a search, you can save it. When you save a search, you are saving its criteria, not its current results. After the search is saved, it becomes a virtual subfolder in the Searches folder in your personal folder.

You can configure options to control the behavior of the search engine itself and also to manage the index.

Activity 3.13 | Saving a Search, Managing Search Behavior, and Managing the Index

1 Be sure your **Search Results in Corporate; Montecito** custom search displays, and then on the toolbar, click the **Save search** button.

2 In the displayed **Save As** dialog box, in the **File name** box, name the search **Beaches and Gardens** Compare your screen with Figure 3.50.

> The Bell Orchid Hotels plan to collect more information about beaches and gardens to use in new marketing brochures, so they want to save the search.

Figure 3.50

Save As dialog box

Path displays Searches folder in your personal folder (your name will vary)

Previous saved searches display (your list will vary)

File name

Save button

3 Click the **Save** button. If a message displays that the file exists, click Yes to replace it.

4 **Close** ![X] all open windows. Open the **Bell_Orchid** folder window again, and then navigate to **Montecito ▶ Photos**.

5 By selecting the files and typing in the **Tags** box in the **Details pane**, add the tag **Beach** to the following files: **Surfing 3** and **Surfing 4**. Be sure to click the **Save** button at the right end of the **Details pane**.

6 Using the same technique, add the tag **Garden** to **Tours 1**, **Tours 2**, **Tours 3**, and **Tours 4**. **Close** ![X] the folder window.

7 On the taskbar, click the **Windows Explorer** button , and then in the **navigation pane**, under **Favorites**, click your **Beaches and Gardens** saved search. In the **Details pane**, notice that 35 items display. Compare your results with Figure 3.51.

Recall that when you save a search, you are saving its criteria, not its current results. Thus, each time you reopen the Search folder, Windows 7 reruns the search with the most current results.

Figure 3.51

Saved search in the Searches folder

New results of the search

8 **Start** 🏁 the **Snipping Tool** program, click the **New arrow**, and then click **Window Snip**. Click anywhere in the window. In the **Snipping Tool** mark-up window, click the **Save Snip** button 💾. In the displayed Save As dialog box, if necessary navigate to your **Windows 7 Chapter 3** folder on your USB flash drive and click to select it so that it displays in the address bar.

9 Using your own name, name the file **Lastname_Firstname_3B_Saved_Search_Snip** be sure the file type is **JPEG**, and press Enter. **Close** ❌ the **Snipping Tool** mark-up window. Hold this file until you finish Project 3B, and then submit this file as directed by your instructor.

10 On the toolbar, click the **Organize** button, and then click **Folder and search options**. In the **Folder Options** dialog box, click the **Search tab**.

Here you can manage how the Search feature behaves. You can make changes to what is searched, how the search is conducted, and include additional files and directories when searching non-indexed locations.

You will probably want to maintain the default settings, although you might decide to include the natural language search that you have already practiced.

11 At the bottom of the **Folder Options** dialog box, click **Cancel**.

12 Close ![X] all open windows. Click **Start** ![icon], and then on the right, click **Control Panel**. In the **search** box, type **indexing options**, and then in the results, click **Indexing Options**. Compare your screen with Figure 3.52.

At the top of this dialog box, you can see if your index is up to date. For example, if you just added a number of new folders and files—perhaps by copying them into your Documents folder from another source—you might have to wait a short time for the index to be complete.

Figure 3.52

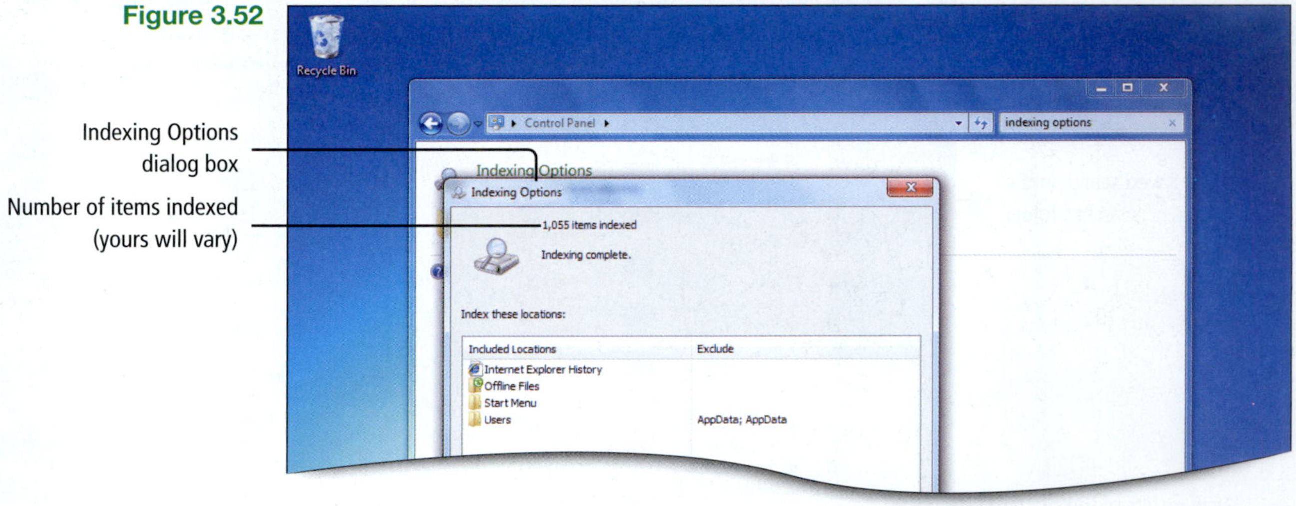

Indexing Options dialog box

Number of items indexed (yours will vary)

13 Close ![X] all open windows. Display the **Windows Explorer Jump List**, and unpin the **Bell_Orchid** folder. On the taskbar, click the **Windows Explorer** button, open the **Documents** library, and then delete the **Bell_Orchid** folder from the **Documents** library. In the **navigation pane**, delete the saved Search *Beaches and Gardens* from Favorites. Submit the four snip files from the project to your instructor as directed.

More Knowledge | Federated Search

In large organizations, files are commonly stored on large servers and managed by systems such as Microsoft SharePoint. If you have access to such files from your own computer, a technology called *Federated Search* enables you to search a remote server or Web service from Windows Explorer using the same techniques that you use to search for files that are stored on your own computer or in the libraries you have set up on your own computer.

End **You have completed Project 3B** ————————————————

Content-Based Assessments

Summary

In this chapter you practiced using the address bar and other navigation techniques to locate files when you are working outside of an application program. The Favorites area is another area from which you can easily navigate to your folders and files. You also practiced techniques to personalize how folders display on your computer and to personalize the view of a folder window by changing the arrangement. You set folder properties and associated files with programs.

Search is one of the most powerful features in Windows 7. By using the search feature efficiently, you are relieved from tediously drilling down into your folder structure to find files that you are looking for. In this chapter, you practiced advanced search techniques and observed how to manage the behavior of the search feature and the index.

Key Terms

Matching

Match each term in the second column with its correct definition in the first column. Write the letter of the term on the blank line in front of the correct definition.

_____ 1. A sequence or path of folders that leads to a specific file or folder.

_____ 2. Another term for a path.

_____ 3. A button on the address bar that depicts the location—library, disk drive, folder, and so on—that you are currently accessing.

_____ 4. A button on the address bar that displays a list of recently accessed locations; the current location is indicated by a check mark.

_____ 5. Locations that you frequently need to access to manage your computer including Libraries, Homegroup, your personal folder, Computer, Network, Control Panel, and Recycle Bin.

_____ 6. A folder that does not represent a physical location but rather contains the results of a search.

_____ 7. A folder option which, when applied, displays a small square box to the left of folders and files.

A Application

B Arrange by

C Base locations

D Check box feature

E Directory

F File association

G File name extension

H File properties

I Location icon

J Metadata

K Path

L Program

M Recent Pages

N Split button

O Virtual folder

Content-Based Assessments

_____ 8. In a folder window, a feature that enables you to arrange the items by Author, Date modified, Tag, Type, or Name; the default arrangement is Folder.

_____ 9. A set of characters at the end of a file name that helps Windows 7 understand what kind of information is in the file and what program should open the file.

_____ 10. A set of instructions that a computer uses to perform a specific task, such as word processing, accounting, or data management.

_____ 11. Another term for a program.

_____ 12. A button, for example on the toolbar, that when pointed to, displays in two parts—an arrow that displays a list and a button that starts the command.

_____ 13. The association between a file and the program that created the file.

_____ 14. Information about your files, such as the name of the author and the date that the file was last modified.

_____ 15. The data that describes other data; for example, the collective group of a file's properties, such as its title, subject, author, and file size.

Multiple Choice

Circle the correct answer.

1. A button with two parts—an arrow that displays a list and a button that starts the command—is a:
   A. dual button
   B. split button
   C. partial button

2. The relationship between a file and the program that created the file is referred to as the file:
   A. association
   B. application
   C. directory

3. Information about your files, such as the name of the author and the date that the file was last modified, is referred to as the file's:
   A. path
   B. metadata
   C. properties

4. The data that describes other data—tags, title, subject, author, and file size—is referred to as:
   A. properties
   B. extensions
   C. metadata

5. A collection of detailed information about the files on your computer that Windows 7 maintains for the purpose of conducting fast searches is the:
   A. directory
   B. index
   C. path

6. All of the locations in your personal folder (Documents, Pictures, and so on) and offline files, if any, that Windows 7 includes in a search are referred to as the indexed:
   A. locations
   B. folders
   C. filters

7. The terms AND, OR, and NOT that govern the logical functions and express a condition that is either true or false are referred to as Boolean:
   A. programs
   B. operators
   C. properties

8. When used in a search, the Boolean filter that finds files that contain both search terms, even if those terms are not next to each other, is the:
   A. AND filter
   B. NOT filter
   C. OR filter

9. When used in a search, the Boolean filter that finds files that contain the first word but that do not contain the second word is the:
   A. AND filter
   B. NOT filter
   C. OR filter

10. When used in a search, the Boolean filter that finds files that contain either search term is the:
   A. AND filter
   B. NOT filter
   C. OR filter

Apply **3A** skills from these Objectives:

1. Navigate by Using the Address Bar
2. Create and Navigate Favorites
3. Personalize the Display of Folders and Files
4. Recognize File Types and Associate Files with Programs

Skills Review | Project **3C** Using Advanced File Management Techniques

Project Files

For Project 3C, you will need the following files:

> **Student Resource CD (or a USB flash drive containing these files)**
> **win03_3C_Answer_Sheet (Word document)**

You will save your file as:

> **Lastname_Firstname_3C_Answer_Sheet**

Project Results

1 **Close** [x] all open windows. On the taskbar, click the **Windows Explorer** button. In the **navigation pane**, click the drive that contains the student files for this textbook, and then navigate to **Chapter_Files ▶ Chapter_03**. Double-click the Word file **win03_3C_Answer_Sheet** to open Word and display the document. Press F12 to display the **Save As** dialog box in Word, navigate to your **Windows 7 Chapter 3** folder, and then using your own name, save the document as **Lastname_Firstname_3C_Answer_Sheet** If necessary, click OK if a message regarding formats displays.

On the taskbar, click the **Word** button to minimize the window and leave your Word document accessible from the taskbar. **Close** the **Chapter_03** folder window. As you complete each step in this project, click the Word button on the taskbar to open the document, type your one-letter answer in the appropriate cell of the Word table, and then on the taskbar, click the **Word** button again to minimize the window for the next step.

Insert the Student Resource CD in the appropriate drive, and then copy the **Bell_Orchid** folder to your **Documents** folder—you will need a *new* copy for this project. Display your **Documents** folder, and then navigate to **Bell_Orchid ▶ Corporate ▶ Information_Technology ▶ Future_Hotels**. At the left end of the **address bar**, click the **location icon**. What is your result?

A. All of the files in the Future_Hotels folder are selected.

B. In the address bar, the path that describes the folder's location displays separated by backslashes and is highlighted.

C. The Documents folder window displays.

2 Press Esc. In the **address bar**, click **Corporate** to display this folder window. In the **address bar**, to the immediate right of the **location icon**, click ▶. What is your result?

A. A list of available base locations displays below the separator line.

B. A list of the subfolders within the Corporate folder displays.

C. The path that describes the folder's location displays and is highlighted.

3 Display the **Bell_Orchid** folder window. On the toolbar, click **New folder**, and then create a new folder named **Florida_Keys** Drag the **Florida_Keys** folder to become the first item under **Favorites**. Which of the following is true?

A. The Florida_Keys folder no longer displays in the file list.

B. The Florida_Keys folder window opens.

C. The Florida_Keys folder displays in the Favorites area with a buff-colored folder.

4 On the **toolbar**, click the **Organize** button, and then click **Folder and search options**. Click the **General tab**. Which of the following is true?

(Project 3C Using Advanced File Management Techniques continues on the next page)

Skills Review | Project **3C** Using Advanced File Management Techniques (continued)

A. On this tab, you can change folder behavior so that every folder opens in a new window.

B. On this tab, you can set programs to open with a single click.

C. On this tab, you can change folder behavior so that no folders display in the file list.

5 In the **Folder Options** dialog box, click the **View tab**. Which of the following settings can be adjusted on your computer?

A. Hiding or showing file extensions.

B. Displaying a folder in the view used when the folder was last displayed.

C. Both A and B.

6 **Close** the **Folder Options** dialog box. Navigate to **Corporate** ▶ **Information_Technology** ▶ **Future_Hotels**. Be sure the view is **Details**, and then **Arrange** the files by **Type**. How many different stacks display?

A. Four

B. Five

C. Six

7 How many files are in the **PowerPoint** stack?

A. Three

B. Four

C. Five

8 **Arrange** the files by **Tag**. How many files are in the **Garden** stack?

A. Two

B. Three

C. Four

9 **Arrange** the files by **Folder**, and then navigate to **Corporate** ▶ **Food_Beverage**. In the **file list**, right-click the **Restaurants** folder, and then click **Properties**. How many *folders* are in the **Restaurants** folder?

A. 35

B. 0

C. 2

10 Click the **Cancel** button. In the **file list**, select the file **CO_FB_Menu_Presentation**. On the **toolbar**, click the **Open button arrow**, and then click **Choose default program**. What is the file extension for this file?

A. .docx

B. .ppt

C. .pptx

Click the **Cancel** button, under **Favorites**, right-click **Florida_Keys** and click **Remove**. Delete the **Bell_Orchid** folder in the **Documents** window. Be sure you have typed all of your answers in your Word document. **Save** and **Close** your Word document, and submit as directed by your instructor. **Close** all open windows.

End **You have completed Project 3C** _____

Content-Based Assessments

Apply **3B** skills from these Objectives:

5 Filter Searches in the Search Box

6 Search by Using the Search Folder

7 Save a Search, Manage Search Behavior, and Manage the Index

Skills Review | Project **3D** Using Advanced Search Techniques

Project Files

For Project 3D, you will need the following files:

Student Resource CD (or a USB flash drive containing these files)
win03_3D_Answer_Sheet (Word document)

You will save your file as:

Lastname_Firstname_3D_Answer_Sheet

Project Results

1 Close all open windows. On the taskbar, click the **Windows Explorer** button. In the **navigation pane**, click the drive that contains the student files for this textbook, and then navigate to **Chapter_Files ▶ Chapter_03**. Double-click the Word file **win03_3D_Answer_Sheet** to open Word and display the document. Press F12 to display the **Save As** dialog box in Word, navigate to your **Windows 7 Chapter 3** folder, and then using your own name, save the document as **Lastname_Firstname_3D_Answer_Sheet** If necessary, click OK if a message regarding formats displays.

On the taskbar, click the **Word** button to minimize the window and leave your Word document accessible from the taskbar. **Close** the **Chapter_03** folder window. As you complete each step in this project, click the Word button on the taskbar to open the document, type your one-letter answer in the appropriate cell of the Word table, and then on the taskbar, click the button again to minimize the window for the next step.

From the Student Resource CD or other device that contains the Student Resource files, copy the **Bell_Orchid** folder to your **Documents** folder—you will need a *new* copy for this project. Display your **Documents** folder, and then navigate to **Bell_Orchid ▶ Corporate ▶ Food_Beverage ▶ Restaurants**. Hold down Ctrl, and then select the following group of files: **Breakfast_Continental**, **Breakfast_Menus**, **Brunch_Menus**, **Grill_Menu**, and **Refreshments**. Right-click any of the selected files, click **Properties**, and then as a group, apply the tag **Menu** Click **OK**, and then in the **search** box, type **menu** How many files display?

A. 5

B. 6

C. 7

2 Clear the **search** box, and then type **tag:menu** How many files display?

A. 4

B. 5

C. 6

3 Clear the **search** box, and then type **costs** How many files display?

A. 4

B. 5

C. 6

(Project 3D Using Advanced Search Techniques continues on the next page)

Content-Based Assessments

Skills Review | Project **3D** Using Advanced Search Techniques (continued)

4 **Clear** the **search** box, and then type **type:xlsx** How many files display?

A. 5

B. 15

C. 16

5 **Clear** the **search** box, and then type **costs NOT overtime** How many files display?

A. 3

B. 4

C. 7

6 **Clear** the **search** box, and then type **menu AND breakfast** How many files display?

A. 4

B. 3

C. 2

7 **Clear** the **search** box, and then type **menu OR breakfast** How many files display?

A. 4

B. 6

C. 8

8 **Clear** the **search** box, and then type **costs type:Excel** How many files display?

A. 4

B. 3

C. 2

9 On the toolbar, click **Organize**, and then click **Folder and search options**. Click the **Search tab**. Which of the following is *not* true?

A. In terms of how the Search feature performs a search, you have the option to find or not find partial matches.

B. In terms of how the Search feature performs, you must always use Boolean operators instead of natural language.

C. When searching non-indexed locations, you have the option to include system directories.

10 **Close** the **Folder Options** dialog box. On the toolbar, click the **Save search** button. Which of the following is true?

A. By default, a saved search is saved in your Documents folder.

B. By default, a saved search is saved in your Searches folder.

C. By default, a saved search is saved in your Desktop folder.

In the **Save As** dialog box, click **Cancel**. Clear the **search** box, display the **Documents** folder, and then delete the **Bell_Orchid** folder in the **Documents** window. Be sure you have typed all of your answers in your Word document. **Save** and **Close** your Word document, and submit as directed by your instructor. **Close** [x] all open windows.

End **You have completed Project 3D**

Mastering Windows 7 | Project 3E Using Advanced File Management Techniques

In the following Mastering Windows 7 project, you will change the way a folder displays. You will capture and save a screen that will look similar to Figure 3.53.

Project Files

For Project 3E, you will need the following files:

Student Resource CD (or a USB flash drive containing these files)
New Snip file

You will save your file as:

Lastname_Firstname_3E__HR_Snip

Project Results

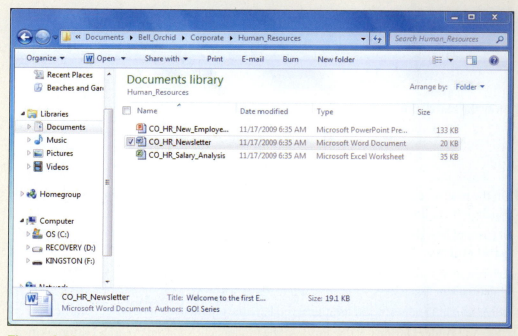

Figure 3.53

(Project 3E Using Advanced File Management Techniques continues on the next page)

Content-Based Assessments

Mastering Windows 7 | Project **3E** Using Advanced File Management Techniques (continued)

1 Copy the **Bell_Orchid** folder from your Student Resource CD to your **Documents** folder. Navigate to **Documents ▶ Bell_Orchid**. Change the folder options so that check boxes display.

2 Navigate to **Bell_Orchid ▶ Corporate ▶ Human_Resources**, and then select the check box for the **CO_HR_Newsletter** file.

3 Create a **Window Snip** in your chapter folder and save it as **Lastname_Firstname_3E_HR_Snip**

4 Change the folder options so that check boxes do **not** display. **Close** all open windows, and delete the **Bell_Orchid** folder from your **Documents** folder. Submit this file as directed by your instructor.

 You have completed Project 3E ——————

Apply **3B** skills from these
Objectives:

5 Filter Searches in the
Search Box

6 Search by Using the
Search Folder

7 Save a Search, Manage
Search Behavior, and
Manage the Index

Mastering Windows 7 | Project **3F** Using Advanced Search Techniques

In the following Mastering Windows 7 project, you will create a search. You will capture and save a screen that will look similar to Figure 3.54.

Project Files

For Project 3F, you will need the following files:

Student Resource CD (or a USB flash drive containing these files)
New Snip file

You will save your file as:

Lastname_Firstname_3F_OR_Snip

Project Results

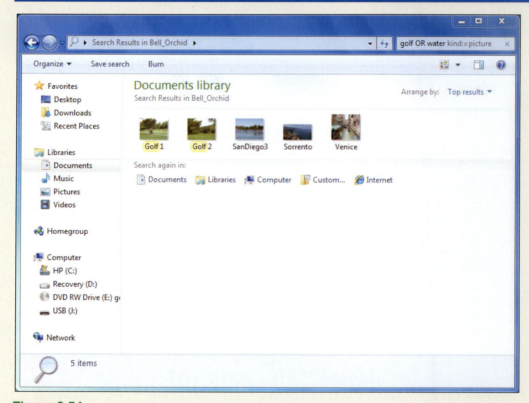

Figure 3.54

(Project 3F Using Advanced Search Techniques continues on the next page)

Content-Based Assessments

Mastering Windows 7 | Project **3F** Using Advanced Search Techniques (continued)

1 Copy *two* folders to your **Documents** folder as follows: First, if necessary, *delete* the Bell_Orchid folder from your Documents folder—for this project you will need a new copy of the files. Insert the Student Resource CD or other device that contains the student files that accompany this textbook. By using the **Send to** command, copy the **Bell_Orchid** folder from the Student Resource CD (or other device) to your **Documents** folder. Leave the window open.

2 On your Student Resource CD (or other device) navigate to **Chapter_Files ▶ Chapter_03**. Right-click the **Montecito** folder, point to **Send to**, and then click **Documents**.

3 When the copy operation is complete, in the **navigation pane**, under **Libraries**, click **Documents** to display your **Documents** folder window. Move the **Montecito** folder into the **Bell_Orchid** folder.

4 Display the **Bell_Orchid** folder window. Conduct a search to find all the files that contain the word **golf** *OR* the word **water** After the search displays a list of results, with your insertion point still in the **search** box, press Spacebar and then type **kind:** Select **Picture** as the kind of file to search by. Change the view to **Medium Icons**.

5 Create a **Window Snip** and save it as **Lastname_Firstname_3F_OR_Snip**

6 Change the view back to **Details**. Delete the **Bell_Orchid** folder from your **Documents** folder, and then **Close** all open windows. Submit your file to your instructor as directed.

 You have completed Project 3F ─────────────────────

Outcomes-Based Assessments

Rubric

The following outcomes-based assessments are *open-ended assessments*. That is, there is no specific correct result; your result will depend on your approach to the information provided. Make *Professional Quality* your goal. Use the following scoring rubric to guide you in *how* to approach the problem, and then to evaluate *how well* your approach solves the problem.

The *criteria*—Software Mastery, Content, Format and Layout, and Process—represent the knowledge and skills you have gained that you can apply to solving the problem. The *levels of performance*—Professional Quality, Approaching Professional Quality, or Needs Quality Improvements—help you and your instructor evaluate your result.

	Your completed project is of **Professional Quality** if you:	Your completed project is **Approaching Professional Quality** if you:	Your completed project **Needs Quality Improvements** if you:
1-Software Mastery	Choose and apply the most appropriate skills, tools, and features and identify efficient methods to solve the problem.	Choose and apply some appropriate skills, tools, and features, but not in the most efficient manner.	Choose inappropriate skills, tools, or features, or are inefficient in solving the problem.
2-Content	Construct a solution that is clear and well organized, contains content that is accurate, appropriate to the audience and purpose, and is complete. Provide a solution that contains no errors in spelling, grammar, or style.	Construct a solution in which some components are unclear, poorly organized, inconsistent, or incomplete. Misjudge the needs of the audience. Have some errors in spelling, grammar, or style, but the errors do not detract from comprehension.	Construct a solution that is unclear, incomplete, or poorly organized; contains some inaccurate or inappropriate content; and contains many errors in spelling, grammar, or style. Do not solve the problem.
3-Format and Layout	Format and arrange all elements to communicate information and ideas, clarify function, illustrate relationships, and indicate relative importance.	Apply appropriate format and layout features to some elements, but not others. Overuse features, causing minor distraction.	Apply format and layout that does not communicate information or ideas clearly. Do not use format and layout features to clarify function, illustrate relationships, or indicate relative importance. Use available features excessively, causing distraction.
4-Process	Use an organized approach that integrates planning, development, self-assessment, revision, and reflection.	Demonstrate an organized approach in some areas, but not others; or, use an insufficient process of organization throughout.	Do not use an organized approach to solve the problem.

Outcomes-Based Assessments

Apply a combination of the **3A** and **3B** skills.

Problem Solving | Project **3G** Help Desk

Project Files

For Project 3G, you will need the following file from the Student Resource CD:

win03_3G_Help_Desk

You will save your file as:

Lastname_Firstname_3G_Help_Desk

From the student files that accompany this textbook, open the **Chapter_Files** folder, and then in **Chapter_03** folder, locate and open the Word document **win03_3G_Help_Desk**. Save the document in your chapter folder as **Lastname_Firstname_3G_Help_Desk**

The following e-mail question has arrived at the Help Desk from an employee at the Bell Orchid Hotel's corporate office. In the Word document, construct a response based on your knowledge of Windows 7. Although an e-mail response is not as formal as a letter, you should still use good grammar, good sentence structure, professional language, and a polite tone. Save your document and submit the response as directed by your instructor.

To: Help Desk

I can navigate all over the Internet without having to double-click to display what I want to look at. Is there a way to avoid double-clicking so often when I am navigating in Windows 7?

End **You have completed Project 3G** ⎯⎯⎯⎯⎯⎯⎯⎯⎯⎯⎯⎯⎯

Outcomes-Based Assessments

Apply a combination of the
3A and **3B** skills.

Problem Solving | Project **3H** Help Desk

Project Files

For Project 3H, you will need the following file from the Student Resource CD:

    win03_3H_Help_Desk

You will save your file as:

    Lastname_Firstname_3H_Help_Desk

From the student files that accompany this textbook, open the **Chapter_Files** folder, and then in the **Chapter_03** folder, locate and open **win03_3H_Help_Desk**. Save the document in your chapter folder as **Lastname_Firstname_3H_Help_Desk**

The following e-mail question has arrived at the Help Desk from an employee at the Bell Orchid Hotel's corporate office. In the Word document, construct a response based on your knowledge of Windows 7. Although an e-mail response is not as formal as a letter, you should still use good grammar, good sentence structure, professional language, and a polite tone. Save your document and submit the response as directed by your instructor.

To: Help Desk

I just received over one hundred new photo files of golf courses, restaurants, and scenic mountain views of Palm Springs, California, where we are considering opening a new resort hotel. First, I want the photos to open in the Microsoft Picture Manager program, but every time I open a photo, it opens with the Windows Photo Viewer program. How can I change my system so that photos open in Microsoft Picture Manager? Second, I don't want to rename all the photos. Is there a way I could add identifying information so I could search for them by *golf* or by *restaurants*, and so on?

 You have completed Project 3H ———————————————————————

Outcome-Based Assessments

Apply a combination of the **3A** and **3B** skills.

Problem Solving | Project **3I** Help Desk

Project Files

For Project 3I, you will need the following file from the Student Resource CD:

> win03_3I_Help_Desk

You will save your document as

> Lastname_Firstname_3I_Help_Desk

From the student files that accompany this textbook, open the **Chapter_Files** folder, and then open the Word document **win03_3I_Help_Desk**. Save the document in your chapter folder as **Lastname_Firstname_3I_Help_Desk**

The following e-mail question has arrived at the Help Desk from an employee at the Bell Orchid Hotel's corporate office. In the Word document, construct a response based on your knowledge of Windows 7. Although an e-mail response is not as formal as a letter, you should still use good grammar, good sentence structure, professional language, and a polite tone. Save your document and submit the response as directed by your instructor.

To: Help Desk

I am the Corporate Director of Food and Beverage. I have hundreds of files from all of our different facilities that deal with various aspects of the Food and Beverage operation. I need to find files by location and also by type of menu. Is there a way I could find, for example, only files that pertain to brunch menus at our Orlando facility or only files that pertain to dinner menus at both the Honolulu and Montecito locations?

End **You have completed Project 3I** ———————————————————

Personalizing Your Windows 7 Environment and Using Windows Media Player

OUTCOMES

At the end of this chapter you will be able to:

PROJECT 4A

Create an environment on your computer that reflects your personal preferences and that makes it easier to manage your computer tasks.

PROJECT 4B

Use Windows Media Player to play, rip, and burn music and to watch videos.

OBJECTIVES

Mastering these objectives will enable you to:

Holger Mette/Shutterstock

In This Chapter

In this chapter, you will personalize your computer environment. Your physical desk—at home or at your office where you do your work—is as personal as you are. You probably have your own personal coffee mug, pens and pencils, reference books, and photos of family members or friends or pets. You can personalize your Windows 7 desktop too, by adding your own colors, backgrounds, photos, and tools that you work with most often.

In this chapter, you will also use Windows Media Player, which enables you to play music, look at pictures, watch videos, and watch recorded television shows. It also enables you to organize your digital media, rip CDs, burn CDs from your own playlists, synchronize with your portable media player, and purchase media content from online sources.

The projects in this chapter relate to the **Bell Orchid Hotels**, headquartered in Boston, and which own and operate resorts and business-oriented hotels. Resort properties are located in popular destinations, including Honolulu, Orlando, San Diego, and Santa Barbara. The resorts offer deluxe accommodations and a wide array of dining options. Other Bell Orchid hotels are located in major business centers and offer the latest technology in their meeting facilities. The company plans to open new properties and update existing properties over the next ten years.

Project 4A Personalizing Your Windows 7 Environment

Project Activities

In Activities 4.01 through 4.09, you will work with Barbara and Steven, employees in the Information Technology department at the headquarters office of Bell Orchid Hotels, as they explore how to personalize the desktop and arrange Windows 7 tools for a productive computer environment. Your completed screens will look similar to Figure 4.1.

Project Files

For Project 4A, you will need the following files:

Student Resource CD (or a USB flash drive containing these files)
New Snip files

You will save your files as:

Lastname_Firstname_4A_Desktop_Snip
Lastname_Firstname_4A_Customize_Snip
Lastname_Firstname_4A_Links_Snip
Lastname_Firstname_4A_Gadgets_Snip
Lastname_Firstname_4A_Steps_Snip

Project Results

Figure 4.1
Project 4A Personalizing Your Windows 7 Environment

Objective 1 | Personalize the Desktop and Screen Saver

Recall that the *desktop* simulates the top of an actual desk and acts as your work area in Windows 7. The desktop is the main screen area that you see after you turn on your computer and log on. The desktop includes the taskbar at the bottom and the Start button in the lower left corner.

A *screen saver* is a moving picture or pattern that displays on your screen after a specified period of inactivity—that is, when the mouse or keyboard has not been used.

Activity 4.01 | Personalizing the Desktop Background

Selecting a desktop background—sometimes referred to as the *wallpaper*—is one of the easiest ways to personalize your computer environment. Many attractive backgrounds are included with Windows 7, including photos, graphic designs, and solid colors. Creating a background from one of your own photos is a nice way to personalize to your desktop background.

A *theme* is a combination of pictures, colors, and sounds on your computer. A theme includes a desktop background, a screen saver, a window border color, and a sound scheme. Some themes include specific types of desktop icons and mouse pointers. Windows comes with several themes that you can use, or you can create your own customized themes. Additionally, you can download themes created by others from various Internet sites.

1 If necessary, *delete* the Bell_Orchid folder from your Documents folder—for this project, you will need a new copy of the files. Insert the Student Resource CD or other device that contains the student files that accompany this textbook. By using the **Send to** command that you have practiced, copy the **Bell_Orchid** folder to your **Documents** folder.

Another Way

From the Start menu, display the Control Panel, and then under Appearance and Personalization, click Change desktop background.

2 **Close** ![x] all open windows to display your desktop. Point anywhere on your desktop, right-click, and then on the shortcut menu, click **Personalize**.

3 At the bottom of the displayed **Personalization** window, click **Desktop Background**, and then compare your screen with Figure 4.2.

Figure 4.2

Desktop Background window (your arrangement may differ if others have used this computer)

Picture location arrow

Scroll box

Current desktop background checked (yours may differ)

4 Move the scroll box up or down as necessary, and take a moment to view the various photos, designs, and graphics that are provided as **Windows Desktop Backgrounds**—some may be provided by your computer's manufacturer and display a stylized version of a logo.

Any theme that is included with Windows 7, for example the *Architecture* theme, will provide a changing background of the six pictures that will cycle on the desktop background, a complementary window color, and the Cityscape sound scheme.

5 Click the **Picture location arrow**, click **Solid Colors**, and then in the lower left corner, click **More**.

By using the tools provided, you can create any custom color. This is useful if you are trying to match your desktop background to a set of organization colors, for example the school colors of your college or university or the colors of your favorite sports team.

6 **Close** ▣ the **Color** dialog box, click the **Picture location arrow**, and then click **Pictures Library**. At the bottom of the window, click the **Picture position arrow**, and notice that there are five arrangements by which Windows 7 can display a selected picture as a desktop background.

Behind this window, your desktop might display various pictures that accompany Windows 7.

Here, you can also select how often to change the background picture if you have selected multiple pictures.

7 Click in a white area of the dialog box to close the **Picture position** menu. To the right of the **Picture location** box, click the **Browse** button, and then compare your screen with Figure 4.3.

Browsing is a term used to describe the process of navigating within Windows 7 to look for a specific program, file, e-mail, Control Panel feature, or Internet favorite.

Your desktop might display one of the sample pictures.

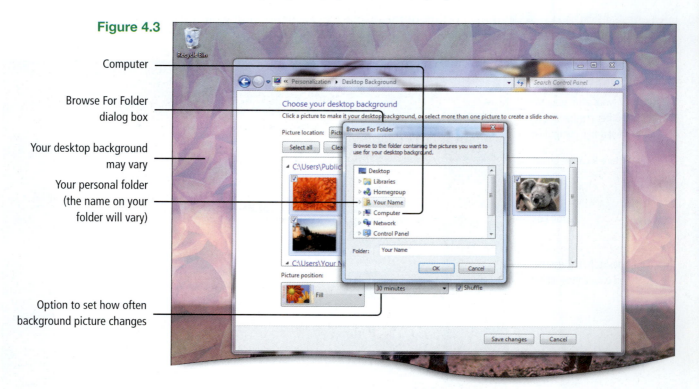

Figure 4.3

Computer

Browse For Folder dialog box

Your desktop background may vary

Your personal folder (the name on your folder will vary)

Option to set how often background picture changes

8 In the **Browse For Folder** dialog box, click **Computer** to expand it. Scroll down as necessary, and then click the location that contains your student files, either the CD/DVD drive or a USB flash drive.

9 Scroll down as necessary, click the **Chapter_Files** folder, scroll down again, and then click **Chapter_04**. Compare your screen with Figure 4.4.

Figure 4.4

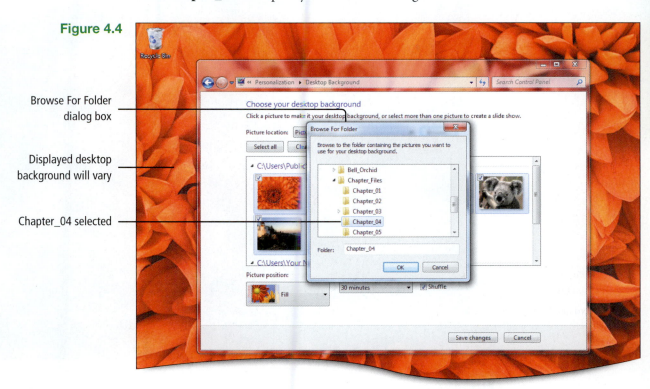

Browse For Folder dialog box

Displayed desktop background will vary

Chapter_04 selected

10 Click **OK**, and then compare your screen with Figure 4.5. Notice that one of the two displayed pictures might display on your desktop.

Figure 4.5

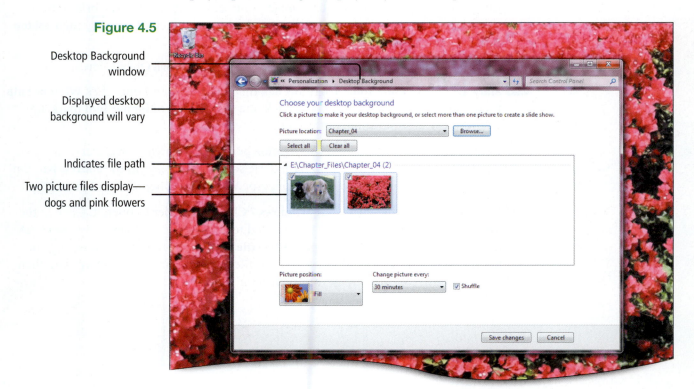

Desktop Background window

Displayed desktop background will vary

Indicates file path

Two picture files display—dogs and pink flowers

11 Click the picture of the two dogs, and then in the upper right corner of the **Desktop Background** dialog box, click the **Minimize** button  to minimize the window. Compare your screen with Figure 4.6.

Figure 4.6

Selected picture displays as background (your picture placement could vary depending on screen resolution)

Control Panel window minimized to taskbar

Word and Excel pinned to taskbar; yours may differ

12 On the taskbar, click the **Control Panel** button to redisplay the **Desktop Background** window.

13 Click the **Picture location arrow**, click **Windows Desktop Backgrounds**, scroll down to the **Nature** category, and then click **img2**—the second image that is a bright green plant. In the lower right corner, click **Save changes**, and then **Close** the **Desktop Background** window.

This would be an appropriate image for computers at the Bell Orchid Hotels.

14 **Start** the **Snipping Tool** program, click the **New arrow**, and then click **Window Snip**. Point anywhere on the desktop and click one time. In the **Snipping Tool** mark-up window, click the **Save Snip** button.

15 In the **Save As** dialog box, in the **navigation pane**, scroll down as necessary, and then under **Computer**, click your USB flash drive so that it displays in the **address bar**. On the toolbar, click the **New folder** button, type **Windows 7 Chapter 4** and press Enter.

16 In the **file list**, double-click your **Windows 7 Chapter 4** folder to open it. Click in the **File name** box, and then replace the selected text by typing **Lastname_Firstname_4A_Desktop_Snip** Be sure the file type is **JPEG file**, and then press Enter. **Close** the **Snipping Tool** mark-up window. Hold this file until you finish Project 4A, and then submit this file as directed by your instructor.

17 Point anywhere on the desktop, right-click, and then click **Personalize**. Under **Aero Themes**, click **Windows 7**, and then compare your screen with Figure 4.7.

Aero refers to the desktop experience that features a translucent glass design for windows, attractive graphics, taskbar previews of open windows, and the Aero features you practiced in Chapter 1 such as Snap and Aero Peek.

Figure 4.7

The theme you created displays under My Themes.

Aero Themes

Windows 7 selected

Desktop background displays the default Windows 7 background

18 Under **My Themes**, point to the **Unsaved Theme** and right-click, and then click **Delete theme**. Click **Yes**.

On your own computer, experiment and create as many themes as you want.

19 Close ⊠ the **Personalization** window.

> **More Knowledge** | Storing Personal Photos to the Picture Location
>
> In the manner that you practiced in this activity, you can click Browse and navigate to any personal photo you have stored in your personal folders or on a removable device, and then use it as your desktop background. If you would like to have your personal photos available immediately when you click Pictures from the Picture location arrow, store them in the Pictures subfolder of your personal folder. Recall that your personal folder is the folder created for your user account name, and contains subfolders for Documents, Pictures, Music, and so on.

Activity 4.02 | Personalizing the Screen Saver

Using a screen saver is a way to personalize your computer, keep others from viewing your screen when it is inactive, and enhance security by offering password protection.

1 Right-click on the desktop, and then click **Personalize**. In the displayed **Personalization** window, in the lower right corner, click **Screen Saver**.

The Screen Saver Settings dialog box displays. In the default Windows Aero theme, no screen saver is selected.

2 Click the **Screen saver arrow**, in the displayed list, click **Ribbons**, and then compare your screen with Figure 4.8.

> **Alert! | If the small screen displays a message**
>
> If the small screen indicates *This screen saver can't run because it requires a newer video card*, skip this step and move to Step 3.

You can view the screen savers that come with Windows 7 in this manner, and if you want to use one, select it by clicking OK. Or, click the Preview button to preview the full-screen view of the screen saver; move the mouse to cancel the full-screen preview and redisplay the dialog box.

Figure 4.8

Screen Saver Settings dialog box

Small preview of *Ribbons* screen saver

Click to see a full-screen preview—move mouse to cancel

Use spin box to change amount of time until screen saver displays

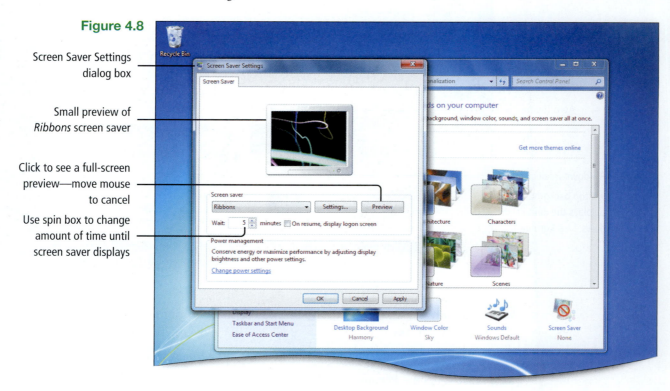

> **Note | A screen saver is not required**
>
> If you do not want a screen saver, but instead prefer that your screen is always displayed, in the Screen Saver Settings dialog box, click the Screen saver arrow, and then in the displayed list, click (None).

3 Click the **Screen saver arrow** again, and then in the displayed list, click **Photos**.

Use this screen saver to personalize your computer with one or more of your own photos. If no other pictures have been selected on the computer at which you are working, the default photos are those that come with Windows 7 in the Sample Pictures folder in the Pictures library.

4 In the center of the dialog box, click the **Settings** button.

The Photos Screen Saver Settings dialog box displays. Here you can select photos to use as your screen saver. Place the photos you want to use in a folder, and then browse for the folder by clicking the Browse button.

For more information about customizing your screen saver, you can click the **How do I customize my screen saver?** link in the lower left corner.

5 In the lower right corner, click **Cancel** to redisplay the **Screen Saver Settings** dialog box. Locate, but do *not* select, the check box next to **On resume, display logon screen**.

On your own computer, you might decide to select this check box to add additional security to your computer. By enabling this feature, you will be required to type your user password to cancel the screen saver display and continue using your computer. As soon as you move the mouse or press a key, the screen saver will close, and the log on screen will display requesting your password.

6 At the bottom of the **Screen Saver Settings** dialog box, click **Cancel** to close the dialog box without making any changes to the existing screen saver. **Close** ![X] the **Personalization** window.

More Knowledge | Downloading Screen Savers

Screen savers are available on the Internet for download. When you search for the term *screen savers*, you will find many to choose from. For example, you can search for *golf screen saver* to find screen savers with a golf theme. Only download screen savers from a trusted source. Screen savers have the potential to contain malicious software or *spyware*. Spyware is software that sends information about your Web surfing habits to a Web site without your knowledge.

Objective 2 | Personalize the Start Menu

The *Start menu* is a list of choices that provides access to your computer's programs, folders, and settings. In Windows 7, you have control over the programs and files that appear there. Organize and customize the Start menu so that it is easy to find the programs, folders, and features that you use frequently.

You have already practiced many of the common tasks for which the Start menu is useful, for example to:

- Start programs
- Open commonly used folders
- Search in the search box for files, folders, and programs
- Adjust computer settings from the Control Panel
- Access the Windows 7 Help system
- Turn off your computer
- Log off from Windows or switch to a different user account

Activity 4.03 | Personalizing the Start Menu

1 In the lower left of your keyboard, press ⊞ —this is the keyboard method to display the Start menu. Take a moment to review the main parts of the default Start menu by comparing your screen with Figure 4.9.

On the left, the *programs list* displays recently used programs on the bottom, programs that you have pinned to the Start menu at the top, and a button to display all the programs on your computer. On the right, **common folders and features** provide quick access to the folders and features you use most often.

At the lower left, you can type in the **search box** to search your entire computer for files, folders, e-mail messages, or programs. At the lower right, the **Shut down button** displays a menu for switching users, logging off, restarting, or shutting down.

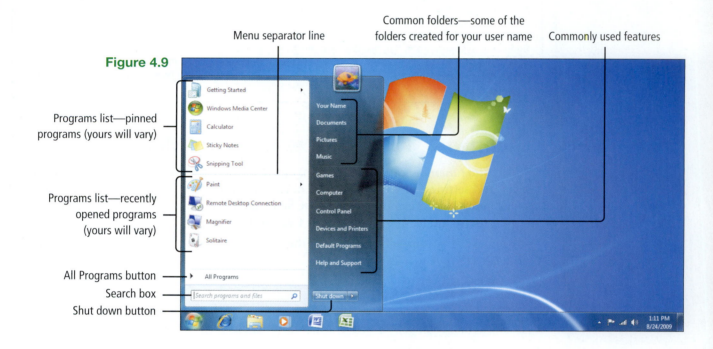

Figure 4.9

Menu separator line

Common folders—some of the folders created for your user name

Commonly used features

Programs list—pinned programs (yours will vary)

Programs list—recently opened programs (yours will vary)

All Programs button

Search box

Shut down button

Note | The Recently Used Programs Area on a New Computer

On a new computer, the lower left portion of the Start menu might display programs that your computer manufacturer wants you to see and possibly purchase. As you begin to use your own programs, the list will display your recently opened programs.

2 On the displayed **Start menu**, click **All Programs**, and then click **Accessories**. Point to the **Notepad** program, right-click, and then click **Pin to Start Menu**. Click on the desktop to close the Start menu, and then display the **Start menu** 🔵 again. Compare your screen with Figure 4.10.

The Notepad program is pinned to the Start menu and will remain there until you unpin it. All programs above the menu separator line are pinned programs. Recall that you practiced this technique previously by pinning Snipping Tool to the Start menu. If you use a program frequently, pin it to the Start menu so it is always readily available. For programs that you use every day, pin them to the taskbar.

Figure 4.10

Pinned programs (your list may vary)

Notepad pinned to Start menu

Menu separator line

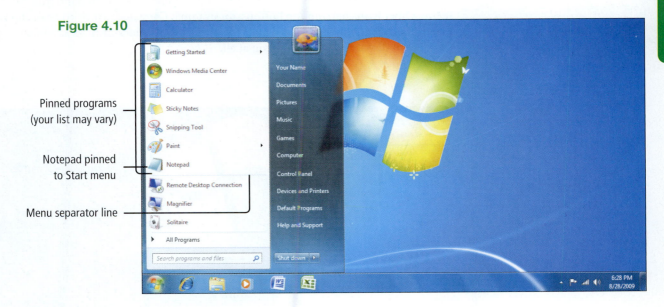

3 In the **Pinned programs area**, right-click **Notepad**, and then click **Unpin from Start Menu**.

4 Point to the **Start** button 🔵, and then right-click. On the displayed shortcut menu, click **Properties**. Compare your screen with Figure 4.11.

The Taskbar and Start Menu Properties dialog box displays. Here you can customize the appearance of your Start menu.

Figure 4.11

Start Menu tab

Taskbar and Start Menu Properties dialog box

Customize button

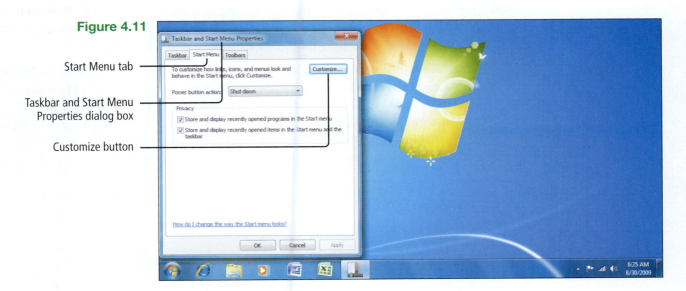

Another Way

To display this dialog box, on the desktop, right-click, click Personalize, and then in the lower left corner of the Personalization window, under See also, click Taskbar and Start Menu. Or, display the Control Panel, click Appearance and Personalization, and then click Taskbar and Start Menu.

5 On the **Start Menu tab**, click the **Customize** button. In this alphabetical list, under **Control Panel**, click the **Display as a menu** option button. Compare your screen with Figure 4.12.

On this list, you can customize how links, icons, and menus look and behave on your Start menu.

For items that have only a check box, for example *Devices and Printers*, removing the check mark—referred to as *clearing the check box*—removes the command from your Start menu. Other items have option buttons, for example *Computer*, which you can choose to determine if the item displays as a link that opens in a window, displays as a menu listing, or does not display on the Start menu at all.

Figure 4.12

Display as a menu option button selected

Option buttons—display as a link, display as a menu, or don't display

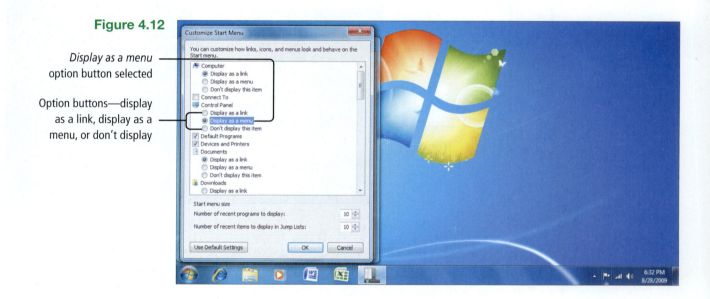

6 **Start** the **Snipping Tool** program, click the **New arrow**, and then click **Window Snip**. Point anywhere in the **Customize Start Menu** dialog box, and click one time. In the **Snipping Tool** mark-up window, click the **Save Snip** button.

7 In the **Save As** dialog box, in the **navigation pane**, scroll down as necessary, and then under **Computer**, click your USB flash drive so that it displays in the **address bar**. Navigate to your **Windows 7 Chapter 4** folder, and then as the file name, type **Lastname_Firstname_4A_Customize_Snip** Be sure the file type is **JPEG file**, and then press [Enter]. **Close** the **Snipping Tool** mark-up window. Hold this file until you finish Project 4A, and then submit this file as directed by your instructor.

8 Click **OK** two times. Display the **Start menu** 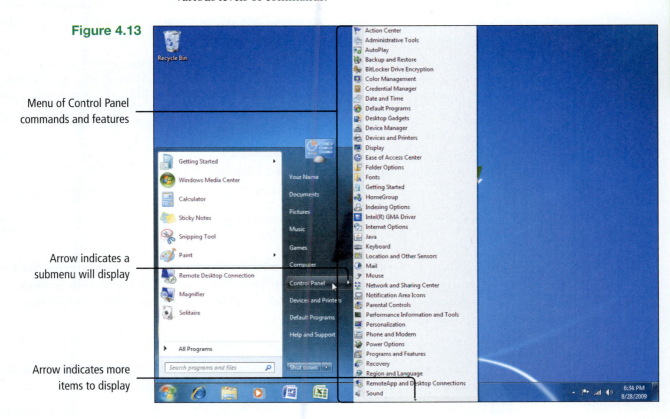, and then notice that to the right of **Control Panel**, an arrow indicating a submenu displays. Point to **Control Panel**, and then compare your screen with Figure 4.13.

> A menu of Control Panel features and commands displays.
>
> From this submenu, you can click a menu item to move directly to the Control Panel area instead of displaying the Control Panel window and locating the item by clicking through various levels of commands.

Figure 4.13

Menu of Control Panel commands and features

Arrow indicates a submenu will display

Arrow indicates more items to display

9 At the bottom of the menu, point to the **arrow** and notice that the menu scrolls to display more items. At the top of the menu, point to the **arrow** to scroll in the opposite direction. In the displayed list, click **Power Options**.

> If you use the commands on the Control Panel frequently, for example if you manage a small network, you may find it easier to change the Start menu in this manner.

10 **Close** ![X] the **Power Options** window. Right-click the **Start** button ![icon], and then display the **Taskbar and Start Menu Properties** dialog box again. On the **Start Menu tab**, click the **Customize** button. Under **Control Panel**, click the **Display as a link** option button to return your Start menu to the default setting.

> To remove an item from the Start menu completely, you can click the *Don't display this item* option button.

11 In the **Customize Start Menu** dialog box, at the top of the list under **Computer**, click the **Display as a menu** option button. Click **OK** two times to apply this change, display the **Start menu** ![icon], and then point to **Computer**.

> Displaying Computer as a menu is probably not as useful as displaying it as a link. Displaying an item as a link opens the item in Windows Explorer, where you have more options for navigating. Thus, most of the defaults are set as links, which means the items open in a window, rather than display as a menu.

Note | You Can Display Items Both as a Link and as a Menu

If you set an item to display as a menu, you can still open it in a window. On the Start menu, point to the item, right-click, and then click Open.

---

12 Redisplay the **Taskbar and Start Menu Properties** dialog box, and then on the **Start Menu tab**, click the **Customize** button. In the lower left, click **Use Default Settings**, and then notice that under **Computer**, the default **Display as a link** option button is selected.

> Use this button to return the Start menu settings to the default settings.

13 By using the scroll bar on the right, scroll down and examine the items that you can customize on the **Start menu**.

14 Position the scroll box approximately in the middle of the scroll bar, and then locate the check box for **Highlight newly installed programs**.

> You can control some Start menu *behaviors* in this dialog box. For example, the first time you display the Start menu after installing a new program on your computer, the All Programs button on the Start menu is highlighted, and the program name is highlighted on the list of programs. This feature is controlled here. Because it is a helpful feature, you probably will choose to leave this feature enabled.

15 In the lower portion of the dialog box, locate the **spin box** under **Start menu size**, and then compare your screen with Figure 4.14.

> By clicking the arrows in this spin box, you can increase or decrease the number of recently used programs on your Start menu.

> If you like to have a large number of *pinned* programs, you might consider decreasing this number to enlarge the space available for pinned programs.

> Here you can also control the number of recent items to display in Jump Lists, which are also available on the Start Menu.

Figure 4.14

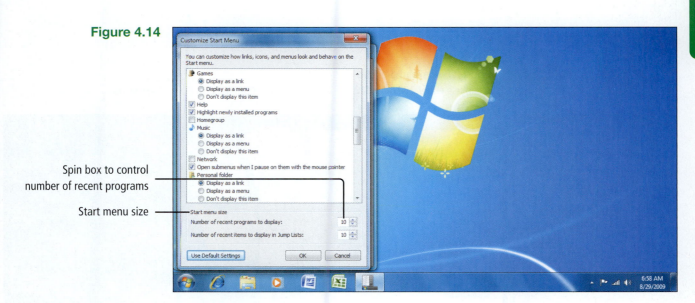

Spin box to control number of recent programs

Start menu size

16 In the list of Start menu items that you can change, scroll to the end of the list and notice the **Use large icons** check box.

> Windows 7 uses large icons on the Start menu by default, but if you have a large number of programs and want more programs to display on your Start menu, clear this check box to display smaller icons.

17 Click the **Use Default Settings** button to return any settings you may have changed on the Start menu to the default settings. Click **OK** two times to close both dialog boxes.

Activity 4.04 | Displaying Jump Lists from the Start Menu

The Jump Lists that you have displayed from programs open on the taskbar and pinned to the taskbar can also be displayed from programs you have pinned to the Start Menu. You can pin a program to both the Start Menu and the taskbar, and you will always see the same items in your Jump List for a program, regardless of whether you are viewing it on the Start menu or on the taskbar. For example, if you pin a file to a program's Jump List on the taskbar, the item also displays in that program's Jump List on the Start menu.

Another Way

On the Start menu, click All Programs, click the Microsoft Office folder, and then point to Microsoft PowerPoint and right-click.

1 Click the **Start** button 🪟, and then in the **Search** box, type **PowerPoint** On the displayed list, point to the **PowerPoint** program and right-click. Compare your screen with Figure 4.15.

Microsoft PowerPoint program
(you can use either 2007 or 2010)

Command to Pin to Start Menu

Figure 4.15

Results of search for
PowerPoint (yours
will vary)

Program name typed
in search box

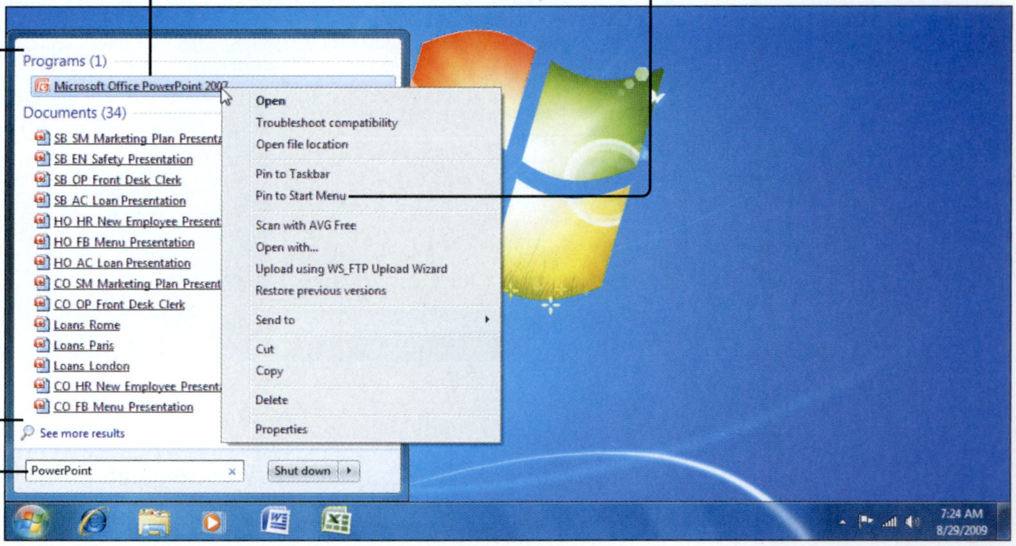

2 On the displayed shortcut menu, click **Pin to Start Menu**. Click anywhere on the desktop to close the **Start** menu.

3 On the taskbar, click the **Windows Explorer** button 📁, and then navigate to **Documents ▶ Bell_Orchid ▶ Corporate ▶ Operations**. Double-click the PowerPoint file **CO_OP_Front_Desk_Clerk** to open the file in PowerPoint.

The Front Desk Staff Training Presentation displays in the PowerPoint program.

4 In the upper right corner, click the **Close** button 🔴 to close the PowerPoint file. **Close** 🔴 the **Operations** folder window.

5 Click the **Start** button 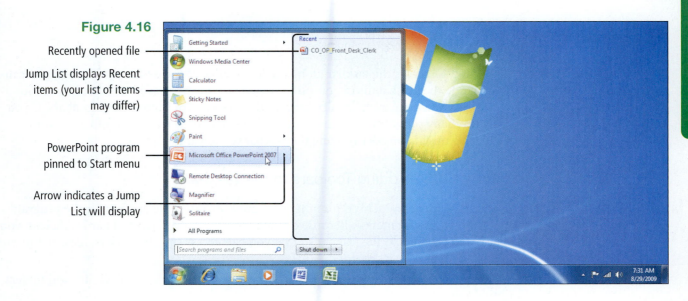, point to your pinned **PowerPoint** program, and then compare your screen with Figure 4.16.

> The arrow to the right of a program pinned to the Start menu indicates that a Jump List of recently opened files will display.

Figure 4.16

Recently opened file

Jump List displays Recent items (your list of items may differ)

PowerPoint program pinned to Start menu

Arrow indicates a Jump List will display

6 From the **Start** menu , drag the **PowerPoint icon** to an empty area on the taskbar, and then when the ScreenTip *Pin to Taskbar* displays, release the mouse button.

7 On the taskbar, point to the **PowerPoint** icon you just pinned, right-click to display the **Jump List**, and then compare your screen with Figure 4.17.

> The file you just opened, CO_OP_Front_Desk_Clerk, displays under **Recent**. Recall that recent and pinned items on a Jump List will display regardless of whether you are viewing the Jump List from the program pinned to the Start menu or to the taskbar.

Figure 4.17

Jump List displayed from taskbar (your list of Recent files may vary)

PowerPoint program pinned to taskbar

8 On the **Jump List**, click **Unpin this program from taskbar**.

9 Display the **Start** menu , right-click the **PowerPoint** icon, and then click **Unpin from Start Menu**. Click anywhere on the desktop to close the Start menu.

Objective 3 | Personalize the Taskbar

Recall that the *taskbar* contains the Start button and a button for all open programs. A program that has multiple windows open will display multiple overlapping program buttons on the taskbar. The important uses of the taskbar are to:

- Keep track of your windows
- Minimize and restore windows
- See previews of your open windows

Windows 7 places the taskbar along the lower edge of the desktop. Although you can move or hide the taskbar, most computer users leave the taskbar in its default location. You can also resize the toolbar to create additional space for buttons and toolbars. If you work with many programs regularly, and also like to add convenient toolbars to your taskbar, you might consider resizing the taskbar to view more items.

Activity 4.05 | Adding Toolbars to the Taskbar

You have already practiced pinning program buttons to the taskbar for the programs you know you use frequently. Because driving your work from the taskbar is efficient, you can also add toolbars to the taskbar so that you can access specific folders, files, or Internet sites directly from the taskbar.

Take advantage of toolbars to further reduce the time it takes to find files and folders and sites that you use frequently.

1 **Close** [×] any open windows to display your desktop. Point to an empty area of your taskbar and right-click, point to **Toolbars**, and then compare your screen with Figure 4.18.

The toolbars shown in Figure 4.18 are included with Windows 7—others might display on your list.

Figure 4.18

List of available toolbars (your list may differ)

2 In the displayed list of available toolbars, click **Address**. Compare your screen with Figure 4.19.

The Address toolbar provides a space to enter an Internet address or the name and path of a program, document, or folder.

Figure 4.19

Address toolbar

3 Be sure your system is connected to the Internet, click in the **Address** box on the taskbar, type **www.bls.gov** and press Enter to display the Web site for the **U.S. Bureau of Labor Statistics**.

4 Point to an empty area of the taskbar, right-click, point to **Toolbars**, and then click **Links**. At the top of your screen, in the Web site's address in your Internet browser software, locate the Web page's icon—a blue and red star. Drag the Web page icon onto the **Links** toolbar, as shown in Figure 4.20, and release the mouse button when you see the text *Create link in Favorites bar*.

This action not only places the link on the Links toolbar on your taskbar, but also places the link on the Favorites bar in Internet Explorer. Thus, if you choose to have the Links toolbar on your taskbar, any links you add to the Favorites toolbar in Internet Explorer will also be accessible directly from your taskbar.

Figure 4.20

Web page icon and URL (your page content will differ)

ScreenTip indicates that link will be placed on *Favorites Bar*

Links toolbar on the taskbar

5 At the top of the **Internet Explorer** window, under the **address bar**, notice that the link to the U.S. Bureau of Labor Statistics displays on the **Favorites bar**. On the taskbar, to the right of **Links**, click the **double chevrons** >> to display a shortcut menu containing the link to U.S. Bureau of Labor Statistics. Compare your screen with Figure 4.21.

Figure 4.21

Link displays on Favorites bar in Internet Explorer (your page content will differ)

Link to U.S. Bureau of Labor Statistics that you placed on toolbar

Double chevrons (>>) display list of links on the Links toolbar

6 **Start** 🟦 the **Snipping Tool** program, click the **New arrow**, and then click **Full-screen Snip**. In the **Snipping Tool** mark-up window, click the **Save Snip** button 🖫. In the displayed **Save As** dialog box, if necessary navigate to your **Windows 7 Chapter 4** folder on your USB flash drive and click to select it so that it displays in the address bar.

7 Click in the **File name** box, and then using your own name, type **Lastname_Firstname_4A_Links_Snip** Be sure the file type is **JPEG file**, and then press Enter. **Close** ❎ the **Snipping Tool** mark-up window. Hold this file until you finish Project 4A, and then submit this file as directed by your instructor.

8 On the taskbar, to the right of the word *Links*, click the **double chevrons** >>. In the displayed list, right-click **U.S. Bureau of Labor Statistics**, and then click **Delete** to remove the link from the list. Click **Yes** in the displayed dialog box.

The link is removed from both your Links toolbar and the Favorites bar in Internet Explorer.

9 **Close** ❎ the **U.S. Bureau of Labor Statistics** Web site and close Internet Explorer. Click in an open area of the taskbar, right-click, point to **Toolbars**, and then click the **Address** toolbar to remove it from the taskbar. Use the same technique to remove the **Links** toolbar from the taskbar.

You can see that it is easy to add and remove toolbars to the taskbar. Consider using such toolbars either permanently or on a short-term basis, for example when you are working on a project that requires visiting specific Web sites repeatedly.

10 Right-click the taskbar, point to **Toolbars** to display the list of available toolbars, and then notice the **Desktop** and **Tablet PC Input Panel** toolbars.

> The Desktop toolbar provides copies of all the icons currently on your desktop and access to your computer's resources. Some computer users add this toolbar. However, recall that it is better not to clutter your desktop with icons and files, but rather to pin frequently used programs to your taskbar and use the toolbars to access frequently used folders.
>
> If you have a tablet PC, you can use the Tablet PC Input Panel to enter text by using a tablet pen. It includes a writing pad and a character pad to convert handwriting into typed text, and an on-screen keyboard to enter individual characters.

11 On the list of available toolbars, click **New toolbar**. In the **New Toolbar – Choose a folder** dialog box, navigate to **Libraries ▶ Documents ▶ Bell_Orchid.** In the lower right corner, click the **Select Folder** button. Compare your screen with Figure 4.22.

> Any folder on your system can become a toolbar, including a Windows system folder such as Control Panel. The folder's name displays on the taskbar, and by clicking the double chevrons, each item in the folder becomes accessible. Then by pointing to submenus, you can navigate within each folder.

Figure 4.22

Toolbar created from
Bell_Orchid folder

12 On the taskbar, to the right of **Bell_Orchid**, click the **double chevrons** >>. On the displayed menu, *point* to **Corporate**, and then *point* to **Information_Technology**. Compare your screen with Figure 4.23.

> Consider using a toolbar like this for quick browsable access to the contents of a folder, especially if it is a folder that you access frequently.

Figure 4.23

Bell_Orchid folder and
subfolders displayed for
quick browsable access

13 Right-click in an empty area of the taskbar, point to **Toolbars**, and then click the **Bell_Orchid** toolbar to remove it from the taskbar.

Enable the toolbars that are convenient for you when it makes sense to do so, and remove them when they are no longer useful. With your new knowledge about these convenient features, you can personalize your computer whenever it suits your needs.

Activity 4.06 | Controlling the Display of Icons in the Notification Area

Recall that the *notification area*—also referred to as the *system tray* or the *status area*—at the right end of your taskbar contains program icons and notifications. A *notification*, which is a small pop-up window providing information about status, progress, and the detection of new devices, might display from time to time. For example, notifications about things like incoming e-mail, updates, and network connectivity display here.

The *Action Center* lists important messages about security and maintenance settings on your computer that need your attention. It is a central place to view alerts and take actions, for example to view and install updates.

Some programs, upon installation, have an icon that you can add to the notification area if you want to do so. You can choose which icons and notifications display in the notification area and change the order in which they display.

1 At the right end of the taskbar, locate and then click the **Show hidden icons** arrow ▲, and then click **Customize**. Compare your screen with Figure 4.24.

Here you can select which icons and notifications display on the taskbar. By default, both icons and notifications display for Action Center, Network, and Volume.

For other installed programs that include a system tray icon, for example security software such as AVG as shown in this Figure, you can decide how you want the program to behave in the notification area.

Figure 4.24

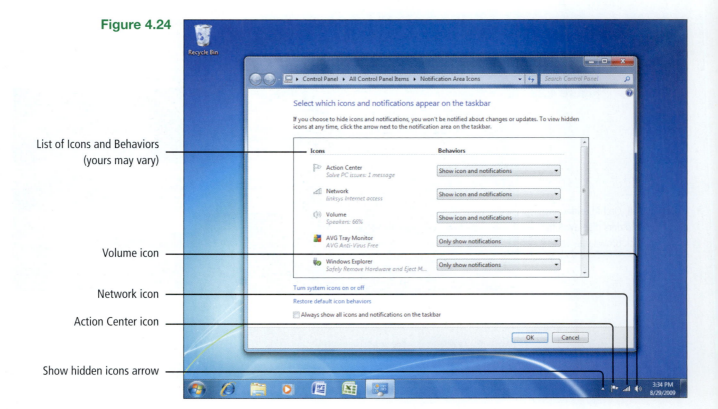

List of Icons and Behaviors (yours may vary)

Volume icon

Network icon

Action Center icon

Show hidden icons arrow

2 In the **Notification Area Icons** window, to the right of **Action Center**, click the arrow, and then compare your screen with Figure 4.25.

> Here, for each available icon, you can choose to see both the icon and notifications, to see only the notifications, or to hide both the icon and the notifications.

Figure 4.25

List of behaviors for an icon

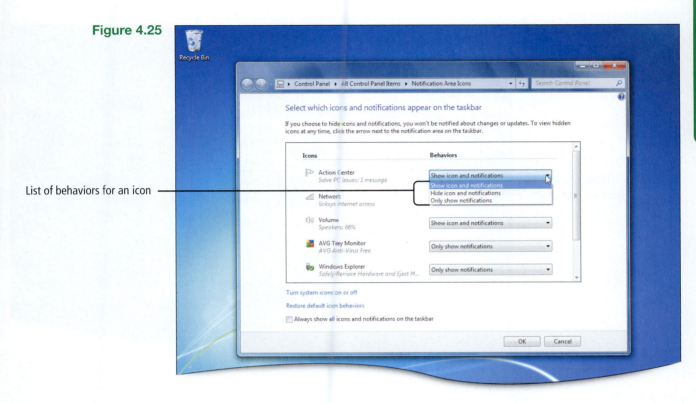

3 Click the arrow again to close the list, and then at the bottom of the **Notification Area Icons** window, click **Turn system icons on or off**.

> Here you can control the behavior of the system icons if you want to make any changes.

4 **Close** the **System Icons** window.

5 On the taskbar, click the **Action Center** icon, and then click **Open Action Center**.

> Here you can attend to any messages or notifications that display.

6 **Close** the **Action Center** window.

Objective 4 | Personalize the Desktop by Adding Gadgets

A *gadget*, also referred to as a *desktop gadget*, is a mini-program that offers information and provides easy access to tools that you use frequently. A gadget can display continuously updated information and enable you to perform common tasks without opening a window.

For example, you can install gadgets that display regularly updated weather forecasts, news headlines, traffic maps, Internet radio streams, or a picture slide show of your favorite photos. Gadgets can also integrate with your programs. For example, you can display a list of all your online instant messaging contacts and view who is online, or display the Day view from your Outlook calendar.

Activity 4.07 | Adding Gadgets to Your Desktop

1 **Close**  any open windows. Right-click anywhere on the desktop, and then click **Gadgets**. Point to the **Clock** gadget, right-click, and then compare your screen with Figure 4.26.

Figure 4.26

Default gadgets (your list may vary)

Another Way

Double-click a gadget to add it to the desktop.

2 On the shortcut menu, click **Add**, and notice that the clock displays in the upper right corner of your desktop. Using the same technique, add the **Weather** gadget and the **Slide Show** gadget. Compare your screen with Figure 4.27.

Clock gadget

Figure 4.27

Three gadgets display (your desktop may differ if you have already added gadgets)

Weather gadget

Slide Show gadget (your pictures will vary)

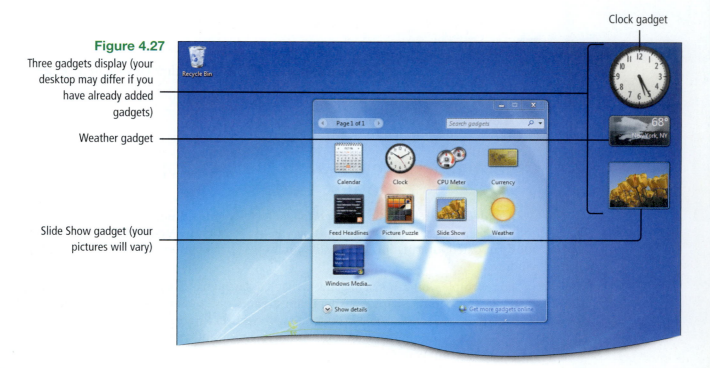

3 **Close** ❎ the **Gadgets** window. Point to the **Weather** gadget to display a small toolbar to the right, and then right-click to display a shortcut menu. Click **Options**.

4 In the **Search** box, type **Boston** and then click the **Search** button 🔍. On the displayed list, click **Boston, Massachusetts**, and notice that at the top of the window, your new locations displays. Compare your screen with Figure 4.28.

Figure 4.28

Weather options window —

Current location indicates
Boston, Massachusetts

5 Click **OK** and notice the information in the **Weather** gadget, which displays the current temperature in Boston.

> **Note | You Can Have More Than One Gadget of the Same Type**
>
> You can have duplicates of the same gadget. For example, if you want to monitor weather in multiple locations, you can add multiple weather gadgets.

6 Point to the **Clock** gadget and right-click.

Here you can choose to always display the gadget on top of open windows, engage the Move pointer to move the gadget to another location, close (remove) the gadget, and set the Opacity.

7 Point to **Opacity**, and then click **60%**. Notice that the gadget dims. Point to the **Clock** gadget and notice that it displays with no transparency.

In this manner, you can make a gadget less prominent.

8 **Start** 🪟 the **Snipping Tool** program, click the **New arrow**, and then click **Full-screen Snip**. In the **Snipping Tool** mark-up window, click the **Save Snip** button 💾. In the displayed **Save As** dialog box, if necessary navigate to your **Windows 7 Chapter 4** folder on your USB flash drive and click to select it so that it displays in the address bar.

9 Click in the **File name** box, and then using your own name, type **Lastname_Firstname_4A_Gadgets_Snip** Be sure the file type is **JPEG file**, and then press Enter. **Close**  the **Snipping Tool** mark-up window. Hold this file until you finish Project 4A, and then submit this file as directed by your instructor.

10 Click on the **Slide Show** gadget, and notice that in addition to the toolbar, some controls display directly on the gadget. Point to each control to view its ScreenTip.

> The controls on the Slide Show enable you to view the *Previous* picture, *Pause* on the current picture, move to the *Next* picture, or to *View* an enlargement of the picture on your screen.

11 Try out the controls, and when you are finished, on the small toolbar, click the **Options** button for the **Slide Show** gadget. In the displayed **Slide Show** dialog box, to the right of the **Folder arrow**, click the **Browse** button, and then compare your screen with Figure 4.29.

> By default, Slide Show displays items in the Sample Pictures folder that comes with Windows 7. You may want to create a selection of pictures of your own to display here. To do so, create a folder of pictures on your computer, and then browse for and select the folder in this dialog box.

Figure 4.29

Slide Show settings

Browse For Folder dialog box

Set time between pictures

Set transition effects

Display pictures in random order

12 In the **Browse For Folder** window, click **Cancel**. Notice the **Show each picture** arrow and the **Transition between pictures** arrow.

> If you have browsed and selected your folder of personal photos, you can use these options to set the time between the display of each picture and the transition effect to use when a new picture displays. The transition effects are similar to the slide transition effects in PowerPoint.
>
> Here you can also choose to shuffle the pictures so that they display in random order.

13 Click **Cancel** to close the **Slide Show** dialog box. Right-click on the desktop, click **Gadgets**, and then in the lower right corner of the window, click **Get more gadgets online**. Scroll down as necessary to display the section for **Desktop gadgets**.

If you are connected to the Internet, the Microsoft site *Personalization Gallery* displays. Explore this site to find many other useful and entertaining gadgets to display on your desktop. Be aware that the arrangement of this site changes periodically.

14 Close [X] the Microsoft Web site. Point to the **Weather** gadget, and in the upper right corner, click the white **X** to close and remove the gadget from the desktop. Right-click the **Clock** gadget, and then click **Close gadget**. Use either technique to close the **Slide Show** gadget.

If you install a new gadget, for example from the Microsoft site, it will display in the Gadgets window. Removing a gadget from the desktop does not uninstall it—it will remain available in the Gadgets window.

15 Close [X] the Gadgets window.

More Knowledge | How does the Feed Headlines gadget work?

Feeds, also known as *RSS* feeds, XML feeds, syndicated content, or Web feeds, contain frequently updated content published by a Web site. RSS is an acronym for *Really Simple Syndication*, and is a syndication format popular for collecting updates to blogs and news sites. A syndication format is a publishing format that lets you view headlines of the latest updates from your favorite blogs and Web sites all from within a single newsreader program.

By default, the Feed Headlines gadget will not display any headlines, but you can get started by clicking *View headlines* on the gadget.

To choose a feed from the Web, first display a Web page that has feeds, for example *www.microsoft.com/rss* and then click the square orange Feeds button. On the displayed Web page, click Subscribe to this feed, and then depending on the site, click Subscribe (or Subscribe to this feed, which might display a second time). If an Internet Explorer dialog box displays, click Subscribe. The feed should now be available to the Feed Headlines gadget.

On the gadget, display Options. In the Display this feed list, click the feed to which you subscribed, and then close the dialog box.

Objective 5 | Personalize the Ease of Access Center and Use the Problem Steps Recorder

The *Ease of Access Center* is a centralized location for accessibility settings and programs that can make your computer easier and more comfortable for you to use.

Activity 4.08 | Personalizing Settings in the Ease of Access Center

1 **Close** ▣ any open windows. From the **Start menu** 🏁, display **Control Panel**, at the lower right click **Ease of Access**, and then click **Ease of Access Center**. **Maximize** ▣ the window, and then compare your screen with Figure 4.30.

> **Alert!** | Voice Commands Might be Audible
>
> You might hear some voice commands if your speakers are enabled.

Figure 4.30

Ease of Access Center window

Questionnaire

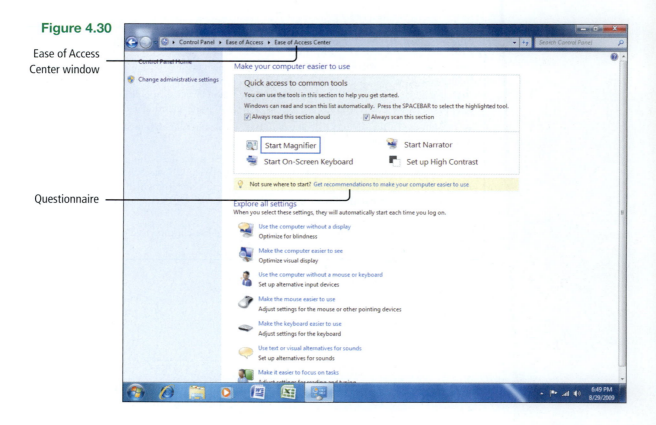

2 In the center of the screen, locate the yellow bar, and then click **Get recommendations to make your computer easier to use**.

> If you are unsure what features might be useful to you, begin with this questionnaire to answer questions about how you interact with your computer in terms of your sight, dexterity, hearing, speech, and reasoning.

3 In the lower right corner, click **Cancel**. In the upper portion of the screen, click the **Start Magnifier** command.

> *Magnifier* is a screen enlarger that magnifies a portion of the screen. This feature is helpful for computer users with impaired vision and for those who require occasional screen magnification for such tasks as editing art.

4 Move your mouse into each corner of your screen, and notice that the window is magnified. Then, point to the magnifying glass and click >>. Compare your screen with Figure 4.31.

Figure 4.31

Magnifier dialog box—
screen magnified (your
screen portion may differ)

Close button

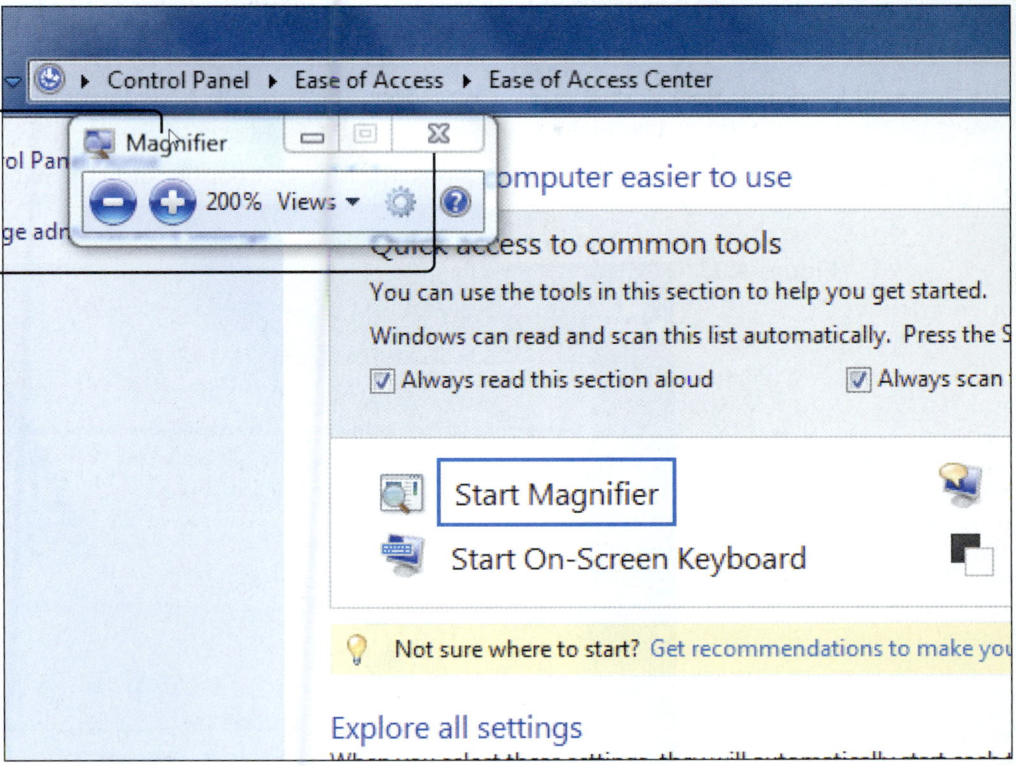

5 **Close** the **Magnifier** dialog box to turn off the **Magnifier**. In the upper right corner of the window, click the **Restore Down** button, and then **Close** the **Ease of Access Center**.

> Use the Ease of Access Center as necessary to make your computer comfortable to use.

Activity 4.09 | Using the Problem Steps Recorder

The *Problem Steps Recorder* captures the steps you perform on your computer, including a text description of where you clicked and a picture of the screen during each click—referred to as a *screenshot*. After you capture the steps, you can save them to a file, and then send them in an e-mail to your Help Desk or someone else who can help you with a computer problem. Conversely, if you are helping a friend, colleague, or family member with a computer problem, they can send a file to you so that you can view the steps they performed.

1 **Close** any open windows. Display the **Start menu**, and then type **problem steps** On the list of search results, click **Record steps to reproduce a problem**. Compare your screen with Figure 4.32.

Figure 4.32

Problem Steps
Recorder window

2 Click **Start Record**. Click the **Start** button , in the **Search** box type **printer** and then on the list click **Add a printer**.

The steps you are performing are being recorded.

3 In the **Problem Steps Recorder** window, click **Add Comment**, and then in the **Highlight Problem and Comment** box, type **I'm not sure which one to choose.** Then click **OK**.

4 In the **Problem Steps Recorder** window, click **Stop Record**. Compare your screen with Figure 4.33.

The recording stops. The Save As dialog box displays, and the file type is set to ZIP Files.

Figure 4.33

Problem Steps Recorder dialog box

Save As dialog box

File type is ZIP Files

5 In the **Save As** dialog box, in the **navigation pane**, navigate to your **Windows 7 Chapter 4** folder on your USB flash drive. Then, as the **File name**, type **Lastname_Firstname_4A_Steps** and click **Save**.

6 **Close** the **Problem Steps Recorder** window and the **Add Printer** dialog box. On the taskbar, click the **Windows Explorer** button, navigate to your chapter folder, and then compare your screen with Figure 4.34.

Figure 4.34

Address bar displays path

ZIP file displays

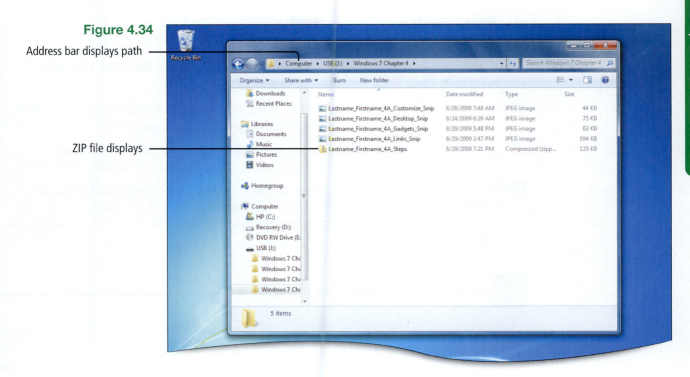

7 Point to your ZIP file, double-click, and then double-click to open the **Problem** file in Internet Explorer. Then, scroll down to display **Problem Step 4** on your screen, and notice that your comment displays, as shown in Figure 4.35.

Figure 4.35

Recorded Problem Steps displays in Internet Explorer

Problem Step 4 with your comment (your display may differ but you can see your comment)

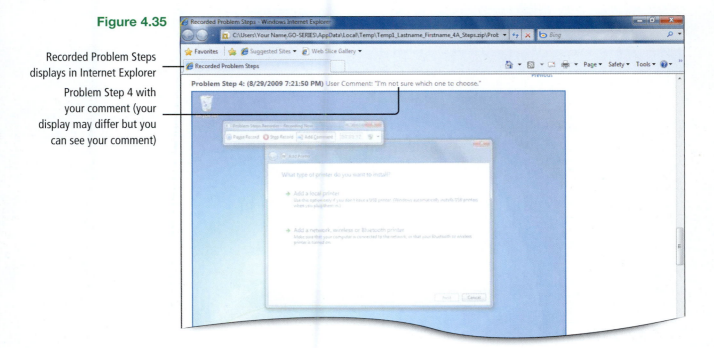

8 **Start** 🪟 the **Snipping Tool** program, click the **New arrow**, and then click **Window Snip**. Click anywhere in the window, and then in the **Snipping Tool** mark-up window, click the **Save Snip** button 💾. In the displayed **Save As** dialog box, if necessary navigate to your **Windows 7 Chapter 4** folder on your USB flash drive and click to select it so that it displays in the **address bar**.

9 Click in the **File name** box, and then using your own name, type **Lastname_Firstname_4A_Steps_Snip** Be sure the file type is **JPEG file**, and then press [Enter]. **Close** [✖] the **Snipping Tool** mark-up window.

10 Press [Ctrl] + [Home] to move to the top of the displayed file. Notice that you can view the recorded steps as a slide show. Click **Review the additional details**.

Here error messages and other technical details about the steps you performed are recorded, which can assist your Help Desk in helping you solve problems.

11 **Close** [✖] Internet Explorer. Delete the **Bell_Orchid** folder from your **Documents** folder. Close all open windows. Submit the five snip files from this project as directed by your instructor. Unless your instructor tells you otherwise, you need not submit the ZIP file you created.

End **You have completed Project 4A** ————————————

Project 4B Using Windows Media Player

In Activities 4.10 through 4.16, you will familiarize yourself with the Windows Media Player interface. You will view and play a music CD, rip a CD, create a playlist, and burn a CD. Your captured screens will look similar to Figure 4.36.

Project Files

For Project 4B, you will need the following files:

Student Resource CD or a USB flash drive containing the student files
One of your own music CDs (for one Optional activity if assigned)
One blank recordable CD (for one Optional activity if assigned)
New Snip files

You will save your files as:

Lastname_Firstname_4B_Playlist_Snip
Lastname_Firstname_4B_Rip_Snip (Optional)
Lastname_Firstname_4B_Burn_Snip (Optional)
Lastname_Firstname_4B_Video_Snip

Project Results

Figure 4.36
Project 4B Using Windows Media Player

Objective 6 | Explore Windows Media Player

Windows Media Player is an application in Windows 7 that provides an easy-to-use way for you to play digital media files, organize your digital media collection, ***burn*** CDs of your favorite music, ***rip*** music from CDs, ***sync*** digital media files to a ***portable device***, and shop for digital media content from online stores.

To burn a CD means to copy files to a recordable CD or DVD. To rip means to copy digital media content from an audio CD. Sync, in Windows Media Player, is the process of maintaining digital media files on your portable device based on specific rules. A portable device is any mobile electronic device that can exchange files or other data with a computer or device; for example, a smartphone or a portable music player.

Activity 4.10 | Getting Started with Windows Media Player

The Windows Media Player window looks similar to a window in Windows Explorer. The category of multimedia that you choose—music, pictures, or video—determines the appearance of the Windows Media Player window.

> **Another Way**
>
> Display the Start menu, in the Search box type *Windows Media Player*, and then click the program name on the list of search results.

1 On the taskbar, click the **Windows Media Player** icon. If a Welcome screen displays, click the Recommended settings option button, and then click Finish.

2 **Maximize** the window. In the upper right corner, click the **Play tab** to display the **list pane** on the right side of your screen, on the left, if necessary click Music, and then compare your screen with Figure 4.37.

When you start the Player for the first time, it automatically searches certain default folders included in Music, Pictures, Videos, and Recorded TV libraries on your computer.

Figure 4.37

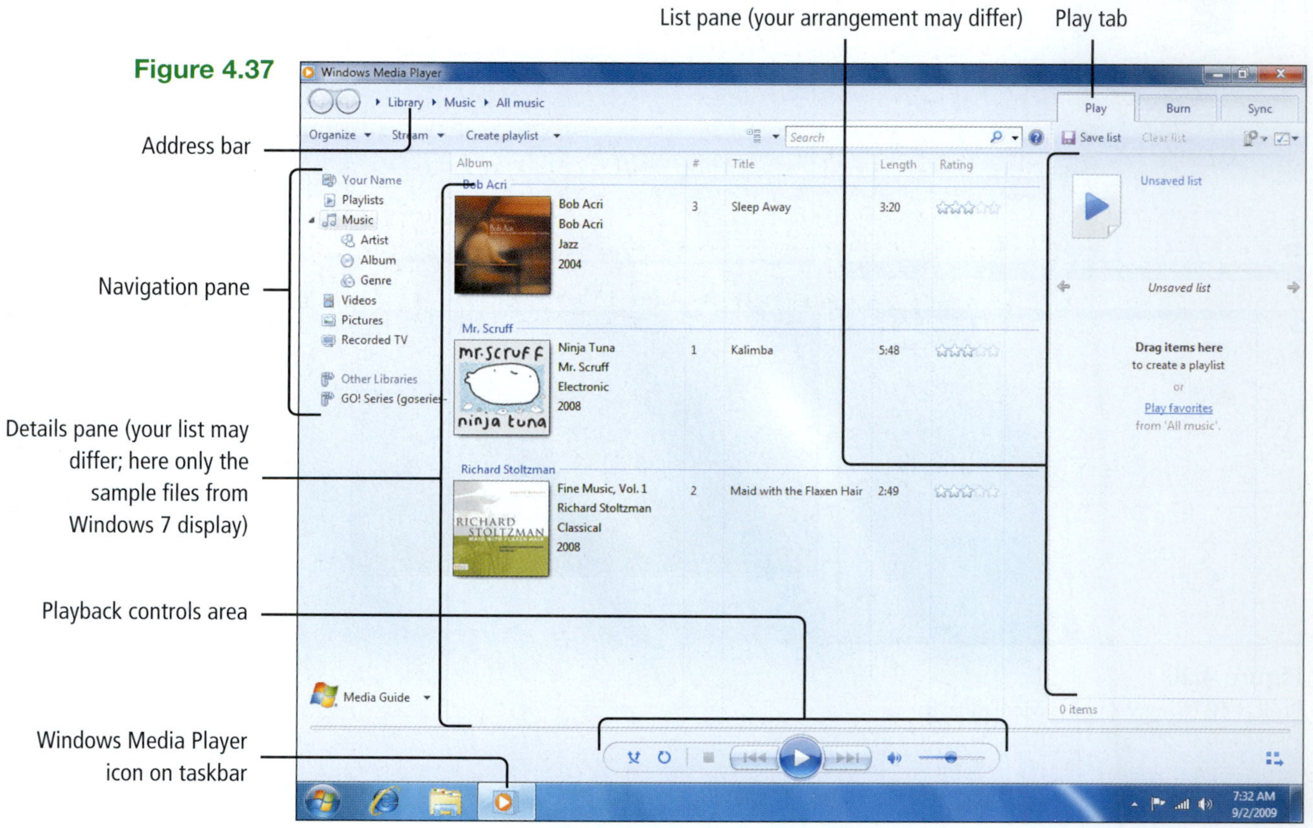

List pane (your arrangement may differ)
Play tab
Address bar
Navigation pane
Details pane (your list may differ; here only the sample files from Windows 7 display)
Playback controls area
Windows Media Player icon on taskbar

> **Alert! | Your screen will differ in content and arrangement**
>
> Most of the figures in this project use the files included in the Sample Music folder that comes with Windows 7. Your figures may differ. For example, iTunes selections might display, or podcasts that you have downloaded might display.

3 In the **navigation pane**, click **Videos**. If no videos have been added to your computer, the sample video included with Windows 7 will display.

4 Leave **Windows Media Player** open for the next activity.

Objective 7 | Play Music Using Media Player

You can use Windows Media Player to play music that you have stored on your computer or to play music directly from a CD. You can also set the Player window to display splashes of color and geometric shapes that change with the music, or you can minimize the Player window and let it play in the background while you are performing other tasks on your computer. This is referred to as the *Now Playing mode*.

Activity 4.11 | Playing Music

Windows Media Player can play pre-recorded CDs. For this activity, you will need a music CD of your choice.

> **Alert! | This activity is optional**
>
> If you do not have a music CD of your own for this activity, you can either read through the steps without actually performing them, or try this activity on your own at a later time.

1 In the **navigation pane**, click **Music** to return to the Music library. In the **details pane**, notice that items are referred to as *Albums*.

The default sort order is by Album name and the default view is Expanded tile.

2 Turn on your speakers or plug headphones into your computer. Place an audio CD in your computer's CD/DVD drive. If the CD cover does not display, click the View options button ⊞, and then click Expanded tile. Compare your screen with Figure 4.38.

The details pane displays the cover, the name of the CD, the name of the artist, the type of music, a list of titles, and the length of each title.

CD title   Length of each title

Figure 4.38

Cover art (does not display for all CDs; yours will differ)

Artist name

Year recorded (if known)

Type of music

List of songs on the CD

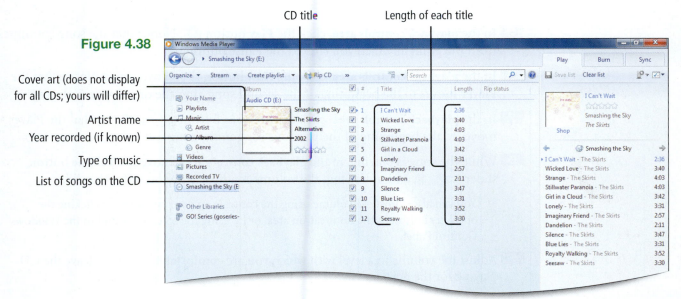

3 If the CD is not already playing, in the **playback controls area**, click the **Play** button [▶].

> Unless you clicked a song title other than the first one, the CD begins playing the first title, and will continue to play until the last title is finished. Information about the CD name, the artist, the composer, and the title name display on the left side of the playback controls area. The number of minutes and seconds the song has been playing displays, and a slider at the top of the playback controls area displays the progress of the song.

4 In the **playback controls area**, click the **Pause** button [❚❚], and then compare your screen with Figure 4.39.

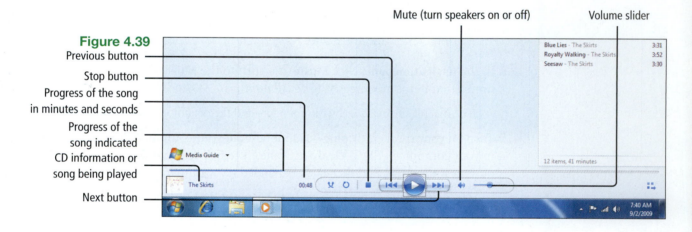

Figure 4.39
Previous button
Stop button
Progress of the song in minutes and seconds
Progress of the song indicated
CD information or song being played
Next button

Mute (turn speakers on or off)   Volume slider

5 In the **playback controls area**, click the **Play** button [▶]. Notice that the song continues from the point at which you clicked the Pause button.

6 In the **playback controls area**, click the **Next** button [▶▶❘] two times. Notice that the Player moves to the beginning of the second song after the one that was playing.

7 In the **playback controls area**, click the **Previous** button [❘◀◀]. Notice that the Player moves to the beginning of the previous song in the song list.

8 While the song is playing, in the **playback controls area**, move the **Volume** button slider [━●━], and notice that the volume is adjusted as you move the slider.

> You can also adjust the volume using the controls on your speakers, by clicking the Speakers button in the notification area, or by using the software found in the Windows Control Panel.

9 Adjust the volume to a level with which you are comfortable, and then leave the CD playing for the next activity.

Activity 4.12 | Using Now Playing Modes

The *Player Library mode*, which is currently displayed, gives you comprehensive control over the numerous features of the Player. If you do not plan to use your computer for any other activities while the CD is playing, you can alter the window to display interesting visuals that are integrated with the music. If you are going to use your computer for other tasks while the CD is playing, you can switch to Now Playing mode, which gives you a simplified view.

1 With your CD still playing, in the lower right corner, click the **Switch to Now Playing** button. Move your pointer into the small window to display the **playback controls area**, and then *point* to but do not click the **Stop** button. Compare your screen with Figure 4.40.

The Player switches to and displays in the Now Playing mode.

Figure 4.40

Player displays in
Now Playing mode

Playback controls area

ScreenTip for Stop button

2 Point slightly to the left of the **Stop** button ![Stop button] in an empty area of the **playback controls area**, right-click, and then point to **Enhancements**. Compare your screen with Figure 4.41.

Figure 4.41

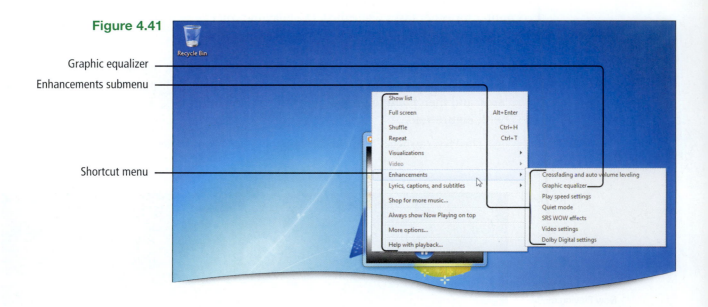

Graphic equalizer

Enhancements submenu

Shortcut menu

3 Click **Graphic equalizer**, and then compare your screen with Figure 4.42.

A *graphic equalizer* enables you to adjust the bass and treble that you hear. For example, listeners to classical music commonly enhance the low frequency ranges on the left side of the graphic equalizer. The sliders on the left control the bass; the sliders on the right control the treble.

Figure 4.42

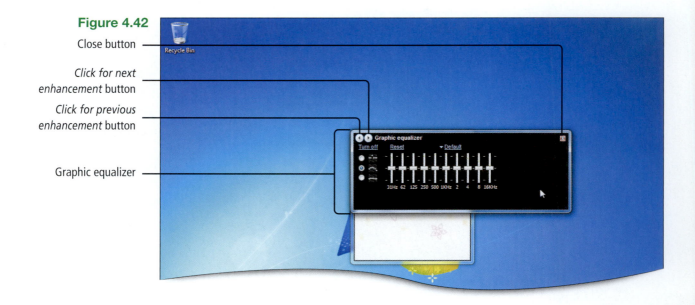

Close button

Click for next enhancement button

Click for previous enhancement button

Graphic equalizer

4 **Close**  the **graphic equalizer**. Display the shortcut menu again, point to **Visualizations**, point to **Battery**, and then click **kaleidovision**. Then, **Maximize** the window, and compare your screen with Figure 4.43.

The active *visualizations*—splashes of color and geometric shapes—are available from three categories—*Alchemy*, *Bars and Waves*, and *Battery*—or from the Web.

The patterns change along with the rhythm and intensity of the music; this is more obvious in some visualizations than in others.

Figure 4.43

Restore down button

Kaleidovision visualization (yours may differ in color and pattern)

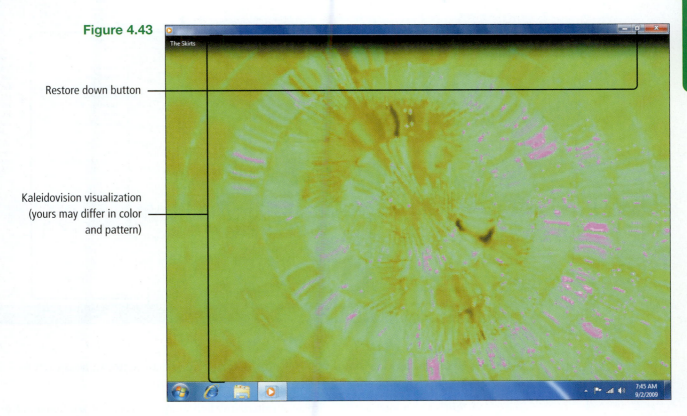

5 In the upper right corner, click the **Restore Down** button. Redisplay the shortcut menu, point to **Visualizations**, and then click **Album art** to return to the default view.

6 Point in the upper right corner of the album art; click the **Switch to Library** button ⊞ to return to the Player Library mode. In the **playback controls area**, point slightly above the counter, right-click, and then point to **View**. Compare your screen with Figure 4.44.

Figure 4.44

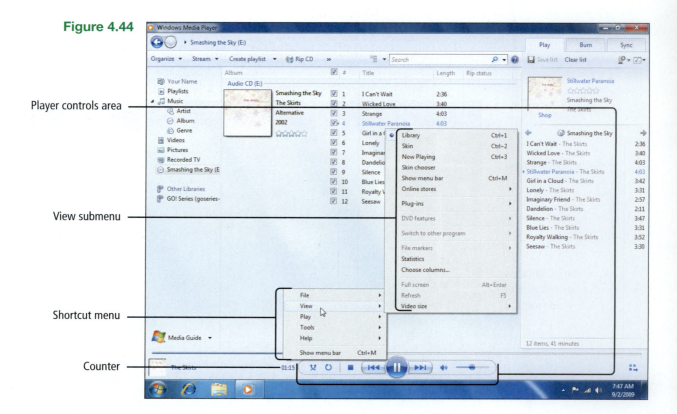

Player controls area

View submenu

Shortcut menu

Counter

7 Click **Skin**, and notice that the Player now displays in a small window, as shown in Figure 4.45.

A *skin* is a user interface that displays an alternative appearance and customized functionality for software such as Windows Media Player. The *skin mode*—a display mode in which the user interface is displayed as a skin—displays a small Media Player window that includes a menu, a video area, and playback controls.

Menu   Switch to Library button

Figure 4.45

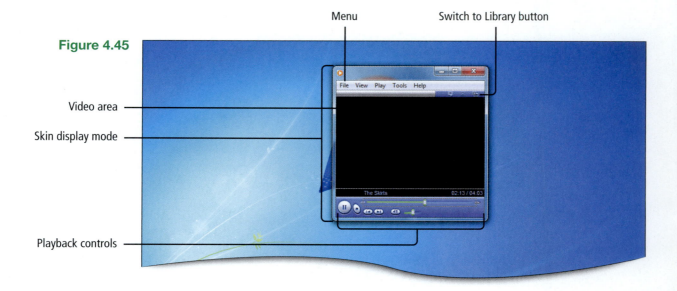

Video area

Skin display mode

Playback controls

8 On the menu bar, click **View**, and then on the menu click **Now Playing** to return to this mode. In the upper right corner, click the **Switch to Library** button ⊞ to return to the Player Library mode.

Note | To Keep the Windows Media Player in Front of Other Windows

When you are listening to music while performing other tasks on your computer, you might want to keep the small window for the Now Playing mode in front of other windows. To do this from Player Library mode, right-click an open area of the player controls area. From the displayed menu, point to Tools, and then click Options. In the Options dialog box, click the Player tab, and then under Player settings, select the *Keep Now Playing on top of other windows* check box.

---

9 In the **playback controls area**, click the **Stop** button ◾. Leave Windows Media Player open for the next activity.

More Knowledge | Minimizing the Media Player to the Taskbar

If you want to keep control of the Windows Media Player, but do not want the window in your desktop work area, start playing your music, and then click the Minimize button. The Windows Media Player icon on the taskbar will display with a glass frame indicating an open program. If you point to the button, the thumbnail displays a small set of player controls that you can use from the thumbnail image.

Activity 4.13 | Creating and Saving a Playlist

A *playlist* is a list of digital media items that you create and save. A playlist is useful when you want to group items that you like to listen to or view frequently. An auto playlist continuously updates automatically based on the music in the Player Library. A regular playlist is a list you save that contains one or more digital files—any combination of songs, videos, or pictures in the Player Library.

1 Be sure you have stopped the CD that was playing. In the **navigation pane**, click **Music** to return to your Music library.

2 If the **list pane** does not display on the right side of your window, in the upper left corner, click **Organize**, point to **Layout**, and then click **Show list**.

3 In the **list pane** on the right side of your screen, at the top of the pane click **Clear list**. Notice that you can drag items to the list pane area to create a playlist.

Note | Using Windows Media Library Sample Files

When you install Windows 7, a group of sample files is installed in the Player Library. These include sample cuts from three CDs, but not the entire CDs. If your computer does not display the sample files shown, use other audio files in their place.

---

4 In the **details pane**, under **Bob Acri**, drag the **Sleep Away** title into the **list pane**, and then when the ScreenTip + *Add to list* displays, as shown in Figure 4.46, release the mouse button. If the song begins to play, in the playback controls area, click Stop.

The song displays in the **list pane** area, but still displays in the **details pane**.

Figure 4.46

Title selected

ScreenTip + *Add to list* displays

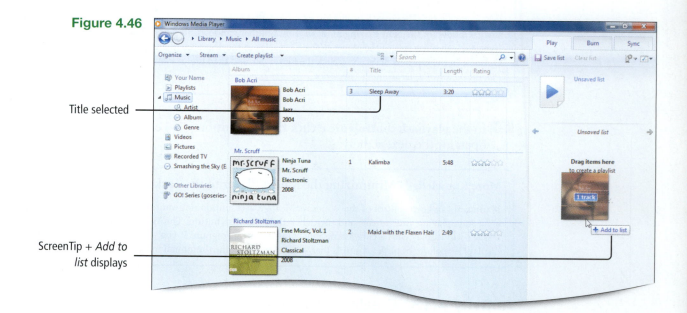

5 Use the same technique to drag two more songs to the playlist. Use songs of your choice, or, from the **Mr. Scruff album**, drag *Kalimba* and from the **Richard Stoltzman album**, drag *Maid with the Flaxen Hair*.

6 At the top of the **list pane**, click **Save list**, and then using your own name type **Lastname_Firstname_4B_Playlist** and press Enter. Compare your screen with Figure 4.47.

Figure 4.47

Playlist named

Playlist name displays in navigation pane

Playlist created (your list may differ)

7 Start the **Snipping Tool** program, click the **New arrow**, and then click **Full-screen Snip**. In the **Snipping Tool** mark-up window, click the **Save Snip** button. In the displayed **Save As** dialog box, if necessary navigate to your **Windows 7 Chapter 4** folder on your USB flash drive and click to select it so that it displays in the **address bar**.

8 Click in the **File name** box, and then using your own name, type **Lastname_Firstname_4B_Playlist_Snip** and press Enter. **Close** the **Snipping Tool** mark-up window. Hold this file until you finish Project 4B, and then submit this file as directed by your instructor.

9 At the top of the **list pane**, click the **Clear list** button to clear the list pane—this does not delete your playlist, but rather, clears it from the list pane. Leave the Player open for the next activity.

Objective 8 | Rip a CD

If you want to add songs to your computer from CDs, you can rip the CD—copy digital media tracks from a music CD to a format that can be played on your computer. You can rip an entire CD, or you can select only the tracks that you want.

Activity 4.14 | Ripping a CD

In this activity, you will rip tracks from a CD to your computer. You will need a CD of your own to complete this activity, and the songs and CD title displayed on your screens will not match the figures shown below.

> **Alert! | This activity is optional**
>
> If you do not have a music CD of your own for this activity, you can either read through the steps without actually performing them, or try this activity on your own at a later time.

1 With **Windows Media Player** still active, put an audio CD in your CD drive. If you already have a CD in the drive from the previous activities, find its name in the lower portion of the navigation pane, under Recorded TV and click the name.

2 At the top of the window, click **Rip CD**. Compare your screen with Figure 4.48.

During the process, each title will indicate *Pending*, or when complete, *Ripped to library*. When complete, the song's checkbox is also cleared.

To rip only specific titles, clear the checkbox before beginning the rip process.

Figure 4.48

Checkmark cleared after each song is ripped

Rip status

Name of CD in navigation pane (yours will differ)

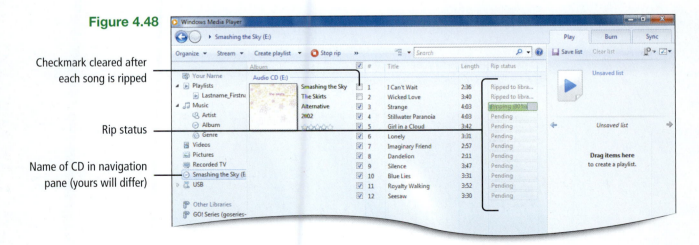

3 When your rip process is complete, to the right of **Rip CD**, click **Rip settings**, or click the **double chevrons** >>, point to **Rip settings**, and then point to **Format**. Compare your screen with Figure 4.49, and then take a moment to review the audio formats described in the table in Figure 4.50.

Figure 4.49

Format submenu —

Figure 4.50

Audio Formats	
Type	**Description**
Windows Media Audio	Balances sound quality and file size. This is the default Windows audio format, and will be used if you do not change the settings.
Windows Media Audio Pro	Saves the audio files in smaller files; often used for portable devices with limited storage capacities.
Windows Media Audio (Variable Bit Rate)	Varies the amount of information stored depending on the music being played. This format is used infrequently.
Windows Media Audio Lossless	Results in the best sound quality, but also creates the largest files.
MP3	Compresses the data used to record songs while keeping the sound quality relatively high.
WAV (Lossless)	Results in an uncompressed song format used for high-quality audio; this format can be read by both Windows and Apple computers. File sizes are relatively large.

Note | Choosing a Bit Rate

From the Rip settings submenu, if you point to Audio Quality, you can also choose a bit rate for your ripped audio files. The *bit rate* is the amount of information saved per second. The higher the bit rate, the better the sound, and the larger the files.

4 Click in an empty area of the window to close the menu.

5 **Start** 🏁 the **Snipping Tool** program, click the **New arrow**, and then click **Window Snip**. Click anywhere in the window, and then in the **Snipping Tool** mark-up window, click the **Save Snip** button 🖫. In the displayed **Save As** dialog box, if necessary navigate to your **Windows 7 Chapter 4** folder on your USB flash drive and click to select it so that it displays in the address bar.

6 Click in the **File name** box, and then using your own name, type **Lastname_Firstname_4B_Rip_Snip** Be sure the file type is **JPEG**, and press Enter. **Close** ❎ the **Snipping Tool** mark-up window. Hold this file until you finish Project 4B, and then submit this file as directed by your instructor.

7 Leave the Player open for the next activity.

Alert! | Copyright issues

Commercial CDs are almost always protected by copyright laws. If you are ripping CDs that you own, and are making these copies for your own personal use, most people agree that this is legal. If, however, you use these files to create a CD for someone else, or if you trade or make the files available on the Internet, you are violating copyright laws. When ripping music from a CD to your own computer, be sure the CD you use is one that you own. If you are ripping the CD in a lab or on someone else's computer, in Windows Explorer, open the Music library folder and delete the files.

Objective 9 | Burn a CD

Windows Media Player can burn—write files to—CDs and DVDs. You can burn data CDs or music CDs. There are two types of CDs you can use. CD-Rs are CDs that can be written to one time. CD-RWs are rewritable discs that can be used over and over again.

Activity 4.15 | Burning a Music Disc by Using Windows Media Player

In this activity, you will burn a CD using the sample files included with Windows 7. If you prefer to use other audio files, substitute those for the ones indicated in the steps below. Your screens will differ from the ones shown.

Alert! | This activity is optional

If you do not have a blank CD of your own for this activity, you can either read through the steps without actually performing them, or try this activity on your own at a later time.

1 Remove the audio CD from your CD/DVD drive. Insert your Student Resource CD, or the device that contains the student files that accompany this textbook. Wait a few moments, and then **Close** ❎ the **AutoPlay** dialog box.

2 From the taskbar, open **Windows Explorer** 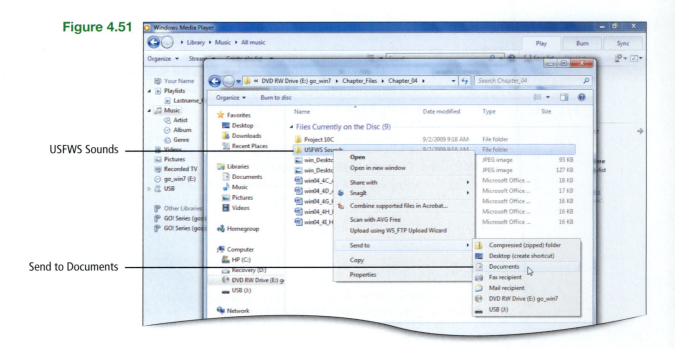. Display the student files, navigate to **Chapter_Files ▶ Chapter_04**. Select the folder **USFWS Sounds**, right-click, and then by using the **Send to** command, copy the files to your **Documents** folder, as shown in Figure 4.51.

Figure 4.51

USFWS Sounds

Send to Documents

3 In the **navigation pane**, click **Documents**. Select the **USFWS Sounds** folder, hold down Ctrl, and then as shown in Figure 4.52, drag the folder into your **Music** folder in the **navigation pane** until the ScreenTip + *Copy to My Music* displays, and then release the mouse button and release Ctrl. **Close** the Documents window.

Figure 4.52

Folder in Documents library

ScreenTip

4 In the Player window, in the **navigation pane**, click **Music**, and then scroll down to view the new titles, which may be near the end of the list. Compare your screen with Figure 4.53.

> No cover art or artist will display. These are sounds from the U.S. Fish and Wildlife Service.

> Use this technique to get music into the Music library so that you can burn a music CD.

Figure 4.53

Five titles —

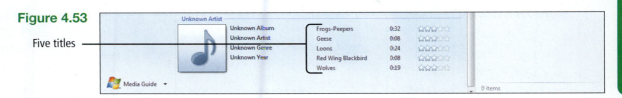

5 Remove the Student CD from your CD/DVD drive, and insert a blank recordable CD.

6 In the upper right corner, click the **Burn tab**, and notice that *Burn list* displays in the **list pane**.

7 In the **Title** column, click **Frogs-Peepers**, hold down Shift, click **Wolves**, release Shift, and then drag the entire selection into the **Burn list** until the ScreenTip + *Add to Burn List* displays, as shown in Figure 4.54.

> A burn list area displays in the list pane. At the top of the list pane, the drive with the blank CD displays, along with the amount of time used by the files and the amount of time left on the CD.

Figure 4.54

Burn tab —

ScreenTip —

Five titles selected —

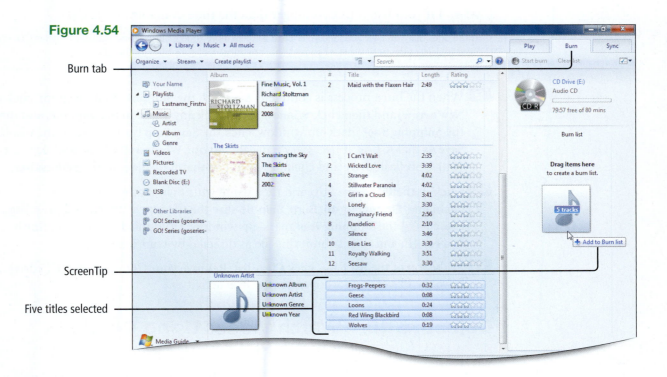

8 At the top of the **list pane**, click the **Start burn** button. Compare your screen with Figure 4.55.

> A progress bar displays the burn process. When the burning process is complete, the CD will eject.

Figure 4.55

Burn progress indicated ——

Alert! | If your list of titles is longer than the time available on the CD

If the titles that you have added to your Burn list take more time than the time available on your CD, you will need to delete titles until you have enough space to burn all of your titles on the CD.

---

9 When the burn process is complete, **Start** 🟢 the **Snipping Tool** program, click the **New arrow**, and then click **Window Snip**. Click anywhere in the window, and then in the **Snipping Tool** mark-up window, click the **Save Snip** button 🖫. In the displayed **Save As** dialog box, if necessary navigate to your **Windows 7 Chapter 4** folder on your USB flash drive and click to select it so that it displays in the **address bar**.

10 Click in the **File name** box, and then using your own name, type **Lastname_Firstname_4B_Burn_Snip** Be sure the file type is **JPEG**, and press Enter. **Close** ❎ the **Snipping Tool** mark-up window. Hold this file until you finish Project 4B, and then submit this file as directed by your instructor.

11 At the top of the **list pane**, click **Clear list**. Remove your CD, close your CD drive, and leave the Player window open for the next activity.

Objective 10 | Watch Videos Using Windows Media Player

Windows Media Player provides a basic method for viewing pictures and videos. You can build playlists that include a combination of videos and pictures, and play them in the same manner in which you played audio files.

Activity 4.16 | Watching Videos

1 In the **navigation pane**, click **Videos**. In the **details pane**, scroll as necessary to see the title **Wildlife in HD**, which is a sample video that comes with Windows 7. Or, insert a DVD of your own and click its name in the navigation pane.

2 Click the video to select it, and then in the **playback controls area**, click the **Play** button. If necessary, **Maximize** the window, and then compare your screen with Figure 4.56.

Figure 4.56

Video playing in Media Player window (your scene may differ)

3 With the video playing (if necessary click Play again), **Start** the **Snipping Tool** program, click the **New arrow**, click **Window Snip**, click in the window, and then in the **Snipping Tool** mark-up window, click the **Save Snip** button. In the displayed **Save As** dialog box, if necessary navigate to your **Windows 7 Chapter 4** folder on your USB flash drive and click to select it so that it displays in the **address bar**.

4 Click in the **File name** box, and then using your own name, type **Lastname_Firstname_4B_Video_Snip** Be sure the file type is **JPEG**, and press Enter. **Close** the **Snipping Tool** mark-up window.

5 After the video completes, in the dark screen that displays, click **Go to Library**.

6 **Close** Windows Media Player. Delete the **USFWS Sounds** folder from your **Documents** folder and also from your **Music** folder, and then submit the four snip files that you created in this project as directed by your instructor.

End **You have completed Project 4B**

Summary

Windows 7 is your personal environment for computing. From the Control Panel, you can click Appearance and Personalization and see many different areas of your computer that you can customize to fit your computing needs.

Your computer can reflect your personality by customizing the desktop and screen saver, and by adding gadgets. You gain productivity, however, when you customize your computing environment to make your computer easier and faster to use. For example, in this chapter, you practiced techniques to customize the Start menu and the taskbar in various ways to place your programs, files, and folders within easy reach. You also explored ways to make your computing environment physically more comfortable.

In this chapter, you also used Windows Media Player to play music, rip and burn CDs, and watch videos.

Key Terms

Matching

Match each term in the second column with its correct definition in the first column. Write the letter of the term on the blank line in front of the correct definition.

_____ 1. The main screen area that you see after you turn on your computer and log on, and which acts as your work area in Windows 7.

_____ 2. A moving picture or pattern that displays on your screen after a specified period of inactivity—that is, when the mouse or keyboard has not been used.

_____ 3. The background of the desktop.

_____ 4. A combination of pictures, colors, and sounds on your computer; includes a desktop background, a screen saver, a window border color, and a sound scheme.

_____ 5. A term used to describe the process of navigating within Windows 7 to look for a specific program, file, e-mail, Control Panel feature, or Internet favorite.

_____ 6. The term that refers to the desktop experience that features a translucent glass design for windows, attractive graphics, taskbar previews of open windows, and features such as Snap and Peek.

A Aero

B Browsing

C Common folders and features

D Desktop

E Desktop background

F Notification area

G Programs list

H Screen saver

I Search box

J Shut down button

K Spyware

L Start menu

M System tray

N Taskbar

O Theme

_____ 7. Software that sends information about your Web surfing habits to a Web site without your knowledge.

_____ 8. A list of choices that provides access to your computer's programs, folders, and settings.

_____ 9. The left side of the Start menu that displays recently used programs on the bottom, programs that you have pinned to the Start menu at the top, and a button to display all the programs on your computer.

_____ 10. The right side of the Start menu that provides quick access to the folders and features you use most often.

_____ 11. An area on the Start menu from which you can search for programs, files, folders, and e-mail messages.

_____ 12. On the Start menu, a button that displays a menu for switching users, logging off, restarting, or shutting down.

_____ 13. The area along the lower edge of the desktop that contains the Start button, a button for all open programs, and the notification area.

_____ 14. The area at the right end of the taskbar that contains some program icons and notifications.

_____ 15. Another term for the notification area.

Multiple Choice

Circle the correct answer.

1. A small pop-up window with information about the status of your computer or the detection of new devices is:
   A. a warning   **B.** a notification   **C.** an action

2. A central place to view alerts and take actions related to your computer is the:
   A. Ease of Access Center   **B.** taskbar   **C.** Action Center

3. A mini-program that offers information and provides easy access to tools that you use frequently is a:
   A. gadget   **B.** magnifier   **C.** toolbar

4. Frequently updated content published by a Web site is referred to as:
   A. comments   **B.** feeds   **C.** blogs

5. A central location for accessibility settings and programs that can make your computer easier to use is the:
   A. Action Center   **B.** Ease of Access Center   **C.** Accessibility Center

6. The process of copying files _to_ a recordable CD or DVD is called:
   A. burning   **B.** ripping   **C.** syncing

7. The process of copying digital media content _from_ a CD is called:
   A. burning   **B.** ripping   **C.** syncing

8. A simplified Windows Media Player view that enables you to play music in the background while you are performing other tasks is:
   A. Player Library mode   **B.** Skin mode   **C.** Now Playing mode

9. A list of digital media items that you create and save is a:
   A. library   **B.** playlist   **C.** visualization

10. The default format for audio in Windows Media Player is:
    A. Windows Media Audio   **B.** MP3   **C.** WAV

Skills Review | Project 4C Personalizing Your Windows 7 Environment

Project Files

Student Resource CD or a flash drive containing the student data files:

    win04_4C_Answer_Sheet (Word document)

You will save your file as:

    Lastname_Firstname_4C_Answer_Sheet

■1 **Close** [✖] all open windows. On the taskbar, click the **Windows Explorer** button. In the **navigation pane**, click the drive that contains the student files for this textbook, and then navigate to **Chapter_Files ▶ Chapter_04**. Double-click the Word file **win04_4C_Answer_Sheet** to open Word and display the document. Press F12 to display the **Save As** dialog box in Word, navigate to your **Windows 7 Chapter 4** folder, and then using your own name, save the document as **Lastname_Firstname_4C_Answer_Sheet** If necessary, click OK if a message regarding formats displays.

On the taskbar, click the **Word** button to minimize the window and leave your Word document accessible from the taskbar. **Close** the **Chapter_04** folder window. As you complete each step in this project, click the Word button on the taskbar to open the document, type your one-letter answer in the appropriate cell of the Word table, and then on the taskbar, click the button again to minimize the window for the next step.

Insert the Student Resource CD in the appropriate drive, and then copy the **Bell_Orchid** folder to your **Documents** folder—you will need a new copy for this project. On your desktop, right-click, and then click **Personalize**. Which window displays?

A. Desktop Background window

B. Personalize Appearance and Sounds window

C. Personalization window

■2 From the displayed window, what would you click to display a solid blue color as your desktop background?

A. Desktop Background, Picture location arrow, Windows Wallpapers

B. Desktop Background, Picture location arrow, Solid Colors

C. Screen Saver, Solid Colors

■3 Display the **Screen Saver Settings** dialog box, and then select the **Bubbles** screen saver in the dialog box. Click the **Preview** button, and then press Esc to return to the dialog box. Which of the following best describes the behavior of this screen saver?

A. The background is black and a large bubble fills the screen.

B. The background is black and small bubbles float on the screen.

C. The screen continues to display and transparent bubbles float on top.

■4 **Cancel** the **Screen Saver Settings** dialog box so that no changes are made and close all open windows. Display the **Taskbar and Start Menu Properties** dialog box, click the **Start Menu** tab, and then click the **Customize** button. What action would be necessary to remove the Pictures folder from the Start menu?

A. Under Personal folder, click *Don't display this item.*

(Project 4C Personalizing Your Windows 7 Environment continues on the next page)

Skills Review | Project **4C** Personalizing Your Windows 7 Environment (continued)

B. Clear the Pictures check box.

C. Under Pictures, click *Don't display this item*.

5 From this dialog box, how could you prevent *Devices and Printers* from displaying on the Start menu?

A. It is not possible to remove Devices and Printers from the Start menu.

B. Clear the Devices and Printers check box.

C. Change Devices and Printers to Control Panel.

6 Click the **Use Default Settings** button to undo any changes you have made, and then close all open windows. Display the **Taskbar tab** of the **Taskbar and Start Menu Properties** dialog box. How many screen locations can you choose from to display the taskbar?

A. Four

B. Three

C. Two

7 **Close** the dialog box and then display the **Problem Steps Recorder** window. Which of the following is *not* true?

A. There is a button to add voice recording.

B. There is a timer display.

C. There is a Help button.

8 **Close** the **Problem Steps Recorder**. Right-click the taskbar, and then add a **New toolbar**. From your **Bell_Orchid** folder, select the **Honolulu** folder, and then click **Select Folder**. On the taskbar, click the double chevrons >> to the right of *Honolulu*. Your result is:

A. A Jump List displays.

B. The Bell_Orchid folder window displays.

C. The subfolders in the Honolulu folder display.

9 Close all open windows. Delete the **Honolulu** toolbar from the taskbar. Add the **Calendar gadget** to your desktop. Right-click the **Calendar**, point to **Size**, and then click **Large size**. Your result is:

A. The calendar displays only the month.

B. The calendar displays both the month and the day.

C. The calendar displays only the day.

10 Remove the **Calendar** from the desktop; close all open windows. From the **Control Panel**, open the **Ease of Access Center**. Regarding how to make the mouse easier to use, which of the following is true?

A. You can change the color of the mouse pointer to red.

B. You can change the shape of the mouse to a star.

C. You can use the numeric keypad to move the mouse pointer around the screen.

Leave the **Bell_Orchid** folder in your **Documents** folder *only if* you plan to complete Project 4E; otherwise delete it. Be sure you have typed all of your answers in your Word document. **Save** and **Close** your Word document, and submit as directed by your instructor. **Close** [X] all open windows.

End **You have completed Project 4C** —————————

Content-Based Assessments

Apply **4B** skills from these Objectives:

- ◻ Explore Windows Media Player
- ◻ Play Music Using Media Player
- ◻ Rip a CD
- ◻ Burn a CD
- ◻ Watch Videos Using Windows Media Player

Skills Review | Project **4D** Using Windows Media Player

Project Files

Student Resource CD or a flash drive containing the student data files:

win04_04D_Answer_Sheet (Word document)

You will save your file as:

Lastname_Firstname_4D_Answer_Sheet

1 **Close** ▣ all open windows. On the taskbar, click the **Windows Explorer** button. In the **navigation pane**, click the drive that contains the student files for this textbook, and then navigate to **Chapter_Files** ▶ **Chapter_04**. Double-click the Word file **win04_4D_Answer_Sheet** to open Word and display the document. Press F12 to display the **Save As** dialog box in Word, navigate to your **Windows 7 Chapter 4** folder, and then using your own name, save the document as **Lastname_Firstname_4D_Answer_Sheet** If necessary, click OK if a message regarding formats displays.

On the taskbar, click the **Word** button to minimize the window; redisplay the document as necessary to type your answers. By using the **Send to** command, from the **Chapter_04** folder, copy the **Project 4D** folder to your **Documents** library. Navigate to **Documents** ▶ **Project 4D**. Hold down Ctrl, and then drag the **Pr04D Audio** folder into your **Music** library. Hold down Ctrl, and then drag the **Pr04D Video** folder into your **Videos** library. **Close** the window and start **Windows Media Player**. **Maximize** the window if necessary.

Be sure the **Play tab** is active. In the **navigation pane**, click **Videos**, and then in the **details pane**, locate **Flight into Grand Canyon**. What is the length, in minutes, of this video?

A. 7 minutes

B. 8 minutes

C. 9 minutes

2 Double-click the video **Flight into Grand Canyon** to being playing it. **Maximize** the window, and then move the mouse pointer into the lower portion of the screen to display the playback controls area. What displays to indicate how much of the video has played?

A. A thin blue bar moves from left to right.

B. A counter displays in minutes and seconds.

C. Both A. and B.

3 Point to the upper left corner of the screen. What displays?

A. The title of the video

B. A counter

C. Both A. and B.

4 In the **player controls area**, click the **Stop** button. What is your result?

A. The viewing area displays a thumbnail image of the video.

B. The viewing area displays the name of the video you just played.

C. A dark screen displays with options to *Play again* and *Go to Library*.

(Project 4D Using Windows Media Player continues on the next page)

Content-Based Assessments

Skills Review | Project **4D** Using Windows Media Player (continued)

5 Click **Go to Library**. In the **navigation pane**, click **Music**. Scroll down to **Unknown Artist**, and then in the **Title list**, locate **WolfHowl**. What is the length of this audio file?

A. 18 seconds

B. 28 seconds

C. 19 seconds

6 On the menu bar, click **Organize**. Which of the following is *not* listed on the menu?

A. Manage libraries

B. Sort by

C. Create Auto Playlist

7 On the **Organize** menu, click **Options**, and then click the **Rip Music tab**. Under **Rip settings**, click the **Format** arrow. Which of the following is *not* a format you can use to rip a CD?

A. MP3

B. Window Media Audio

C. Windows Music Player

8 **Close** the **Options** dialog box. Click the **Start** button, click **Help and Support**, type **burn a cd** and press Enter. Click **Burn a CD or DVD in Windows Media Player**. Scroll down and click **Types of discs you can burn**. According to this information, which type of disc has the largest capacity?

A. Data CD

B. Data DVD

C. Audio CD

9 **Close** the **Windows Help and Support** window. In the search box at the top of the Player window, type **elk** What is your result?

A. The ElkBellow audio file begins to play.

B. *ElkBellow* displays in the list pane.

C. Only the title *ElkBellow* displays in the Title list.

10 In the lower left corner, click **Media Guide**. In the navigation bar across the top, click **Internet Radio**, under **Genres**, click **Jazz**, and then click **SKY.fm** or some other station. What is your result?

A. The station plays on your computer's speakers.

B. The station plays with accompanying visualizations.

C. Both A. and B.

Leave the **Pr04D Audio** folder in your **Music** library and the **Pr04 Video** folder in your **Videos** library *only if* you plan to complete Project 4F; otherwise delete the two folders from their respective libraries. Be sure you have typed all of your answers in your Word document. **Save** and **Close** your Word document, and submit as directed by your instructor. **Close** Windows Media Player and all open windows.

 You have completed Project 4D ———————————————

Apply **4A** skills from these Objectives:

1 Personalize the Desktop and Screen Saver

2 Personalize the Start Menu

3 Personalize the Taskbar

4 Personalize the Desktop by Adding Gadgets

5 Personalize the Ease of Access Center and Use Problem Steps Recorder

Mastering Windows 7 | Project **4E** Personalizing Your Windows 7 Environment

In the following Mastering Windows 7 project, you will create two toolbars for your taskbar and add a gadget to your desktop. You will capture and save a screen that will look similar to Figure 4.57.

Project Files

For Project 4E, you will need the following file:

New Snip file

You will save your file as:

Lastname_Firstname_4E_Orlando_Snip

Project Results

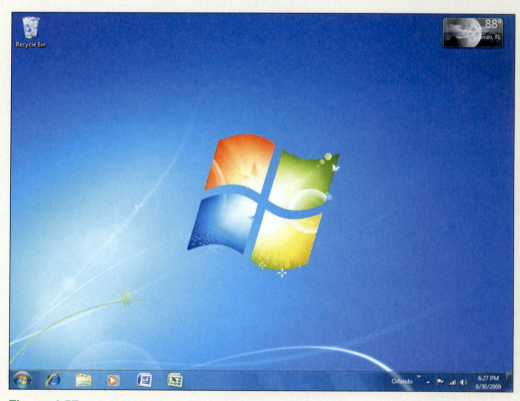

Figure 4.57

(Project 4E Personalizing Your Windows 7 Environment continues on the next page)

Mastering Windows 7 | Project **4E** Personalizing Your Windows 7 Environment (continued)

1 If necessary, copy the **Bell_Orchid** folder to your **Documents** library. Create a **New toolbar** on your taskbar to display the **Orlando** folder from your Bell_Orchid folder.

2 Add the **Weather** gadget to your desktop, close the **Gadget** window, and then set the Weather location to Orlando, Florida. Close the Gadgets window.

3 Create a **Full-screen snip** and save it as **Lastname_Firstname_4E_Orlando_Snip**

4 Delete the toolbar that you created, and then remove the **Weather** gadget from your desktop. Delete the **Bell_Orchid** folder from the **Documents** library. Submit your snip file as directed by your instructor.

 You have completed Project 4E _____

Mastering Windows 7 | Project **4F** Using Windows Media Player

In the following Mastering Windows 7 project, you will create a playlist that includes both audio and video files. You will capture and save a screen that will look similar to Figure 4.58.

Project Files

For Project 4F, you will need the following file:

New Snip file

You will save your file as:

Lastname_Firstname_4F_Media_Snip

Project Results

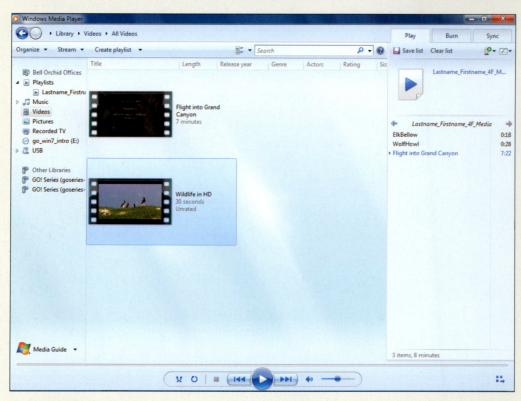

Figure 4.58

(Project 4F Using Windows Media Player continues on the next page)

Content-Based Assessments

Mastering Windows 7 | Project **4F** Using Windows Media Player (continued)

1 If necessary, by using the **Send to** command, copy the **Project 4D** folder to your **Documents** library. Navigate to **Documents ▶ Project 4D**. Hold down Ctrl, and then drag the **Pr04D Audio** folder into your **Music** library. Hold down Ctrl, and then drag the **Pr04D Video** folder in your **Videos** library. **Close** the window.

2 Start **Windows Media Player**. **Maximize** the window. Click the **Play tab**, clear the **list pane**, and then from your

Music library, drag **ElkBellow** and **WolfHowl** into the **list pane**. From your **Videos** library, drag **Flight into Grand Canyon** into the **list pane**. Save the playlist as **Lastname_Firstname_4F_Media**

3 Create a **Full-screen snip** and save it as **Lastname_Firstname_4F_Media_Snip** Submit this file as directed by your instructor. Close all open windows. Delete the **Pr04D Audio** and **Pr04D Video** folders from their respective libraries.

 You have completed Project 4F

Outcomes-Based Assessments

Rubric

The following outcomes-based assessments are *open-ended assessments*. That is, there is no specific correct result; your result will depend on your approach to the information provided. Make *Professional Quality* your goal. Use the following scoring rubric to guide you in *how* to approach the problem, and then to evaluate *how well* your approach solves the problem.

The criteria—Software Mastery, Content, Format and Layout, and Process—represent the knowledge and skills you have gained that you can apply to solving the problem. The levels of performance—Professional Quality, Approaching Professional Quality, or Needs Quality Improvements—help you and your instructor evaluate your result.

	Your completed project is of Professional Quality if you:	Your completed project is of Approaching Professional Quality if you:	Your completed project Needs Quality Improvements if you:
1-Software Mastery	Choose and apply the most appropriate skills, tools, and features and identify efficient methods to solve the problem.	Choose and apply some appropriate skills, tools, and features, but not in the most efficient manner.	Choose inappropriate skills, tools, or features, or are inefficient in solving the problem.
2-Content	Construct a solution that is clear and well organized, contains content that is accurate, appropriate to the audience and purpose, and is complete. Provide a solution that contains no errors of spelling, grammar, or style.	Construct a solution in which some components are unclear, poorly organized, inconsistent, or incomplete. Misjudge the needs of the audience. Have some errors in spelling, grammar, or style, but the errors do not detract from comprehension.	Construct a solution that is unclear, incomplete, or poorly organized, contains some inaccurate or inappropriate content, and contains many errors of spelling, grammar, or style. Do not solve the problem.
3-Format and Layout	Format and arrange all elements to communicate information and ideas, clarify function, illustrate relationships, and indicate relative importance.	Apply appropriate format and layout features to some elements, but not others. Overuse features, causing minor distraction.	Apply format and layout that does not communicate information or ideas clearly. Do not use format and layout features to clarify function, illustrate relationships, or indicate relative importance. Use available features excessively, causing distraction.
4-Process	Use an organized approach that integrates planning, development, self-assessment, revision, and reflection.	Demonstrate an organized approach in some areas, but not others; or, use an insufficient process of organization throughout.	Do not use an organized approach to solve the problem.

Outcomes-Based Assessments

Apply a combination of the **4A** and **4B** skills.

Problem Solving | Project **4G** Help Desk

Project Files

For Project 4G, you will need the following file:

win04_4G_Help_Desk

You will save your file as

Lastname_Firstname_4G_Help_Desk

From the student files that accompany this textbook, open the **Chapter_Files** folder, and then in the **Chapter_04** folder, locate and open the Word document **win04_4G_Help_Desk**. Save the document in your chapter folder as **Lastname_Firstname_4G_Help_Desk**

The following e-mail question has arrived at the Help Desk from an employee at the Bell Orchid Hotel's corporate office. In the Word document, construct a response based on your knowledge of Windows 7. Although an e-mail response is not as formal as a letter, you should still use good grammar, good sentence structure, professional language, and a polite tone. Save your document and submit the response as directed by your instructor.

To: Help Desk

My supervisor sent me some DVDs that contain video training. Will these play on Windows Media Player? If so, how do I start the player and view the video?

End **You have completed Project 4G**

Apply a combination of the **4A** and **4B** skills.

Problem Solving | Project **4H** Help Desk

Project Files

For Project 4H, you will need the following file:

    win04_4H_Help_Desk

You will save your file as

    Lastname_Firstname_4H_Help_Desk

From the student files that accompany this textbook, open the **Chapter_Files** folder, and then in the **Chapter_04** folder, locate and open **win04_4H_Help_Desk**. Save the document in your chapter folder as **Lastname_Firstname_4H_Help_Desk**

The following e-mail question has arrived at the Help Desk from an employee at the Bell Orchid Hotel's corporate office. In the Word document, construct a response based on your knowledge of Windows 7. Although an e-mail response is not as formal as a letter, you should still use good grammar, good sentence structure, professional language, and a polite tone. Save your document and submit the response as directed by your instructor.

To: Help Desk

I am working on a project where I am researching three specific government Web sites and then storing all of my notes in several documents that I have created. Is there any way that I could make it easier to access these three Web sites and three documents without opening a lot of windows every time I need to start and stop work on this project?

 You have completed Project 4H ———————————————

Outcomes-Based Assessments

Apply a combination of the **4A** and **4B** skills.

Problem Solving | Project 4I Help Desk

Project Files

For Project 4I, you will need the following file:

> **win04_4I_Help_Desk**

You will save your document as

> **Lastname_Firstname_4I_Help_Desk**

From the student files that accompany this textbook, open the **Chapter_Files** folder, and then in the **Chapter_04** folder, locate and open **win04_4I_Help_Desk**. Save the document in your chapter folder as **Lastname_Firstname_4I_Help_Desk**

The following e-mail question has arrived at the Help Desk from an employee at the Bell Orchid Hotel's corporate office. In the Word document, construct a response based on your knowledge of Windows 7. Although an e-mail response is not as formal as a letter, you should still use good grammar, good sentence structure, professional language, and a polite tone. Save your document and submit the response as directed by your instructor.

To: Help Desk

I need to make my computer easier to see. Can you tell me how to find out about the ways I can do that?

End **You have completed Project 4I** —————————————————————————

Exploring the World Wide Web with Internet Explorer 8

Charles Zachritz/Shutterstock

In This Chapter

In this chapter, you will browse the Web using Internet Explorer 8. Browsing the Web is one of the most common activities of computer users. You will use tabbed browsing, in which you can open multiple Web sites in one window. You will also use Web Slices and Accelerators to speed your Web browsing.

Internet Explorer 8 includes features to make printing and saving Web pages easy. You can also save and print pictures from a Web site. You will discover how to locate, subscribe to, and view RSS feeds. Internet Explorer 8 provides for inline toolbar searching, which allows you to conduct a search without actually navigating to the Web site of the search provider. You will practice conducting searches from multiple search providers from the Internet Explorer Search box.

The projects in this chapter relate to the **Bell Orchid Hotels**, headquartered in Boston, and which own and operate resorts and business-oriented hotels. Resort properties are located in popular destinations, including Honolulu, Orlando, San Diego, and Santa Barbara. The resorts offer deluxe accommodations and a wide array of dining options. Other Bell Orchid hotels are located in major business centers and offer the latest technology in their meeting facilities. The company plans to open new properties and update existing properties over the next ten years.

Project 5A Browsing the Web with Internet Explorer 8

In Activities 5.1 through 5.10, you will work with Barbara Hewitt and Steven Ramos, employees in the Information Technology department at the headquarters office of Bell Orchid Hotels, as they explore how to browse and navigate the World Wide Web by using Internet Explorer 8. Bell Orchid Hotels is investigating a new hotel opportunity in Miami, Florida, which will be geared to both business travelers and family vacations. Barbara and Steven have the assignment to conduct research on the Web for this new hotel. Your completed screens will look similar to Figure 5.1.

For Project 5A, you will need the following files:

New Snip files

You will save your files as:

Lastname_Firstname_5A_Florida_Snip
Lastname_Firstname_5A_Favorites_Snip
Lastname_Firstname_5A_Print_Snip
Lastname_Firstname_5A_Picture_Snip

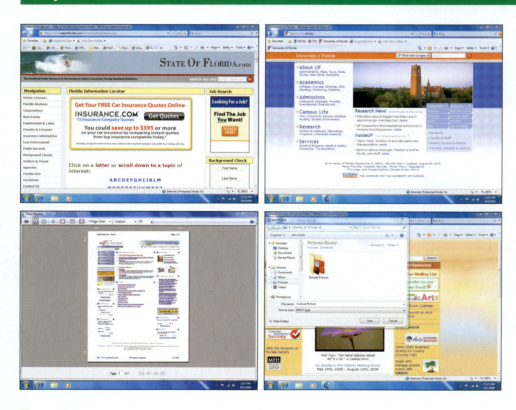

Figure 5.1
Project 5A Browsing the Web with Internet Explorer 8

Objective 1 | Use Tabbed Browsing

A **Web browser** is a software program that you use to display Web pages and navigate the Internet. **Internet Explorer 8** is the Web browser software developed by Microsoft Corporation and that is included with Windows 7. **Browsing** is the term used to describe the process of using your computer to view Web pages. **Surfing** refers to the process of navigating the Internet either for a particular item or for anything that is of interest, and quickly moving from one item to another.

Browsing the Web is one of the most common activities performed by individuals who use computers. Common tasks that you perform on the Internet might include looking at your favorite news sites, managing your finances with your bank, conducting research, shopping, sending e-mail, using social media sites such as Facebook or Twitter, or reading or writing entries in a **blog**. A blog—short for **Web log**—is an online journal or column used to publish personal or company information in an informal manner. For example, the developers of Microsoft Word maintain a blog of information about using Word at *http://blogs.msdn.com/microsoft_office_word*.

Activity 5.01 | Using Tabbed Browsing

Tabbed browsing is a feature in Internet Explorer that enables you to open multiple Web sites in a single browser window. You open each new Web page in a new tab, and then switch among your open Web pages by clicking the tab that displays in the upper portion of the screen. The advantage to using tabbed browsing is that you have fewer items open on the taskbar.

In this activity, you will work with Barbara and Steven, who are conducting research on the new hotel in Miami.

> **Another Way**
>
> On the Start menu, in the Search box, type Internet Explorer, and then click the program name.

1 On the taskbar, click the **Internet Explorer** button. If a Welcome screen displays, in the lower right, click **Ask me later**.

The **home page** that is set on your computer displays. On your computer, *home page* refers to whatever Web page you have selected—or is set by default—to display on your computer when you start Internet Explorer. When visiting a Web site, *home page* refers to the starting point for the remainder of the pages on that site.

For example, your computer manufacturer may have set its company site as the default home page. At your college, the home page of your college's Web site might be the home page on the computer at which you are working.

More Knowledge | Consider Downloading These Additional Windows 7 Programs

Some programs that were included in Windows Vista and Windows XP are no longer included in Windows 7. Instead, you can decide which programs you need and download them for free by using **Windows Live Essentials**. The new free programs include: Windows Live Mail (replaces Windows Mail and Outlook Express), Windows Live Messenger, Windows Live Photo Gallery, Windows Live Movie Maker, and Windows Live Family Safety. You can also download for free Office Outlook Connector, Office Live Add-in, and Microsoft Silverlight. To get information about and download any of these free programs, go to www.download.live.com.

2 At the top of your screen, click in the **address bar** to select (highlight) the current Web address, and then compare your screen with Figure 5.2.

The *address bar* is the area at the top of the Internet Explorer window that displays, and where you can type, a *URL—Uniform Resource Locator*—which is an address that uniquely identifies a location on the Internet.

A URL is usually preceded by *http://* and can contain additional details, such as the name of a page of hypertext, which often has the extension *.html* or *.htm*.

Figure 5.2

URL in address bar highlighted (your selected URL may differ)

Address bar

Another Way

Instead of pressing Enter, you can click the small blue arrow at the end of the address bar.

3 In the **address bar**, with the current URL selected, type **www.usa.gov** and then press Enter. Notice the URL in the **address bar**, and then compare your screen with Figure 5.3.

The Web site for the United States Government displays. By typing in the address bar, the new URL opens and the original URL—whatever your home page site was—closes.

A URL contains the *protocol prefix*—in this instance *http*—which stands for *HyperText Transfer Protocol*. HTTP represents the set of communication rules used by your computer to connect to servers on the Web. Internet Explorer defaults to the *http* prefix, so it is not necessary to type it, even though it is part of the URL for this site.

The protocol prefix is followed by a colon and the separators //.

A URL also contains the *domain name*—in this instance *www.usa.gov*. A domain name is an organization's unique name on the Internet, and consists of a chosen name combined with a *top level domain* such as *.com* or *.org* or *.gov*.

Figure 5.3

Address bar indicates URL for United States Government

Tab for *USA.gov* Web site

> **Alert! | Web Sites Update Content Frequently**
>
> As you progress through the projects in this chapter, the pictures of various Web sites in this textbook may not match your screens exactly, because Web site administrators frequently update content. This will not affect your ability to complete the projects successfully.

4 Take a moment to study the table in Figure 5.4 to become familiar with top level domains.

There are two types of top level domains—the generic top level domains, such as *.com*, *.org*, and so on, and the **country codes** such as *.ca* for Canada, *.cn* for China, and *.uk* for United Kingdom.

Common Domain Name Extensions and Organization Types

Domain Name Extension	Organization Type
.com	Commercial businesses and companies
.net	Internet service providers and other communications-oriented organizations
.org	Usually nonprofit organizations
.edu	U. S. educational only
.gov	U. S. government only
.info	Information services
.mobi	Mobile devices
.name	Individuals and families
.biz	Usually small businesses

Figure 5.4

5 Click in the **address bar** to select the URL text, and then type **miamibeachfl.gov** and press Enter.

The acronym *www*, which stands for *World Wide Web*, is used for uniformity on the Web. You can usually omit typing *www* and its following dot, because most Web servers are configured to handle a URL with or without it. If a Web page does not display without typing *www*, retype the URL and include *www*.

6 To the immediate right of the **Forward** button ⊙, locate and click the **Recent Pages** button ▾. Compare your screen with Figure 5.5.

The *Recent Pages* button displays a list of recently accessed locations, and the current location is indicated by a check mark. By clicking an item on this list, you can jump to a recently accessed location quickly. The list is limited to the current session; thus, only locations you have accessed since starting Internet Explorer display on the list.

Recent Pages button   New Tab button

Figure 5.5

List of Recent Pages

Current location indicated by check mark

Forward button

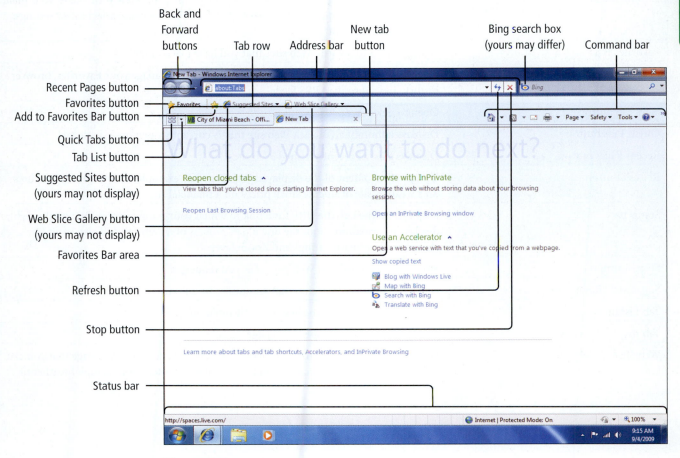

7 Click the **Recent Pages** button again to close the list, and then locate and point to the **New Tab** button , which is to the immediate right of the **City of Miami Beach tab**. Click the **New Tab** button one time. Compare your screen with Figure 5.6, and then take a moment to study the parts of the Internet Explorer window in the table in Figure 5.7.

The screen for a new tab displays, and in the address bar, *about:Tabs* is selected. This *What do you want to do next?* page will display a list of sites that you have opened and then closed during this session, which is useful if you have closed a browser window by mistake and want to go back to it.

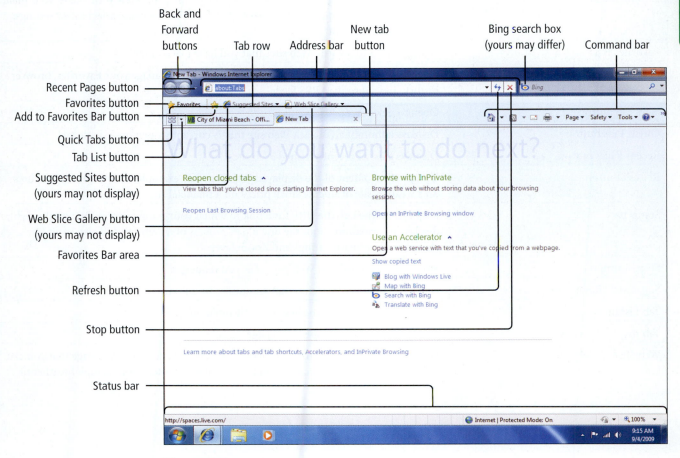

Figure 5.6

Parts of the Internet Explorer Window

Window Element	Function
Add to Favorites Bar button	Places the active URL on the Favorites Bar.
Address bar	Displays the URL of the currently active Web page.
Back and Forward buttons	Display Web pages you have previously visited.
Bing search box	Provides an area in which you type a search term to conduct an Internet search; Bing is the default search engine but you can select a different one.
Command bar	Contains, by default, the buttons to view your Home page; view your Feeds; view mail; print Web pages; manipulate Web pages, for example by saving; select safety settings; and to display a list of Tools.
Favorites Bar	Displays links to favorite Web sites that you have placed there.
Favorites button	Opens the Favorites Center pane, which is an area to manage your Favorites, browser history, and subscribed RSS feeds.
New Tab button	Opens a new tab.
Quick Tabs button	Displays a thumbnail of each Web site that is currently open on a single tab.
Recent Pages button	Displays a list of recently visited Web sites.
Refresh button	Updates the content of the displayed Web page; for example, to update temperatures on a weather site or update stock prices on a financial site.
Status bar	Displays, on the left, the URL for a link to which your mouse is pointing; on the right, displays information about the download process of a Web site and also icons to change your security settings and Zoom level.
Stop button	Stops the download of a Web page that you requested.
Suggested Sites button	Helps you discover Web sites that are similar to the sites you visit.
Tab List button	Lists the names of all Web sites currently open on a tab.
Tab row	Displays a tab for each open Web page.
Web Slice Gallery button	Enables you to subscribe to Web Slices—a specific portion of a Web page that you can subscribe to, and which enables you to see updated content, for example weather or traffic.

Figure 5.7

8 With the text in the **address bar** selected, type **miamigov.com/cms** and then press Enter to display the Web site for the **City of Miami**. Click the **New Tab** button, type **doh.state.fl.us** and then press Enter. Compare your screen with Figure 5.8.

The Web site for the Florida Department of Health opens in the new tab.

Figure 5.8

Three tabs open

City of Miami Beach tab

City of Miami tab

Florida Department of Health tab active

9 On the **tab row**, click the first open tab—the **City of Miami Beach tab**.

> The Web site for Miami Beach redisplays. Recall that by opening multiple sites on tabs, you can switch between Web sites easily by clicking a tab.

10 On the taskbar, *point to* the **Internet Explorer** icon 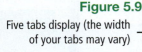 to display a thumbnail for each open tab.

> Here you can see the Web sites that you have open in Internet Explorer, and can navigate to a site by clicking its thumbnail.

11 At the end of the **tab row**, click the **New Tab** button, type **hsmv.state.fl.us** and then press Enter to display the site for the **Florida Department of Highway Safety and Motor Vehicles**. Open another **New Tab**, type **leg.state.fl.us** and then press Enter to display the site for the **Florida Legislature**. Compare your screen with Figure 5.9.

> Depending on the size of your screen and its resolution, the tabs might display differently than shown in Figure 5.9, but you can see that five Web pages are open.

Figure 5.9

Five tabs display (the width of your tabs may vary)

12 Click the **New Tab** button, and then type **myflorida.com** and press Enter. Click the **New Tab** button, and then type **visitflorida.com** and press Enter.

> Seven Web sites are open and seven tabs display in your tab row. As you open more tabs, the width of each tab decreases slightly and you can no longer read all the text on the tab.

13 By clicking the **New Tab** button ⬜ for each, open the following five sites, waiting a moment for each site to display completely. Then, compare your screen with Figure 5.10.

> **dep.state.fl.us**
>
> **stateofflorida.com**
>
> **floridastateparks.org**
>
> **florida.edu**
>
> **mdc.edu**

Twelve Web sites are open, however on some screens, Internet Explorer will display only nine or ten tabs in the tab row, plus the New Tab button. On larger screens, you might be able to display more tabs.

Figure 5.10

Open tabs

Small tabs with double chevrons

New tab button

More Knowledge | Using the Address Bar Efficiently

The address bar, based on the first few characters that you type, will search across your History, Favorites, and RSS Feeds, displaying matches from the address or any part of the URL. When you see a match, click it to avoid retyping the entire URL of a site you have previously visited.

---

14 On the **tab row**, to the *left* of the first visible tab, click the ⟪ button, and then compare your screen with Figure 5.11.

When you have more sites open than Internet Explorer can display on the tab row, the small tabs with double chevrons indicate that more tabs are available. When the double chevrons are black, this indicates that additional tabs are open to the left (<<) or to the right (>>). If the double chevrons are dimmed, no additional tabs are open in the direction of the chevrons.

Figure 5.11

Indicates more tabs are available to the right (your displayed site may differ)

Activity 5.02 | Using the Tab List, Quick Tabs, and Shortcuts to Navigate Among Open Tabs

When you have multiple Web pages open at once, each one is displayed on a separate tab. When many Web pages are open and the width of each tab is decreased, it may become difficult to determine which tab represents a specific site. In this activity, you will practice various ways to navigate the open tabs to find the one you want easily.

1 On the left end of the **tab row**, click the **Tab List** button ⌄, and then compare your screen with Figure 5.12.

> The Tab List displays. When multiple tabs are open, the Web site name on each tab is truncated—cut short. By clicking the Tab List button, you can see a list of all open Web sites, in the order they were opened, and you can see the complete name of each Web site that is open on a tab.
>
> Additionally, the highlighted section indicates tabs that are visible on the tab row; tabs outside of the highlighted area, for example at the bottom in Figure 5.12, are open, but their tabs are not in view on the tab row.
>
> From this list, you can click a site to move to another tab, regardless of whether the tab is visible on the tab row.

Web sites outside highlighted area are open but tab is not in view

Web sites in highlighted area have visible tabs in tab row

Figure 5.12

Tab List button

Tab List

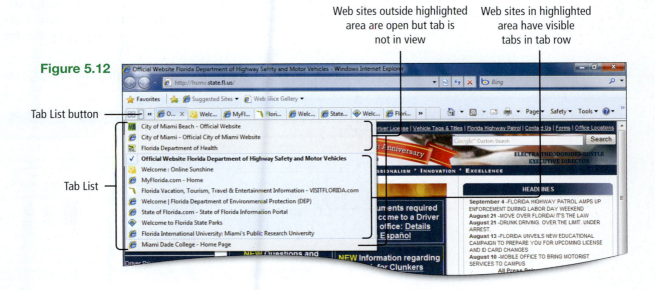

2 On the displayed **Tab List** menu, at the top, click **City of Miami Beach**. Notice that to the immediate left of the **Miami Beach tab**, *no* small tab with double chevrons displays, because all tabs to the left are in view. Point to the **City of Miami Beach tab**, and then notice that a ScreenTip displays the site name and the site's URL. Notice also that because this is the active tab, the **Close Tab** button ⊠ displays, as shown in Figure 5.13.

Figure 5.13

Close Tab button displays in active tab

ScreenTip displays site name and URL

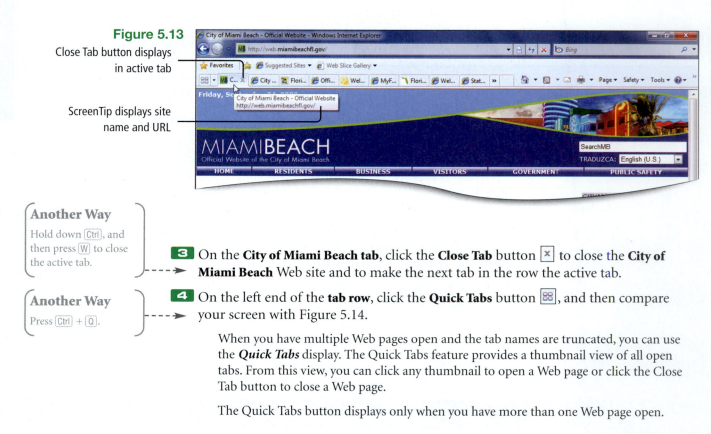

Another Way

Hold down ⌃Ctrl, and then press W to close the active tab.

3 On the **City of Miami Beach tab**, click the **Close Tab** button ⊠ to close the **City of Miami Beach** Web site and to make the next tab in the row the active tab.

Another Way

Press ⌃Ctrl + Q.

4 On the left end of the **tab row**, click the **Quick Tabs** button ⊞, and then compare your screen with Figure 5.14.

When you have multiple Web pages open and the tab names are truncated, you can use the *Quick Tabs* display. The Quick Tabs feature provides a thumbnail view of all open tabs. From this view, you can click any thumbnail to open a Web page or click the Close Tab button to close a Web page.

The Quick Tabs button displays only when you have more than one Web page open.

Figure 5.14

Quick Tabs button in tab row

Tab Close buttons display for each site (your sites may vary in appearance)

5 In the **Quick Tabs** display, click the thumbnail for **State of Florida.com** to display its site.

In this manner, you can display any open site from the Quick Tabs display.

6 **Start** 🟢 the **Snipping Tool** program, click the **New arrow**, and then click **Full-screen Snip**. In the **Snipping Tool** mark-up window, click the **Save Snip** button 💾.

7 In the **Save As** dialog box, in the **navigation pane**, scroll down as necessary, and then under **Computer**, click your USB flash drive so that it displays in the **address bar**. On the toolbar, click the **New folder** button, type **Windows 7 Chapter 5** and press Enter.

8 In the **file list**, double-click your **Windows 7 Chapter 5** folder to open it. Click in the **File name** box, and then replace the selected text by typing **Lastname_Firstname_5A_Florida_Snip** Be sure the file type is **JPEG file**, and then press Enter. **Close** ❎ the **Snipping Tool** mark-up window. Hold this file until you finish Project 5A, and then submit this file as directed by your instructor.

More Knowledge | The Display of Quick Tabs Scales to the Number of Open Tabs

The Quick Tabs display scales to the number of tabs that you have open. For example, if you have nine tabs open, Quick Tabs shows thumbnail images of all nine tabs. If you have more than 20 tabs open, you will see smaller thumbnail images of each tab, but you can still see all the tabs in a single view.

---

9 Click the **Quick Tabs** button 🔲 again. In the **Quick Tabs** display, point to the **Close Tab** button ☒ for the **State of Florida.com** site as shown in Figure 5.15.

Figure 5.15

Close button in Quick Tabs display

10 Click the **Close Tab** button ⊠ to close the Web page, and notice that in the display, the thumbnails rearrange to fill the blank space. *Except* for the **City of Miami** site (do not close it), use the same technique to close all the other sites. Then click the thumbnail image for the **City of Miami** to display the site. Compare your screen with Figure 5.16.

Although the content of this Web page may differ from what you currently have displayed, you can see that this Web page contains various links—other pages in this Web site that you can display. Groups of links are sometimes referred to as a *navigation bar*.

Figure 5.16

Navigation bar with links (yours may differ)

Navigation bar with links (yours may differ)

Link to City Officials (yours may differ)

11 On the navigation bar on the left, click **Business**; or, click any link on the page. Compare your screen with Figure 5.17.

When you click a link on a Web page, the new page opens on the same tab.

Figure 5.17

Back button active

Link opens on *same* tab— only one tab displays

12 In the upper left corner, click the **Back** button one time to return to the previous page. Then, click the **Forward** button to redisplay the page regarding Business information in the City of Miami.

In this manner, you can click the Back and Forward buttons as necessary to redisplay pages you have visited.

Another Way
Point to a link on the page and right-click, and then click Open in New Tab.

13 Hold down Ctrl, and then in the navigation bar in the upper portion of the page, click **city directory**. Notice that a new tab opens for the **City Directory** page but the page itself does not display. Notice also that the two tabs display in the same color.

In this manner, you can open links in separate tabs without actually displaying them. When you are finished viewing the active page, you can investigate the other links you opened. Additionally, the tabs are colored to match so that you know they are related.

14 In the same navigation bar in the upper portion of the page, hold down both Ctrl and Shift, point to **employment**, and then click. Release the keys.

The link opens in a new tab, and the color coding continues to indicate that the tabs originated from the same site.

Use this technique to open a link in a new tab and simultaneously display the link.

Another Way
Double-click an empty space in the tab row to open a new tab.

15 Hold down Ctrl and press T to open a new tab. Type **sunbiz.org** and press Enter. In the **tab row**, point to the **City Directory tab**. If you have a mouse wheel, also referred to as the *middle mouse button*, click it and notice that the tab is closed. Otherwise, point to the tab, right-click, and click Close Tab.

16 Point to the middle tab—for the city's **Employee Relations Department**, right-click, and then click **Close Tab**.

Use either of these techniques to close a tab without first making it the active tab. This is useful when you have some tabs open that you no longer need and want to close them quickly.

17 Press Ctrl + T to open a new tab, and then compare your screen with Figure 5.18.

After you have opened and closed sites, you can view a list of all the sites you have visited in this session by opening a new tab. Then, if you want to do so, you can click a site name to open it on this tab.

Figure 5.18

Reopen closed tabs list (your list may vary)

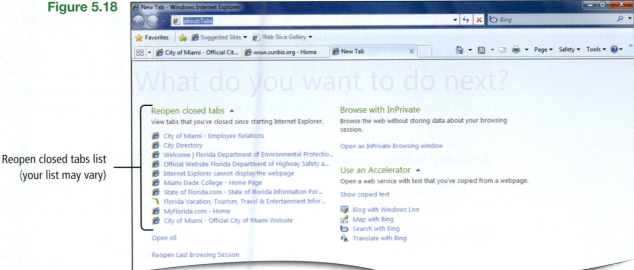

18 In the upper right corner of the Internet Explorer window, click the **Close** 🔲 button.

> When you close Internet Explorer, you are prompted to close all the tabs, or you can close only the current tab.

19 In the displayed **Internet Explorer** dialog box, click **Close all tabs**.

20 Take a moment to examine some additional shortcuts that you can use when navigating in Internet Explorer as shown in the table in Figure 5.19.

Keyboard and Mouse Shortcuts When Working with Tabs in Internet Explorer

To do this:	Press or do this:
Open links in a new tab in the background	Ctrl + click; or point to the link, right-click, and click Open In New Tab.
Open links in a new tab in the foreground	Ctrl + Shift + click using the left or middle mouse button.
Open a new tab in the foreground	Ctrl + T
Switch between tabs	Ctrl + Tab or Ctrl + Shift + Tab (right to left and left to right).
Close current tab (or current window when there are no open tabs)	Ctrl + W
Switch to a specific tab number	Ctrl + n (where n is a number between 1 and 8).
Switch to the last tab	Ctrl + 9.
Open Quick Tabs (thumbnail view)	Ctrl + Q.
Open a link in a tab with a wheel mouse	Click the link with the mouse wheel.
Close a tab with a wheel mouse	Click the tab with the mouse wheel.
Reorder tabs in the tab row	Point to the tab you want to move, and then drag it to the desired position.

Figure 5.19

Objective 2 | Organize Favorites

The *Favorites Center* is a list of links to Web sites that is saved in your Web browser. Saving a Web site as a favorite allows you to return to it quickly. For example, if you have a favorite health site that you visit frequently, you can save that site's address as a Favorite. Returning to the site requires only one or two clicks instead of typing a complete URL.

You can create a folder to organize your favorite links into groups that are meaningful to you. Then, you can either open one site from the folder, or open all the sites in the folder with a single click.

Activity 5.03 | Organizing Favorites and Creating a Favorites Folder

In this activity, you will help Barbara and Steven organize a number of sites that they believe will be useful to those who are conducting research for the new hotel in Miami.

1 **Close** 🔲 any open windows and display your Windows 7 desktop. On the taskbar, click the **Internet Explorer** button 🔵, click in the **address bar**, and then type **mdc.edu** and press Enter.

2 Click the **New Tab** button, type **florida.edu** and then press Enter.

Barbara and Steven know that one thing managers will be looking for are institutions of higher learning where employees can gain additional knowledge and credentials in management, computer science, and tourism management.

3 In the upper left corner, click the **Favorites** button, and then at the top of the pane, to the right of *Add to Favorites*, click the ▾ **arrow**. On the displayed list, click **Add Current Tabs to Favorites**.

4 In the **Add Tabs to Favorites** dialog box, in the **Folder Name** box, type **Colleges and Universities** If necessary, click the Create in arrow and click Favorites. Compare your screen with Figure 5.20.

Figure 5.20

Two tabs open

Add Tabs to Favorites dialog box

Folder name

Tab group will be created in *Favorites*

Add button

5 In the dialog box, click the **Add** button. **Close** Internet Explorer and all tabs.

6 Open **Internet Explorer** again, and then in the upper left corner, click the **Favorites** button. If necessary, at the top of the displayed list, click the Favorites tab. Scroll down as necessary, click **Colleges and Universities** to expand the list, and then point to the arrow to the right of **Colleges and Universities** to display the ScreenTip. Compare your screen with Figure 5.21.

ScreenTip

Your home page background displays (yours will differ)

Figure 5.21

Colleges and Universities folder expanded

Favorites List (yours may vary)

Folders created by Microsoft (yours may vary)

7 To the right of **Colleges and Universities**, click the arrow to open the entire group of sites on individual tabs; notice that because they are in a group, the tabs are colored to match. Point to the tab for your home page, right-click, and then click **Close Tab** so that only the two Florida college tabs display.

> From the Favorites List, you can also click one of the links individually to open just one of the links.

8 Display the tab for **Florida International University**, and then on the navigation bar on the left of this site, click **Colleges & Schools**. Locate and click the link for the **College of Business Administration**.

9 Click the **Favorites** button, click **Add to Favorites**, and then in the **Add a Favorite** dialog box, click the **Create in arrow**. Compare your screen with Figure 5.22.

Figure 5.22

Add a Favorite dialog box

Create in arrow

Colleges and Universities folder (other folders on your list will vary)

10 From the displayed list, click the **Colleges and Universities** folder, and then click the **Add** button.

> The link to the College of Business Administration at Florida International University is added to the folder *Colleges and Universities*.

11 Open a **New Tab**, type **miamidade.gov** and then press Enter.

12 Hold down Ctrl and press D—this is a keyboard shortcut for the Add to Favorites command. In the **Add a Favorite** dialog box, click the **New Folder** button.

13 In the **Folder Name** box, type **County Govt Miami-Dade** Click the **Create in arrow**, and then click **Favorites** so that you create the folder at the same level as other folders. Click the **Create** button.

14 In the displayed **Add a Favorite** dialog box, select the text in the **Name** box, and then replace it by typing **Miami-Dade County** Compare your screen with Figure 5.23.

> You need not accept the default name of a Web site stored in your Favorites list. Change the name as necessary so that you can easily identify the site.

Figure 5.23

Name changed ——————
New folder name ——————
Add button ——————

15 In the **Add a Favorite** dialog box, click the **Add** button.

> In this manner, you can create folders for your favorite sites at the time you save the site as a Favorite. Be sure to notice where the folder is being stored, and place it either at the Favorites level or within other folders if you want to do so.

16 In the upper left corner, click the **Favorites** button, to the right of *Add to Favorites* click the ▾ **arrow**, click **Organize Favorites**, and then from this dialog box, create a **New Folder** named **Florida Tourism** Press Enter, and then in the lower right corner of the dialog box, click the **Close** button.

17 Open a **New Tab** 🔲, type **visitflorida.com** and then press Enter. Click the **Favorites** button, click **Add to Favorites**, in the displayed dialog box, click the **Create in arrow**, click the **Florida Tourism** folder, and then **Add** this site.

18 Hold down Alt and press Z to display the **Add to Favorites** menu. Click **Organize Favorites**, click the **County Govt Miami-Dade** folder to select it, and then in the lower portion of the dialog box, click **Rename**. Type **Florida Government** and then press Enter.

19 Point to **Colleges and Universities** and click one time to expand the list. Click **Colleges and Universities** again to collapse the list. Point to **Florida Tourism**, and then right-click.

> From the displayed shortcut menu, you can see that you can take many additional actions on the list of folders such as sorting the list of folders by name, creating a new folder, and deleting a folder.

20 Click **Colleges and Universities** to expand the list. Then point to **Florida International University** and right-click.

> From the displayed menu, you can perform similar commands related to a specific site in the list.

21 **Close** ![X button] the **Organize Favorites** dialog box; **Close** ![X button] Internet Explorer.

> **More Knowledge** | Copying Favorites from One Computer to Another and Printing Favorites
>
> You can save your Favorites from one computer and then import that list to another computer. To do so, open Windows Help and Support, type export Favorites, and follow the instructions for exporting, importing, and printing favorites.

Activity 5.04 | Using the Favorites Bar

The *Favorites bar* is a toolbar that displays directly below the address bar and to which you can add or drag Web addresses you use frequently. You can also use the Favorites bar to monitor RSS feeds to which you have subscribed and to store your Web Slices.

1 On the taskbar, click the **Internet Explorer** button ![IE icon]. Click in the **address bar** to select the existing URL, type **weather.gov** and then press Enter.

2 Directly below the **address bar**, click the **Add to Favorites Bar** ![icon] button. Compare your screen with Figure 5.24.

URL typed in address bar

Figure 5.24

Add to Favorites Bar button

NOAA's site displays on Favorites bar

3 Click in the **address bar**, type **fsu.edu** and press Enter. At the left end of the **address bar**, point to the **Florida State University logo**, hold down the left mouse button, and then drag the logo onto the **Favorites bar** until a black line displays to the right of the NOAA's site, as shown in Figure 5.25. Then release the mouse button.

Figure 5.25

Logo being dragged

Vertical line

ScreenTip

4 On the **Favorites bar**, point to the **NOAA's** site, right-click, and then click **Rename**. In the **Rename** box, type **NOAA** and then click **OK**. Using the same technique, rename *The Florida State University* link **FSU** Compare your screen with Figure 5.26.

> You can change and shorten the names on your Favorites bar to make additional space. When you have more Favorites than the bar can accommodate, double chevrons will display at the right, which when clicked will display a continuation of the list.

Figure 5.26

Link names shortened on Favorites bar

5 Click in the **address bar**, type **ufl.edu** and press Enter, and then drag its logo to the **Favorites bar** to the right of FSU.

6 **Start** the **Snipping Tool** program, click the **New arrow**, and then click **Full-screen Snip**. In the **Snipping Tool** mark-up window, click the **Save Snip** button .

7 In the **Save As** dialog box, in the **navigation pane**, scroll down as necessary, and then under **Computer**, click your USB flash drive so that it displays in the **address bar**. Navigate to your **Windows 7 Chapter 5** folder, and then as the file name, type **Lastname_Firstname_5A_Favorites_Snip** Be sure the file type is **JPEG file**, and then press Enter. **Close** the **Snipping Tool** mark-up window. Hold this file until you finish Project 5A, and then submit this file as directed by your instructor.

8 Point to the **University of Florida** link on the **Favorites bar**, right-click, click **Delete**, and then click **Yes**. By using the same technique, delete the links for **FSU** and **NOAA**.

9 **Close** Internet Explorer.

> On your own computer, place links to the sites you use most frequently on the Favorites bar, and for other favorite sites, add them to the Favorites Center.

More Knowledge | Additional Tools to Manage Your Favorites

There are additional free tools available to manage your favorites. These tools are sometimes referred to as *bookmark managers*. Windows Live Favorites (*http://favorites.live.com*) is a free web-based service from Microsoft. The Favorites you place on this list are available from any online connection—not just from your own computer. Another service is *delicious* (delicious.com) where you can maintain a collection of Web site addresses and publish it. You can also download a toolbar button as an add-on for Internet Explorer, so it is easy and quick to add a site to your collection.

Objective 3 | Manage Browsing History and Browse with InPrivate

As you browse the Web, Internet Explorer stores information about the Web sites you visit. It also stores information that you are frequently asked to provide. For example, if you type your name and address into a Web site, Internet Explorer stores that information. All of this information is referred to as your **browsing history**.

Usually it is useful to have this information stored on your computer, because it speeds your Web browsing and might automatically provide information so that you do not have to type it over and over.

Internet Explorer stores the following types of information:

- *Temporary Internet files*, which are copies of Web pages, images, and media that you have downloaded from the Web. Storing this information makes viewing faster the next time you visit a site that you have visited before.
- *Cookies*, which is the term used to refer to small text files that Web sites put on your computer to store information about you and your preferences, for example login information.
- A history of Web sites that you have visited.
- Information that you have entered into Web sites or the address bar, including your name and address if you have entered it into a site, and the URLs that you have visited before.
- Saved Web passwords.

Activity 5.05 | Viewing and Deleting Browsing History

You might want to delete your browsing history to make more space on your own computer. If you are using a public computer, such as in your college classroom or lab, you will want to delete your browsing history so that you do not leave any of your personal information stored there.

1 On the taskbar, click the **Internet Explorer** button ![IE icon]. Click the **Favorites** button, and then at the top of the pane click the **History tab**. Under **History**, click the **arrow**, and then if necessary, click **View By Date**. Display the list again, click **Today**, and then compare your screen with Figure 5.27.

Here you can view a list of the sites you visited today.

Figure 5.27

Favorites button —

History tab —

Arrow —

List of sites visited today (yours will vary) —

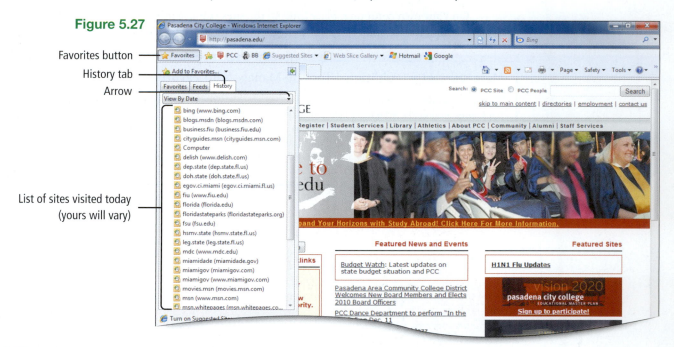

2 At the top of the pane, to the right of *View By Date*, click the **arrow**. On the displayed list, click **Search History**, and then in the displayed **Search for** box, type **Miami** Click the **Search Now** button, and then notice that a list of sites that you have visited related to *Miami* displays.

3 To the right of *Search History*, click the **arrow** again, and then click **View By Order Visited Today**.

4 In the upper right portion of your screen, on the **Command bar**, click the **Safety** button, and then click **Delete Browsing History**. Compare your screen with Figure 5.28.

> Here you can delete all of your web browsing history, or individually select one or more categories of files to delete.

Figure 5.28

Your displayed home page will differ

Delete Browsing History dialog box

Categories of files that you can delete

Delete button

5 Unless you are working on your own computer and you do not want to delete any files, click the **Delete** button, and then wait a few moments for the deletion to complete.

> Deleting all browsing history does not delete your list of Favorites or feeds to which you have subscribed. This action deletes only temporary files, your browsing history, cookies, and saved form information passwords—if their checkboxes are selected.

> If you perform this action on your own computer, it might take a few seconds longer to display sites again the first time you access them. After that, the system will rebuild your browsing history as you browse the Web.

6 **Close** Internet Explorer.

More Knowledge | Close Internet Explorer After Deleting Browser History

You should close Internet Explorer after deleting your browser history to clear cookies that are still in memory from your current browsing session. This is especially important when using a public computer such as in your college computer lab.

Activity 5.06 | Using InPrivate Browsing

Use **InPrivate Browsing** to browse the Web without storing data about your browsing session. This feature is useful because it prevents anyone else who might be using your computer from seeing what sites you visited.

1 On the taskbar, click the **Internet Explorer** button 🔵. Click the **New Tab** button 🔲. On the right, click **Browse with InPrivate**. Compare your screen with Figure 5.29.

The InPrivate indicator displays on the address bar and the tab indicates *InPrivate*.

Figure 5.29
Address bar indicates *InPrivate*

InPrivate tab

2 With the text in the **address bar** selected, type **gatorzone.com** and press Enter. (This site may play sound if your speakers or headphones are enabled.)

3 Click the **New Tab** button 🔲; notice that **InPrivate Browsing** is still in effect. Type **fsu.edu/athletics** and press Enter.

In the current Internet Explorer window, you can open as many tabs as you want, and they will be protected by InPrivate Browsing.

4 Click the **Favorites** button, and then click the **History tab**. Click the **arrow**, click **View By Order Visited Today**. Notice that the two sites you accessed while using InPrivate Browsing do *not* display on the list.

While using InPrivate Browsing, Internet Explorer stores some information. For example, cookies are kept in memory so pages work properly, but are cleared when you close the browser window. Temporary Internet files are also stored so pages work properly, but are deleted when you close the browser window. Web page history, form data, and passwords are not stored at all.

5 Close ❎ Internet Explorer.

Cookies are cleared and temporary Internet files are discarded.

Objective 4 | Print, Zoom, and Change the Text Size of Web Pages

By default, Internet Explorer 8 will shrink a Web page's text just enough to ensure that the entire page prints properly. The Page Zoom feature enables you to increase or decrease the page size for easier viewing. You can also adjust the size of displayed text.

Activity 5.07 | Printing Web Pages

Internet Explorer 8 provides useful options for formatting and then printing a Web page. In the following activity, you will work with Barbara and Steven to print a Web page.

1 **Close** ❎ any open windows. On the taskbar, click the **Internet Explorer** button ,
click in the **address bar**, type **myflorida.com** and then press Enter.

> The home page that serves as the official *portal* for the State of Florida displays. A portal is a Web site that displays news, content, and links that are of interest to a specific audience; for example, individuals who need information about Florida.

2 On the **Command bar**, locate and click the **Print button arrow** to display a menu.
Compare your screen with Figure 5.30.

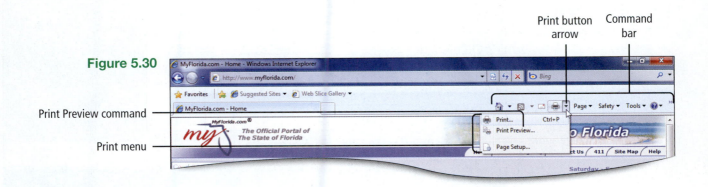

Figure 5.30

Print button arrow

Command bar

Print Preview command

Print menu

3 On the menu, click **Print Preview**. Compare your screen with Figure 5.31, and then take a moment to study the parts of the Print Preview window described in the table in Figure 5.32.

Recall that Internet Explorer will shrink the page as necessary to fit horizontally on the selected paper size. You can also drag the margins by using the adjust margin buttons on this Print Preview screen.

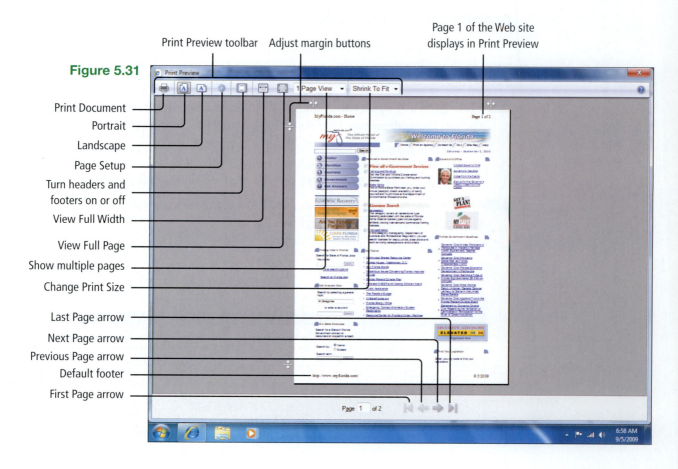

Figure 5.31

Print Preview toolbar   Adjust margin buttons   Page 1 of the Web site displays in Print Preview

Print Document
Portrait
Landscape
Page Setup
Turn headers and footers on or off
View Full Width
View Full Page
Show multiple pages
Change Print Size
Last Page arrow
Next Page arrow
Previous Page arrow
Default footer
First Page arrow

Parts of the Print Preview Window in Internet Explorer 8

Adjust margin buttons	Adjusts the left, right, top, and bottom margins by dragging.
Change Print Size	Stretches or shrinks the page size to fill the printed page.
First Page arrow	Displays the first page of a multiple-page preview screen.
Landscape	Prints the page in landscape orientation, in which the paper is wider than it is tall.
Last Page arrow	Displays the last page of a multiple-page preview screen.
Next Page arrow	Displays the next page of a multiple-page preview screen.
Page indicator	Indicates the page displayed and the total number of pages.
Page Setup	Opens the Page Setup dialog box, in which you can change paper size, orientation, margins, and header and footer options.
Portrait	Prints the page in portrait orientation, in which the paper is taller than it is wide.
Previous Page arrow	Displays the previous page of a multiple-page preview screen.
Print Document	Opens the Print dialog box, enabling you to print the page using the current settings.
Show multiple pages	Displays multiple pages on the preview screen.
Turn headers or footers on or off	Turns the display of headers and footers off or on in the manner of a toggle button.
View Full Page	Zooms the Web page to show the full Web page in the preview screen.
View Full Width	Zooms the Web page to the width of the preview screen.

Figure 5.32

4 On the **Print Preview** toolbar, click the **Show multiple pages arrow** ⌄ , and then click **2 Page View.**

This Web page, as currently formatted, will print on two pages.

Another Way

Experiment with percentages on the list, or by typing in the Custom box, to shrink the page to print the way you want it to-on one or more pages.

5 On the toolbar, to the right of *Shrink To Fit*, click the **Change Print Size button arrow** ▾, and then from the displayed list, click **Custom.** In the **% box,** type **75** and press Enter. Compare your screen with Figure 5.33.

Figure 5.33

Print size changed to 75% (your percentage may differ)

Headers display

Page 1 of 1 indicated

Page resized to fit on one sheet (your page content may differ)

Footer displays

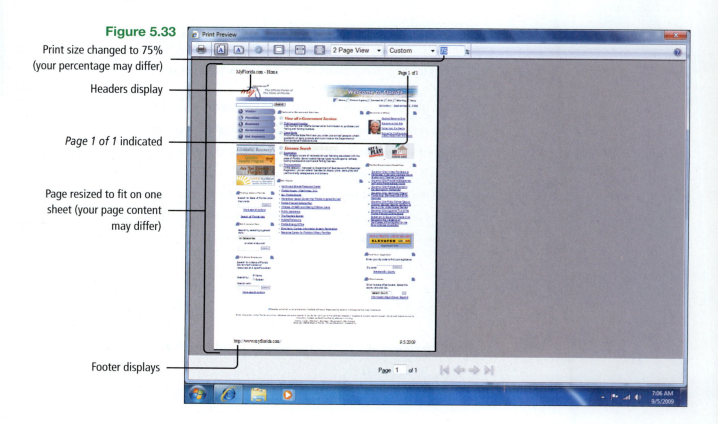

6 On the toolbar, to the right of *2 Page View*, click the **Show multiple pages button arrow** ▾, and then click **1 Page View** to return to that view and center the page on the Preview screen.

7 On the toolbar, click the **Page Setup** button 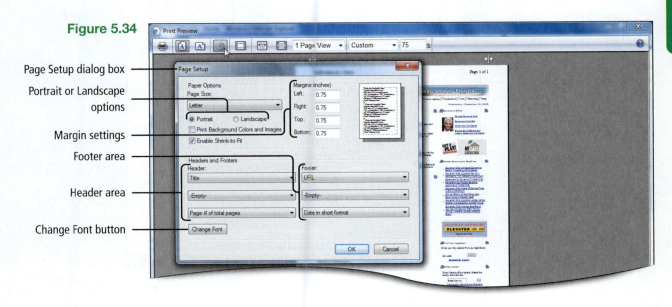. Compare your screen with Figure 5.34.

Here you can change or add to the headers and footers on a printed Web page.

By default there are two headers, one left aligned and one right aligned, which will display the page title and the URL. Similarly, there are two footers, one left aligned and one right aligned, which will display the page number with total pages and the date in short format.

The default setting for the centered header and footer is *Empty*. You can change any of the headers and footers by clicking the arrow and selecting an item or by selecting Custom and creating a new entry. You can also change the font of the headers and footers.

Figure 5.34

Page Setup dialog box

Portrait or Landscape options

Margin settings

Footer area

Header area

Change Font button

8 Under **Footer,** click the second arrow, and then point to **Custom,** as shown in Figure 5.35.

Here you can enter a centered footer.

Footer area   Control for centered header

Figure 5.35

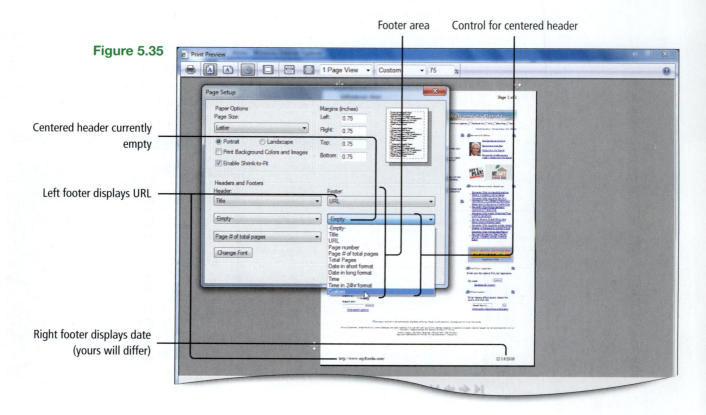

Centered header currently empty

Left footer displays URL

Right footer displays date (yours will differ)

9 Click **Custom.** In the Custom dialog box, using your own name, type **Firstname Lastname** Compare your screen with Figure 5.36.

Figure 5.36

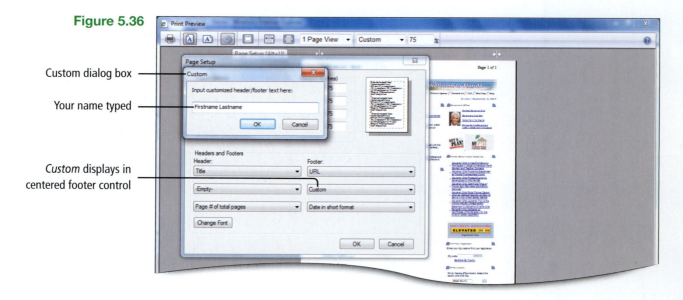

Custom dialog box

Your name typed

Custom displays in centered footer control

10 In the **Custom** dialog box, click **OK**. In the **Page Setup** dialog box, click **OK.**

In the Print Preview screen, your name displays as a centered heading.

11 **Start** 🪟 the **Snipping Tool** program, click the **New arrow**, and then click **Full-screen Snip.** In the **Snipping Tool** mark-up window, click the **Save Snip** button 💾.

12 In the **Save As** dialog box, in the navigation pane, scroll down as necessary, and then under Computer, click your USB flash drive so that it displays in the address bar. Navigate to your **Windows 7 Chapter 5** folder, and then as the file name, type **Lastname_Firstname_5A_Print_Snip** Be sure the file type is **JPEG** file, and then press Enter. **Close** ❎ the **Snipping Tool** mark-up window. Hold this file until you finish Project 5A, and then submit this file as directed by your instructor.

13 **Close** ❎ the **Print Preview** screen, and then **Close** ❎ Internet Explorer.

More Knowledge | Printing Specific Parts of a Web Page

To print only a specific part of a Web page, use your mouse to select the content that you want to print. Then, click the Print button arrow, click Print, and then in the Print dialog box, click the Selection option button. Click Print.

Activity 5.08 | Zooming and Changing the Text Size of Webpages

1 **Close** ❎ any open windows. On the taskbar, click the **Internet Explorer button** 🌐, click in the **address bar,** type **miamigov.com** and press Enter. On the **Command bar,** click the **Page** button, point to *Zoom,* and then click **200%.**

The view of the page is increased to 200%. Increasing the Zoom level increases the size of everything on the page, including graphics and controls.

2 Using the technique you just practiced, change the Zoom level to 50%.

3 Hold down Ctrl and then turn your mouse wheel backward and forward to increase and decrease the zoom.

This is a useful technique if you want to briefly magnify some text that is difficult to read or to examine a photo closely.

4 In the lower right corner of your screen, point to the **Change zoom level button** 🔍, and then click as many times as necessary to return the zoom level to 100%.

5 Open a **New Tab** 🗔, type **myflorida.com** and then press Enter. On the **Command bar,** click the **Page** button, and then point to **Text Size**.

The default text size is Medium, but if you would like to see more text on the screen you can set a smaller text size. If you have difficulty reading Web pages on your screen, you can set a larger text size.

Changing the text size affects only the text—graphics and controls continue to display in their original size.

6 On the displayed submenu, click **Largest,** and notice that the text on your screen is enlarged. Compare your screen with Figure 5.37.

Figure 5.37

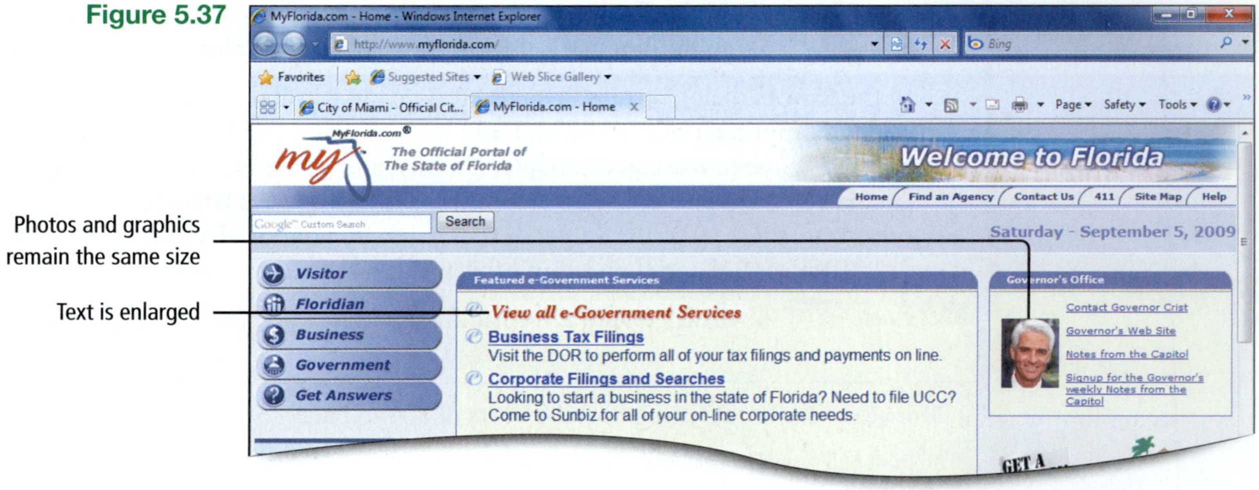

Photos and graphics remain the same size

Text is enlarged

7 Using the technique you just practiced, return the **Text Size** to **Medium**.

Note | Text Size is Set at Page Creation

The text size of some Web pages is set by the person who created the page.

The creator of the Web page may set a specific text size that you cannot change with the Text Size command. If you want to do so, you can override this setting as follows: click the Tools button on the Command bar, click Internet Options, on the General tab, click the Accessibility button, and then select the Ignore font sizes specified on Web pages check box.

---

8 **Close** Internet Explorer.

More Knowledge | Using Full Screen Mode

You can view a Web page in Full Screen mode, which will hide the title bar, the address bar, the Favorites Bar, the tab row, and the Command bar—unless you point to them. Full Screen mode will give you another inch or so of vertical screen space. To view Full Screen mode, press F11 ; or, from the Tools menu, click Full Screen. Press F11 again to return to normal view.

Objective 5 | Save Web Page Information

You can save an entire Web page, an image on a Web page, or selected text from a Web page. Doing so is a good way to capture information to which you want to refer later without accessing the Internet.

Activity 5.09 | Saving Web Page Information

1 **Close** any open windows. On the taskbar, click the **Internet Explorer** button, click in the **address bar**, type **florida-arts.org** and then press Enter. Compare your screen with Figure 5.38. If you cannot locate this page, navigate to any page that has a picture or graphic.

Because the content of Web pages changes frequently, the content and images on the displayed page will likely differ from Figure 5.38.

Figure 5.38

Florida Division of Cultural Affairs (your text and images will differ)

Various images on the page

Alert! | The Content of Web Pages is Protected by Copyright Laws

Nearly everything you find on the Web is protected by copyright law, which protects authors of original works, including text, art, photographs, and music. If you want to use text or images that you find online, you will need to get permission. One of the exceptions to this law is the use of small amounts of information for educational purposes, which falls under Fair Use guidelines.

Copyright laws in the United States are open to different interpretations, and copyright laws can be very different in other countries. As a general rule, if you want to use someone else's material, always get permission first.

2 Point to any picture or image on the page (scroll down if necessary to find a picture, or navigate to some other page with a picture), right-click, and then from the displayed menu, click **Save Picture As**. If necessary, navigate to the **Pictures** library in your personal folder, and then in the **File name** box, type **Cultural_Picture** Compare your screen with Figure 5.39.

> You can save a picture displayed on a Web page in this manner.

Figure 5.39

Save Picture dialog box

Pictures library active

File name typed

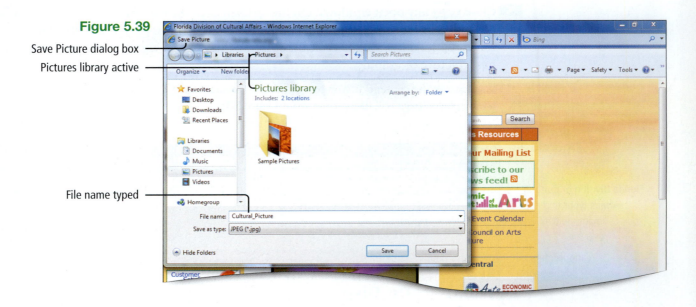

3 With the **Save Picture** dialog box displayed, **Start** the **Snipping Tool** program, click the **New arrow**, and then click **Full-screen Snip**. In the **Snipping Tool** mark-up window, click the **Save Snip** button.

4 In the **Save As** dialog box, in the **navigation pane**, scroll down as necessary, and then under **Computer**, click your USB flash drive so that it displays in the **address bar**. Navigate to your **Windows 7 Chapter 5** folder, and then as the file name, type **Lastname_Firstname_5A_Picture_Snip** Be sure the file type is **JPEG** file, and then press Enter. **Close** the **Snipping Tool** mark-up window. Hold this file until you finish Project 5A, and then submit this file as directed by your instructor.

5 In the **Save Picture** dialog box, click **Cancel**.

> You can use this technique to save images on Web pages.

Note | Printing a Picture from a Web Page

To print a picture from a Web page, point to the image and right-click. From the displayed menu, click Print Picture, and then in the Print dialog box, click Print.

---

6 On the **Command bar**, click the **Page** button, and then click **Save As**. At the bottom of the displayed **Save Webpage** dialog box, click the **Save as type arrow**, and then compare your screen with Figure 5.40.

To save all files associated with the page, including graphics, frames, and style sheets in their original format, you can use the file format *Webpage, complete (*.htm;*.html)*.

To save all information as a single file, you can use the file format *Web Archive, single file (*.mht)*.

To save just the current HTML page, without graphics, sounds, or other files, you can use the file format *Webpage, HTML only (*.htm;*.html)*. To save just the text from the current Web page, you can use the file format *Text File (*.txt)*.

Figure 5.40

Save Webpage dialog box —

Save as type arrow —

File types —

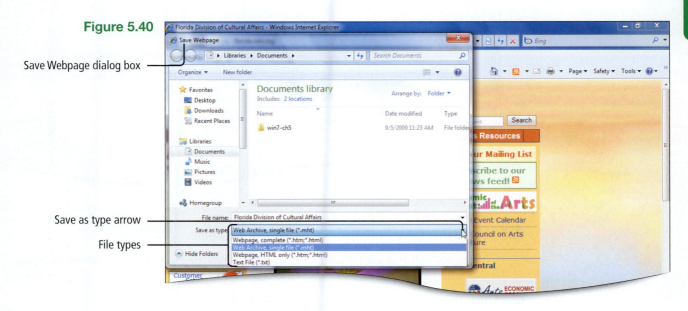

7 **Close** [x] the **Save Webpage** dialog box without saving, and then **Close** [x] Internet Explorer.

More Knowledge | E-mailing a Web Page

You can e-mail a Web page in two ways. From the Page button menu, click Send Page by E-mail; or, click Send Link by E-mail. Your default e-mail program will display. The first option inserts the entire page in the text of the e-mail. The second option inserts only the URL in the text of the e-mail message.

To set a program to use for e-mail within Internet Explorer, on the Command bar, click the Tools button, click Internet Options, click the Programs tab, and then under Internet programs, click the Set programs button.

Objective 6 | Manage Add-ons

An ***add-on*** is a program that adds features to a Web browser such as Internet Explorer. Examples of add-ons include additional toolbars, animated mouse pointers, and interactive Web content. Most add-ons come from the Internet and most require that you give permission to install them on your computer. It is possible that an add-on is installed without your knowledge, for example as part of another program. Some add-ons are installed with Microsoft Windows 7.

Activity 5.10 | Managing Add-ons

1 **Close** ▣ any open windows. On the taskbar, click the **Internet Explorer** button ⬡, click in the **address bar**, type **florida.edu** and press ⬚Enter⬚. On the **Command bar**, click the **Tools** button, and then click **Manage Add-ons**. Compare your screen with Figure 5.41.

Figure 5.41

Manage Add-ons dialog box

Add-on types

Show button

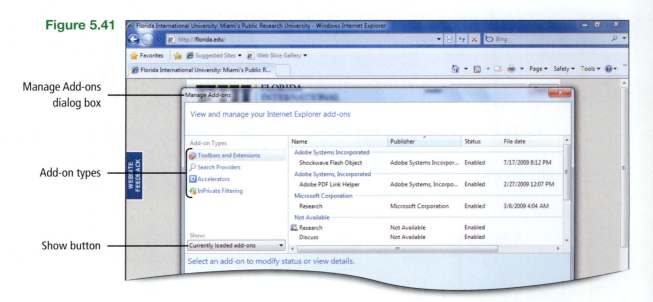

2 Be sure that **Show** indicates *Currently loaded add-ons.*

The add-ons that are necessary for the current Web page or a recently viewed Web page display on this list.

3 Click the **Show arrow**, and then click **All add-ons**.

A complete list of the add-ons that reside on your computer displays. If for any reason you need to do so, from this list you can either disable a selected add-on by selecting the add-on, and then clicking the Disable button that will display in the lower right corner of the dialog box. Or, you can delete a selected add-on by clicking the Delete button.

4 Click the **Show arrow,** and then click **Run without permission.**

A list of add-ons that are pre-approved by Microsoft, by your computer manufacturer, or by a service provider displays. All pre-approved add-ons are checked and most are digitally signed.

A *digital signature* is an electronic security mark that can be added to files. It enables you to verify the publisher of a file and helps verify that the file has not changed since it was digitally signed. If *(Not verified)* displays in the Publisher column, the add-on itself is not digitally signed.

5 Click the **Show arrow** again, and then click **Downloaded controls**.

A list of 32-bit *ActiveX* controls displays. ActiveX is a technology for creating interactive Web content such as animation sequences, credit card transactions, or spreadsheet calculations. An *ActiveX control* is a type of add-on.

Upon displaying some Web pages, you might see an *Information bar* (usually a yellow bar) display below the address bar. An information bar commonly displays information about downloads, blocked pop-up windows, and installing ActiveX controls.

Use caution when asked to download an ActiveX control. Such controls can enhance your Web browsing, but could also be a security risk. Be sure you trust the site that is asking you to install the control.

6 In the lower left corner of the **Manage Add-ons** dialog box, click **Find more toolbars and extensions**.

The Microsoft site for Internet Explorer Add-ons displays.

7 Take a moment to examine this page.

You can see that there are many interesting and useful add-ons that you can add to Internet Explorer.

8 **Close**  all open windows, and then **Close** Internet Explorer. Submit the four snip files from this project to your instructor as directed.

End **You have completed Project 5A** ────────────────

Project 5B Searching with Search Tools and Using the Web Safely

Project Activities

In Activities 5.11 through 5.17 you will train with Steven Ramos and Barbara Hewitt, employees in the Information Technology Department at the Bell Orchid Hotel, so that you will be able to search the Web from the Internet Explorer window and maintain the safety and security of data and computer users. Your completed screens will look similar to Figure 5.42.

Project Files

For Project 5B, you will need the following files:

New Snip files

Your will save your files as:

    Lastname_Firstname_5B_Searches_Snip
    Lastname_Firstname_5B_RSS_Snip
    Lastname_Firstname_5B_Slice_Snip
    Lastname_Firstname_5B_Accelerator_Snip

Project Results

Figure 5.42
Project 5B Searching with Search Tools and Using the Web Safely

Objective 7 | Search the Internet

The Internet can connect you to a vast amount of information, but first you have to find the information that you need. From within Internet Explorer, there are two ways in which you can search for information on the Internet without navigating to a specific Web site. The easiest method is to type a **search term** in the Search box in the upper right corner of the Internet Explorer screen. A search term is a word or phrase that describes the topic about which you want to find information. You can also type a search term directly in the address bar.

Activity 5.11 | Searching the Internet

A **search provider** is a Web site that provides search capabilities on the Web. The default search provider in Internet Explorer is Microsoft's Bing; however, you can change the default and easily switch among providers.

1 On the taskbar, click the **Internet Explorer** button 🅮. If a Welcome screen displays, close it. In the upper right corner, locate the **Search** box, and then at the right end of the box, click the **Search arrow** ▼. Compare your screen with Figure 5.43.

Search box, *Bing* indicated as
default (your default may differ)

Figure 5.43

Search arrow

Your home page
may differ

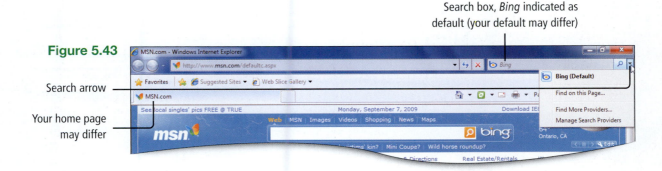

Note | If Bing is not your default

If Bing is not the default, set it as the default for this project as follows: On the displayed menu, click Find More Providers, and then click Bing Search. Click Add to Internet Explorer, and then click Add. Then, click the search arrow, click Manage Search Providers, click Bing, and then in the lower right corner, click Set as default. Click the Close button.

---

2 With **Bing** set as your default search provider, click in a blank area of the screen to close the Search menu. Then hold down Ctrl and press E to place the insertion point in the **Search** box; or, just click in the Search box.

3 Type the following, including the quotation marks: **"florida tourism"** and then press Enter. In the list of results, notice that your exact term *florida tourism* displays in bold.

Bing displays the search results, and on the right, displays **sponsored links**—paid advertisements shown as a links, typically for products and services related to your search term. Sponsored links are the way that search sites like Bing, Google, and others earn revenue. On the left, related searches are suggested.

Use quotation marks to search for specific phrases. Surrounding terms with quotation marks limits the search results to only those Web pages that contain the exact phrase that you typed. Without the quotation marks, the search results will include any page that contains the terms that you typed, regardless of the order of the words.

4 In the **Search** box, click the **Search arrow** ▼, and then on the displayed list, click **Find More Providers**. Compare your screen with Figure 5.44.

Figure 5.44

Search the Gallery box

Click to view more pages

Search providers you can add to Internet Explorer 8 (your list may vary)

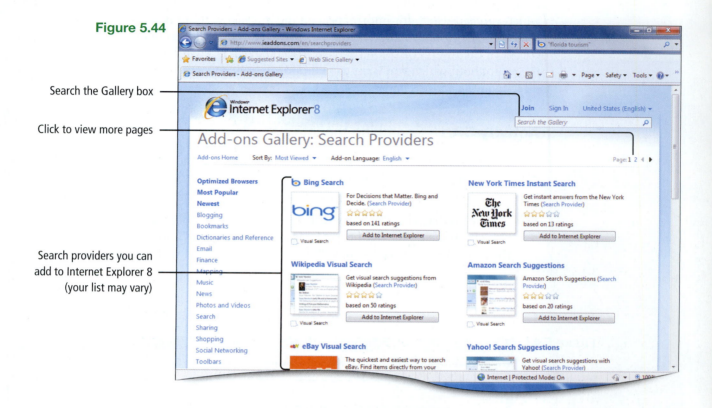

5 In the upper right corner, click in the **Search the Gallery** box, type **ask.com** and then press Enter. When the **Ask.com** logo displays, click the **Add to Internet Explorer** button. Then click **Add**. If the provider is already installed, click OK or Cancel.

6 In the upper right corner, in the **Search** box, click the **Search arrow** ▼, and then compare your screen with Figure 5.45.

Figure 5.45

Ask.com added to the list of providers

7 On the displayed list, click **Ask.com**, and notice that the same search is conducted in the Ask.com site. Compare your screen with Figure 5.46.

> Internet Explorer conducts your search for *florida tourism* in the Ask.com search engine. If you do not find what you are looking for with a particular search provider, you can search using a different provider.

Figure 5.46

Search conducted using the term "*florida tourism*"

Results from Ask.com search provider

8 Using the same technique, add the **Google** provider (you may have to go to the second page of listings; use *Google Search Suggestions*). Click the **Search arrow ▼**, and then click **Google**.

> Results for "florida tourism" from your Google search display.

9 In the **Search** box, click the **Search arrow ▼**, and then on the displayed list, click **Bing** to redisplay those results. Press Ctrl + E to select the text in the search box. Type the following but do *not* press Enter: **"Miami Hotels"** Hold down Alt and press Enter.

> The search results display in a new tab. Use this technique to keep the results of various searches displayed.

10 Start the **Snipping Tool** program and create a **Full-screen** snip. **Save** the snip in your **Window 7 Chapter 5** folder as a **JPEG** file with the name **Lastname_Firstname_5B_Searches_Snip Close** ▣ the **Snipping Tool** mark-up window. Hold this file until you complete Project 5B, and then submit it as directed by your instructor.

11 Open a **New Tab** ▣, in the **address bar** type **Florida Keys** and then press Enter.

> When you type a search term directly in the address bar, Internet Explorer tries to find a URL that matches; if it cannot do so, the default search provider conducts the search.

12 Open a **New Tab** ▣ and then in the **address bar** type **Find Miami Chamber of Commerce** and press Enter.

> In the Internet Explorer address bar, you can type *Find* or *Go* or ? followed by a keyword, a Web site name, or a phrase, and then press Enter. To display the results in a new tab, press Alt + Enter after typing the phrase.

13 Open a **New Tab** and then type **cnet.com** and press **Enter**. Wait for any ads to complete, and then in the displayed Web site, locate the **Search** box in the upper portion of the screen. Click in the **Search** box, and in all uppercase letters type **TEST** and press **Enter**.

14 Click in the **address bar** to select the entire URL, point to the selected URL and right-click, and then click **Copy**. In the Internet Explorer **Search** box, click the **Search arrow** ▼, and then click **Find More Providers**.

15 Scroll to the bottom of the page, and then click **Create your own Search Provider**. Under **Step 3**, point to the **URL** box, right-click, and then click **Paste**. Click in the **Name** box and type **CNET** Click the **Install Search Provider** button, and then click **Add**.

16 In the **Search** box, click the **Search arrow** ▼, and then on the displayed list, notice that **CNET** has been added as a search provider. Compare your screen with Figure 5.47.

Use the CNET search provider to search for computer related information.

Figure 5.47

CNET displays as a provider

Create your own Search Provider site

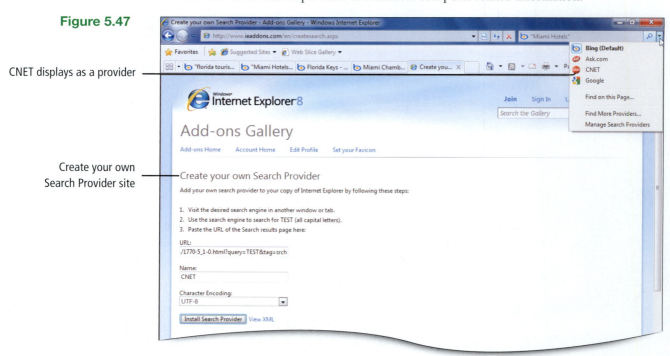

17 **Close** Internet Explorer.

Objective 8 | Subscribe to and View an RSS Feed

RSS is an acronym for *Really Simple Syndication*, which is a syndication format popular for aggregating—gathering together—updates to blogs and news sites.

An *RSS feed*—also known as an *XML feed*, *syndicated content*, or a *Web feed*—contains frequently updated content published by a Web site. The feed consists of a list of new articles from a specific site, each with a headline, summary information, usually a date and time stamp, and a link to the full article for each item.

The advantage of an RSS feed is that you can view new information from your favorite Web sites instead of navigating to the site and scanning it for any new information. You do not have to constantly check a news site, for example, to see if anything new has been posted.

For example, if you regularly visit several sites daily—such as a national news site, a site related to your job, and a site with financial or stock market information—you can subscribe to an RSS feed for those sites and the new articles will be delivered to you as they become available.

Getting started with RSS involves two steps:

- Get an **RSS viewer.** An RSS viewer, also referred to as a *feed reader*, is a program that displays RSS feeds to which you have subscribed. There are a number of RSS viewers available, including the one that comes with Internet Explorer.
- Subscribe to feeds: Most Web sites let you know that you can syndicate their content by displaying an orange button. Clicking the button adds the feed to your feed reader list.

Activity 5.12 | Subscribing to and Viewing an RSS Feed

To subscribe to an RSS feed, click the orange RSS icon on any Web page, or look for an orange button that indicates *XML*.

1 **Close** 🗙 any open windows. On the taskbar, click the **Internet Explorer** button 🄴, click in the **address bar**, type **usa.gov** and then press Enter. On the **Command bar**, locate the **Feeds** button 🔲, and notice that it is orange.

> Internet Explorer detects the presence of a Web feed on a page that you are viewing by displaying this button in orange—or in orange with a small starburst—instead of in its default gray color. In that manner, you can know immediately if feeds are available from the displayed Web page.

2 On the **Command bar**, click the **Feeds button arrow** 🔽, and then from the displayed list, click **USA.gov Updates: News and Features**. Compare your screen with Figure 5.48.

Figure 5.48

Subscribe to this feed button

Your content will differ

3 In the upper left portion of the screen, click **Subscribe to this feed**.

> An Internet Explorer dialog box displays, indicating that if you subscribe, the feed will be added to your Favorites Center and kept up to date. The feed will be created in the Feeds folder.

> Here, using the same techniques you use when saving a new Favorite, you can give the feed a more descriptive name, and, optionally file it in a subfolder of the Feeds folder or create a new folder.

4 In the dialog box, click the **Subscribe** button, and notice that in the upper portion of the screen, the message *You've successfully subscribed to this feed!* displays. Just below that message, click **View my feeds**. In the displayed list in the **Favorites Center**, point to the new feed name to display its ScreenTip, and then compare your screen with Figure 5.49.

> When you subscribe to the feed, Internet Explorer automatically checks the Web site and downloads new content so you can see what is new since you last visited the feed.

> When a new post appears, the link for that site displays in bold and clicking it shows the unread material in your browser window.

Figure 5.49

The *USA.gov* feed displays in your Favorites center (your list may differ)

ScreenTip (yours will differ)

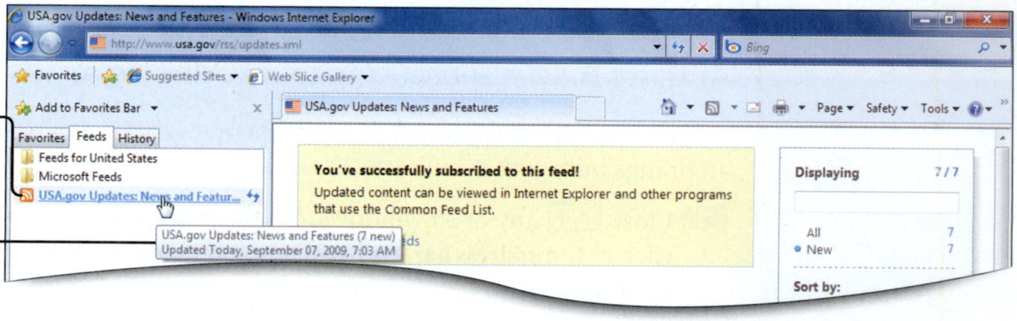

5 In the upper right corner of the **Favorites Center** pane, click the **Close** button ⊠.

> All feeds that you open from within the Favorites Center of Internet Explorer will display in this uniform manner.

> On the right, you can click various options for displaying and sorting the articles. You can also open the link to the Feed Properties dialog box, where you can adjust how often the feed is updated and the number of updates to display.

> Use the *Mark feed as read* link so that if you return to this page, no current entries will be marked as new. This is useful because you do not have to remember if you have already seen an article.

6 Close [×] Internet Explorer. Be sure your **Windows 7** desktop displays. Right-click on the desktop, and then click **Gadgets**. Double-click the **Feed Headlines** gadget to add it to your desktop.

> **Alert! | Does your screen differ?**
>
> If you are unable to display the *Feed Headlines* gadget, skip the remainder of this activity; or, just read the steps and examine the figures.

7 Wait a few moments for the gadget to load. Then, on the desktop, point to the **Feed Headlines** gadget, right-click, and click **Options**. In the displayed **Feed Headlines** dialog box, click the **Display this feed arrow**, and then compare your screen with Figure 5.50.

> The feeds to which you subscribed in Internet Explorer display on the list—others might also display.

Figure 5.50

Feed Headlines dialog box

List of available feeds (yours may vary)

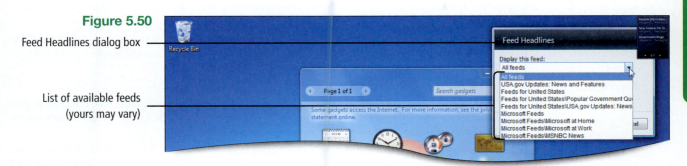

8 From the displayed list, click **USA.gov Updates: News and Features**, and then click **OK**. Notice that only headlines from this feed display. Click any headline, and then compare your screen with Figure 5.51.

> To view a summary of an interesting headline, you can click any headline, as shown in Figure 5.51. In this manner, you can use a gadget to view feeds from a single source quickly. To view the entire article, click the headline in the title bar above the summary to open the Web page that contains the entire article, or click *Read online*.

Figure 5.51

Title bar, when clicked, will display webpage for entire article

Summary of article

Article headline

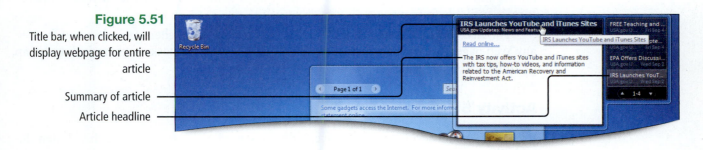

9 Click on the desktop to cancel the headline display.

10 **Start** the **Snipping Tool** program and create a **Full-screen** snip. **Save** the snip in your **Windows 7 Chapter 5** folder as a **JPEG** file with the name **Lastname_Firstname_5B_RSS_Snip Close** the **Snipping Tool** mark-up window. Hold this file until you complete Project 5B, and then submit it as directed by your instructor.

11 Point to the gadget on your desktop and right-click. Click **Close gadget** to delete it from your desktop. **Close** the Gadgets window.

12 On the taskbar, click the **Internet Explorer** button . In the upper left corner, click the **Favorites** button, and then if necessary, click the **Feeds tab**.

13 Point to the **USA.gov Updates** feed and right-click. Click **Delete**, and then click **Yes**.

14 **Close** [×] Internet Explorer.

More Knowledge | **What else should I know about RSS Feeds?**

Feeds are different than a Web site: A feed can have the same content as a Web page, but the feed is usually formatted differently—in the form of headline topics. Additionally, when you subscribe to a feed, Internet Explorer automatically checks the Web site and downloads new content so you can see what is new since you last visited the feed.

The downside of seeing a feed instead of the actual Web site is that you do not get to benefit from the design of the Web page itself, where the format of the information or the photos and graphics could add to or possibly change your interpretation of the information.

Feeds are usually free: It is usually free to subscribe to a feed.

Other programs can display your feeds: Internet Explorer provides the Common Feed List to other programs, so you can subscribe to feeds with Internet Explorer and then read them in other programs such as your e-mail client or in one of the feed readers available as a gadget.

Feeds come in two common formats: Two common formats for feeds are RSS and Atom. Feed formats are constantly being updated with new versions, and Internet Explorer supports most RSS and Atom versions. All feed formats are based on XML (Extensible Markup Language), which is a text-based computer language used to describe and distribute structured data and documents.

Objective 9 | Use Web Slices, Accelerators, and Suggested Sites

An RSS feed enables you to get frequently changing content automatically by subscribing to the feed. A technology that is similar to, and based on, RSS technology, is a **Web Slice**. A Web Slice is a specific *portion*—a slice—of a Web page to which you can subscribe, and which enables you to see when updated content, such as the current temperature, is available from a site.

The **Accelerators** feature displays a blue Accelerator icon when you select text from any Web page, which when clicked enables you to accomplish tasks such as finding a map, defining a word, or e-mailing content to others.

Activity 5.13 | Using Web Slices

After you subscribe to a Web Slice, it displays as a link on the Favorites bar. When the Web Slice is updated, the link displays in bold, at which time you can click the link to see the updated content.

Another Way

If displayed on your
Favorites bar, click
Web Slices or Get more
Add-ons; or, display the
Manage Add-ons dialog
box, and click Find
more toolbars and
extensions.

A Web slice is useful for things that you like to check frequently throughout the day
without actually navigating to a specific site. Popular Web Slices include those for weather,
traffic, and sports scores.

1 **Close** ❎ any open windows. On the taskbar, click the **Internet Explorer** button ,
click in the **address bar**, type **ieaddons.com** and then press Enter. Scroll to the bottom
of the page, and locate **Web Slices**, as shown in Figure 5.52.

Figure 5.52

Tab indicates *Add-ons Gallery*

Favorites bar indicates *Get More Add-ons* (yours may differ)

Web Slices link

2 Click the **Web Slices** link to display the **Web Slices Add-ons Gallery**. Notice that on
the left, there are many categories to choose from when looking for a Web Slice.
Compare your screen with Figure 5.53.

Figure 5.53

Weather from Bing

Add to Internet Explorer button

3 Under **Weather from Bing**, click the **Add to Internet Explorer** button. If you do not see this link, scroll to view the bottom of the page, and then on the left, click Weather.

4 In the new window, *point* to the text *change location*, notice the green button on the **Command bar** and on the page, and then compare your screen with Figure 5.54.

On pages where a Web Slice is available, the Feeds button on the Command bar will light up in green, and a related button on the page will also light up in green.

Figure 5.54

Feeds button lights up in green on Command bar

Green button on page (your location will differ)

5 Click **change location**. In the **Current location** box, delete the existing text, and then type **Miami, Florida** Compare your screen with Figure 5.55.

Figure 5.55

Miami, Florida typed

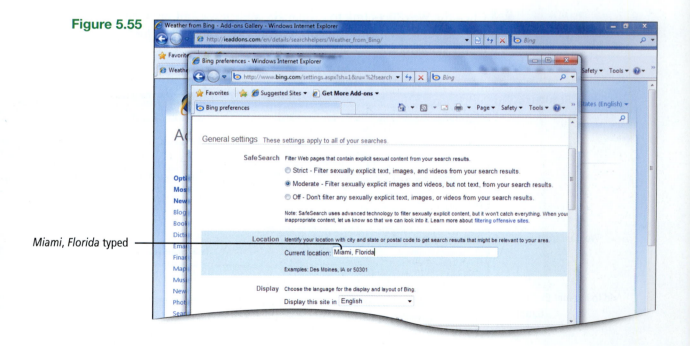

6 Press [Enter] to change the location to **Miami**. On the **Command bar**, point to the green **Web Slice** button and click one time. Compare your screen with Figure 5.56.

Figure 5.56

Weather in Miami, Florida indicated

Add to Favorites Bar button

7 Click the **Add to Favorites Bar** button. If necessary, **Maximize** your window.

The Web Slice displays on your Favorites bar.

8 Click in the **address bar**, type **myflorida.com** and then press [Enter]

9 On the **Favorites bar**, click the **Weather in Miami** link, and then compare your screen with Figure 5.57.

When you click on a Web slice, you do not navigate to a new page; rather a small *slice* of another Web page displays in a small window that you can quickly close. Or, you can click any link in the small window to navigate to the actual site.

Figure 5.57

Current weather conditions in Miami display

10 Click in a blank area of the screen to close the small window.

The next time the weather conditions change, the link will display in bold, and you can view the updated information.

11 **Start** 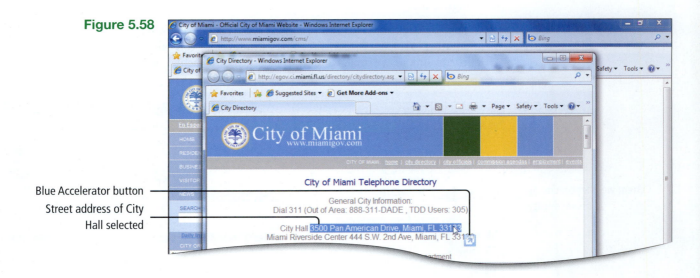 the **Snipping Tool** program and create a **Full-screen** snip. **Save** the snip in your **Windows 7 Chapter 5** folder as a **JPEG** file with the name **Lastname_Firstname_5B_Slice_Snip Close** the **Snipping Tool** mark-up window. Hold this file until you complete Project 5B, and then submit it as directed by your instructor.

12 On the **Favorites bar**, point to the **Weather in Miami** link, right-click, click **Delete**, and then click **Yes**.

You can add and delete Web Slices as you need them.

13 **Close** all Internet Explorer windows.

Activity 5.14 | Using Accelerators

To use an Accelerator, select some appropriate text on a Web page, click the blue Accelerator button, and then select the appropriate service to do what you want to do, such as searching, mapping, shopping, or language translation.

1 **Close** any open windows. On the taskbar, click the **Internet Explorer** button, click in the **address bar**, type **miamigov.com** and then press Enter.

2 In the site's navigation bar, click **city directory**.

The directory opens in a new window.

3 Hold down the left mouse button, and then drag to select the **street address** of **City Hall**, as shown in Figure 5.58. Notice that a **blue Accelerator button** displays.

Figure 5.58

Blue Accelerator button
Street address of City Hall selected

4 Click the **blue Accelerator** button to display a shortcut menu, and then click **Map with Bing**. **Maximize** 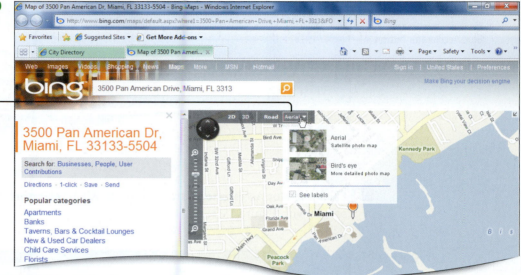 the window.

> A map of the street address displays. In the Bing mapping application, you can click various views of the address you selected, for example Bird's eye displays an overhead picture of the address.

5 As shown in Figure 5.59, point to **Aerial**.

Figure 5.59

Views that you can select ⸺

6 On the displayed list, click **Bird's eye**.

7 **Start** the **Snipping Tool** program and create a **Full-screen** snip. **Save** the snip in your **Windows 7 Chapter 5** folder as a **JPEG** file with the name **Lastname_Firstname_5B_Accelerator_Snip Close** the **Snipping Tool** mark-up window. Hold this file until you complete Project 5B, and then submit it as directed by your instructor.

8 Open a **New Tab** , in the **address bar** type **ieaddons.com** and press Enter. Scroll to the bottom of the page, on the left click **Accelerators**, and then in the upper right corner, click in the **Search the Gallery** box. Type **define** and press Enter.

9 Under **Define with Bing**, click **Add to Internet Explorer**, and then click **Add**.

10 Click in the **address bar**, type **miamigov.com** and then press ⟨Enter⟩. In the site's navigation bar, click **City Organizations**. Under the heading **City Marinas**, in the first sentence, point to the word *marinas* and double-click to select the word and display the blue Accelerator button. Compare your screen with Figure 5.60.

Figure 5.60

Blue Accelerator button ——

marinas selected ——

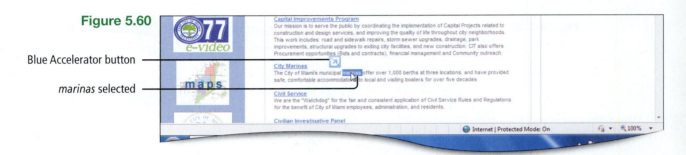

11 Click the **blue Accelerator** button, point to **All Accelerators**, and then compare your screen with Figure 5.61.

Figure 5.61

Define with Bing ——

List of available Accelerators ——

12 Click **Define with Bing**, and then compare your screen with Figure 5.62.

You can see that there are many ways to use Accelerators.

Figure 5.62

marina defined in Bing ——

13 **Close** ❌ all Internet Explorer windows.

More Knowledge | Using the Suggested Sites Feature

Suggested Sites is an optional online service that suggests other Web sites in which you might be interested based on the Web sites you visit most. First, you must activate the feature by clicking it on the Favorites bar, and then clicking Turn on Suggested Sites. Or, from the Tools menu, click Suggested Sites. Once activated, your Web browsing history is sent to Microsoft. Then, as you browse the Web, you can click the Suggested Sites link to see a list of related sites. For example, after browsing the Web in Project 5A, the feature might suggest additional sites related to Miami and Florida. If you do not plan to use this feature, you can right-click the link on the Favorites bar and delete it. You can also turn it off at any time, and even if activated, it does not record any information when InPrivate Browsing is turned on.

Objective 10 | Block Pop-up Windows and Use the Information Bar

A *pop-up* is a small Web browser window that displays on top of the Web site you are viewing; pop-ups are usually created by advertisers. *Pop-up Blocker* is a feature in Internet Explorer that enables you to limit or block most pop-ups. The Information bar displays information about downloads, blocked pop-up windows, and other activities.

Activity 5.15 | Using the Internet Explorer 8 Pop-up Blocker and Information Bar

Pop-up Blocker is enabled by default. To turn it off or change the settings, display the Tools menu as shown in Figure 5.63.

Figure 5.63

Command to turn off Pop-up Blocker

Command to display Pop-up Blocker Settings dialog box

Tools menu

By displaying the Pop-up Blocker Settings dialog box, you can *allow* pop-ups from specific Web sites as shown in Figure 5.64. You can also select the Blocking level and decide whether to play a sound or show the Information bar when a pop-up is blocked. These default settings are appropriate for most computer users. Some sites request that you allow pop-ups from their site, and if you trust the site, it is safe to do so. For example, the learning management system known as *Blackboard*, which is used by many colleges and universities, requests that you allow pop-ups from its site.

Because the Information bar displays on a site when a pop-up is blocked, you always have the choice of viewing the pop-up message if you want to do so. Click the Information bar and then click Show Blocked Pop-up. From the Information bar, you can also click to temporarily accept pop-ups from a specific site.

Figure 5.64

Pop-up Blocker Settings dialog box

List of allowed sites (yours will vary)

Blocking level

The Information bar will display at the top of the screen if:

- A site tries to install an ActiveX control, install an updated ActiveX control, install an add-on program, run an ActiveX control in an unsafe manner, or run active content.
- A site tries to download a file to your computer.
- Your security settings are below the recommended levels.
- You started Internet Explorer with add-ons disabled.

One advantage of the Information bar is that you are not required to attend to it. For example, if you display a site by mistakenly typing an incorrect URL, you can ignore the Information bar. If you want to proceed with using a feature of the displayed site, click the message and then take appropriate action. For a complete list of messages that you might see in the Information bar, display the Windows Help and Support window, and search for *information bar*.

To check how well you can identify pop-up blocking functions, take a moment to answer the following questions:

1 By default, Pop-up Blocker is _____.

2 You always have the choice of _____ a pop-up message if you want to do so.

3 One common reason that the Information bar will display is if a Web site tries to install, update, or run in an unsafe manner any type of _____ control.

4 The Information bar commonly displays if a site tries to _____ a file to your computer.

5 One advantage of the Information bar is that you are not _____ to do anything with it.

Objective 11 | Protect Against Malware

Internet Explorer will warn you when Web pages try to install software by displaying the Information bar. There are additional ways in which Internet Explorer provides safety features to protect your computer against malware.

Activity 5.16 | Protecting Against Malware

Internet Explorer's *protected mode* makes it more difficult for malicious software to be installed on your computer by preventing a downloaded program from making any direct changes to the system. It also allows you to install *wanted* ActiveX controls or add-ons when you are logged on as an administrator. Protected mode is on by default and you will see it indicated in the status bar. One way that protected mode helps protect your computer from malicious downloads is by restricting where files can be saved without your consent.

Windows Defender is a spyware scanning and removal tool included with Windows 7. By default, Windows Defender, when enabled, scans your computer for spyware automatically daily at 2:00 a.m. During the scan, Windows Defender takes automatic action on various items, depending on your preferences. If any spyware is found, you are prompted with options to deal with each threat by selecting Ignore, Quarantine, Remove, or Always Allow. Windows Defender constantly updates it definitions so that it can find new spyware threats that emerge on the Internet.

The first step in using Windows Defender is to make sure it is enabled on your computer. To do so, open the Control Panel, type defender in the Search box, and then click Windows Defender. To enable or change the settings of Windows Defender, click the Tools button as shown in Figure 5.65.

Figure 5.65

Tools and Settings in Windows Defender

To check how well you understand protecting against malware, take a moment to answer the following questions:

1 Protected mode makes it difficult for malicious software to be installed on your computer by preventing a downloaded program from making direct _____ to the system.

2 Protected mode is on by default and is indicated on the _____.

3 Protected mode restricts where a downloaded file can be stored without your _____.

4 When enabled, Windows Defender scans your computer for spyware daily at _____.

5 Windows Defender constantly updates its _____ so that it can find new spyware threats that emerge on the Internet.

Objective 12 | Protect Your Data

Windows 7 provides a variety of ways to protect your personal data and your electronic transactions.

Activity 5.17 | Protecting Your Data

A **certificate** is a digital document that verifies the identity of a person or indicates the security of a Web site. Certificates are issued by trusted companies known as **Certification Authorities.** Certificates make secure transactions on the Internet possible. When you visit a secure Web site in Internet Explorer, a padlock icon will display in the address bar indicating that a digital certificate identifies the site. As shown in Figure 5.66, you can click the padlock icon to display information about the certificate.

Figure 5.66

Padlock icon in address bar

Information about the certificate

You can see specific information about the issuer of the certificate by clicking *View certificates.* You will commonly see such certificate information on any site where financial transactions are involved.

Phishing is a technique used to trick computer users into revealing personal or financial information through an e-mail message or a Web site. The message or site appears to come from a trusted source but actually directs recipients to provide information to a fraudulent Web site.

SmartScreen Filter is a feature in Internet Explorer that helps detect phishing Web sites and Web sites that distribute malware. SmartScreen Filter runs in the background and protects you by comparing the addresses of Web sites you visit against a list of sites reported to Microsoft as legitimate. This list is stored on your computer. It also analyzes the sites you visit to see if they have characteristics common to a phishing site.

To manually check a Web site that you find suspicious, navigate to the site you want to check, on the Command bar, click Safety, point to SmartScreen Filter, click Check This Website, and then click OK. If a Web site is flagged as suspicious, you should not submit any personal or financial information to it unless you are certain that the site is trustworthy. Suspicious sites are flagged by Internet Explorer by displaying the address bar in yellow along with a message. For more information about how Internet Explorer handles phishing, in the Windows Help and Support window, search for phishing and click SmartScreen Filter: frequently asked questions.

To check how well you understand data protection, take a moment to answer the following questions:

1 A certificate can verify the _____ of a Web site.

2 Certificates make _____ transactions on the Web possible.

3 When you visit a secure Web site, the address bar displays a _____ icon.

4 A technique to trick computer users into revealing personal information is _____.

5 If the SmartScreen Filter in Internet Explorer suspects a Web site of having phishing characteristics, it will display a message and display the address bar in _____.

End **You have completed Project 5B** ————————————————

Summary

In this chapter, you used tabbed browsing to open multiple Web sites in a single browser window. You created and organized Favorites. When you use public computers, it is a good idea to delete your browsing history, which you practiced in this chapter. You also practiced printing and saving information on a Web page.

In this chapter, you practiced locating, subscribing to, and viewing RSS feeds. You also practiced how to use Web Slices and Accelerators. There are many excellent search providers that you can use to search the Web, and in this chapter, you used several providers to search.

Key Terms

Matching

Match each term in the second column with its correct definition in the first column. Write the letter of the term on the blank line in front of the correct definition.

_____ 1. Any software program with which you display Web pages and navigate the Internet.

_____ 2. The Web browser software developed by Microsoft Corporation that is included with Windows 7.

_____ 3. The term used to describe the process of using your computer to view Web pages.

_____ 4. A feature in Internet Explorer that enables you to open multiple Web sites in a single browser window.

_____ 5. The area across the upper portion of the Internet Explorer window in which a tab for each open Web site displays.

A Accelerators

B Browsing

C Cookies

D Favorites bar

E Favorites Center

F InPrivate Browsing

G Internet Explorer 8

H Pop-up

I Quick Tabs

J RSS feed

K Search term

L Tab row

Content-Based Assessments

M Tabbed browsing

N Web browser

O Web Slice

_____ 6. The feature in Internet Explorer that displays, on a single tab, a thumbnail of each Web site that is currently open.

_____ 7. A list of links to Web sites that is saved in your Web browser.

_____ 8. A toolbar in Internet Explorer 8 that displays directly below the address bar and to which you can add or drag Web addresses you use frequently.

_____ 9. Small text files that Web sites put on your computer to store information about you and your preferences, for example logon information.

_____ 10. A feature in Internet Explorer 8 with which you can browse the Web without storing data about your browsing session.

_____ 11. A word or phrase that describes the topic about which you want to find information.

_____ 12. Frequently updated content published by a Web site and delivered to a feed reader.

_____ 13. A specific _portion_—a slice—of a Web page to which you can subscribe, and which enables you to see when updated content, such as the current temperature, is available from a site.

_____ 14. An Internet Explorer feature that displays a blue button when you select text from any Web page, from which you can accomplish tasks such as finding a map or defining a word.

_____ 15. A small Web browser window that displays on top of the Web site you are viewing, and which is usually created by advertisers.

Multiple Choice

Circle the correct answer.

1. An online journal or column used to publish personal or company information is a:
   A. web feed   **B.** blog   **C.** search provider

2. The ending letters of a URL such as _.com_, _.org_, and so on is the:
   A. locator   **B.** country code   **C.** top level domain

3. A Web site that displays news, content, and links that are of interest to a specific audience is a:
   A. portal   **B.** URL   **C.** feed

4. Frequently updated content published by a Web site and delivered to a feed reader is:
   A. an RSS feed   **B.** a blog   **C.** a cookie

5. Programs that add features to a Web browser such as Internet Explorer are:
   A. bookmark managers   **B.** temporary Internet files   **C.** add-ons

6. A Web site that provides search capabilities on the Web is called a:
   A. sponsored link   **B.** search provider   **C.** domain

7. An example of an Accelerator is a:
   A. domain name   **B.** digital signature   **C.** mapping site

8. A feature in Internet Explorer that makes it difficult for malicious software to be installed on your computer is:
   A. protected mode   **B.** syndicated content   **C.** ActiveX

9. A spyware scanning and removal tool included with Windows 7 is:
   A. Windows Blocker   **B.** Windows Defender   **C.** Windows Security

10. A technique used to trick computer users into revealing personal information is:
    A. hacking   **B.** spying   **C.** phishing

Content-Based Assessments

Apply 5A skills from these Objectives:

1 Use Tabbed Browsing

2 Organize Favorites

3 Manage Browsing History and Browse with InPrivate

4 Print, Zoom, and Change the Text Size of Web Pages

5 Save Web Page Information

6 Manage Add-ons

Skills Review | Project 5C Browsing the Web with Internet Explorer 8

Project Files

For Project 5C, you will need the following files:

> **Student Resource CD or USB flash drive containing the student data files**
> **win05_5C_Answer_Sheet (Word document)**

You will save your document as:

> **Lastname_Firstname_5C_Answer_Sheet**

Project Results

1 **Close** [×] all open windows. On the taskbar, click the **Windows Explorer** button. In the **navigation pane**, click the drive that contains the student files for this textbook, and then navigate to **Chapter_Files ▶ Chapter_05**. Double-click the Word file **win05_5C_Answer_Sheet** to open Word and display the document. Press F12 to display the **Save As** dialog box in Word, navigate to your **Windows 7 Chapter 5** folder, and then using your own name, save the document as **Lastname_Firstname_5C_Answer_Sheet** If necessary, click OK if a message regarding formats displays.

On the taskbar, click the **Word** button to minimize the window and leave your Word document accessible from the taskbar. **Close** the **Chapter_05** folder window. As you complete each step in this project, click the Word button on the taskbar to open the document, type your one-letter answer in the appropriate cell of the Word table, and then on the taskbar, click the button again to minimize the window for the next step.

Open Internet Explorer. Click in the **address bar** and navigate to **doh.state.fl.us** Open a **New Tab**, and then go to the site **miamigov.com** On a **New Tab**, go to the site **hsmv.state.fl.us** On the **tab row**, click the **Quick Tabs** button. What is your result?

A. Thumbnails for each open site display.

B. A list of recently visited Web sites displays.

C. The tabs in the tab row are rearranged in alphabetical order.

2 On the **tab row**, click the **Tab List** button. How many sites display on the list?

A. one

B. two

C. three

3 On a **New Tab**, go to the site **florida.edu** and then click the **Favorites** button. Click **Add to Favorites**. What is your result?

A. The Favorites Center pane displays on the left side of the screen.

B. The Create Favorites Folder dialog box displays.

C. The Add a Favorite dialog box displays.

4 Click **Cancel**. On the displayed home page for **Florida International University**, on the **navigation bar**, point to the link for **Athletics** and right-click. From the displayed shortcut menu, which of the following actions are possible?

A. You can open the Athletics link in a new tab.

B. You can send the Athletics link to your Documents folder.

C. You can create a tab group.

(Project 5C Browsing the Web with Internet Explorer 8 continues on the next page)

Skills Review | Project **5C** Browsing the Web with Internet Explorer 8 (continued)

5 Click in a blank area of the screen to close the shortcut menu. Click the **Favorites** button to open the **Favorites Center** pane. Across the top, which tabs display?

A. Favorites, Tab Groups, Feeds

B. Favorites, Feeds, History

C. Favorites, History, Recent Pages

6 Click the **History tab**, and then click the **arrow**. Which of the following is *not* a viewing arrangement?

A. By Date

B. By Favorites

C. By Most Visited

7 Click in a blank area of the screen to close the **Favorites Center** pane. On the **Command bar**, click the **Safety** button, and then click **Delete Browsing History**. According to this information, cookies consist of:

A. Saved information that you have typed into forms.

B. Buttons added to the tab row.

C. Files stored on your computer by Web sites to save preferences.

8 **Close** the **Delete Browsing History** dialog box. Click the **Tools** button, and then click **Manage Add-ons**. At the bottom of the screen, click **Find more toolbars and extensions**. What is your result?

A. A list of add-ons stored on your computer displays.

B. A list of recently used add-ons displays.

C. The Microsoft site for finding and installing new add-ons displays.

9 **Close** the **Add-ons** site and the **Manage Add-ons** dialog box. Click the **New Tab**, and then click **Browse with InPrivate**. What is your result?

A. The Delete Browsing History dialog box displays.

B. InPrivate displays in the address bar.

C. Both A and B.

10 **Close** the **InPrivate** window. With the **FIU** site displayed, click the **Print button arrow**, and then click **Print Preview**. Click the **Page Setup** button to display the **Page Setup** dialog box. From this dialog box, which of the following can be changed?

A. Left and right margins

B. Headers and footers

C. Both A and B

Be sure you have typed all of your answers in your Word document. **Save** and **Close** your Word document, and submit as directed by your instructor. **Close** [×] all open windows.

End **You have completed Project 5C**

Content-Based Assessments

Skills Review | Project **5D** Searching with Search Tools and Using the Web Safely

Project Files

For Project 5D, you will need the following files:

> Student Resource CD or USB flash drive containing the student data files
> win05_5D_Answer_Sheet (Word document)

You will save your document as:

> Lastname_Firstname_5D_Answer_Sheet

Project Results

1 **Close** all open windows. On the taskbar, click the **Windows Explorer** button. In the **navigation pane**, click the drive that contains the student files for this textbook, and then navigate to **Chapter_Files ▶ Chapter_05**. Double-click the Word file **win05_5D_Answer_Sheet** to open Word and display the document. Press F12 to display the **Save As** dialog box in Word, navigate to your **Windows 7 Chapter 5** folder, and then using your own name, save the document as **Lastname_Firstname_5D_Answer_Sheet** If necessary, click OK if a message regarding formats displays.

On the taskbar, click the **Word** button to minimize the window and leave your Word document accessible from the taskbar. **Close** the **Chapter_05** folder window. As you complete each step in this project, click the Word button on the taskbar to open the document, type your one-letter answer in the appropriate cell of the Word table, and then on the taskbar, click the button again to minimize the window for the next step.

Close Internet Explorer if it is open, and then **Start** Internet Explorer again. In the **Search** box, click the **Search arrow** ▼, and then click **Manage Search Providers**. If necessary, set **Bing** as the default and close the Manage Add-ons dialog box. What is your result?

A. *Bing* displays in the Search box.

B. *Default Search* displays in the Search box.

C. *Start your search here* displays in the Search box.

2 In the **Search** box, click the **Search arrow** ▼, and then click **Find More Providers**. What is your result?

A. A list of recently used search providers displays.

B. The Microsoft site for adding search providers to Internet Explorer 8 displays.

C. Bing conducts an Internet search for search providers.

3 Locate the **New York Times Instant Search**, point to the logo that indicates *The New York Times*, right-click, and then click **Save Picture As**. What is your result?

A. An error message indicates that you cannot save this as a picture.

B. The logo displays in Windows Photo Viewer.

C. The Save Picture dialog box displays.

4 Click **Cancel** to close the dialog box. In the categories of possible add-ons, click **Dictionaries and Reference**. Which of the following is true?

A. Google Define is *not* among the available dictionaries.

B. There are at least two Wikipedia sites that you can add.

C. Both A. and B. are true.

(Project 5D Searching with Search Tools and Using the Web Safely continues on the next page)

Content-Based Assessments

Skills Review | Project **5D** Searching with Search Tools and Using the Web Safely (continued)

5 Click in the **address bar**, type **noaa.gov** and then press Enter. On this page, what signifies that an RSS Feed is available from this site?

A. The Feeds button lights up in green.

B. The Feeds button lights up in orange.

C. The Feeds button blinks on and off.

6 **On the Command bar**, click the **Feeds** button. What is your result?

A. The Feed Headlines gadget displays.

B. The NOAA News Releases displays as a feed to which you can subscribe.

C. The Feeds tab of the Favorites Center displays.

7 On the **Command bar**, click the **Tools** button, point to **Pop-up Blocker**, and then click **Pop-up Blocker Settings**. What does the **Medium blocking level** do with pop-ups?

A. Allows pop-ups from secure sites

B. Blocks most automatic pop-ups

C. Blocks all pop-ups

8 What notifications are available to notify you when a pop-up has been blocked?

A. Play a sound

B. Display the Information bar

C. Both A and B

9 **Close** the **Pop-up Blocker Settings** dialog box. From the **Start menu**, click **Help and Support**, and then in the **Search Help** box type **information bar** and press Enter. In the displayed list, click **Internet Explorer Information bar: frequently asked questions**. Under what circumstances might the Information bar display on your computer?

A. If a Web site tries to open in a new window

B. If a Web site tries to install an ActiveX control

C. If a Web site tries to install an RSS feed

10 At the top of the **Windows Help and Support** window, delete the text *information bar*, type **protected mode** and press Enter. Which of the following is *not* true about protected mode?

A. Protected mode is turned on by default.

B. Protected mode allows you to install wanted ActiveX controls or add-ons when you are logged on as an administrator.

C. Protected mode prevents you from entering credit card information into a Web site.

Be sure you have typed all of your answers in your Word document. **Save** and **Close** your Word document, and submit as directed by your instructor. **Close**  all open windows.

End **You have completed Project 5D** ———————————————

Content-Based Assessments

Apply 5A skills from these Objectives:

■1 Use Tabbed Browsing

■2 Organize Favorites

■3 Manage Browsing History and Browse with InPrivate

■4 Print, Zoom, and Change the Text Size of Web Pages

■5 Save Web Page Information

■6 Manage Add-ons

Mastering Windows 7 | Project **5E** Browsing the Web with Internet Explorer 8

In the following Mastering Windows 7 project, you will open related sites on separate tabs. You will capture and save a screen that will look similar to Figure 5.67.

Project Files

For Project 5E, you will need the following file:

New Snip file

You will save your document as:

Lastname_Firstname_5E_Sites_Snip

Project Results

Figure 5.67

(Project 5E Browsing the Web with Internet Explorer 8 continues on the next page)

Mastering Windows 7 | Project **5E** Browsing the Web with Internet Explorer 8 (continued)

1 Open Internet Explorer and be sure only the tab for your home page displays. Click in the **address bar**, type **miamicityballet.org** and press [Enter]. Hold down [Ctrl], and then in the navigation bar in this site, click **MCB School** so that a new tab is created for the link and the two tabs are color coded.

2 On a **New Tab**, go to the site **miamisymphony.org** Hold down [Ctrl], and then in the navigation bar of this site, click **Season** so that a new tab is created for the link and the two tabs are color coded.

3 Create a **Full-screen Snip**, and then **Save** the snip in your **Windows 7 Chapter 5** folder as a **JPEG** file with the name **Lastname_Firstname_5E_Sites_Snip** Submit this file as directed by your instructor.

4 **Close** all open windows and **Close** Internet Explorer.

End **You have completed Project 5E** —————————

Content-Based Assessments

Apply **5B** skills from these Objectives:

- **7** Search the Internet
- **8** Subscribe to and View an RSS Feed
- **9** Use Web Slices and Accelerators, and Suggested Sites
- **10** Block Pop-up Windows and Use the Information Bar
- **11** Protect Against Malware
- **12** Protect Your Data

Mastering Windows 7 | Project **5F** Searching with Search Tools and Using the Web Safely

In the following Mastering Windows 7 project, you will use an Accelerator. You will capture and save a screen that will look similar to Figure 5.68.

Project Files

For Project 5F, you will need the following file:

New Snip file

You will save your document as:

Lastname_Firstname_5F_Aerial_Snip

Project Results

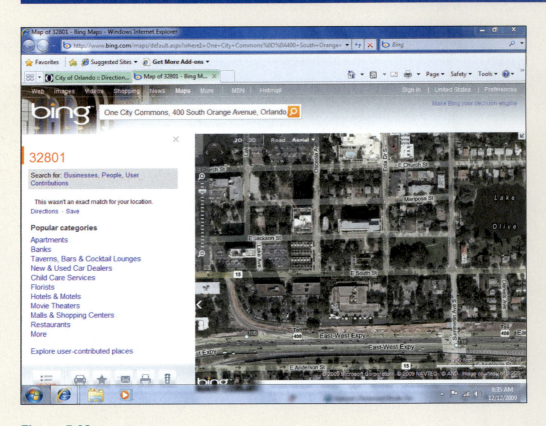

Figure 5.68

(Project 5F Searching with Search Tools and Using the Web Safely continues on the next page)

Mastering Windows 7 | Project **5F** Searching with Search Tools and Using the Web Safely (continued)

1 Open Internet Explorer. In the **address bar**, type **cityoforlando.net** and press [Enter]. On the site's **Information Center** navigation bar, click **City Hall Hours & Directions**.

2 Select the City Hall address (include the city, state, and ZIP code), click the **Accelerator** button, and then click **Map with Bing**.

3 Set the view to **Aerial** and then **Satellite photo map**. Create a **Full-screen Snip** and **Save** it as **Lastname_Firstname_5F_Aerial_Snip** Submit this file as directed by your instructor.

4 **Close** all open windows and **Close** Internet Explorer.

 You have completed Project 5F ——————————————————

Outcomes-Based Assessments

Rubric

The following outcomes-based assessments are open-ended assessments. That is, there is no specific correct result; your result will depend on your approach to the information provided. Make Professional Quality your goal. Use the following scoring rubric to guide you in how to approach the problem and then to evaluate how well your approach solves the problem.

The *criteria*—Software Mastery, Content, Format and Layout, and Process—represent the knowledge and skills you have gained that you can apply to solving the problem. The *levels of performance*—Professional Quality, Approaching Professional Quality, or Needs Quality Improvements—help you and your instructor evaluate your result.

	Your completed project is of Professional Quality if you:	Your completed project is of Approaching Professional Quality if you:	Your completed project Needs Quality Improvements if you:
1-Software Mastery	Choose and apply the most appropriate skills, tools, and features and identify efficient methods to solve the problem.	Choose and apply some appropriate skills, tools, and features, but not in the most efficient manner.	Choose inappropriate skills, tools, or features, or are inefficient in solving the problem.
2-Content	Construct a solution that is clear and well organized, contains content that is accurate, appropriate to the audience and purpose, and is complete. Provide a solution that contains no errors of spelling, grammar, or style.	Construct a solution in which some components are unclear, poorly organized, inconsistent, or incomplete. Misjudge the needs of the audience. Have some errors in spelling, grammar, or style, but the errors do not detract from comprehension.	Construct a solution that is unclear, incomplete, or poorly organized, or that contains some inaccurate or inappropriate content, and contains many errors of spelling, grammar, or style. Do not solve the problem.
3-Format and Layout	Format and arrange all elements to communicate information and ideas, clarify function, illustrate relationships, and indicate relative importance.	Apply appropriate format and layout features to some elements, but not others. Overuse features, causing minor distraction.	Apply format and layout that does not communicate information or ideas clearly. Do not use format and layout features to clarify function, illustrate relationships, or indicate relative importance. Use available features excessively, causing distraction.
4-Process	Use an organized approach that integrates planning, development, self-assessment, revision, and reflection.	Demonstrate an organized approach in some areas, but not others; or, use an insufficient process of organization throughout.	Do not use an organized approach to solve the problem.

Apply a combination of the **5A** and **5B** skills.

Problem Solving | Project **5G** Help Desk

Project Files

For Project 5G, you will need the following file:

> win05_5G_Help_Desk

You will save your document as:

> Lastname_Firstname_5G_Help_Desk

From the student files that accompany this textbook, open the **Chapter_Files** folder, and then in the **Chapter_05** folder, locate and open the Word document **win05_5G_Help_Desk**. Save the document in your chapter folder as **Lastname_Firstname_5G_Help_Desk**

The following e-mail question has arrived at the Help Desk from an employee at the Bell Orchid Hotel's corporate office. In the Word document, construct a response based on your knowledge of Windows 7. Although an e-mail response is not as formal as a letter, you should still use good grammar, good sentence structure, professional language, and a polite tone. Save your document and submit the response as directed by your instructor.

To: Help Desk

I have asked my research assistant to conduct some Internet research about what hotels around the country are doing in regard to designing innovative restaurants. Is there a way he could organize the sites he wants me to review by geographic location and by type of restaurant?

End **You have completed Project 5G** ————————————————

Outcomes-Based Assessments

Apply a combination of
the **5A** and **5B** skills.

Problem Solving | Project **5H** Help Desk

Project Files

For Project 5H, you will need the following file:

    win05_5H_Help_Desk

You will save your document as:

    Lastname_Firstname_5H_Help_Desk

From the student files that accompany this textbook, open the **Chapter_Files** folder, and then in the **Chapter_05** folder, locate and open **win05_5H_Help_Desk**. Save the document in your chapter folder as **Lastname_Firstname_5H_Help_Desk**

The following e-mail question has arrived at the Help Desk from an employee at the Bell Orchid Hotel's corporate office. In the Word document, construct a response based on your knowledge of Windows 7. Although an e-mail response is not as formal as a letter, you should still use good grammar, good sentence structure, professional language, and a polite tone. Save your document and submit the response as directed by your instructor.

To: Help Desk

Guests who use the computers in our hotel Business Centers have inquired about how they can prevent others from seeing the sites they visited and potentially seeing personal information. What instructions could we post at each of these computers to advise guests how to remove any such information from these public computers?

 You have completed Project 5H ————————————————

Outcomes-Based Assessments

Apply a combination of the **5A** and **5B** skills.

Problem Solving | Project 5I Help Desk

Project Files

For Project 5I, you will need the following file:

> win05_5I_Help_Desk

You will save your document as:

> Lastname_Firstname_5I_Help_Desk

From the student files that accompany this textbook, open the **Chapter_Files** folder, and then in the **Chapter_05** folder, locate and open the Word document **win05_5I_Help_Desk**. Save the document in your chapter folder as **Lastname_Firstname_5I_Help_Desk**

The following e-mail question has arrived at the Help Desk from an employee at the Bell Orchid Hotel's corporate office. In the Word document, construct a response based on your knowledge of Windows 7. Although an e-mail response is not as formal as a letter, you should still use good grammar, good sentence structure, professional language, and a polite tone. Save your document and submit the response as directed by your instructor.

To: Help Desk

Guests commonly stop by the Front Desk at our hotels and inquire about what the weather will be like in the next few days. Is there a way we could have something on all of the Front Desk computers that would provide the Desk Clerks with constantly updated weather information?

 You have completed Project 5I ——————————————

Glossary

Accelerators An Internet Explorer feature that displays a blue Accelerator icon when you select text from any Web page, and which when clicked enables you to accomplish tasks such as finding a map, defining a word, or e-mailing content to others.

Action Center A central place to view alerts and take actions, for example to view and install updates and view important messages about security and maintenance settings on your computer.

ActiveX A technology for creating interactive Web content such as animation sequences, credit card transactions, or spreadsheet calculations.

ActiveX control A type of add-on that uses ActiveX technology.

Add-on A program that adds features to a Web browser such as Internet Explorer.

Address bar (Windows Explorer) Displays your current location in the folder structure as a series of links separated by arrows.

Address bar (Internet Explorer) The area at the top of the Internet Explorer window that displays, and where you can type, a URL.

Administrator account A user account that lets you make changes that will affect other users of the computer; the most powerful of the three types of accounts, because it permits the most control over the computer.

Aero The term that refers to the desktop experience that features a translucent glass design for windows, attractive graphics, taskbar previews of open windows, and the Aero features such as Snap and Aero Peek.

Aero Flip 3D A feature that arranges your open windows in a three-dimensional stack that you can flip through quickly without having to click buttons on the taskbar.

Aero Peek A technology that assists you when you have multiple windows open by allowing you to *peek* at either the desktop that is behind open windows or at a window that is hidden from view by other windows; then, you can move the mouse back into the taskbar to close the peek.

Aero Shake A feature in which you can shake an active window by moving the mouse vigorously back and forth on the title bar to have all other open windows minimize; you can then restore all the windows by shaking the open window again.

All Programs An area on the Start menu that displays all the programs on your computer system that are available to you; some groups of programs display in a folder.

AND filter When used in a search, finds files that contain both search terms even if those terms are not next to each other.

Application Another term for a program.

Arrange by In a folder window, a feature that enables you to arrange the items by Author, Date modified, Tag, Type, or Name; the default arrangement is Folder.

AutoPlay A Windows 7 feature that lets you choose which program to use to start different kinds of media, such as music CDs, or CDs and DVDs containing photos; it displays when you plug in or insert media or storage devices.

Base locations Locations that you frequently need to access to manage your computer including Libraries, Homegroup if you have one, your personal folder, Computer, Network, Control Panel, and Recycle Bin.

Bing An Internet search engine by Microsoft.

BIOS (Basic Input/Output System) A program installed by a computer's manufacturer that runs at startup, checks the hardware devices, and then loads the operating system.

Bit rate The number of bits transferred per unit of time, typically expressed in bits per second.

Blog An online journal or column used to publish personal or company information in an informal manner.

Bookmark managers Free Web tools available to manage your favorites.

Boolean operators The terms AND, OR, and NOT that govern the logical functions and express a condition that is either true or false.

Booting the computer The process of turning on a computer when the computer has been completely shut down and during which the BIOS program will run.

Browsing (Windows Explorer) A term used to describe the process of navigating within Windows 7 to look for a specific program, file, e-mail, Control Panel feature, or Internet favorite.

Browsing (Internet Explorer) The term used to describe the process of using your computer to view Web pages.

Browsing history The information stored by Internet Explorer about the sites you have visited and the information you have typed into a site.

Burning a disc The process of writing files on a CD or DVD.

Cascade An arrangement of open windows on your screen that display in a single stack fanned out so that each title bar is visible.

Case sensitive A requirement, especially for computer passwords, in which capitalization must match each time the characters are typed.

Certificate A digital document that verifies the identity of a person or indicates the security of a Web site.

Certification Authorities Companies, for example Verisign, that issue digital certificates.

Check box feature A folder option which, when applied, displays a check box to the left of folders and files.

Click The action of pressing the left mouse button.

Clipboard A temporary storage area for information that you have copied or moved from one place and plan to use somewhere else.

Common dialog boxes The dialog boxes, such as Save and Save As, provided by the Windows programming interface that enable programs to have a consistent appearance and behavior.

Common folders and features The right side of the Start menu that provides quick access to the folders and features you use most often.

Compress To reduce the size of a file; compressed files take up less storage space and can be transferred to other computers, for example in an e-mail message, more quickly than uncompressed files.

Computer A command on the Start menu that displays a window from which you can you can access disk drives, cameras, printers, scanners and other hardware connected to your computer.

Content view A folder window view in which the files display a vertical list that includes the program icon, the date the file was last modified, the file size, and other properties such as author names or tags.

Control Panel A window from which you can customize the appearance and functionality of your computer, add or remove programs, set up network connections, and manage user accounts.

Cookies Small text files that Web sites put on your computer to store information about you and your preferences, for example logon information.

Country codes Top level domains for countries, for example *.ca* for Canada.

Criteria Text that specifies the conditions that identify the specific files you are looking for in a search.

Custom search A search feature in which you can define a specific scope—range of locations—for your search.

Data All the files—documents, spreadsheets, pictures, songs, and so on—that you create and store during the day-to-day use of your computer.

Data management The process of managing your files and folders in an organized manner so that you can find information when you need it.

Deselect To cancel the selection of one or more selected items.

Desktop Serves as a surface for your work, like the top of an actual desk, and is the main screen area that you see after you turn on your computer; here you can arrange *icons*—small pictures that represent a file, folder, program, or other object—on the desktop such as shortcuts to programs, files, folders, and various types of documents in the same manner you would arrange physical objects on top of a desk.

Desktop background Displays the colors and graphics of your desktop; you can change the desktop background to look the way you want it.

Desktop gadget Another term for a gadget.

Details pane Displays the most common properties associated with the selected file.

Details view A file list view that displays a list of files or folders and their most common properties.

Digital signature An electronic security mark that can be added to files.

Directory A file folder on a disk in which you store files; also called a *path*.

Domain name An organization's unique name on the Internet, which consists of a chosen name combined with a top level domain such as *.com* or *.org* or *.gov*.

Double-click The action of pressing the left mouse button twice in rapid succession while holding the mouse still.

Drag The action of moving something from one location on the screen to another while holding down the left mouse button; the action of dragging includes releasing the mouse button at the desired time or location.

Drilling down The process of navigating downward through multiple levels of your folder structure to find what you are looking for.

Drive An area of storage that is formatted with a file system compatible with your operating system and is identified by a drive letter.

Ease of Access Center A centralized location for accessibility settings and programs that can make your computer easier and more comfortable for you to use.

Extract The action of decompressing—pulling out—files from a compressed form.

Favorites bar A toolbar in Internet Explorer 8 that displays directly below the address bar and to which you can add or drag web addresses you use frequently.

Favorites Center A list of links to Web sites that is saved in your Web browser.

Federated Search A technology that enables you to search a remote server or Web service from Windows Explorer using the same techniques that you use to search for files that are stored on your own computer.

Feed reader Another name for an RSS viewer.

Feeds Frequently updated content published by a Web site.

File A collection of information that is stored on a computer under a single name, for example a text document, a picture, or a program.

File association The association between a file and the program that created the file.

File list Displays the contents of the current folder or library. If you type text into the Search box, only the folders and files that match your search will display here—including files in subfolders.

File name extension A set of characters at the end of a file name that helps Windows 7 understand what kind of information is in a file and what program should open it.

File properties Information about a file such as its author, the date the file was last changed, and any descriptive tags.

Filtered A display of files that is limited based on certain criteria.

Folder A container in which you store files.

Folder structure The hierarchy of folders in Windows 7.

Folder window A window that displays the contents of the current folder, library, or device, and contains helpful parts so that you can navigate—explore within the organizing structure of Windows.

Free-form snip When using Snipping Tool, the type of snip that lets you draw an irregular line, such as a circle, around an area of the screen.

Full-screen snip When using Snipping Tool, the type of snip that captures the entire screen.

Full-Screen Window Preview In the Aero Peek technology, the ability to *peek* at a window that is hidden from view by other windows.

Gadget A mini-program that offers information and provides easy access to tools that you use frequently.

Getting Started In Windows 7, a task-centered grouping of links to tools that can help you get started with and add new features to your computer.

Graphic equalizer In Windows Media Player, the controls that enable you to adjust the bass and treble that you hear.

Graphical user interface The system by which you interact with your computer and which uses graphics such as an image of a file folder or wastebasket that you click to activate the item represented.

Guest account A user account for users who do not have a permanent account on the computer; it permits only temporary access to the computer.

GUI The acronym for a graphical user interface, pronounced *GOO-ee*.

Hard disk drive The primary storage device located inside your computer and where most of your files and programs are typically stored; usually labeled as drive C.

Hierarchy An arrangement where items are ranked and where each level is lower in rank than the item above it.

Home page On your own computer, the Web page you have selected—or that is set by default—to display on your computer when you start Internet Explorer; when visiting a Web site, the starting point for the remainder of the pages on that site.

http The protocol prefix for HyperText Transfer Protocol.

HyperText Transfer Protocol The set of communication rules used by your computer to connect to servers on the Web.

Icons Small images that represent commands, files, or other windows.

Index A collection of detailed information about the files on your computer that Windows 7 maintains for the purpose conducting fast searches; when you begin a search, Windows 7 searches this summary information rather than searching file by file on your hard disk drive.

Indexed Locations All of the folders in your personal folder (Documents, Pictures, and so on) and offline files, if any, that Windows 7 includes in a search.

Information bar A bar at the top of an Internet Explorer screen that displays information about downloads, blocked pop-up windows, and installing ActiveX controls.

InPrivate Browsing A feature in Internet Explorer 8 with which you can browse the Web without storing data about your browsing session; useful when using a public computer.

Insertion point A blinking vertical line that indicates where text or graphics will be inserted.

Internet Explorer 8 The Web browser software developed by Microsoft Corporation that is included with Windows 7.

JPEG The acronym for Joint Photographic Experts Group that is a common file type used by digital cameras and computers to store digital pictures—a popular file type because it can store a high-quality picture in a relatively small file.

Jump List A list that displays when you right-click a button on the taskbar, and which displays locations (in the upper portion) and tasks (in the lower portion) from a program's taskbar button; functions as a mini start menu for a program.

Library A collection of items, such as files and folders, assembled from various locations.

Library pane Enables you to customize the library or arrange files by different *file properties*—information about the files, such as the author, the date the file was last changed, and any descriptive *tags* (a property that you create to help you find and organize your files) you might have added to the file. This pane displays only when you are in a library, such as the Documents library.

Live File System A file storage system with which you can create CDs and DVDs; discs formatted with Live File System allow you to copy files to the disc at any time, instead of copying (burning) them all at once.

Location Any disk drive, folder, or other place in which you can store files and folders.

Location icon A button on the address bar that depicts the location—library, disk drive, folder, and so on—you are accessing.

Lock A process that sets your computer so that your password is required to log back on to your desktop; others can log on to their own desktops while your desktop is locked.

Log off A process that exits the active user account from Windows, and then displays the Welcome screen ready for another user to log on.

Magnifier A screen enlarger that magnifies a portion of the screen in a separate window; helpful for computer users with low vision and for those who require occasional screen magnification for such tasks as editing art.

Mastered A file system with which you can create CDs and DVDs; discs created using the Mastered format are more likely to be compatible with older computers, but an additional step is required to burn the collection of files to the disc.

Menu A list of commands within a category.

Menu bar A group of menus at the top of a program window.

Metadata The data that describes other data; for example, the collective group of a file's properties, such as its title, subject, author, and file size.

Mouse pointer Any symbol that displays on your screen in response to moving your mouse.

Naming convention A plan that provides a consistent pattern for naming files and folders on your computer.

Natural language A search feature than enables you to perform searches with simple language without entering colons or Boolean operators.

Navigate To explore within the folder structure of Windows Vista for the purpose of finding files and folders.

Navigation The actions you perform to display a window to locate a command or display the folder window for a folder whose contents you want to view.

Navigation pane The area on the left side of a folder window; it displays favorites, libraries, and an expandable list of drives and folders.

Network A group of computers or other devices, such as printers and scanners, which communicate either wirelessly or by using a physical connection.

Network notification icon In the notification area, an icon that displays the status of your network.

NOT filter When used in a search, finds files that contain the first word but that do not contain the second word.

Notification A small pop-up window providing information about status, progress, and the detection of new devices.

Notification area Displays notification icons and the system clock; sometimes referred to as the *system tray*.

Now Playing mode A simplified Player view that enables you to play music in the background while you are performing other tasks.

Offline files Files from a network that have been copied to your hard disk drive for easy access when you are not connected to the network.

Operating system A computer program that manages all the other programs on your computer, stores files in an organized manner, and coordinates the use of computer hardware such as the keyboard and mouse.

OR filter When used in a search, finds files that contain either search term.

Paint A program that comes with Windows 7 with which you can create and edit drawings and display and edit stored photos.

Partial matching A technique employed by the Windows 7 search feature that matches your search criteria to part of a word or phrase rather than to whole words.

Path A sequence of folders (directories) that leads to a specific file or folder.

Personal folder A folder created for each user account, labeled with the account holder's name, and which contains the subfolders *Documents*, *Pictures*, *Music*, among others; always located at the top of the Start menu.

Phishing A technique used to trick computer users into revealing personal or financial information through an e-mail message or a Web site.

Pinned Placing programs on the Start menu in a manner that remains until you remove it.

Playback controls area The area in Windows Media Player that enables you to play, pause, stop, rewind, or fast forward multimedia files; also enables you to control the order in which objects play, and to control the volume.

Player Library mode A comprehensive Player view in which you have control over the numerous features of the Player.

Playlist A list of digital media items that you create and save.

Point The action of moving the mouse pointer over something on the screen.

Pointer Any symbol that displays on your screen in response to moving your mouse and with which you can select objects and commands.

Pointing device A mouse, touchpad, or other device that controls the pointer position on the screen.

Pop-up A small Web browser window that displays on top of the Web site you are viewing, and which are usually created by advertisers.

Pop-up Blocker A feature in Internet Explorer that enables you to block most pop-ups.

Portable device Any mobile electronic device that can exchange files or other data with a computer or device; for example, a smartphone or a portable music player.

Portal A Web site that displays news, content, and links that are of interest to a specific audience.

Preview Desktop In the Aero Peek technology, the ability to *peek* at the desktop that is behind open windows.

Preview pane An additional pane on the right side of the file list to display a preview of a file (not a folder) that you select in the file list.

Problem Steps Recorder A Windows 7 feature that captures the steps you perform on your computer, including a text description of where you clicked and a picture of the screen during each click.

Program A set of instructions that a computer uses to accomplish a task, such as word processing, accounting, or data management; also referred to as an *application*.

Programs list The left side of the Start menu that displays recently used programs on the bottom, programs that you have pinned to the Start menu at the top, and a button to display all the programs on your computer.

Progress bar In a dialog box or taskbar button, a bar that indicates visually the progress of a task such as a download or file transfer.

Properties Descriptive pieces of information about a folder or file such as the name, the date modified, the author, the type, and the size.

Protected mode A feature in Internet Explorer that makes it more difficult for malicious software to be installed on your computer by preventing a downloaded program from making any direct changes to the system.

Protocol prefix The letters that represent a set of communication rules used by a computer to connect to another computer.

Quick Tabs The feature in Internet Explorer that displays, on a single tab, a thumbnail of each Web site that is currently open.

Quotes filter When used in a search, finds files that contain the exact phrase placed within the quotes.

Really Simple Syndication A syndication format popular for aggregating updates to blogs and news sites.

Recent Pages A button on the address bar that displays a list of recently accessed locations; the current location is indicated by a check mark.

Rectangular snip When using Snipping Tool, the type of snip that lets you draw a precise box by dragging the mouse pointer around an area of the screen to form a rectangle.

Recycle Bin A folder that stores anything that you delete from your computer, and from which anything stored there can be retrieved until the contents are permanently deleted by activating the Empty Recycle Bin command.

Removable storage device A portable device on which you can store files, such as a USB flash drive, a flash memory card, or an external hard drive, commonly used to transfer information from one computer to another.

Resources A term used to refer collectively to the parts of your computer such as the central processing unit (CPU), memory, and any attached devices such as a printer.

Restart A process that turns your computer off and then on again during which time the system cache is cleared; useful if your computer is operating slowly or having technical problems, or after installing new software or software updates.

Right-click The action of clicking the right mouse button.

Rip The process of copying digital media content from an audio CD.

RSS An acronym for *Really Simple Syndication*, which is a syndication format popular for aggregating—gathering together—updates to blogs and news sites.

RSS feed Frequently updated content published by a Web site and delivered to a feed reader.

RSS viewer A program that displays RSS feeds to which you have subscribed.

Screen capture An image file that contains the contents of a computer screen.

Screen saver A moving picture or pattern that displays on your screen after a specified period of inactivity—that is, when the mouse or keyboard has not been used.

Screenshot The term used for an image of the contents of a computer screen.

ScreenTip Useful information that displays in a small box on the screen when you perform various mouse actions, such as pointing to screen elements.

Scroll arrow Arrows at the top and bottom, or left and right, of a scroll bar that when clicked, move the window in small increments.

Scroll bar A bar that displays on the bottom or right side of a window when the contents of a window are not completely visible; used to move the window up, down, left, or right to bring the contents into view.

Scroll box The box in a vertical or horizontal scroll bar that you drag to reposition the document on the screen.

Search box A box found on the Start menu and in windows that display libraries, folders, and files that provides a way to find specific files and folders by typing search terms.

Search box An area on the Start menu from which you can search for programs, files, folders, and e-mail messages.

Search folder The Windows 7 folder in which you conduct searches in the entire set of indexed locations.

Search provider A Web site that provides search capabilities on the Web.

Search term A word or phrase that describes the topic about which you want to find information.

Select To specify, by highlighting, a block of data or text on the screen with the intent of performing some action on the selection.

SharePoint A Microsoft technology that enables employees in an organization to access information across organizational and geographic boundaries.

Shift Click A technique in which the SHIFT key is held down to select all the items in a consecutive group; you need only click the first item, hold down SHIFT, and then click the last item in the group.

Shortcuts Desktop icons that link to any item accessible on your computer or on a network, such as a program, file, folder, disk drive printer, or another computer.

Show desktop button Displays the desktop by making any open windows transparent (when pointed to) or minimized (when clicked).

Shut down Turning off your computer in a manner that closes all open programs and files, closes your network connections, stops the hard disk, and discontinues the use of electrical power.

Shut down button On the Start menu, a button that displays a menu for switching users, logging off, restarting, or shutting down.

Side by side An arrangement of open windows on your screen that displays side by side.

Skin A user interface that displays an alternative appearance and customized functionality for software such as Windows Media Player.

Skin mode An operational state of Windows Media Player in which its user interface is displayed as a skin.

Sleep Turning off your computer in a manner that automatically saves your work, stops the fan, and uses a small amount of electrical power to maintain your work in memory; the next time you turn the computer on, you need only to enter your password (if required) and your screen will display exactly like it did when you turned off.

SmartScreen Filter A feature in Internet Explorer that helps detect phishing Web sites and Web sites that distribute malware.

Snap A Windows 7 feature that automatically resizes windows when you move—*snap*—them to the edge of the screen.

Snip The image captured using Snipping Tool.

Snipping Tool A program included with Windows 7 with which you can capture an image of all or part of a computer screen, and then annotate, save, copy, or share the image via e-mail.

Speakers icon Displays the status of your speakers (if any).

Split button A button that has two parts—a button and an arrow; clicking the main part of the button performs a command and clicking the arrow opens a menu with choices.

Sponsored links Paid advertisements shown as a links, typically for products and services related to your search term; sponsored links are the way that search sites like Bing, Google, and others earn revenue.

Spyware Software that sends information about your Web surfing habits to a Web site without your knowledge.

Stack An arrangement of open windows on your screen that display each window across the width of the screen in a vertical stack.

Standard user account A user account that lets you use most of the capabilities of the computer, but requires permission from an administrator to make changes that affect other users or the security of the computer.

Start button Displays the Start menu—a list of choices that provides access to your computer's programs, folders, and settings.

Start menu A list of choices that provides access to your computer's programs, folders, and settings when you press the Start button.

Status area Another term for the notification area.

Subfolder A folder within a folder.

Suggested Sites In Internet Explorer 8, an optional online service that suggests other Web sites in which you might be interested based on the Web sites you visit most.

Surfing The process of navigating the Internet either for a particular item or for anything that is of interest, and quickly moving from one item to another.

Sync The process of maintaining digital media files on your portable device based on specific rules.

Syndicated content Another name for an RSS feed.

System cache An area of the computer's memory where Windows 7 stores information it needs to access quickly.

System tray Another name for the notification area on the taskbar.

Tab row The area across the upper portion of the Internet Explorer screen in which a tab for each open Web site displays.

Tabbed browsing A feature in Internet Explorer that enables you to open multiple Web sites in a single browser window.

Tag A custom file property that you create to help find and organize your files.

Taskbar The area of the desktop that contains the Start button, optional program buttons, and buttons for all open programs; by default, it is located at the bottom of the desktop, but you can move it.

Temporary Internet files Copies of Web pages, images, and media that you have downloaded from the Web, which makes viewing faster the next time you visit a site that you have visited before.

Theme A combination of pictures, colors, and sounds on your computer; includes a desktop background, a screen saver, a window border color, and a sound scheme.

Thumbnail A reduced image of a graphic.

TIFF The acronym for Tagged Image File Format that is a file type used when a very high level of visual quality is needed, for example if the file will be used to print 8-by-10-inch enlargements.

Title bar The bar across the top of the window that displays the program name.

Toolbar A row, column, or block of buttons or icons, usually displayed across the top of a window, which contains commands for tasks you can perform with a single click.

Top level domain The ending letters of a URL such as *.com*, *.org*, and so on.

Uniform Resource Locator An address that uniquely identifies a location on the Internet.

URL The acronym for Uniform Resource Locator.

User account A collection of information that tells Windows 7 what files and folders the account holder can access, what changes the account holder can make to the computer system, and what the account holder's personal preferences are.

Virtual folder A folder that does not represent a physical location but rather contains the results of a search.

Visualizations In Windows Media Player and Media Center, splashes of color and geometric shapes that change along with the rhythm and intensity of the music.

Wallpaper Another term for the desktop background.

Web browser A software program with which you display Web pages and navigate the Internet.

Web feed Another name for an RSS feed.

Web log The term from which *blog* is derived; an online journal or column used to publish personal or company information in an informal manner.

Web Slice A specific *portion*—a slice—of a Web page to which you can subscribe, and which enables you to see when updated content, such as the current temperature, is available from a site.

Window A rectangular area on your screen that displays programs and content, and which can be moved, resized, minimized, or closed; the content of every window is different, but all windows display on the desktop.

Window snip When using Snipping Tool, the type of snip that captures the entire displayed window.

Windows 7 An operating system developed by Microsoft Corporation.

Windows Defender A spyware scanning and removal tool included with Windows 7.

Windows Explorer The program within Windows 7 that displays the contents of libraries, folders, and files on your computer, and which also enables you to perform tasks related to your files and folders such as copying, moving, and renaming. Windows Explorer is at work anytime you are viewing the contents of a library, a folder, or a file.

Windows Help and Support The built-in help system for Windows 7.

Windows Media Player A feature in Windows 7 that provides an easy-to-use way for you to play digital media files, organize your digital media collection, burn CDs of your favorite music, rip music from CDs, sync digital media files to a portable device, and shop for digital media content from online stores.

Word wheel A lookup method in which each new character that you type into the search box further refines the search.

Writable disc A CD or DVD disc onto which files can be copied.

XML feed Another name for an RSS feed.

Index

naming/saving, 92–96
Resume_Guide, 111, 112, 113, 114
Staffing_Plan, 101, 103, 104, 107
tags added to, 189
Word files *(Continued)*
Tours, 190
word count and, 177
Word file type icon, 48
Word program (Microsoft Word), 14, 46, 50, 55, 91, 163
word wheel technology, 20, 124, 127, 133

WordPad, 30, 46, 52, 53, 54, 55
World Wide Web (www), 292
writable disc, 116
www. *See* **World Wide Web**

X-Z

XML (Extensible Markup Language) feeds, 249, 328, 329, 332. *See also* **RSS feeds**
Zoom feature, 317–318